11/13

Gun Digest® Book

TACTICAL WEAPONS

ASSEMBLY/DISASSEMBLY

2nd EDITION

Kevin Muramatsu

Published by

Gun Digest® Books, an imprint of F+W Media, Inc.
Krause Publications • 700 East State Street • Iola, WI 54990-0001
715-445-2214 • 888-457-2873
www.krausebooks.com

To order books or other products call toll-free 1-800-258-0929
or visit us online at www.gundigeststore.com

CAUTION: Technical data presented here, particularly technical data on the handloading and on firearms adjustment and alteration, inevitably reflects individual experience with particular equipment and components under specific circumstances the reader cannot duplicate exactly. Such data presentations therefore should be used for guidance only and caution. F+W Media, Inc., accepts no responsibility for results obtained using this data.

ISBN-13: 978-1-4402-3603-7
ISBN-10: 1-4402-3603-8

Cover & Design by Tom Nelsen
Edited by Corrina Peterson

Printed in the United States of America

Acknowledgements

In great deal because of the times, it was necessary to beg and borrow guns like a starving orphan from those who had them available (or didn't). I greatly appreciate the following individuals' efforts in obtaining the firearms included in this revision. Some of you I know personally, and to those I don't, hit me up for a beer at SHOT Show. I owe you one.

The Wolf's Den Gun Shop, John Gangl, David Cammack, David Potvin, Mike Nishalke of Hunter Outdoor Communications, Jessica Kallam and Carlos Martinez from the Freedom Group, Amanda Jackson of IWI USA, Eric Burgess from Laura Burgess Marketing, Derek Kellgren from Kel-Tec CNC, Kristina DeMilt of FNH-USA, Cody Bates from Davidsons, Inc., Troy Bacon from RSR Group, the folks at CDNN who just happened to have a couple 551s left when I really needed one, and her holiness Rachel for letting me keep the guns that I had to buy outright. Hopefully I didn't leave anyone out, but my lack of good sleep and potent caffeine is mind slamming my memory into further uselessness. If I forgot you, find me at SHOT. I'll buy you two beers.

Preface

This book is the final volume in the Assembly/Disassembly series of manuals from Gun Digest. It is final only in that it was the last of the originals to be published, and is coincidentally the last of the originals to be revised. This first revision adds to the initial batch, both in the number of firearms and in the inclusion of an index.

The word "tactical" is one of those things that can have multiple, subjective meanings. In regard to this tome it refers to firearms which might be used in law enforcement or by non-police for personal defense. As such it contains rifles, shotguns, pistols (including some concealable models), and even a few C&R machineguns. Those who wish access to such takedowns with more modern machineguns are, well, pretty much out of luck. Fortunately a number of the inclusions here are identical to their fully automatic counterparts, with the exception of the absence of the happy switch.

An interesting development has been the advent of bullpup rifles. While not a new concept, more and more rifles are being manufactured here or imported that sport the bullpup style of design. That is, to say, (for a lack of an easier description) a long gun that places the chamber behind the trigger. The benefit of this arrangement is a rifle that is much shorter overall than a standard rifle but retains the same length of barrel, allowing similar or better ballistics than the standard rifle designs, and much better carrying balance and handling. This is not without drawbacks. The bullpup design usually has a horrible trigger pull and it places the chamber right beneath the shooter cheek, which causes some consternation among many. For this and other reasons, not the least of which is that these guns really do look kind of funny, the bullpup has really not gained a great following with the gun-owning American public. Following this rather mini-trend, several of the new inclusions in this revision are of the bullpup pattern.

Although it may be noted in the individual texts, there are some firearms, notably the AR-15 and 1911, that have been copied so much it's impossible to list all their manufacturers or incarnations in which they have appeared. It can be taken for granted that if it looks convincingly like one of those guns, it probably is (or 90% is) that gun, and the take down steps will mostly apply.

To some degree a magazine is a magazine is a magazine. The vast majority of magazines are constructed in the very same fashion and so there are only a few magazines specifically addressed with their parent firearms.

Pay attention to the "Tools" section found a few pages in. It cannot be overstressed that the appropriate tools be used, not just any old thing lying around. I highly advise using a digital camera to take photos (or multiple photos) of each step of your disassembly. It is very difficult for an author to take as many photos as he would like of each of these steps. There simply isn't enough space in the allotted pages to fit that many pictures. So it is recommended that when the reader of this manual goes about the process of disassembling one of the guns in this book, that he or she take multiple pictures at each step along the way. There is no downside to this and there could be a very tangible upside.

Before you start playing around the guts of a gun, ensure that the thing is completely unloaded. This obligatory warning has been omitted from each entry to avoid having to write it out forty times. Triple check the gun, especially the chamber, and that the magazine is not present in the gun and is itself empty of cartridges.

At the time of this writing, there is a full court press on politically to restrict gun ownership rights in the USA. A timely confluence of events (from their perspective) has convinced the power grabbers that this is a good time to go for broke. So far, they have met with some success. Most of the illogic and intolerant vitriol is directed at the types of firearms included in this disassembly manual, and at those who own them. It is imperative that anyone who reads or uses this manual understand that, when it relates to gun control, a gun is every gun. An AR is the same as a Citori, is the same as a Winchester 94, is the same as a S&W Model 60, is the same as a 1911, is the same as a Glock, is the same as a Mauser, is the same as great-great granddaddy's black powder rifle. There are those want them all, and the gun owners of this country had better unify and steadfastly and completely resist further useless gun laws or there will be nothing left when they eventually come for the single shot .22s; and if you think the state is pushing their way into your life now, just wait until then, when there is no final means of resistance remaining.

Okay, enough preaching. Use this manual to good effect. I certainly enjoy taking things apart and fiddling with them enough to keep doing these manuals. Don't lose any springs and don't point the gun at your own head.

Kevin Muramatsu,
In the garage shop (lacking caffeine)
WBT, MN

Contents

Handguns

AMT Back-Up 12

Beretta Px4 Storm 18

Colt 1911 Series 25

FNH Five-Seven 34

FNH FNS 43

HK USP Tactical 51

Kel-Tec PLR-16 60

Smith & Wesson Model 459 65

Taurus 45/410 74

Taurus 24/7 82

Wilson ADP 89

Shotguns

Benelli M2 Tactical 97

Benelli M4 105

FNH SLP Mk 1 115

Kel-Tec KSG 125

Remington Model 870R 136

Rifles

Armalite AR-50A1 144

Armalite AR-180 151

Barrett MRAD 161

Benelli MR1 171

Beretta Cx4 Storm 181

Bushmaster ACR 186

Colt AR-15 197

Daewoo DT 200 207

FN FAL 215

FNH FS2000 227

FNH PS90 240

Heckler & Koch HK 91 250

IWI Tavor 260

Kel-Tec RFB 275

Kel-Tec SUB 2000 285

Kel-Tec SU-16 290

Marlin M9 297

Ruger Mini-14 307

Russian AK-47 315

Russian SKS 323

SIG SAUER 551 A1 333

Springfield SOCOM 16 344

Steyr AUG 356

U.S. M-1 Carbine 366

Valmet 76/FS 374

Wilkinson Terry 382

Submachine Guns

Ingram Model 10 391

Reising Model 50 400

Smith & Wesson M76 407

Thompson Model 1921 414

U.S. M3A1 423

Tools

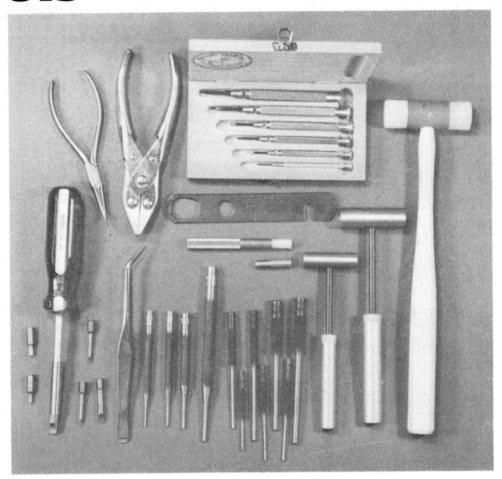

Countless firearms, old and new, bear the marks, burrs and gouges that are the result of using the wrong tools for taking them apart. In the interest of preventing this sort of thing, I am including here a group of tools that are the best types for the disassembly of shotguns. Except for the few shop-made tools for special purposes, all of those shown here are available from one of these sources.

Brownells Inc.
Route 2, Box 1,
200 S. Front St.
Montezuma, Iowa 50171

B-Square Company
P.O. Box 11281
Fort Worth, Texas 761092

General Instructions:

Screwdrivers: Always be sure the blade of the screwdriver exactly fits the slot in the screw head, both in thickness and in width. If you don't have one that fits, grind or file the tip until it does. You may ruin a few screwdrivers, but better them than the screws on a fine shotgun.

Slave pins: There are several references in this book to slave pins, and some non-gunsmith readers may not be familiar with the term. A slave pin is simply a short length of rod stock (in some cases, a section of a nail will do) which is used to keep two parts, or a part and a spring, together during reassembly. The slave pin must be slightly smaller in diameter than the hole in the part, so it will push out easily as the original pin is driven in to retain the part. When making a slave pin, its length should be slightly less than the width of the part in which it is being used, and the ends of the pin should be rounded or beveled.

Sights: Nearly all dovetail-mounted sights are drifted out toward the right, using a nylon, aluminum, or brass drift punch.

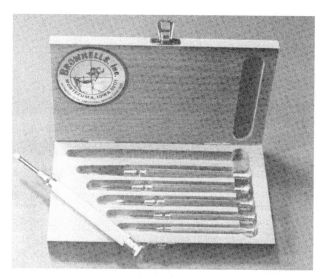

1. The tiniest of these fine German instrument screwdrivers from Brownells is too small for most gun work, but you'll see the rest of them used frequently throughout the book. There are many tight places where these will come in handy.

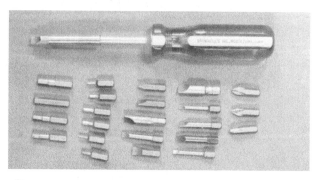

2. When a larger screwdriver is needed, this set from Brownells covers a wide range of blade sizes and also has Phillips- and Allen-type inserts. The tips are held in place by a strong magnet, yet are easily changed. These tips are very hard. With enough force you might manage to break one, but they'll never bend.

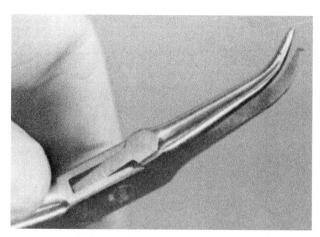

3. You should have at least one good pair of bent sharpnosed pliers. These, from Brownells, have a box joint and smooth inner faces to help prevent marring.

4. For heavier gripping, these Bernard parallel-jaw pliers from Brownells have smooth-faced jaw-pieces of unhardened steel to prevent marring of parts.

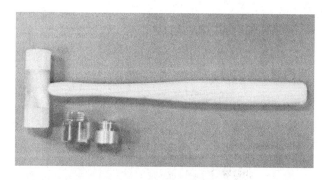

5. For situations where a non-marring rap is needed, this hammer from Brownells is ideal. It is shown with nylon faces on the head, but other faces of plastic and brass are also available. All are easily replaceable.

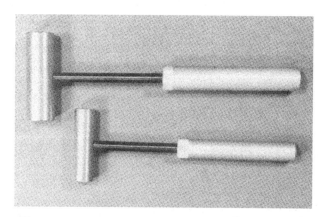

6. For drifting out pins, these small all-metal hammers from B-Square are the best I've seen. Two sizes (weights) are available and they're well worth the modest cost.

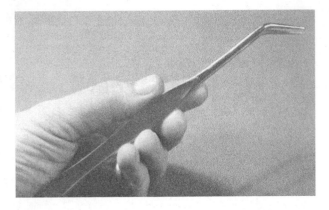

7. For situations where reach and accessibility are beyond the capabilities of sharp-nosed pliers, a pair of large sharp-nosed forceps (tweezers) will be invaluable.

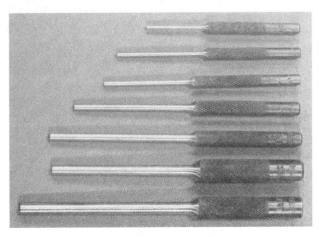

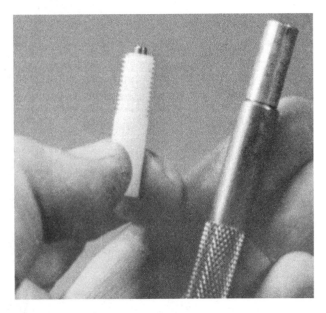

8. One of the most-used tools in my shop is this nylon tipped drift punch, shown with an optional brass tip in place on the handle. It has a steel pin inside the nylon tip for strength. From Brownells, and absolutely essential.

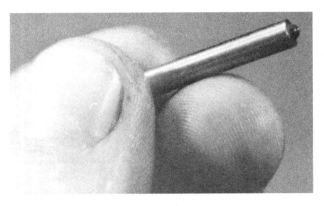

10. These punches by Mayhew are designed specifically for roll pins and have a projection at the center of the tip to fit the hollow center of a roll pin, driving it out without deformation of the ends. From Brownells.

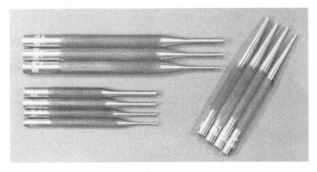

9. A good set of drift punches will prevent a lot of marred pins. These, from Brownells, are made by Mayhew. The tapered punches at the right are for starting pins, the others for pushing them through. Two sizes are available-4 inches or 6 inches.

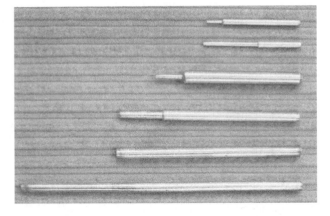

11. Some of the necessary tools are easily made in the shop. These non-marring drift punches were made from three sizes of welder's brazing rod.

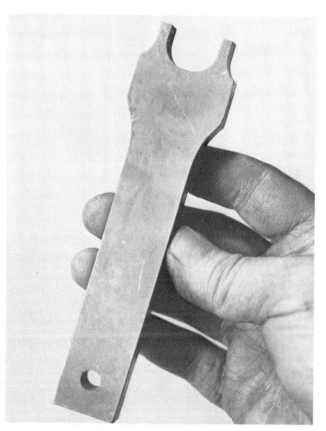

14. These extractor pliers are used in both the removal and replacement of Mauser or Springfield-type extractors, making a difficult job much easier. From Brownells.

12. This heavy wrench from Brownells is designed specifically for removal of the barrel nut in Remington Model 742 and Model 760 rifles. It's a quality tool of 01 steel, hardened to Rockwell C 46-48.

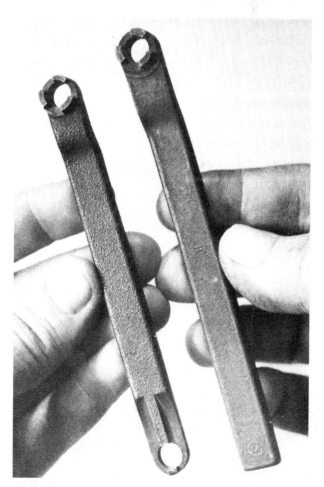

13. Most Remington centerfire rifles have the extractor mounted inside the front of the bolt by a tiny rivet. This special tool from B-square will set these rivets with a minimum of trouble.

15. These wrenches are designed for removal of the piston nut in the .30 U.S. Carbine. The tool at the right is the original military type with three lugs, and the one at the left is a double-end type, to fit both the military guns and the two-slot nut found on some commercial civilian Carbines. These wrenches are available from several military surplus and commercial sources.

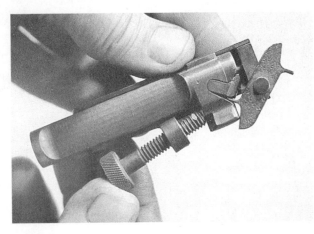

16. Without this tool removal of the firing pin, ejector and extractor from the 30 U.S. Carbine is a tedious job. It is available from military surplus sources. Similar tools are available for M1 Garands and M-14 rifle bolts.

17. This combination tool for the U.S. M-1 rifle (Garand) has provisions for clearing the chamber, installing the extractor and ejector in the bolt, a screwdriver, and other features. A completely-equipped Garand has one of these in the storage trap in the buttstock. They are available from military surplus sources.

18. As more and more rifles begin to use more and more AR-15 parts, the tools for ARs become more necessary to have. This M4 stock wrench is necessary for removing carbine and M4-style stock tubes on many of these guns.

19. A digital camera, even a cheap low-resolution model, can be invaluable. The ability to take a quick, free photo of anything that you are doing, for reference, is a modern convenience that one would be foolish to neglect.

20. Padded vise jaws are a wonderful tool. These puppies lovingly grasp the firearm or part without damaging the metal, wood, or plastic of which the object is made. These jaws are aluminum-based with fiber pads. On the back is a magnet. This is a set made by Wilton and is available from a number of sources.

AMT Back-Up

Data:	AMT Back-Up
Origin:	United States
Manufacturer:	AMT, Inc.
	El Monte, California
Cartridge:	380 ACP
Magazine capacity:	5 rounds
Over-all length:	5 inches
Height:	4 inches
Barrel length:	2⁹⁄₁₆ inches
Weight:	17 ounces

The "Back-Up" is made entirely of stainless steel, and, as its name implies, it is intended as a "back-up" gun for the law officer, for use if his regular sidearm is disabled, empty or lost during a serious social encounter. The little Back-Up is also popular as a self-defense pistol for the private citizen. The excellent and mechanically simple design is the work of John Raymond Wilkinson.

Disassembly:

1. With the magazine removed and the hammer in the fired position, use a non-marring drift to drive out the breechblock cross-pin toward either side.

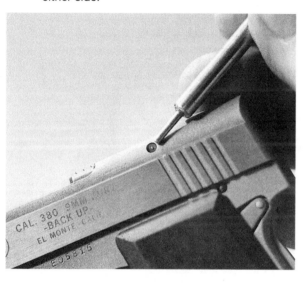

2. With a non-marring tool such as a nylon-tipped punch or a wooden dowel, nudge the breechblock upward, working through the magazine well.

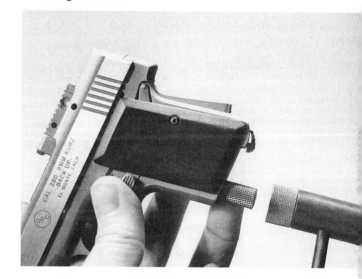

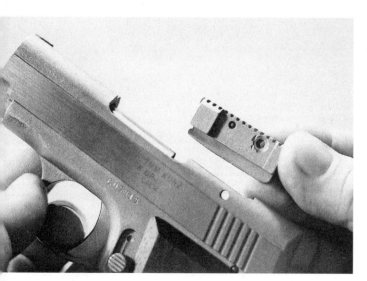

3. Remove the breechblock from the top of the slide.

4. Allow the slide to move forward until it clears the, short slide rails at the rear of the frame, and lift the slide upward at the rear to clear the barrel. Move the slide assembly forward off the barrel and frame. Remove the recoil spring and its guide from the frame.

5. Drifting out the small cross-pin in the breechblock will free the extractor and its coil spring for removal upward. **CAUTION:** *Removal of the extractor will also release the firing pin and its spring, so control the firing pin as the extractor is removed.* The circular spring, which retains the breechblock cross-pin, is staked in place on the left side, and no attempt should be made to remove it.

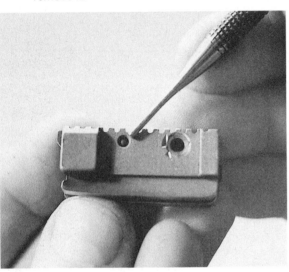

6. Use an Allen wrench of the proper size to back out the grip screws. Lift the grip panels at the rear for removal.

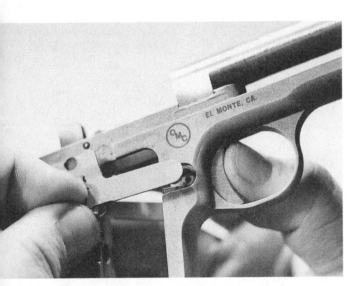

7. With a small tool, detach the trigger bar spring from its groove in the rear lower edge of the trigger bar, and move it inward, behind the bar. Restrain the trigger, and remove the trigger bar toward the left.

8. Removal of the trigger bar will release the trigger and its spring to move forward, and it can then be removed toward either side. Take care that the small trigger spring is not lost.

9. Remove the safety lever toward the left. Take care not to exert outward pressure on the front of the lever.

10. Drift out the small pin at the top of the frame enough to partially release the ejector. It is not removed at this time.

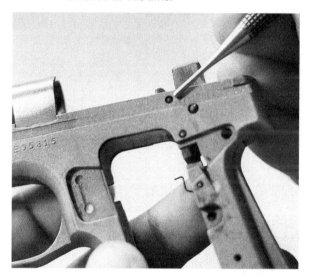

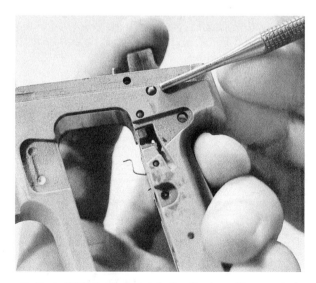

11. With the hammer in the fired position, restrain it, and push out the hammer pivot toward the right.

12. Ease the hammer out upward, along with its strut and spring, and remove the ejector, which will also be released. **CAUTION:** *The hammer spring is under tension.*

13. The hammer strut is easily removable from the hammer by turning it straight out to the rear and sliding it out of its seat in the hammer toward either side.

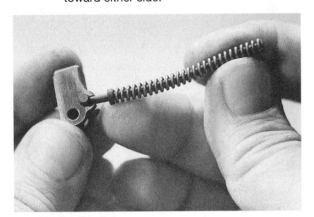

14. Drift out the sear cross-pin, and remove the sear forward, into the magazine well.

15. Push out the pin, which retains the sear spring and the trigger bar spring. Before removal, note the position of the two springs to aid in reassembly.

16. Drift out the cross-pin at the lower rear of the grip frame, and remove the magazine catch downward.

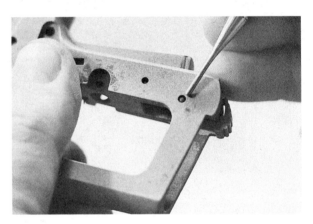

17. Move the grip safety upward to clear its lower lugs from the frame, then remove it downward and toward the rear.

18. The inner tips of the grip safety spring are locked into holes on each side within the backstrap. Squeeze the inner arms of the spring together to clear the tips from the holes, and remove the spring toward the rear.

Reassembly Tips:

1. When replacing the hammer and hammer spring assembly, be sure the spring and strut are attached to the hammer with the double curve of the strut in the orientation shown. When the hammer is in position, start the hammer pin through, then insert the ejector before pushing the hammer pin into place. As the hammer is inserted, be sure the lower tip of the spring strut enters the hole in the top of the magazine catch.

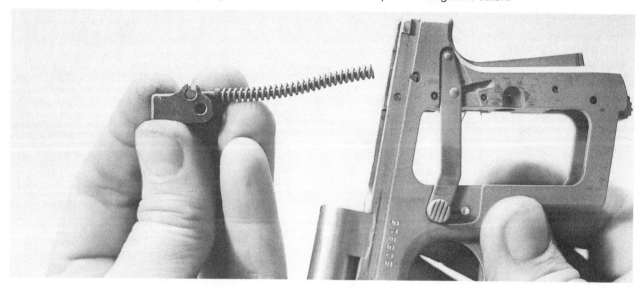

2. After the trigger bar/disconnector is back in place, insert a small tool to re-engage the trigger bar spring with its groove in the rear lower edge of the bar.

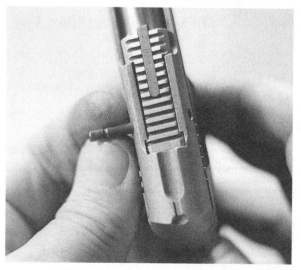

3. Note that the breechblock pin has a groove near one end. This groove must go on the left side of the gun, to engage the spring clip in the breechblock.

Beretta PX4 Storm

Data: Beretta PX4 Storm
Origin: Italy
Manufacturer: Armi Beretta S.p.A.,
Gardone (Brescia)
Cartridge: 9 x 19mm (9mm Luger)
Magazine capacity: 17 rounds
Overall length: 7.55 inches
Height: 5.51 inches
Barrel length: 4.02 inches
Weight: 27.69 ounces

The polymer-frame PX4 was introduced in 2003. It has since been offered in other chamberings, including 40 S&W, and in a compact version. All of these are mechanically the same, and the instructions will apply. I will note that for the non-gunsmith, some aspects of the takedown and reassembly may be difficult.

Field Strip:

1. With the magazine removed and the hammer in cocked position, pull the tabs of the takedown latch down, and move the slide and barrel assembly forward off the frame.

2. Lift the barrel rotation block and remove it, along with the recoil spring assembly.

3. Turn the barrel slightly (counter-clockwise, rear view) to clear the locking lug, and remove it from the slide.

Detail Strip:

4. It is possible to dis-assemble the recoil spring unit by retracting the front ring and its collar and depressing the opposed catches of the endpiece. CAUTION: The compressed spring will be released. In normal takedown, this unit is not taken apart.

5. The extractor and its coil spring are removed by drifting out this vertical roll-pin. Control the spring.

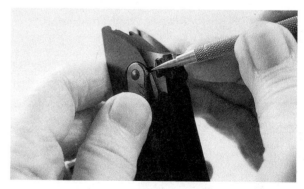

6. Except for repair or refinishing, it is best to avoid takedown of the manual safety and firing pin system. If it is necessary, move the right-side safety lever very slightly to align its retaining roll-pin with an exit track, and drift out the pin. This will allow the lever to be taken off, and the body and left lever of the safety, along with the rear firing pin, can then be turned and taken out to the left. The forward firing pin, the firing pin block, and their springs will then be accessible for removal.

7. Assuming that the manual safety system has been taken out, the firing pin and its spring are removed toward the rear, and the firing pin block, shown here, can then be removed, along with its spring.

10. Remove the back-strap piece toward the rear. Some careful prying may be necessary to free it.

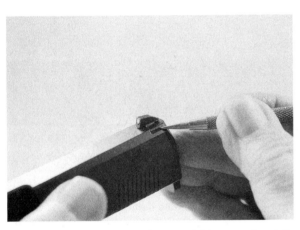

8. Both the front and rear sights are dovetail-mounted, and can be drifted out if necessary.

11. Push out the middle cross-pin at the rear of the grip-frame.

9. Use a sharp screwdriver to lift the back-strap retainer until it can be grasped and removed.

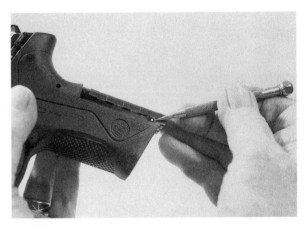

12. Be sure the hammer is in forward position, and push out the cross-pin at lower rear. CAUTION: Restrain the spring base, as the hammer spring will force it out.

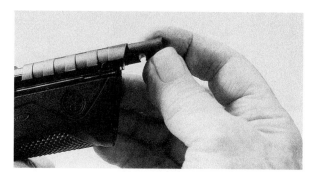

13. Ease out the spring base and remove it.

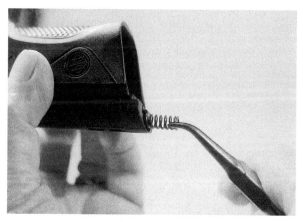

14. Use slim pliers to grip the end of the hammer spring, turn it slightly to free it, and take it out.

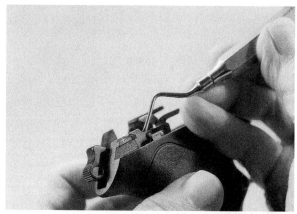

15. This step is one of those that cannot be properly photographed. With the hammer in cocked position, look inside the top of the frame on the right, and use a fork-tipped tool like the one shown to push down the rear of the small rectangular locking spring. While holding it down, use another tool to nudge the tip of the top retaining cross pin toward the left. This slim pin passes through the hammer pivot, and its head is fully recessed into the grip frame on the left side. This is not an easy operation.

16. Remove the upper cross-pin toward the left.

17. With the hammer in forward position, move the rear sub-frame out upward. You will have to dis-engage it form the trigger bar as it exits.

18. If it is necessary to remove the firing pin block lever and sear-trip lever, push this cross pin out toward the left side. CAUTION: a small coil spring and positioning collar will be released, so control them.

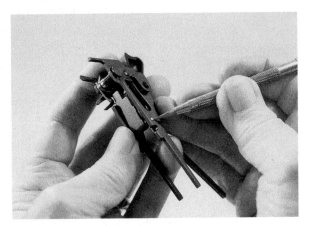

19. The sear and its torsion spring can be removed by pushing out this cross-pin. CAUTION: Control the spring.

20. If the hammer is to be removed, you will have to once again un-latch the lock-spring. The hammer pivot is then pushed out toward the left side. The two-piece hammer spring strut is retained in the hammer by a small roll-pin.

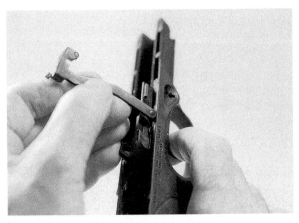

21. Turn the trigger bar upward, and pull the trigger to align it with the exit recess in the frame. Move the bar to the right, and take it out. The trigger bar spring is in a recess inside the magazine well. A hooked tool can be used to remove it upward.

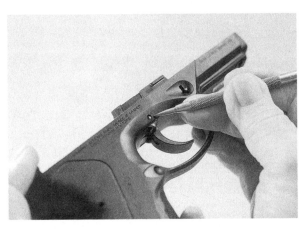

22. Drifting out this cross pin will release the trigger for removal downward. CAUTION: The torsion-type trigger spring will be released inside the frame at the top, so restrain it. In normal takedown, this system is best left in place.

23. If the takedown latch is to be removed, use a very slim tool inside the frame at the top, inserting it in the semi-circular opening at center to depress and hold the spring. The latch can then be taken out either side.

24. To remove the magazine catch system, first insert a small tool in the hole in the release button, and push the lock pin out toward the right side.

25. Remove the lock pin.

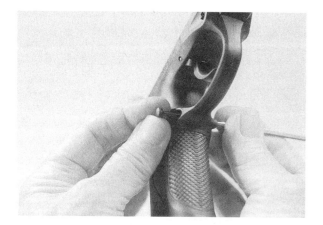

26. Remove the release button and spring toward the left.

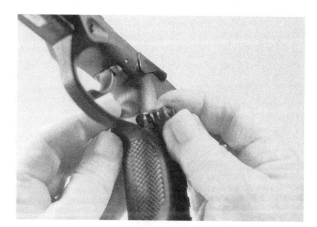

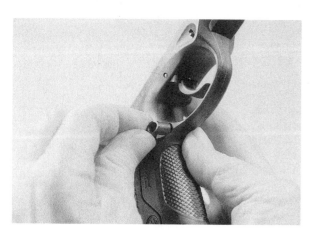

27. Remove the magazine catch piece toward the right.

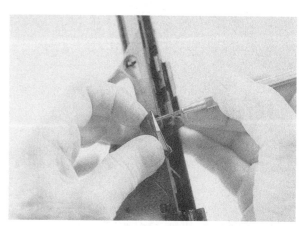

28. If the slide latch needs to be removed, turn it to its uppermost position, and nudge it out toward the left. CAUTION: Control the torsion spring.

Reassembly Tips:

1. As the rear sub-frame is re-installed, be sure the rear tip of the trigger bar is properly engaged before pushing the unit down into place. After the unit is seated, you must hold the trigger bar against the wall of the grip and use a fork-tipped tool to engage the upper arm of the torsion spring with its groove in the underside of the bar.

2. When installing the back-strap retainer, be sure its angled end is toward the front, as shown. A light tap with a non-marring tool will seat it properly.

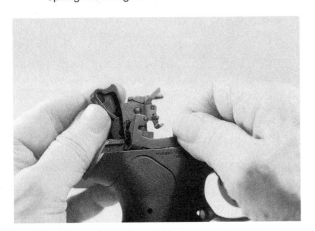

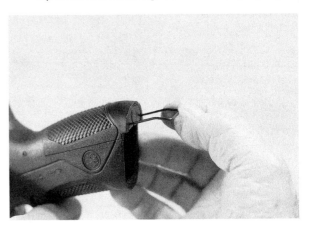

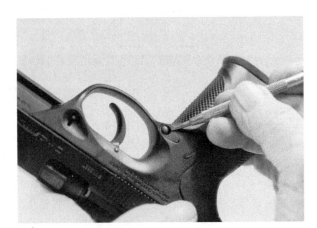

3. Support the magazine release button on a firm surface as the lock pin is pushed back into place. The pin should be checked to be sure it is fully locked.

Colt 1911 Series

Similar/Identical Pattern Guns

The same basic assembly/disassembly steps for the Colt 1911 also apply to the following guns:

AMT Combat Government Model
AMT Skipper

Auto-Ordnance M1911A1 Thompson
Colt Combat Grade Government
Colt Gold Cup
Colt Mark IV Series 70
Colt Super 39
Detonics Scoremaster
Federal Ordnance Ranger M1911A1
Llama Model IXA
Llama Model XV
M-S Safari Arms Model 81 BD

Olympic/Safari Arms Enforcer

Randall Curtis LeMay Four Star
Springfield Armory M1911A1

Springfield Armory M1911A1 Defender

AMT Hardballer
Argentine Model 1927

Colt Combat Commander
Colt Commander
Colt Gold Cup 38 Special
Colt Mark IV Series 80
Colt National Match 45
Essex Model 1911A1
Llama Model IIIA
Llama Model XA
M-S Safari Arms Enforcer
M-S Safari Arms Model 81
BP Super
Olympic/Safari Arms
Matchmaster
Randall Raider
Springfield Armory
M1911A1 Commander
Vega 45

AMT Long Slide
Auto-Ordnance M1911A1
Pit Bull
Colt Combat Elite
Colt Delta Elite
Colt Lightweight Commander
Colt Model 1911
Colt Officers ACP
Falcon Portsider
Llama Model VIII
Llama Model XI
M-S Safari Arms Model 81
M-S Safari Arms Model 81
NM
Randall Compact Service
Model
Randall Service Model
Springfield Armory M1911A1
Compact

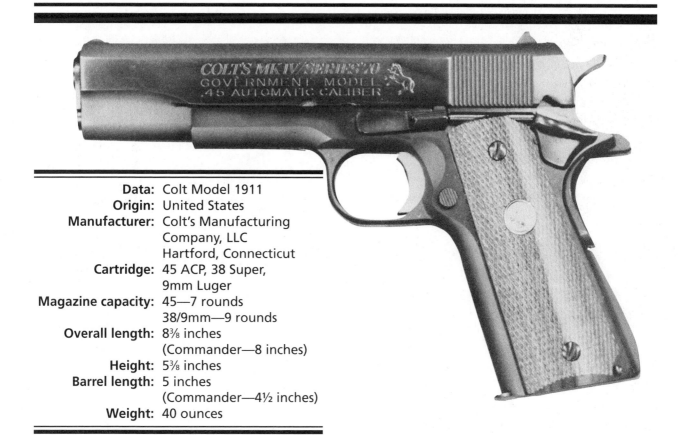

Data:	Colt Model 1911
Origin:	United States
Manufacturer:	Colt's Manufacturing Company, LLC Hartford, Connecticut
Cartridge:	45 ACP, 38 Super, 9mm Luger
Magazine capacity:	45—7 rounds 38/9mm—9 rounds
Overall length:	8⅜ inches (Commander—8 inches)
Height:	5⅜ inches
Barrel length:	5 inches (Commander—4½ inches)
Weight:	40 ounces

Our standard military pistol from 1911 to 1985, the Colt 45 Auto is so well known that it really needs no comment or background data here. The target model, the Gold Cup, has one or two small differences in the internal mechanism. The Series 80 versions have an added firing pin block safety system, consisting of a lever in the frame and a plunger and spring in the slide. These are not complicated, and should cause no takedown problems. The old Government Model has also been copied many times over the years, and the instructions will generally apply to all of these.

Field Strip:

1. With the magazine removed and the hammer down, depress the checkered button below the barrel and turn the barrel bushing toward the right side of the gun until the plug and recoil spring are free to come out. **CAUTION:** *The recoil spring is under tension, so keep strong pressure on the checkered end of the plug and ease it out.* The barrel bushing can ordinarily be turned easily with the fingers, but on some tight older guns, and especially on the new Mark IV Series 70 guns with the barrel-gripping bushing, a special wrench may be necessary.

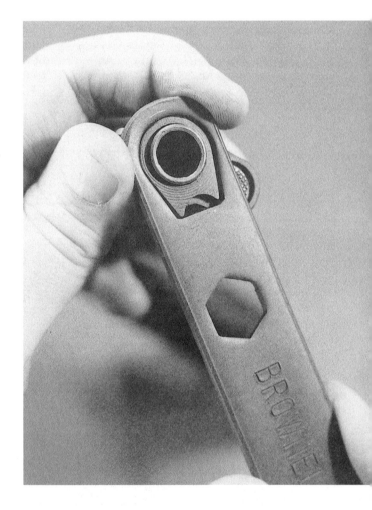

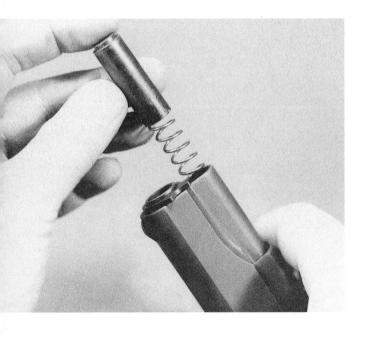

2. After easing out the plug, remove it from the end of the spring. In rare cases, it may be locked on by an internal tab, and a slight turn will be necessary to free it.

3. Cock the hammer, and move the slide back until the small semi-circular cut at its lower edge aligns with the top rear of the slide stop.

4. Push the end of the slide stop shaft, on the right side of the gun, and remove the slide stop from the left side.

5. The slide assembly can now be run forward off the frame.

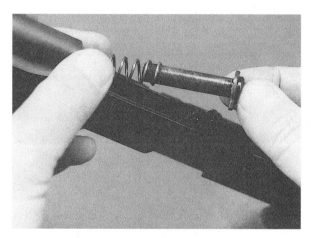

6. Remove the recoil spring and its guide from the slide, together or separately.

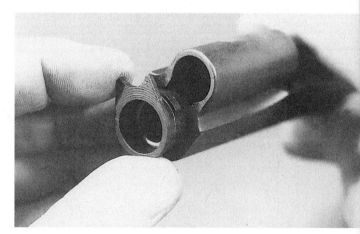

7. Turn the barrel bushing back toward the left side of the slide, until its lug aligns with the opening, and remove the bushing from the front of the slide.

8. Tip the barrel link over forward to clear the recoil spring tunnel.

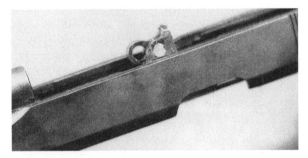

9. Remove the barrel from the front of the slide. **Gun is now field-stripped.**

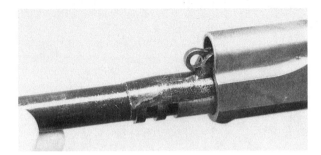

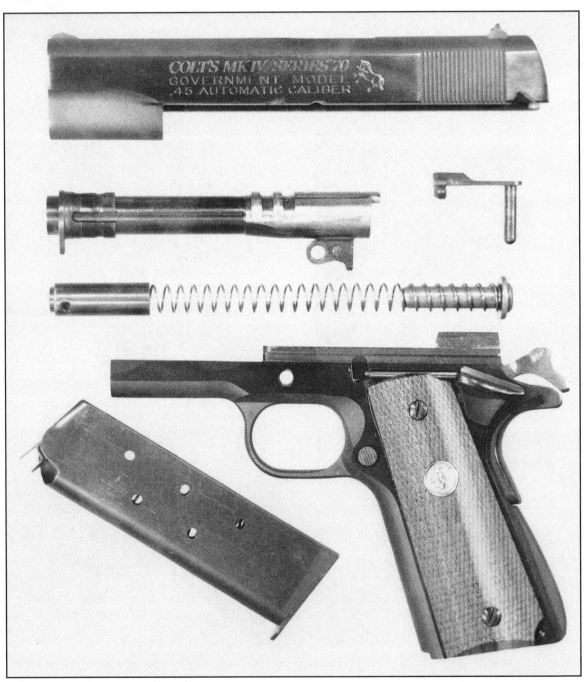

Colt Mk IV/Series 70 field-stripped

Detail Strip:

10. With a tool of appropriate size, depress the firing pin and slide the retainer downward to free the firing pin. **CAUTION:** *The firing pin spring is under some compression, and can eject the firing pin with force when the retainer is removed.*

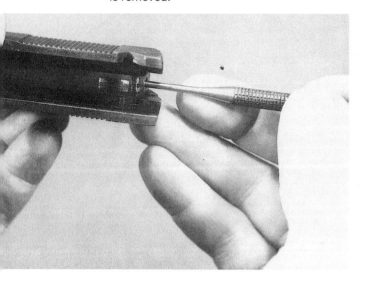

11. After the retainer plate is removed, the firing pin and its return spring can be taken out.

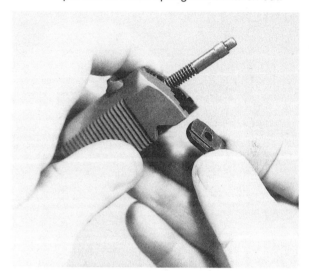

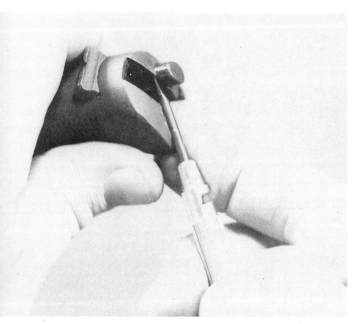

12. Removal of the firing pin retainer plate also frees the extractor. With a small screwdriver pry it gently out, straight to the rear of the slide.

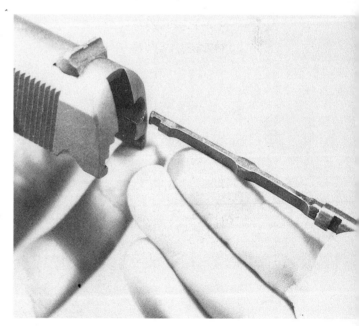

13. When the extractor is pried out past its round headpiece, it can be easily grasped with the fingers and removed from the slide. The rear sight can be drifted out of its dovetail slot from left to right.

14. The initial takedown key for the frame is the mainspring housing retaining pin, located at the lower rear edge of the grip frame.

15. With the hammer at rest, use a drift of the proper size to drive out the mainspring housing retainer pin.

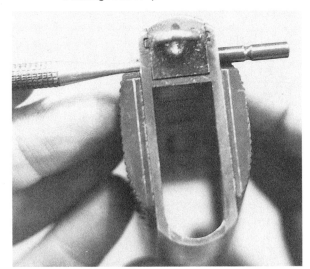

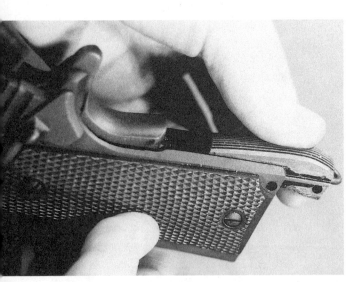

16. The mainspring housing can now be slid down off the frame. If it is tight, cocking the hammer will put pressure on it through the mainspring and help to ease it out.

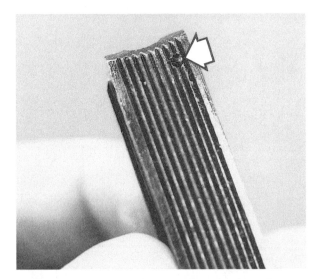

17. Viewing the mainspring housing from the rear, there is a small pin (arrow) at upper right which can be drifted out toward the inside to free the mainspring and its plunger. **CAUTION:** *The mainspring is under quite a bit of tension and can cause injury when released. Use a heavy shop cloth to catch it when driving out the pin.*

18. With the hammer cocked, move the safety almost to the on-safe position while exerting slight outward pressure toward the left. When its internal projection aligns with its cut in the frame, it can easily be taken out.

19. Removal of the safety frees the grip safety and this is now removed to the rear.

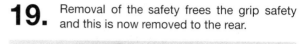

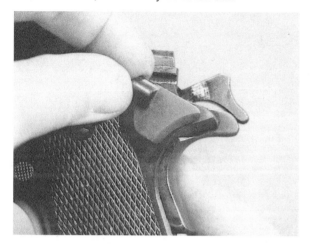

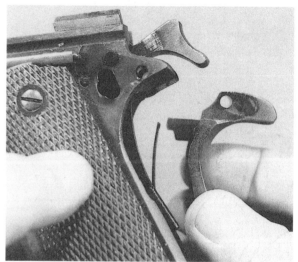

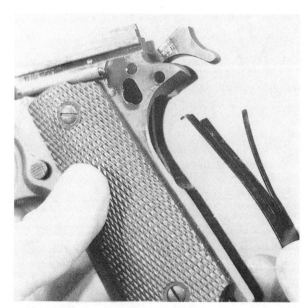

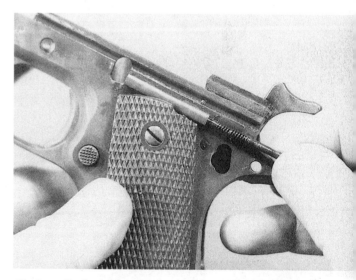

20. The combination leaf spring which powers the sear, trigger, disconnector, and grip safety can now be lifted out at the rear of the grip frame.

21. Pushed from the front with a drift of proper size, the spring and plungers which supply tension to the slide stop and manual safety can now be removed from the rear of its tunnel above the left grip. The spring tunnel is riveted in place inside the magazine well and it is difficult to remove and replace without special tools. Unless removal is absolutely necessary, it should be left in place.

22. Started from the right with a drift of the proper size, the hammer pin is removed from the left side of the grip frame.

23. The hammer can now be lifted out of the frame.

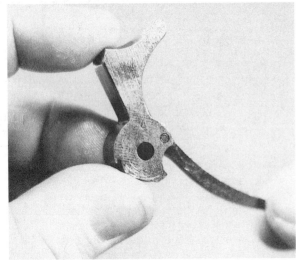

24. Removal of the small pin at lower rear of the hammer will free the hammer strut. Note the direction of its curve, and replace it in the same position.

25. Starting from the right side with a drift, remove the sear/disconnector pin from the left side.

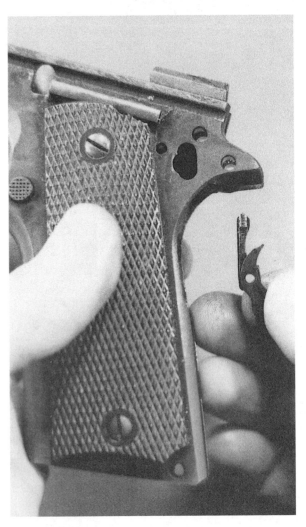

26. The sear and disconnector can now be removed from the rear of the frame. Note their relationship for proper reassembly.

27. With a small screwdriver, turn the slotted head of the magazine release retainer to the left, while keeping the magazine release depressed to the level shown.

28. With the retainer locked into its slot in the magazine release, the release can be taken out toward the right side of the gun. After removal, turning the retainer back to the right will free the retainer and its spring from the release body. These are small parts, so take care that they aren't lost.

29. After the magazine release is taken out, the trigger is free to be removed toward the rear of the frame. The grip screws can be taken out to free the grips.

Reassembly Tips:

When installing the combination spring, slide the mainspring housing partially into the frame to hold the spring in place while replacing the grip safety.

During reassembly, the most difficult operation is often the alignment of the barrel link with the slide latch hole in the frame. The hole is large enough that the proper alignment can be seen, and the link can be edged into position by moving the slide back and forth a very small distance until it drops into place. Don't try aligning the link and the clearance cut for the top of the latch at the same time. Get the latch shaft through the link, then swing the latch up and align it with the clearance cut.

FNH Five-Seven

Data:	FNH Five-seven
Origin:	Belgium
Manufacturer:	Fabrique Nationale, Herstal
Cartridge:	5.7 x 28mm
Magazine capacity:	20 rounds
Overall length:	8.2 inches
Barrel length:	4.8 inches
Weight:	23.3 ounces

The Five-seveN has also been called the IOM (Individual Officer Model), and USG (U.S. Government). The latter designation indicates its use by several agencies. When the pistol was introduced, original ammunition would pierce body armor, and sales were to Law Enforcement only. Later, with different cartridges and a slight re-design, it was offered for regular commercial sales.

Field Strip:

1. With the internal hammer in fired position and the magazine removed, move the slide about a quarter-inch rearward, and hold it there. Push the takedown latch fully to the rear, and keep it in that position.

2. Ease the slide assembly forward about a half-inch, to clear the rails at the rear, and lift it off the frame.

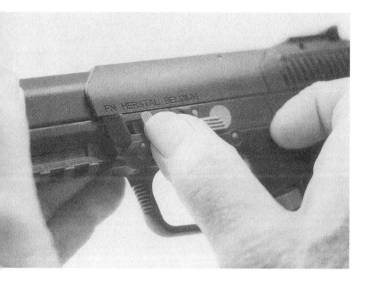

FNH Five-Seven field-stripped

3. Tip the barrel outward at the rear, and remove it from the slide, along with the captive recoil spring.

Detail Strip:

4. It is possible to remove the recoil spring and it's bushing from the barrel by retracting the bushing and spring, then prying off the retaining spring-ring. A vise and extreme caution will be necessary. In normal takedown, this system is left in place.

5. The slide components are contained in a sub-frame that is retained in the cover by this cross pin. It is splined at its right tip, and thus must be drifted out toward the right side. Be sure to use a non-marring brass drift punch.

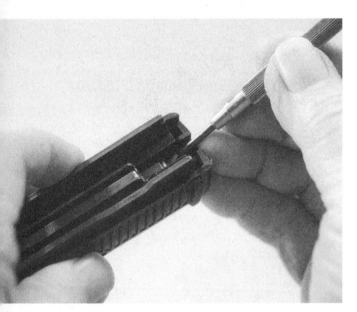

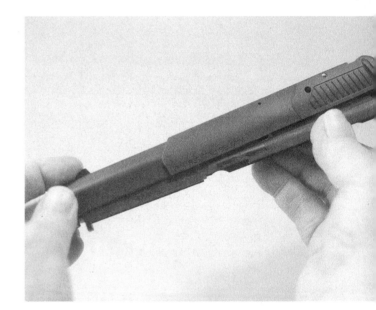

6. Use a tool to gently pry the rear of the sub-frame outward slightly, as shown.

7. When the rear sight has cleared its opening in the cover, push the front sight inward and rearward, to detach the front lug of the sub-frame from its seat in the front of the cover. This will be visible at the front. Remove the sub-frame from the cover.

8. During the sub-frame removal, take care that the loaded-chamber indicator and its small coil spring are not lost. It would probably be wise to remove them at this point.

9. To remove the extractor and its coil spring, depress the extractor slightly at the rear and pull out the pivot pin. Control the spring.

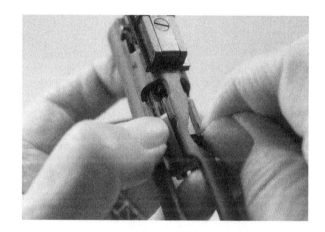

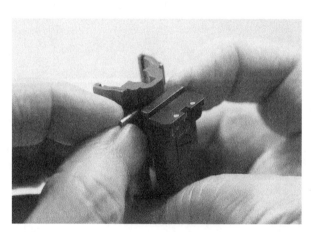

10. Remove the cross pin at the rear of the sub-frame. It can be simply pushed out, no tool required.

11. Remove the firing pin and its return spring toward the rear.

12. If removal of the firing pin safety block and its spring is necessary, these parts can be taken out only upward, and you must first drift the rear sight assembly out of its dovetail-mount. Except for repair, this system is best left in place. This also applies to disassembly of the rear sight. If necessary, the front sight can be drifted out of its dovetail-mount.

13. Unless replacement is necessary, the action locking block and the other forward components should not be removed. If this has to be done, the locking block cross pin is drifted out toward the right. It is under slight spring tension, so control it. If the strong barrel rebound spring must be removed, it will be necessary to insert a spacer of some sort to hold the spring while the cross pin is drifted out toward the right. CAUTION: This spring is very powerful. If the parts above have been removed, the takedown latch can be moved rearward, its rear extension turned upward, and it is then moved inward to be taken out.

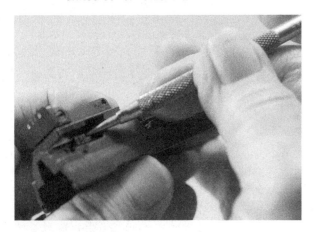

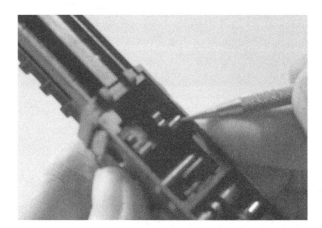

14. The safety levers are retained on their cross-shaft by small roll pins. With the shaft turned to the proper position, these can be drifted out inward and the levers can then be taken out to either side. A positioning plunger and spring will be released on the left side, under the cross-shaft. In normal takedown, this system should be left in place.

15. To remove the rear sub-frame, the two cross pins are pushed out toward the left. First, use a slim tool to lift the front tip of the pin-lock spring upward, and hold it there while the front cross pin is pushed out.

16. The pin-lock spring, which also powers the slide latch, will be released when the front cross pin is removed. It should be taken out now, to prevent loss. The slide latch will also be freed, as the front pin is its pivot, but it is not to be removed.

17. Removal of the slide latch would require that its polymer knob be pried off the internal steel part. In normal takedown, this is not advisable.

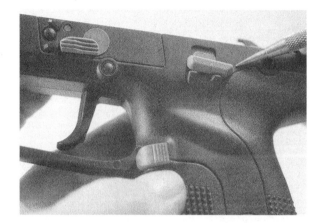

18. Push out the rear cross pin.

19. Remove the sub-frame upward.

20. The firing pin block lever and the sear, and their attendant springs, can be removed by pushing out the two pivot-pins. If this disassembly is done, note the positions and bearing points of the springs, for reassembly. Removal of the sear will require, of course, that the hammer, if cocked, must be eased down to fired position.

21. The last remark also applies if the hammer is to be taken out. Even at rest, the hammer spring is very strong. It must be controlled as the bearing pin is pushed out.

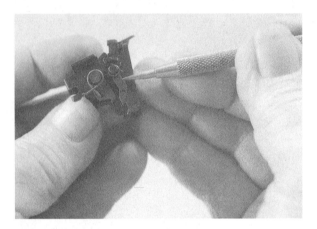

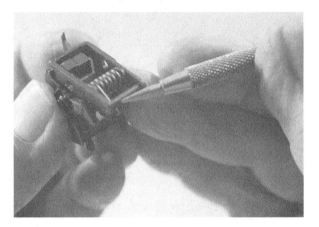

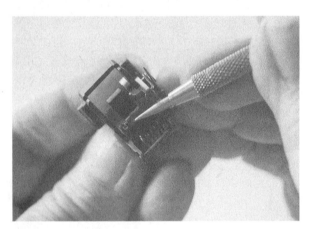

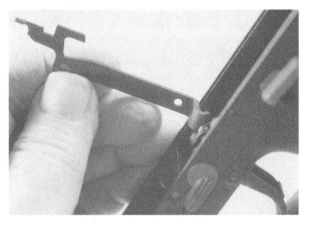

22. If the hammer is removed, note that the rear arm of the hammer spring bears on a small grooved roller, retained by a rear cross pin in the hammer. Take care that this tiny part is not lost.

23. Move the rear of the trigger bar inward, to clear the magazine safety. Then, turn it over toward the front, relieving the spring tension.

24. The trigger cross pin is splined at the left tip, and must be drifted out toward the left. If the manual safety system was previously removed, the removal of this pin will allow the trigger system to be moved out upward.

25. When the safety is still in place, move the trigger assembly upward and rearward until the cross pin at the top is accessible. Pushing out this pin will free the trigger bar and spring for removal. The trigger is then moved downward, and is taken out through the trigger guard opening. Insert a hooked tool under the manual safety cross-shaft on the right side, and push the magazine safety all the way to the rear. Turn its rear tip inward until it is free, and take it out.

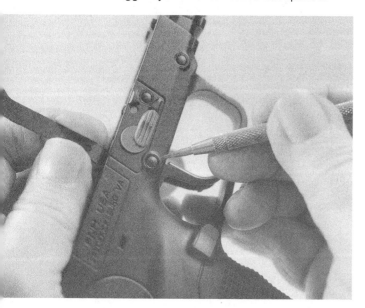

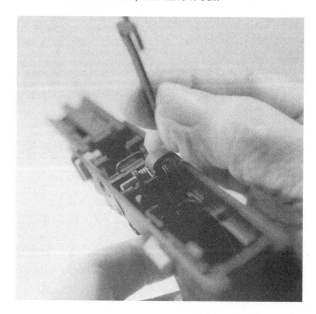

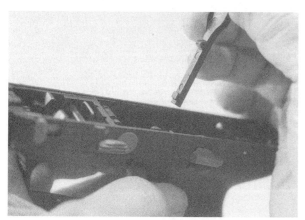

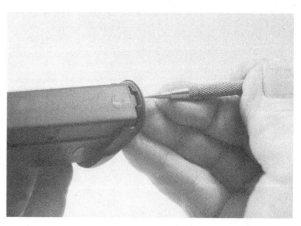

26. A tool is provided with the pistol for removal of the magazine release spring, the round stud on its slim end being used to pull the spring out upward. The release button can then be taken out toward either side. Because of its location, inside the grip frame, a photo of this was not possible.

27. To disassemble the magazine, a sharp rap on a non-marring surface with the back of the floorplate will unlock it and start it off toward the front. CAUTION: The magazine spring is under tension, so control it as the floorplate is taken off.

Reassembly Tips:

1. As the sub-frame unit is put back in, be sure the rear arm of the sear spring contacts its shelf in the frame. When the sub-frame is in place, insert the lock-spring. Remember that its ends must be on top of both pins, and that its center coil goes below the inner flange of the slide latch. Insert the rear cross pin first.

2. When installing the slide sub-frame, align its front lug with the rectangular aperture in the cover, then move it forward and upward into place.

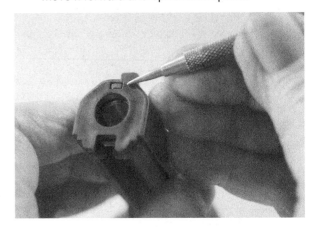

3. The wider end of the supplied tool for the magazine release has a recess that fits and holds the spring for re-insertion.

FNH FNS

Data:	FNH FNS
Origin:	United States
Manufacturer:	FNH USA
Cartridge:	9 mm Luger
Magazine capacity:	17 rounds
Over-all length:	7.25 inches
Barrel length:	4 inches
Weight:	1 pound 9 oz.

The FNS pistol is the descendant of the FNP and FNX series of handguns from Fabrique Nationale of Belgium. The feel and handling is identical but rather than being hammer fired as were the parent models, the FNS is striker fired, with the typical short trigger pull of such types of pistols. FNH began selling these pistols in the US in 2011.

Disassembly:

1. Lock the slide to the rear and rotate the takedown lever down till it stops.

2. Slowly close the slide, pull the trigger, and slide it forward off the front of the frame.

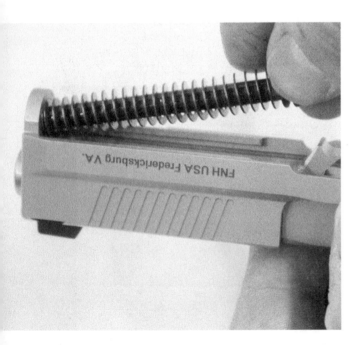

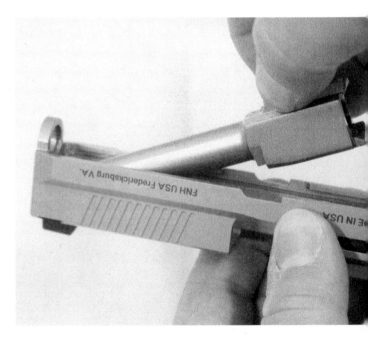

3. Lift the recoil spring and guide rod from the slide.

4. Lift the barrel from the slide.

5. With a small tool depress this plunger into the slide while simultaneously sliding the rear plate down. Control the firing pin as it is released to avoid losing parts.

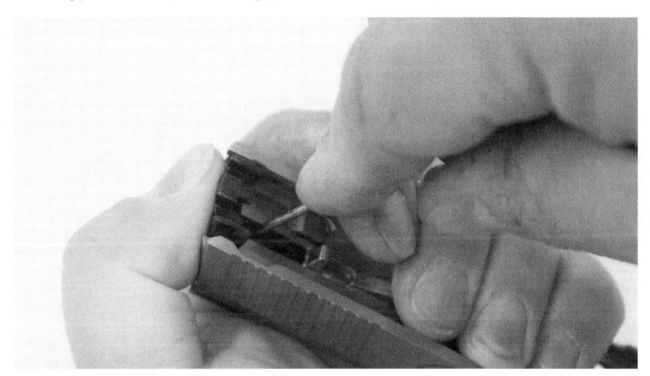

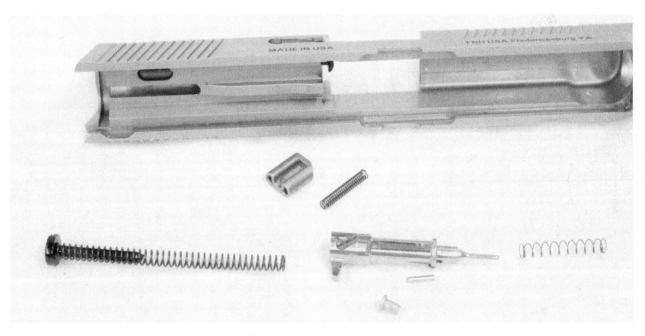

6. The firing pin spring and plunger, the firing pin and the firing pin return spring can now be removed. Note that the firing pin has a small pin that fits transversely that holds a small plunger inside the firing pin.

7. The extractor can be removed by pushing back on the plunger and rolling the extractor forward into the ejection port.

8. If necessary, the front and rear sights can be removed by pushing them out to the right.

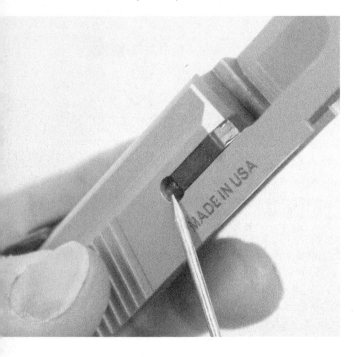

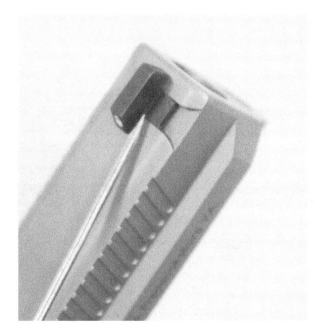

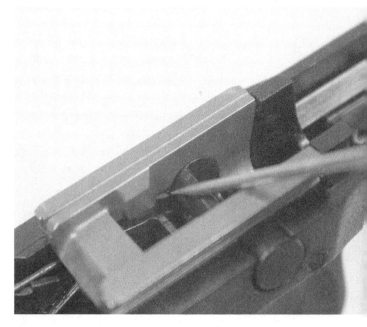

9. Drive out this roll pin at the rear of the frame.

10. Move the takedown lever to the halfway point (about 45 degrees down) and use a small screwdriver to displace the spring leg slightly inward. This will allow the takedown lever to be removed out the left side of the frame.

11. Drive out this pin just forward of the takedown lever. It is very tightly held in place.

12. Drive out the trigger pin.

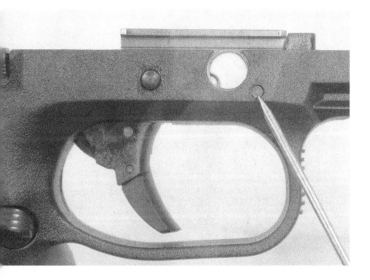

13. Lift the frame rail from the frame.

14. Removed the takedown lever/slide stop spring.

15. Remove the slide stop.

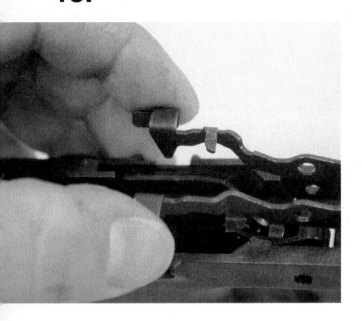

16. Lift out the sear housing and trigger assembly.

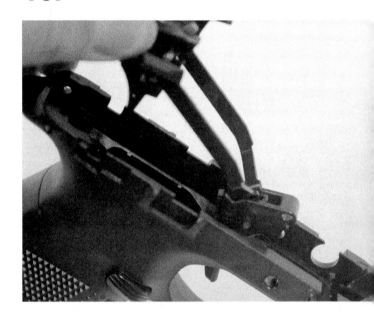

17. The magazine catch can be removed by lifting the spring straight up and pushing the magazine catch out to either side.

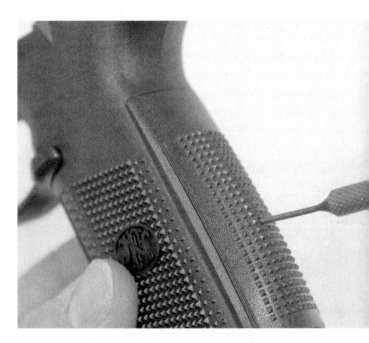

18. The backstrap can be removed by inserting a small punch into the hole in the strap and depressing the light spring inside. Simultaneously push the backstrap down and off the frame.

19. Pull the safety lever from the sear housing. Hold the housing firmly as it will split and fall apart if not held. There is a spring and detent ball on the left side. Do not lose them.

20. Unlatch the trigger bars from their pin.

21. Pull forward slightly on the trigger bar pin to free the disconnector and spring to be pulled from the left side of the housing.

22. Separate one side of the housing from the other. The parts should stay in one or the other. Lift the sear assembly from the housing.

23. Removing this pin will free the sear return spring.

24. Pull this pin to separate the sear assembly.

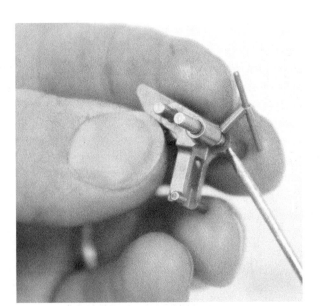

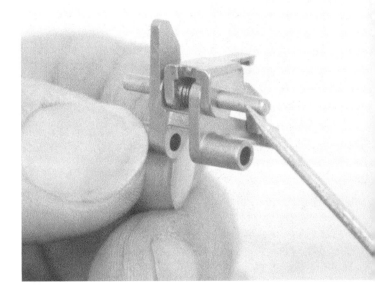

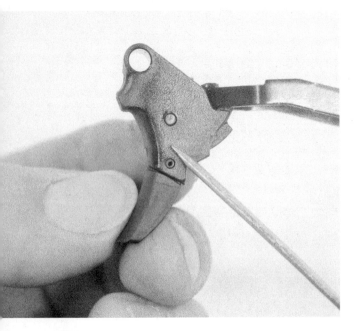

Reassembly Tips:

25. The trigger assembly can be disassembled if necessary, by driving out this roll pin to remove the bottom half of the trigger, and the solid pin to remove the trigger bar.

1. Some force will be required to reseat the frame rail pin that sits in front of the takedown lever. Use care not to damage the frame when reinstalling this pin.

HECKLER & KOCH USP TACTICAL

Data:	HK USP Tactical
Origin:	United States
Manufacturer:	HK Sidearms GmbH, Germany
Cartridge:	.45 ACP
Magazine capacity:	12 rounds
Over-all length:	8.64 inches
Barrel length:	5.09 inches
Weight:	2 pounds 1 oz.

The HK Universal Self-loading Pistol comes in a variety of flavors, from full sized to compact, from 9mm to .45 ACP. The tactical models add a threaded barrel for acceptance of a sound suppressor, and adjustable sights and triggers. Other than that, the Tactical models take down just the same as the standard models. It should be noted that H&K offers all the USP models with a variety of safety/decocking mechanisms. This takedown is based on the Variant 1 design which encompasses a SAFE position and decocker, designed for right-handed users. These are big pistols but are actually quite easy to maintain and shoot.

Disassembly:

1. With the magazine absent, pull back the slide until the squared notch in the left side aligns with the slide stop pin (picture A). Push out the slide stop to the left and remove it from the gun (picture B).

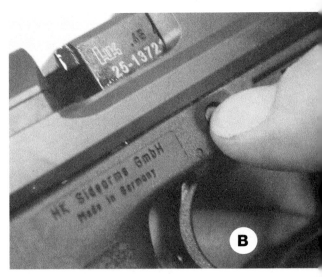

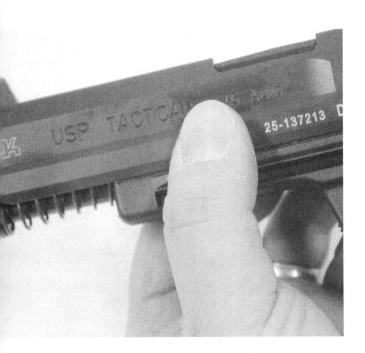

2. Slide the slide assembly forward off the front of the frame.

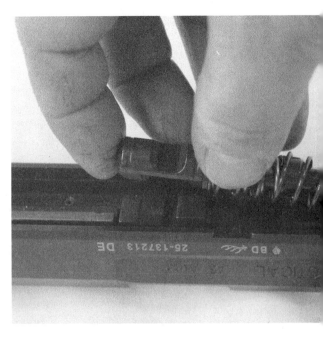

3. Lift the recoil spring and guide rod from the slide.

5. Drive out this pin to remove the extractor and extractor spring.

4. Lift the barrel from the slide.

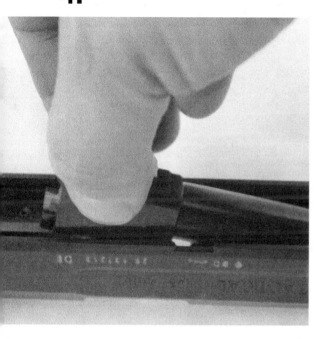

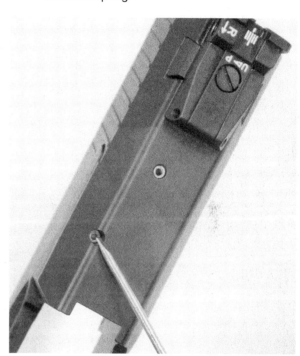

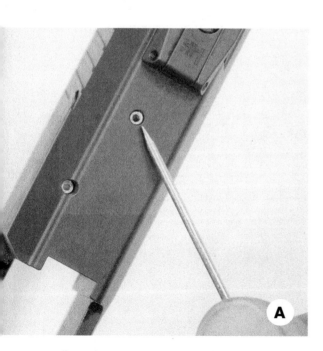

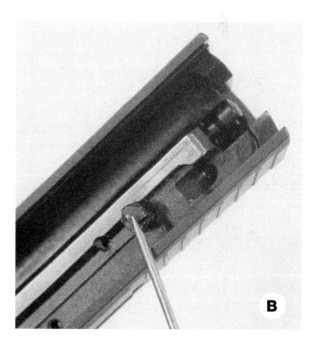

6. Drive out this pin to free the firing pin (picture A). As the firing pin is pulled, the firing pin safety will also be released (picture B). Both the firing pin and the firing pin safety can then be fully removed from the slide.

7. The front and rear sights can be driven out in either direction.

8. The recoil spring assembly can be disassembled by removing this "c" clip. In routine maintenance, this assembly should be left intact.

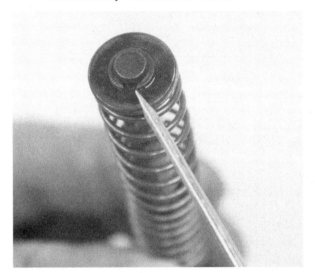

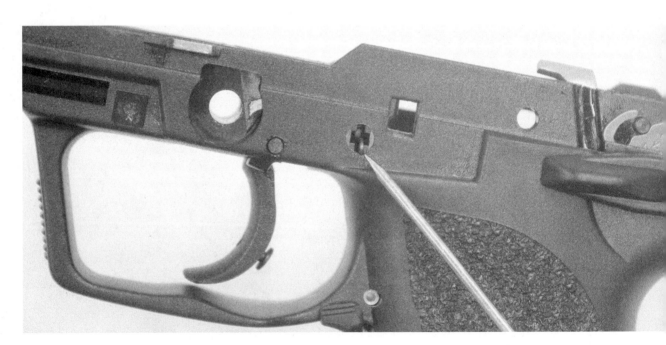

9. The slide stop spring should be left in place unless it is broken.

10. Depress the lanyard loop insert to relieve tension on the hammer spring, then push out the lanyard loop insert pin (picture A). Remove the lanyard loop insert. The hammer spring can also then be removed (picture B).

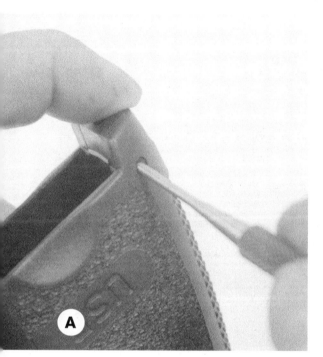

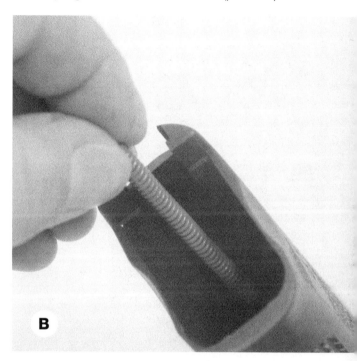

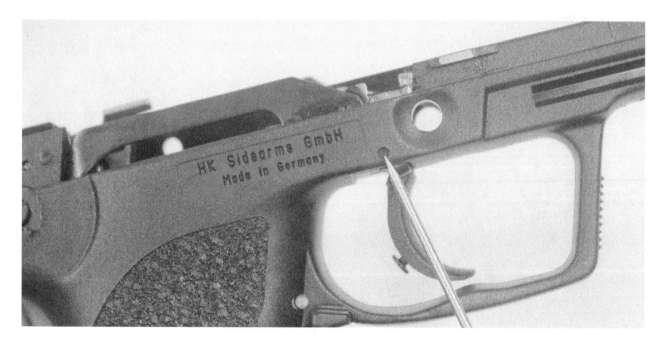

11. Push out the trigger pin from right to left.

12. From the left side, push out the sear axle enough to free the detent plate (picture A). Lift the detent plate from the frame (picture B).

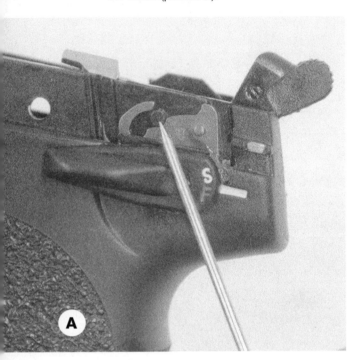

13. From the right, push the sear axle in just far enough to remove the disconnector from the frame.

14. Push the sear axle through from the right all the way out and it will free the next two pieces, the sear actuator latch and the catch. The last piece, the sear, will be freed but will stay in place in the frame.

15. The safety lever can now be pulled out of the frame to the left (picture A). There is a thin detent slide that holds the safety lever in the frame. Use a small tool to depress the spring to allow the safety to be fully removed (picture B). The detent slide and spring can now be removed as well (picture C).

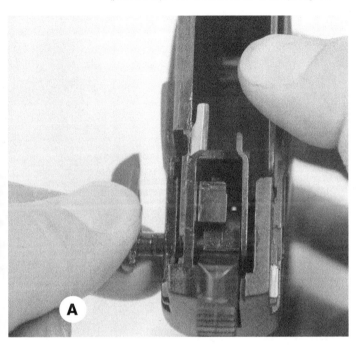

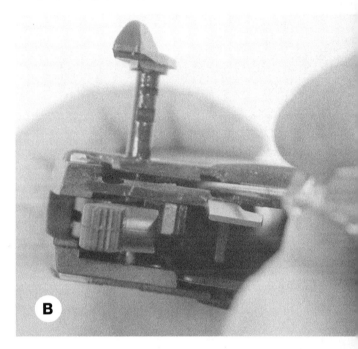

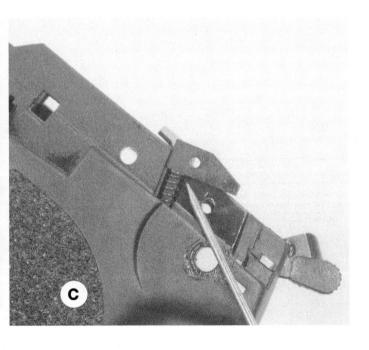

16. Remove the sear from the frame.

17. Push the hammer axis out to the right.

18. Remove the hammer from the frame. The hammer strut can also be removed up out of the frame.

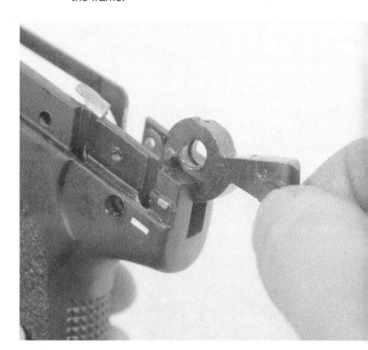

19. Lift the trigger bar. The trigger bar detent and spring can now be lifted from their hole.

20. There is a clearance slot here that will allow the trigger bar to be separated from the trigger. The trigger can be removed down into the trigger guard.

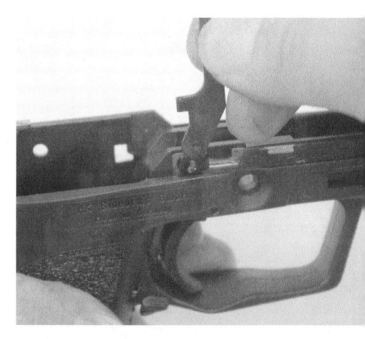

21. The sear spring can be removed if necessary.

22. Drive out this pin to remove the magazine catch and spring.

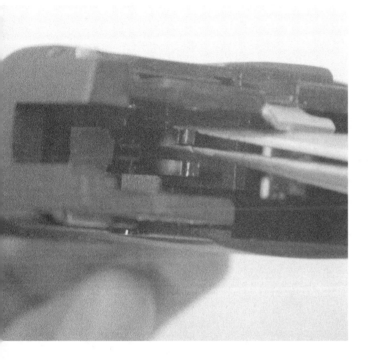

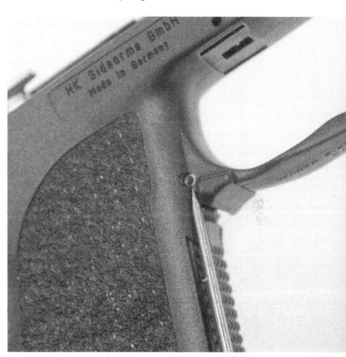

Reassembly Tips:

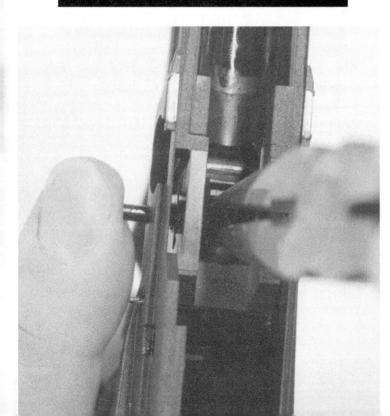

1. Reinstallation of the trigger spring is simplified by the use of needle-nosed pliers. Place the spring leg against the frame and roll the other leg down and onto the trigger to place the coil in line with the pin.

Kel-Tec PLR-16

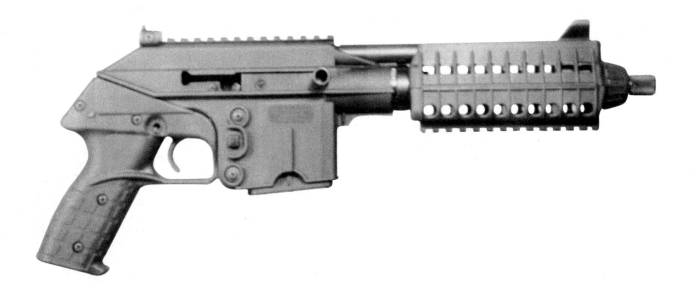

Data:	Kel-Tec PLR-16
Origin:	United States
Manufacturer:	Kel-Tec CNC Industries, Cocoa, Florida
Cartridge:	5.56 x 45mm (223)
Magazine capacity:	10 or 30 rounds
Overall length:	19 inches
Barrel length:	9.2 inches
Weight:	3.2 pounds

The "PLR' designation translates to "Pistol, Long Range", which, in this chambering, it certainly is. The PLR-16 was introduced in 2006. In circumstances where a carbine might be unwieldy, it would be a perfect choice. The one shown here has the optional fore-grip installed. If your gun has it, you'll know how to remove it. The takedown sequence shows a standard version.

Detail Strip:

1. Remove the magazine, cycle the action to cock the internal hammer, and set the manual safety in on-safe position. Push out the large cross pin at the rear of the receiver, and turn the pistol-grip down and forward.

2. Pull the recoil spring tube forward and turn it to align its locking lug with the top of the receiver. When released, the tub should enter the receiver to a depth of about a quarter-inch.

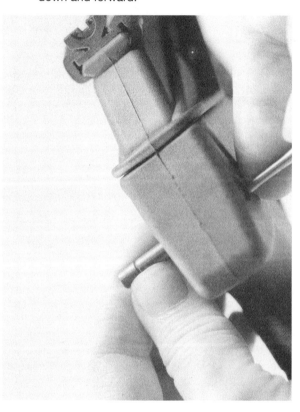

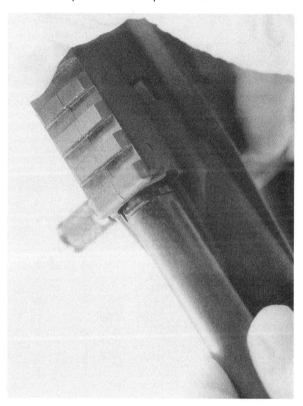

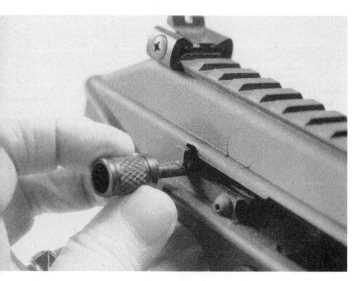

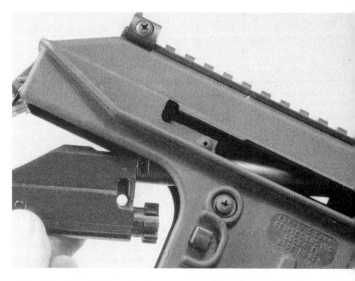

3. Move the bolt and piston assembly all the way to the rear, and turn the bolt handle downward to align it for exit. Remove the bolt handle.

4. Tip the bolt and piston assembly downward at the rear, and remove it.

5. Push out the firing pin retaining pin toward the left.

6. Remove the firing pin.

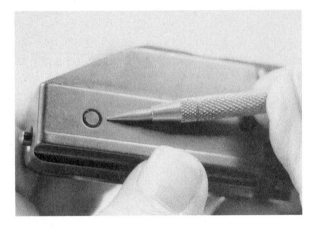

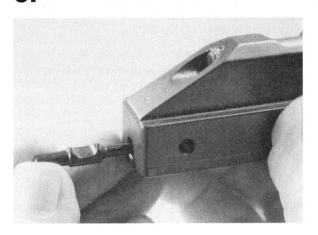

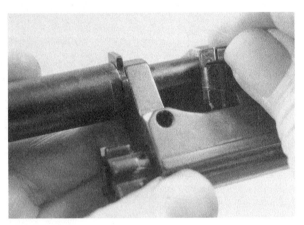

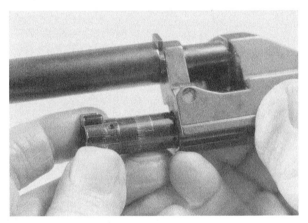

7. Remove the bolt cam piece.

8. Remove the bolt from the carrier unit.

9. If removal of the extractor is necessary for repair, drift out this pin. Control the coil spring, and take care that the small spring buffer is not lost.

10. If the ejector needs to be removed, it is retained by this pin. CAUTION: The coil spring is powerful. Control it and ease it out.

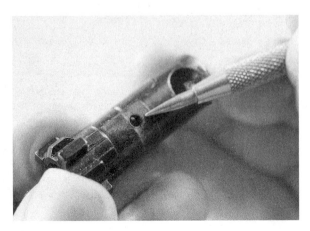

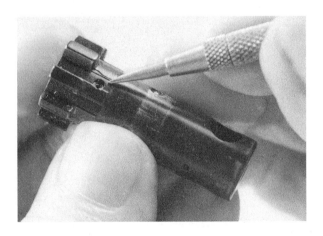

11. To disassemble the piston and recoil spring unit, align the piston head cross pin with the openings in the tube, and push out the pin. CAUTION: This is a strong spring. Keep a good grip on the piston head, and point it away from you.

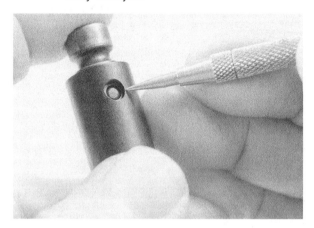

13. If necessary for repair, the lock spring for the takedown pin can be moved out of its recess and turned for removal.

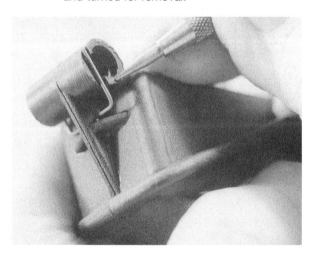

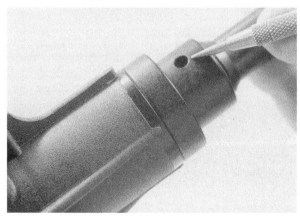

15. Removal of the barrel, its retainer, and extension requires a special two-point wrench to unscrew this barrel nut. This should be considered a factory job.

12. Ease out the piston head and remove it, along with the spring and the tube.

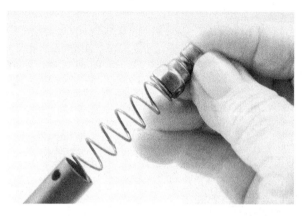

14. The front sight/gas port unit is retained on the barrel by a large roll-pin. This assembly is not routinely removed.

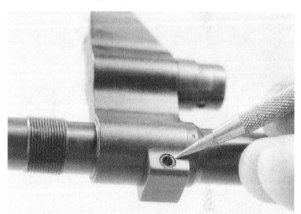

16. The grip frame and the receiver unit are in the same category. Note that the hammer cross pin is not a through-pin. Also, the eight Phillips screws in the grip frame and the four in the receiver require that opposed screwdrivers must be used, and there are several internal spacers involved. With the tension of the hammer spring and other springs, reassembly would be interesting, to say the least. If these areas need attention, it would be best to send them to Kel-Tec.

Reassembly Tips:

1. When reassembling the piston and recoil spring unit, remember that you must align the piston head with the hole at the tip of the guide rod before inserting the retaining pin. Control the piston. Be careful.

2. When inserting the carrier assembly, be sure the bolt stays in its full-forward position, and that the lug on the tube stays at the top. In place, the tube must be parallel with the barrel.

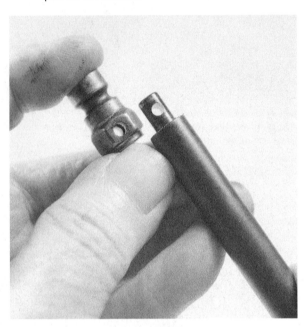

Smith & Wesson 459

Similar/Identical Pattern Guns

The same basic assembly/disassembly steps for the Smith & Wesson 459 also apply to the following guns:

Smith & Wesson Model 439   **Smith & Wesson Model 469**   **Smith & Wesson Model 639**
Smith & Wesson Model 645   **Smith & Wesson Model 659**   **Smith & Wesson Model 669**

Data:	Smith & Wesson Model 459
Origin:	United States
Manufacturer:	Smith & Wesson, Springfield, Massachusetts
Cartridge:	9mm Luger
Magazine capacity:	14 rounds
Overall length:	7$\frac{7}{16}$ inches
Height:	5$\frac{11}{16}$ inches
Barrel length:	4 inches
Weight:	28 ounces

Except for the fully adjustable rear sight in its protective mount, the Model 459 and 439 pistols look very much like the Models 59 and 39 which they replaced. Inside, though, there were extensive mechanical changes which make the takedown and reassembly very different in some areas. One of the most notable additions is an automatic firing pin block safety system. This series of S&W pistols is now being referred to as the "second generation." In addition to the models mentioned above, it also includes Model 639 and 659 (stainless steel), the compact versions, Models 469 and 669, and the 45 ACP, Model 645.

Field Strip:

1. Remove the magazine and cock the hammer. Move the slide toward the rear until the slide-latch notch in its lower edge is aligned with the pivot of the slide latch, and hold it there.

2. Use a non-marring tool to push the right tip of the slide-latch cross-piece toward the left.

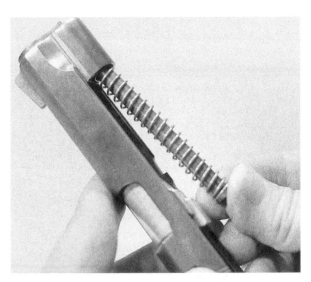

3. Remove the slide-latch toward the left. Move the slide back to its normal position, and use the safety to drop the hammer to the fired position. Return the safety to off-safe, and move the slide assembly forward off the frame.

4. Grip the recoil spring and guide firmly to control the spring tension, and lift the spring assembly away from the barrel, removing it toward the rear. The slide-latch plunger and spring, mounted inside the rear of the recoil spring guide, are staked in and should not be disturbed.

5. Turn the muzzle bushing counterclockwise (front view) until it stops, then remove it toward the front.

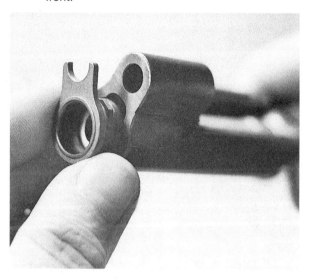

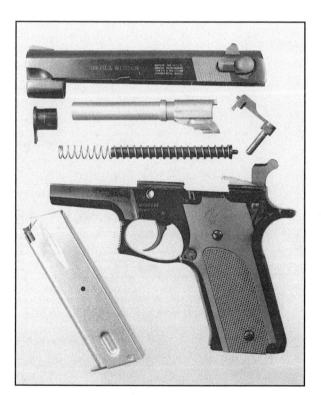

Smith & Wesson 459 field-stripped

6. Move the barrel slightly forward, then tip it downward at the rear and remove it from the bottom of the slide. **Gun is now field-stripped.**

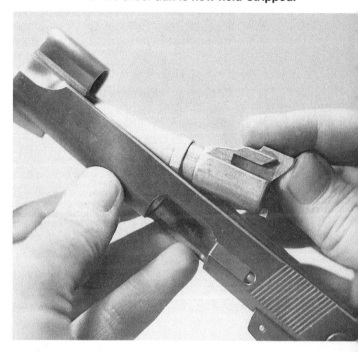

Detail Strip:

7. Depress the firing pin safety block, on the underside of the slide at the right, and use a slim tool to push the firing pin forward until it stops. Release the safety block, and the firing pin will be held forward.

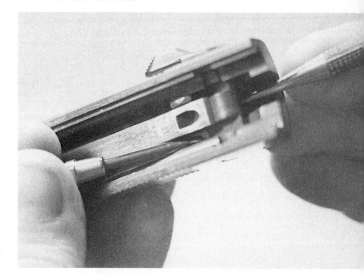

8. In its forward position, the firing pin head will still protrude slightly into the safety cross-piece. Insert a tool to depress it to clear the safety, and push the safety, in off-safe position, toward the left. The small positioning plunger and spring at the lower rear of the safety cross-piece will be released as the safety moves out of the slide, but they will usually stay in their recess. Remove the safety toward the left.

9. Restrain the firing pin at the rear, and once again depress the firing pin safety block. The firing pin and its spring will be released for removal toward the rear.

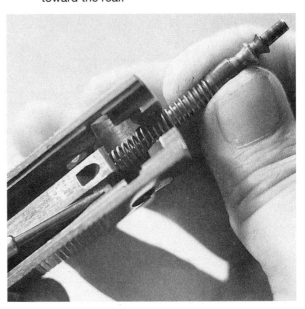

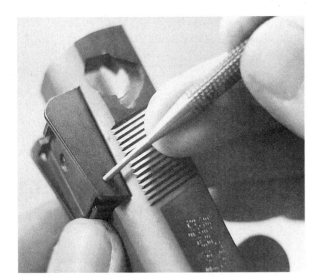

10. Alternately depress the rear sight hinge plungers on each side.

11. Restrain the plungers as they clear the sides of the sight mount, and remove the sight upward and toward the rear. Disassembly of the sight itself is not recommended.

12. With an Allen wrench or screwdriver bit, remove the screw on the left, inside the rear sight mount.

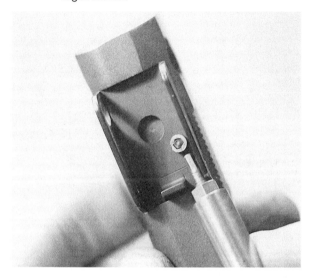

13. Slide the rear sight mount out of its dovetail in the slide, and restrain the two vertical coil springs that will be cleared.

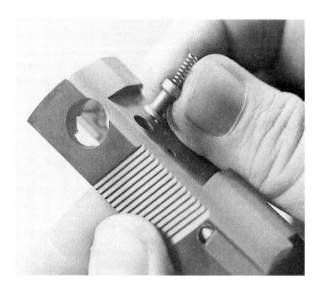

14. Remove the firing pin safety block and its spring from the top of the slide.

15. Remove the magazine safety plunger and spring from the top of the slide.

16. Insert a small sharp screwdriver between the extractor and its plunger, and turn the blade slightly, forcing the plunger toward the rear, and lever the extractor out of its recess. Keep the plunger under control, and ease the spring and plunger out toward the front.

17. With the hammer in the fired position, drift out the cross-pin at the lower rear of the grip frame.

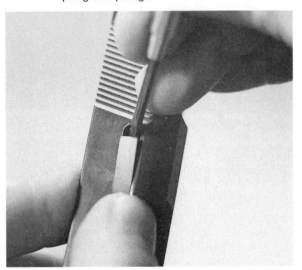

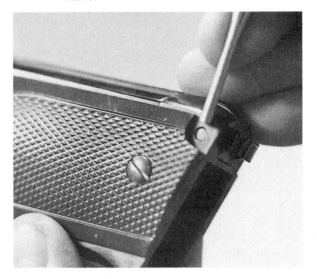

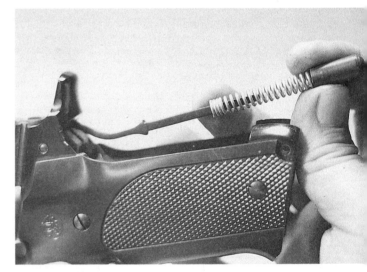

18. Push the lower end of the backstrap insert back until it clears its frame shelf, and it will be forced downward by the pressure of the hammer spring. Remove the insert downward and toward the rear.

19. Remove the hammer spring plunger and the spring from the hammer strut.

20. Remove the grips. Push the hammer pivot about one-third of its length toward the right. Remove the ejector upward, and take out the ejector spring from its well in the frame.

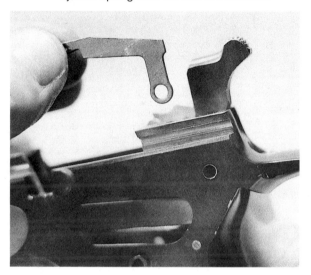

21. Remove the hammer pivot toward the right, and take out the hammer upward. A roll cross-pin joins the strut to the hammer, and this can be removed to separate them, if necessary.

22. Move the sear trip lever slightly toward the left, then remove it upward.

23. Move the firing pin block lever slightly to the left, then rearward, and take it out upward. Remove the spring that powers these two parts from its well in the frame.

24. Drift out the small cross-pin that retains the sear spring, inside the backstrap. This must be drifted out toward the right. Remove the spring toward the rear.

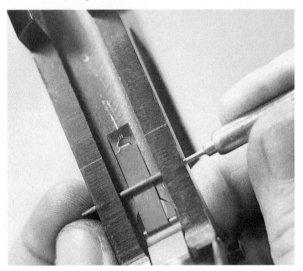

25. Push out the sear cross-pin toward either side, and remove the sear downward.

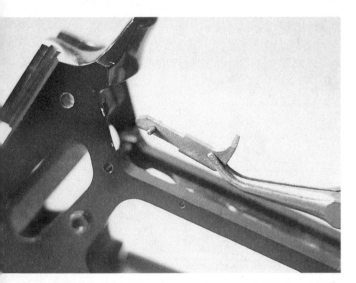

26. Turn the disconnector very slightly toward the right, to clear the trigger bar, and remove the disconnector downward.

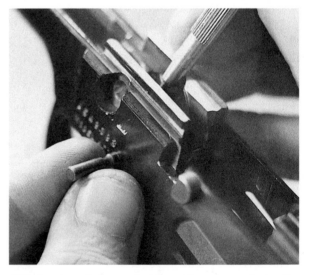

27. Insert a small screwdriver to restrain the trigger spring plunger, and push the trigger pivot pin out toward either side.

28. Allow the trigger to move downward, slowly release the tension of the trigger spring and plunger, and remove the trigger bar toward the rear. The trigger play spring, riveted in place on top of the trigger bar, should not be disturbed.

29. Remove the trigger plunger and spring toward the rear. Move the trigger to the rear of the guard, tilt it forward, and take it out upward. The trigger pivot retaining plunger and spring are mounted inside the trigger, and are retained by a small cross-pin. In normal takedown, these parts are best left in place.

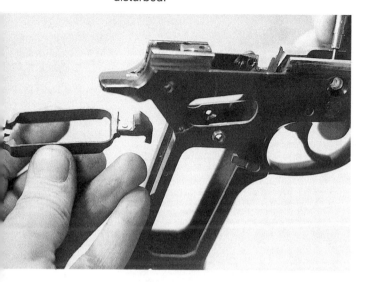

30. Depress the magazine release retainer, and unscrew the release button from the magazine catch cross-piece (counterclockwise, left side view). There is a tool slot in the button, but in most cases the button can be unscrewed with the fingers. The button, retainer, and spring are taken off toward the left, and the catch piece toward the right.

Reassembly Tips:

When replacing the sear cross-pin, note that the reduced tip must go on the right, to mate with the hole in the hammer pivot plate.

When moving the rear sight mount into place, alternately depress the two springs to avoid deformation.

1. When replacing the slide assembly on the frame, the ejector and the two small levers on the right must be depressed to go under the slide.

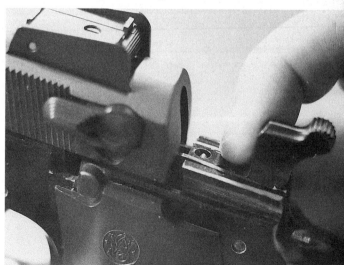

Taurus 45/.410 Revolver

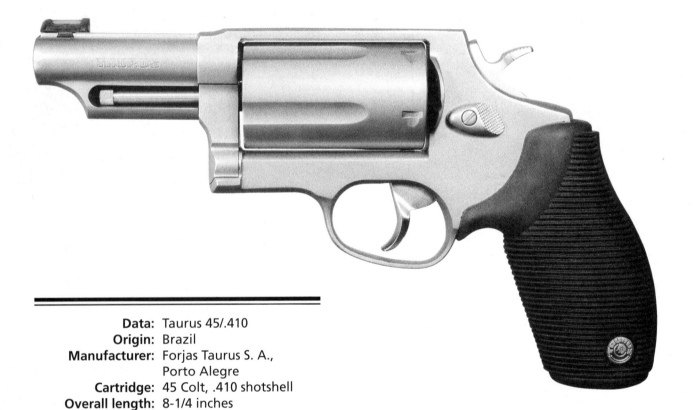

Data: Taurus 45/.410
Origin: Brazil
Manufacturer: Forjas Taurus S. A.,
Porto Alegre
Cartridge: 45 Colt, .410 shotshell
Overall length: 8-1/4 inches
Height: 5-1/4 inches
Barrel length: 3 inches
Weight: 38 ounces

Originally called the "44-Ten Tracker," this big revolver has been more recently titled "The Judge." I can think of several tactical applications, so it certainly deserves inclusion here. Versions are also offered in blue steel, and with a longer barrel.

Disassembly:

1. With an Allen wrench of the proper size, take out the screw at the bottom of the grip, and remove the grip downward.

2. Remove the front sideplate screw.

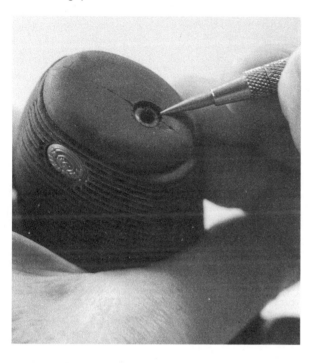

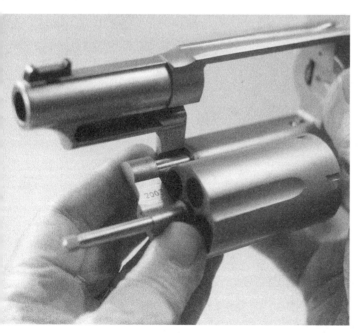

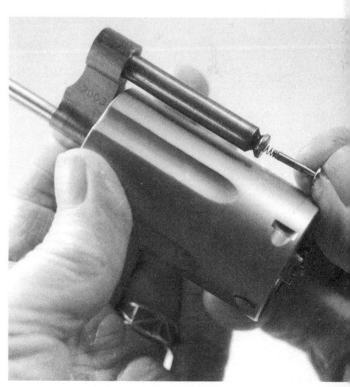

3. Operate the cylinder latch, and swing out the cylinder. Align one of the cylinder flutes with the flange at the front of the frame, and carefully move the crane and cylinder assembly out of the frame toward the front.

4. As this unit is taken out, the cylinder stop plunger and spring will be freed at the rear tip of the crane post, so take care that these small parts are not lost. They are easily removed.

5. To avoid marring the knurling at the end of the ejector rod, use a thick leather pad in the pliers as the rod is unscrewed.   NOTE: This is a left-hand thread. Turn the rod clockwise, front view, for removal.

6. Remove the ejector rod and attached spring.

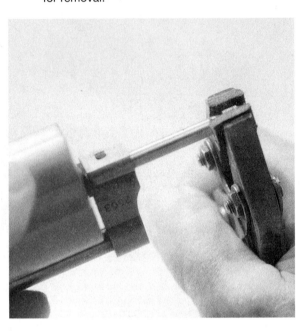

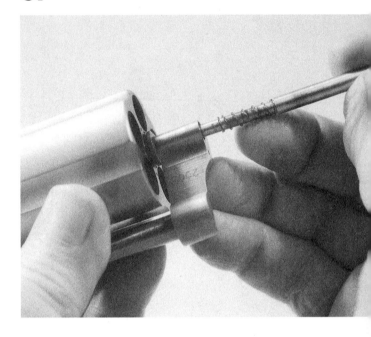

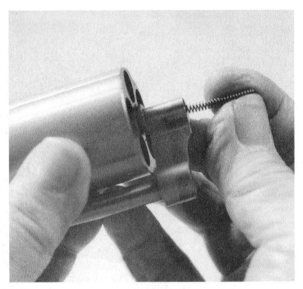

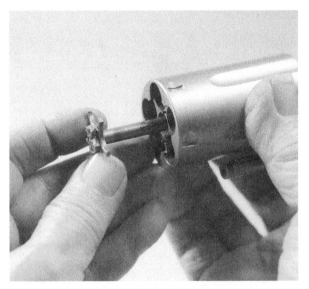

7. Remove the ejector return spring.

8. Remove the ejector/ratchet unit toward the rear.

9. Remove the rear locking pin from the unit. It will probably need a push with a small tool. Take care that this small part is not lost.

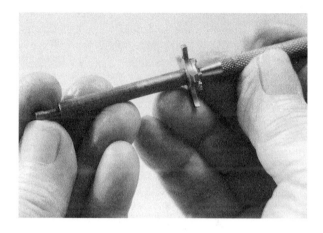

10. The front crane latch and its coil spring are retained by a lengthwise pin in the crane arm, accessible only after removal of the cylinder from its arbor. Doing this requires special tools to avoid damage. If this becomes necessary, it's best to let Taurus do it.

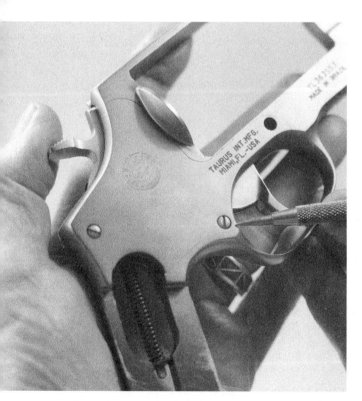

11. Remove the middle and rear sideplate screws. Note that these are not the same as the front screw, so keep them separate for reassembly.

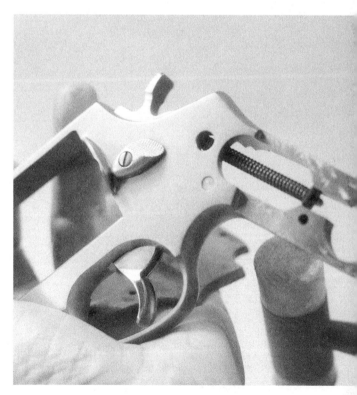

12. Hold the gun as shown, and tap the frame with a rubber or nylon mallet until the sideplate drops into the palm of the hand.

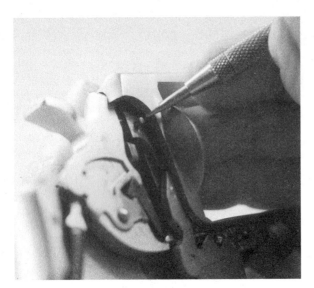

13. The firing pin retaining pin normally protrudes as shown. It is a slip-fit in its aperture, so it might be best to remove it at this point to avoid loss. The firing pin is also lightly staked at the rear, so it won't come out if the pin is removed.

14. Move the cylinder latch thumbpiece rearward so the hammer can be cocked. Insert a slim tool through the hole in the hammer spring strut, as shown.

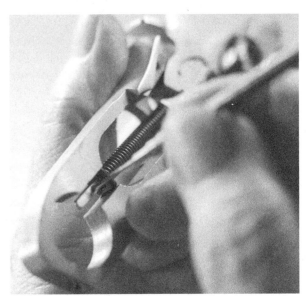

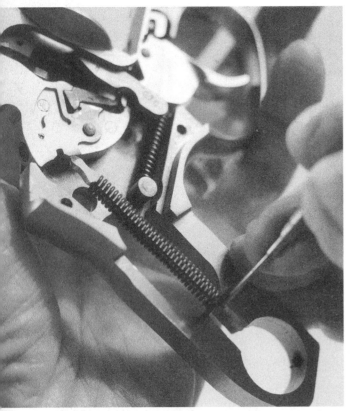

15. Ease the hammer back forward, and remove the strut, its base, and the trapped hammer spring. If this unit is to be disassembled, grip the top of the strut in a vise and be very careful, as the spring is fully compressed.

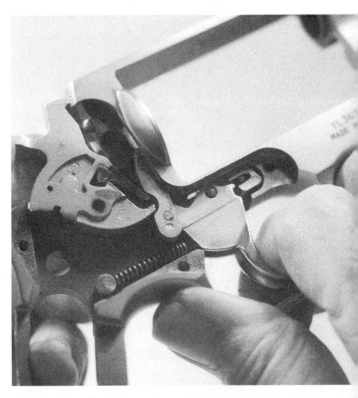

16. Use the trigger to move the hammer very slightly to the rear. The trigger movement will be stopped by the cylinder latch, and this will position the hammer at the right point for taking it off its post toward the right. Note that the hammer must clear the frame at the top, and its lower front must align with an exit cut in the back edge of the cylinder hand.

17. The double-action lever (Taurus: "sear") is easily lifted out of its recess toward the right. CAUTION: The coil spring behind it will be released. The keylock in the back of the hammer can be removed by drifting out its crosspin, but it is best left in place in normal takedown. If it is taken out, a tiny ball and coil spring will be released.

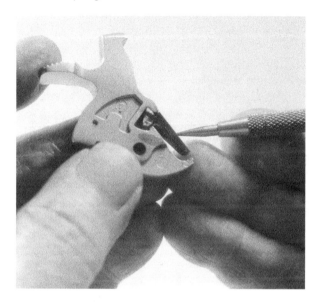

18. Move the cylinder latch thumbpiece rearward so the trigger can be pulled fully to the rear. Insert a slim tool through the hole near the rear tip of the trigger spring guide.

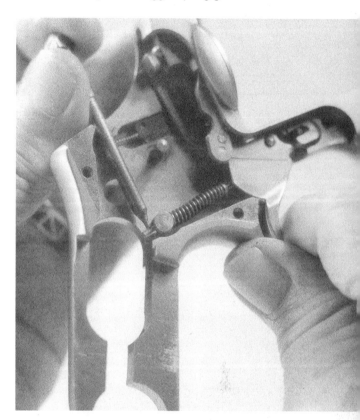

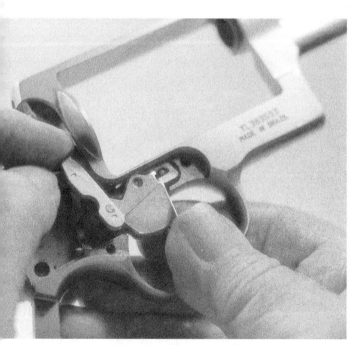

20. Be sure the cylinder stop is in its rearmost and up position, tip the cylinder hand slightly rearward to clear its channel, and remove the trigger from its pivot post.

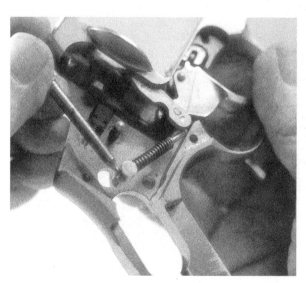

19. Ease the trigger back forward, and remove the spring, guide, and base. If this unit is to be taken apart, remember that you have a fully-compressed spring. Be very careful.

21. The cylinder hand is easily detached, and its plunger and spring can then be taken out of the trigger.

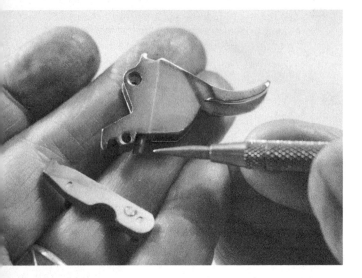

22. Removal of the trigger will also free the transfer bar to be lifted out of the frame.

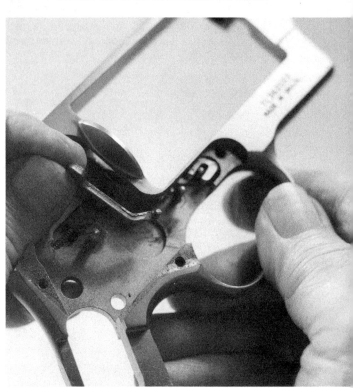

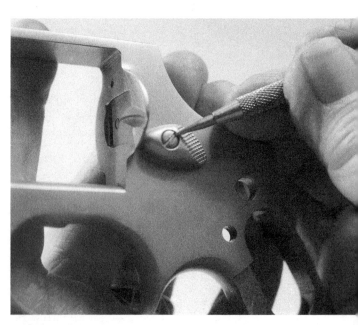

23. Move the cylinder stop to its rearmost position, tip it downward, and remove it toward the right.

24. Removal of this screw will allow the thumbpiece to be taken off toward the left, and the cylinder latch and spring to be removed from inside the frame.

25. As noted earlier, the firing pin is retained not only by a small cross pin, but also by being lightly staked at the rear. If removal of the firing pin and its coil return spring must be done, use a brass drift to gently nudge the parts out rearward, as shown.

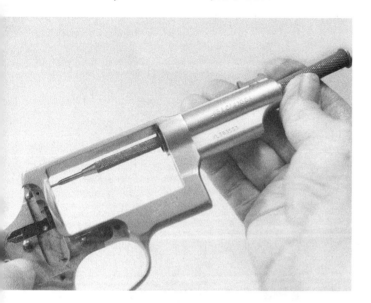

26. The front sight is dovetail-mounted, and can be drifted out if necessary.

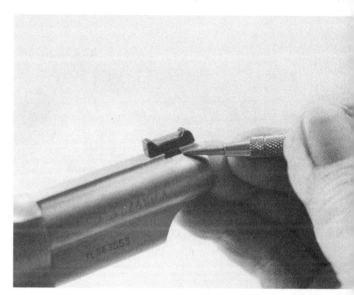

Reassembly Tips:

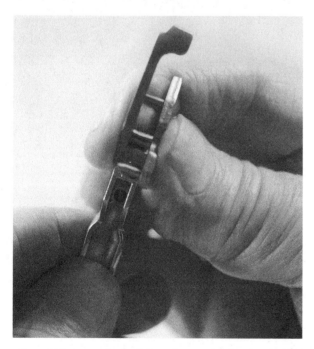

1. This rear view of the trigger shows the proper assembly when it is in place in the gun. The transfer bar is on the left. The cylinder hand is on the right, with its lower cross-piece contacting the plunger and spring.

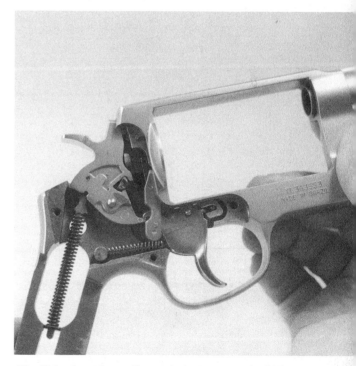

2. This view shows the parts in proper order before the sideplate is re-installed. Note that the sideplate has a flange at the top that must be inserted first. After this, use a rubber or nylon mallet to seat it in place. When installing the cylinder and crane unit, keep the frame pointed downward to insure that the cylinder stop plunger and spring stay in place.

Taurus Model PT24/7

Data: Taurus PT24/7
Origin: Brazil
Manufacturer: Forjas Taurus, S.A.,
Porto Alegre
Cartridge: 9x19mm (9mm Luger)
Magazine capacity: 17 rounds
Overall length: 7.16 inches
Height: 5.62 inches
Barrel length: 4.20 inches
Weight: 27.6 ounces

The PT24/7 arrived in 2004, and has since been offered in 40 S&W and 45 Auto versions. A later pistol, the PT24/7 OSS, has some mechanical differences. With its smooth, short DA trigger pull and manual safety, the T24/7 is perfect for law enforcement use. Many of them are now serving in that capacity.

Field Strip:

1. Lock the slide open, and remove the magazine. Turn the takedown latch down to vertical position, and remove it.

3. Remove the recoil spring unit.

2. Restrain the slide, release the slide latch, and ease the slide forward until it is even with the frame. Pull the trigger, and remove the slide and barrel assembly toward the front.

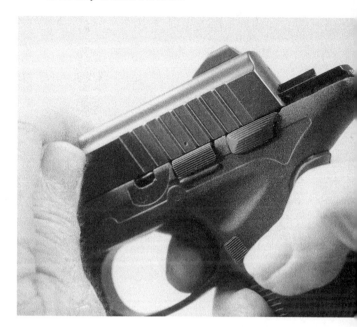

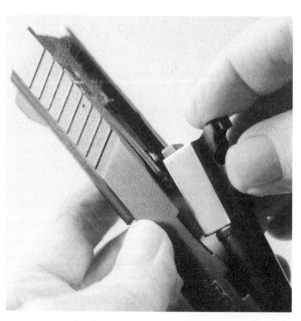

4. Move the barrel slightly forward, then tip it outward for removal.

Taurus Model PT 24/7 field stripped.

Detail Strip:

5. While it is possible to pry the end of the recoil spring around the endcap and turn it off the rod, this is not done in normal disassembly.

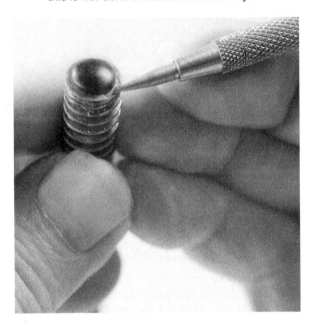

6. The front and rear sights are retained by small vertical screws. In normal takedown, both are best left in place.

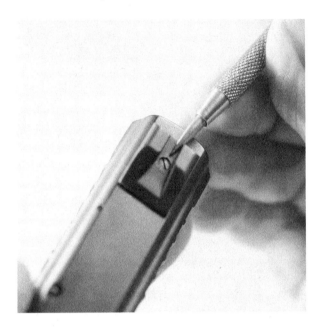

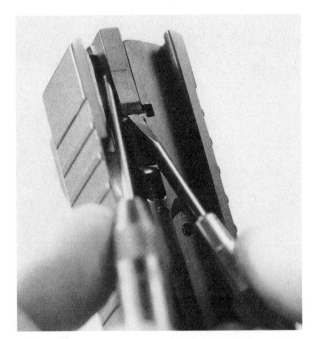

7. To remove the slide endpiece (Taurus: "Slide Cap"), insert a slim tool in the recess on its left side, to push it rearward, and use a small screwdriver to slightly lift its forward locking tab.

8. Depress the striker block (Taurus: "Firing Pin Lock") to allow the striker to be pushed all the way forward, and use a tool to depress the striker spring and lift the retainer for removal.

9. Remove the striker spring assembly. This is a captive unit, and it is not routinely disassembled.

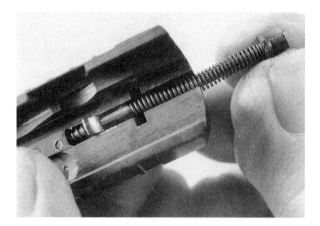

10. Remove the striker (Taurus: "Firing Pin").

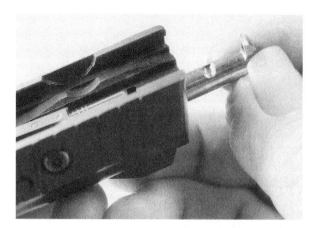

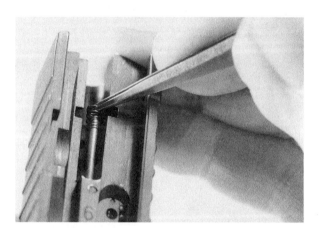

11. Remove the striker rebound spring from the guide post. The guide post is staked in place, and is not routinely removable.

12. Drifting out the vertical pin beside the striker block will allow removal of the extractor, loaded-chamber indicator, striker block, and their attendant coil springs. This should be done only for repair purposes. Control the springs.

13. The key lock is best left in place in normal takedown. If it must be removed for repair, drifting out this small vertical pin will free it for removal. CAUTION: A tiny detent ball and coil spring will be released, so take care that these parts are not lost.

14. To remove the sub-frame from the grip-frame, first drift out the two cross-pins -- one forward of the trigger, and one to its rear.

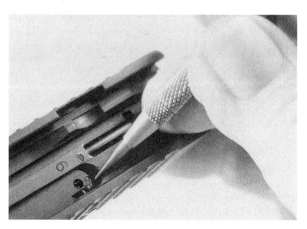

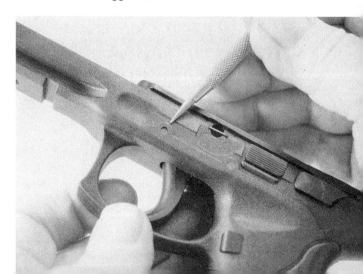

15. After the pins are drifted out, move the subframe upward at the front, then forward, to disengage its rear underlug from the frame. CAUTION: As the unit emerges, restrain the combination slide latch and takedown lever spring on the left side at the front.

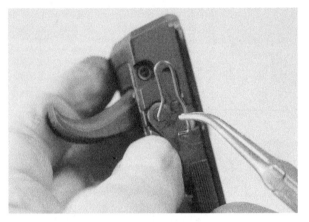

16. Remove the slide latch/takedown lever spring.

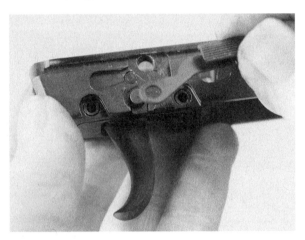

17. Remove the slide latch.

18. Remove the manual safety. Take care that the detent ball behind it does not detach and become lost.

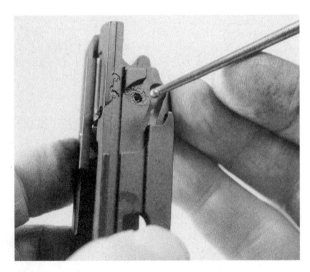

19. Use a magnetized tool to remove the detent ball, and a hooked tool to remove the coil spring under it.

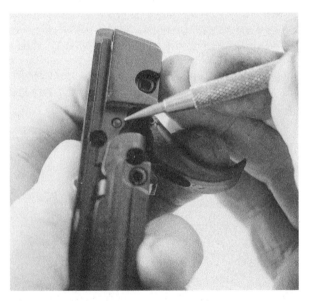

20. With the trigger slightly pulled for clearance, push out the trigger pin toward the left.

21. Move the trigger downward, turn it to the position shown, and remove the trigger assembly toward the right.

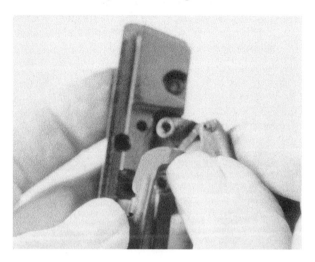

22. If necessary for repair, the trigger bar, trigger safety, and torsion spring can be separated from the trigger by drifting out this cross-pin. The pin is riveted on the right side, and in normal takedown this system should not be disturbed.

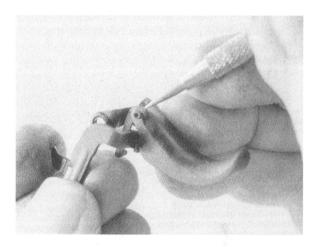

23. If the trigger system housing has to be removed for repair purposes, two retaining bushings must be carefully drifted out. In normal takedown, these parts are left in place.

24. The ejector is retained by two cross-pins on the left side of the sub-frame. Removal should be for repair purposes only. Note that the slide retainer and its coil spring will also be released.

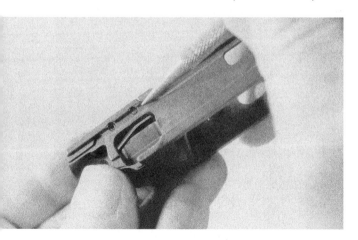

25. On the right side of the sub-frame, two cross-pins retain the trigger bar ramp. Again, removal should be only for repair.

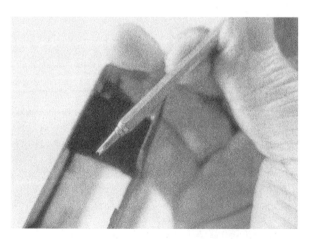

26. Because of its location inside the grip frame, a photo here is not possible. Use a tool with a forked tip, such as the one shown, to push the torsion magazine release spring out of engagement with the catch piece, and this will free it for removal.

Reassembly Tips:

1. If the trigger assembly has been taken apart for repair, this view of the proper arrangement may be helpful.

2. Here is a view of the left side of the sub-frame, with the parts in proper order for re-insertion. As this unit is put back into the grip frame, control the combination spring at the front, and keep the safety pressed snugly in place.

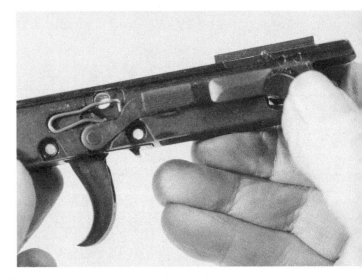

3. When installing the striker retainer, remember that the beveled edge goes toward the rear. Remember also that the striker block must be depressed to allow full forward travel of the striker.

4. When preparing to lock the slide open for insertion of the takedown latch, press the barrel down into its lower position to prevent its following the breech face to the rear.

Wilson Combat ADP

Data:	Wilson Combat ADP
Origin:	United States
Manufacturer:	Wilson Combat, Berryville, Arkansas
Cartridge:	9x19mm (9mm Luger)
Magazine capacity:	10 rounds
Overall length:	6.25 inches
Barrel length:	3-3/4 inches
Weight:	18-1/2 ounces

The "ADP" designation may translate to "Advanced Design Pistol", but the letters are also the initials of the designer, Alex DuPlessis. The gas-brake action, which it shares with the H&K P7, makes for a very small and flat 9mm. This compactness would qualify it as a fine choice for a Law Enforcement back-up pistol. Some of the complete takedown elements are a little difficult, so pay close attention to the instructions.

Field Strip:

1. With the magazine removed, depress the two takedown buttons at the rear of the frame. While holding them pushed in, move the slide slightly rearward, and lift it at the rear. Ease the slide forward off the barrel.

2. Remove the recoil spring from the barrel. Note, for reassembly, that the larger closed coil is toward the front.

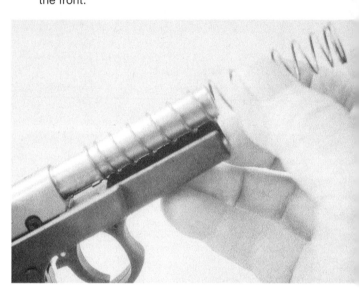

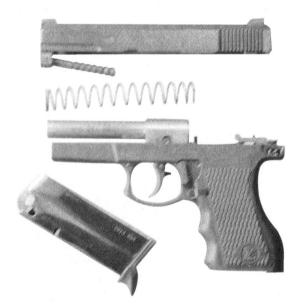

Wilson ADP field stripped.

Detail Strip:

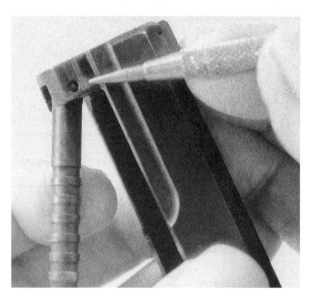

3. In normal takedown, the gas piston is not removed. If this is necessary, the pivot pin must be drifted out toward the right.

4. To remove the breechblock assembly from the slide, begin by drifting out this cross pin. Note also that the front and rear sights can be drifted out of their dovetail mounts, if necessary for repair.

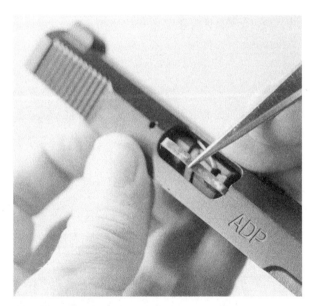

6. Remove the extractor.

8. Remove the combination block lever and pin lock spring.

5. Move the breechblock forward until the extractor is accessible in the ejection port.

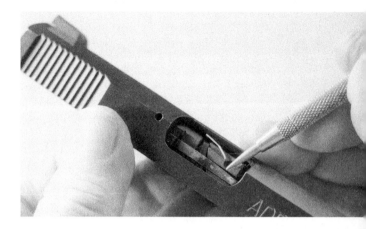

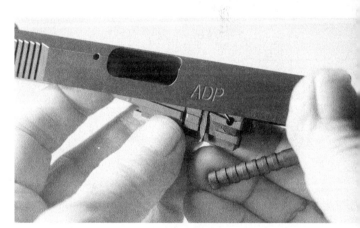

7. Move the breechblock forward until it clears its rails in the slide, and take it out.

9. Remove the striker block lever. Depending on the slide position as the breechblock is taken out, both the lever and the pin lock spring may be detached inside the slide, so take care they are not lost. If necessary, a sharp tool can be used to pry the striker spring off its post inside the rear of the slide. Or, it can be left in place.

10. Remove the striker from the breechblock.

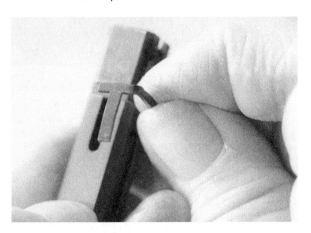

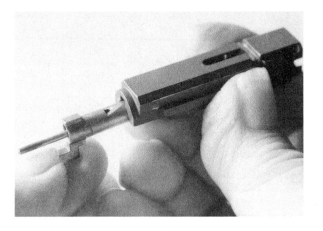

11. If removal of the barrel and trigger assembly is necessary, begin by drifting out the front cross pin. Note that this is a roll-type pin, so be sure to use a proper roll-pin drift. In supporting the polymer frame for this operation, take care that the manual safety lever is not stressed.

12. Turn the manual safety to the on-safe position for clearance, and drift out the rear cross pin.

13. Insert a tapered tool in the piston opening at the front, and use it to nudge the barrel assembly upward in very small increments. CAUTION: As this is being done, depress and hold in the magazine release button, to keep the spring in its recess in the barrel post.

14. As the barrel assembly is moved upward, the magazine release will be freed for removal. CAUTION: Insert a tool on the left side of the barrel post to restrain the magazine release spring, which will be freed as the barrel unit clears the frame.

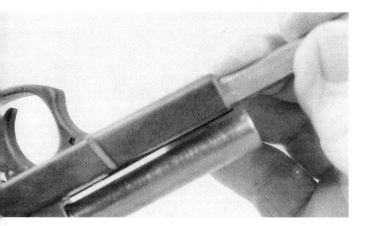

15. Ease out the magazine release spring, and remove it.

16. The doubled-over short upper end of the slide latch spring is mounted in a recess in the under-edge of the barrel housing. Gently pry or pull it out of its recess for removal of the spring and attached slide latch.

17. The trigger assembly can be removed from the barrel unit by drifting out this roll-pin. In normal takedown this system is best left in place, as the polymer trigger could be damaged. If this must be done for repair, be sure the opposite trigger extension is well-supported.

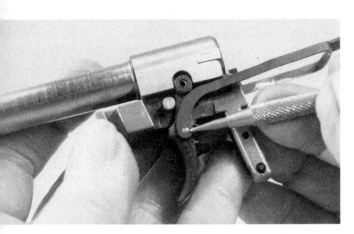

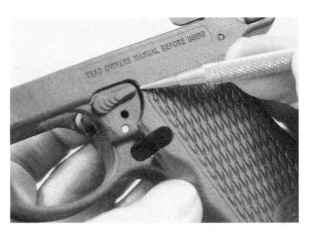

18. If the trigger assembly is removed from the barrel unit the trigger bar can be turned over toward the front, relieving the spring tension. Pushing out this cross pin will allow removal of the trigger bar and spring.

19. Because of its polymer construction, the manual safety system is not routinely removable. The stress of removal could damage the parts.

20. Drift out the rear cross pin toward the right.

21. Remove the disconnector (Wilson: "Catch Transfer") and its torsion spring.

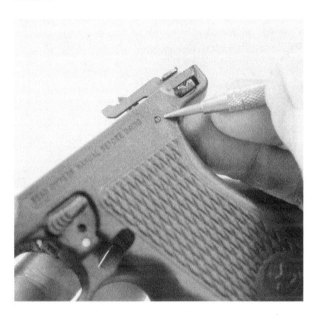

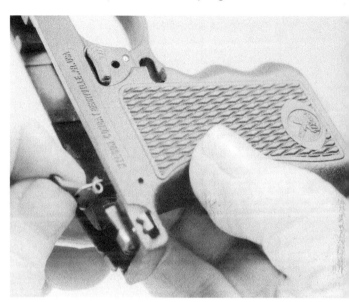

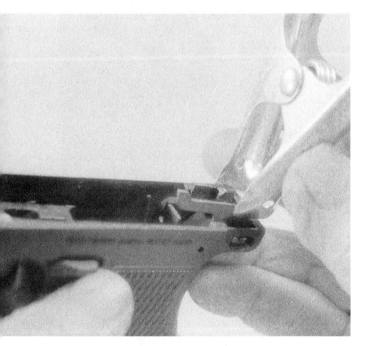

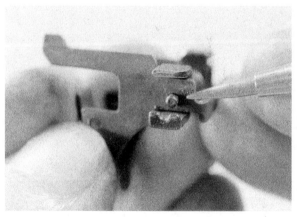

22. Removal of the rear sub-frame will require the use of a clamp to keep the takedown buttons at center.

23. Pushing out this cross pin will allow removal of the takedown buttons and the transverse coil spring.

Reassembly Tips:

1. Installing the disconnector and its spring will be made easier by the use of a slave pin, as shown. Be sure the lower arms of the torsion spring go inside the sub-frame.

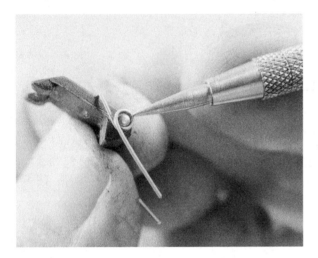

2. As the barrel and trigger assembly are put back into the frame, insert a flat tool on the left side of the barrel post to compress the magazine release spring into its recess.

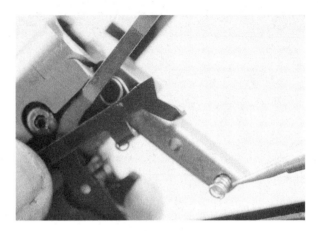

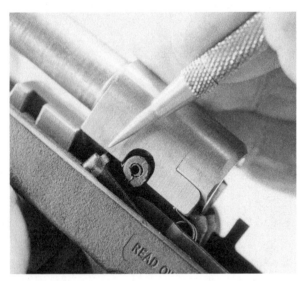

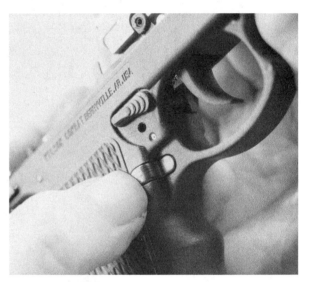

3. As the barrel and trigger assembly are moved downward, be sure the slide latch is fully to the rear, so its pivot end can enter.

4. When the lower tip of the barrel post is visible in the release opening, install the magazine release and hold it precisely even with the sides of the frame as the barrel unit is pushed downward into place.

5. This view of the breechblock shows the striker block and the spring in place, ready for re-insertion in the slide. Remember to install the extractor as the unit is moved rearward. The same slave pin used in the sub-frame can be helpful in lifting the lock-spring ends for re-insertion of the cross pin.

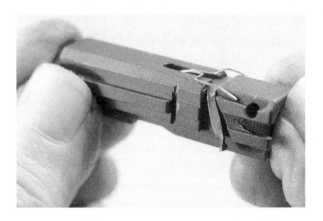

BENELLI M2 TACTICAL

Data:	Benelli M2 Tactical
Origin:	Italy
Manufacturer:	Benelli Armi S.P.A., Urbino
Cartridge:	12 Gauge
Magazine capacity:	5 rounds
Over-all length:	39.75 inches
Barrel length:	18.5 inches
Weight:	6.7 pounds

While in many ways the Benelli shotguns are similar in design, there are often significant deviations. The M2 line, including the Tactical model, are "inertia driven" and essentially identical in function to the hunting and all-purpose lines of semi-auto guns. This differentiates them from the earlier Super 90 models and the M4 and M3 lines, which are gas operated (or pump, as the M3 can be either). Specifically, a large spring internal to the bolt assembly is compressed upon recoil which then energetically pushes the bolt carrier to the rear to initiate the extraction/ejection process. This makes the M2 a very easy-to-maintain gun with a relatively low parts count.

Disassembly:

1. Unscrew the forend retaining cap. This will free the magazine spring, follower, and tube plug. The elastic ring that retains the sling ring should not be removed without necessity. If needed, unscrew the magazine extension from the magazine tube cap.

2. Lock the bolt to the rear and then pull the barrel assembly from the receiver. The forend can them be removed from the barrel by pulling the forend back.

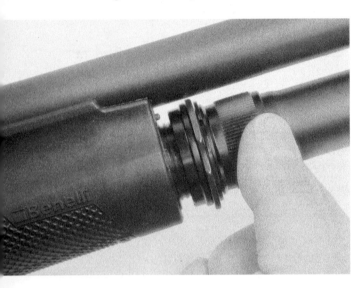

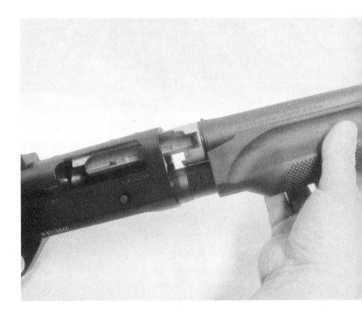

3. Gently allow the bolt to close. Pull the charging handle to the side, jiggling the bolt head to remove the charging handle. Then pull the bolt assembly out the front of the receiver. The hammer must be cocked.

4. Pull out the firing pin retaining pin. Note that the head of the pin incorporates a rubber O-ring. Retain the firing pin with a finger or it will fly forth and be lost with its spring.

5. Pull the firing pin out of the rear of the bolt carrier. The firing pin spring will follow.

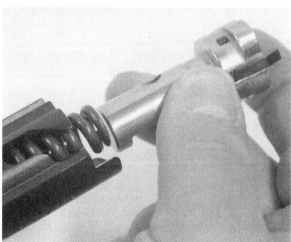

7. Remove the bolt from the bolt carrier. Behind the bolt is the large inertia spring.

6. Remove the cam pin from the bolt.

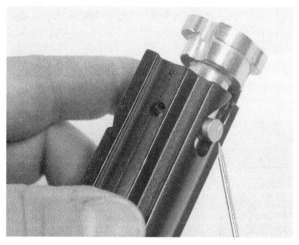

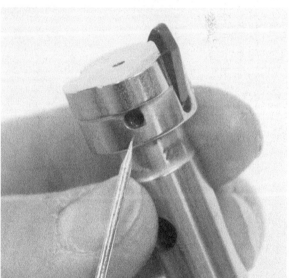

8. The extractor and spring are retained by this pin.

9. The pin that holds the link to the bolt carrier should not be removed without need for replacement as it is heavily staked in place.

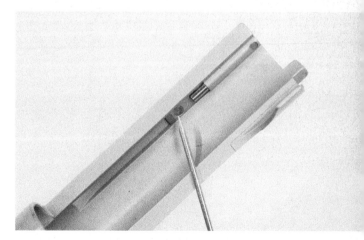

10. The ejector housing is riveted in place and should be left alone unless it needs replacement.

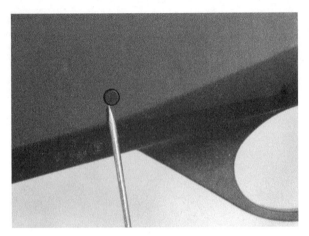

11. Push out the trigger guard pin.

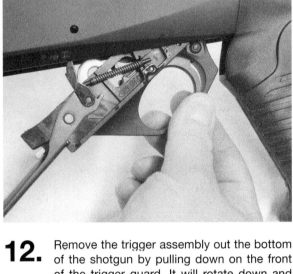

12. Remove the trigger assembly out the bottom of the shotgun by pulling down on the front of the trigger guard. It will rotate down and then it can be pulled forward away from the receiver.

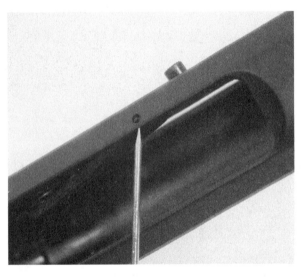

13. The feed latch can be removed by driving out this pin. However, since the receiver and latch can be easily damaged in this process, the pin should be left in place unless the latch or spring needs replacement.

14. To remove the buttstock, pull off the press fit recoil pad. Beneath that is a nut, washer, and the stock plate sling plate, which actually retains the stock. Once the nut and washer are absent, the stock can be pulled off the recoil spring tube, and the sling plate will slide out of the stock to the side.

15. The stock retaining nut screw is usually quite tightly installed. To free the spring assembly, unscrew this retaining nut screw. Any further disassembly, including removing the tube from the receiver, should be reserved for the factory.

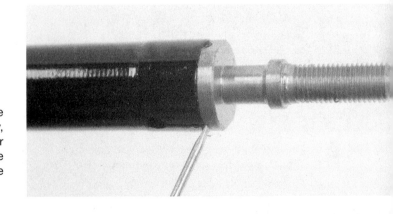

16. The rear sight is held in place by two screws that are very tightly installed (picture A). The front sight post is retained in the base by a nut picture B).

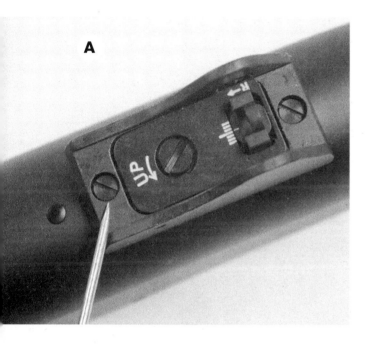

A

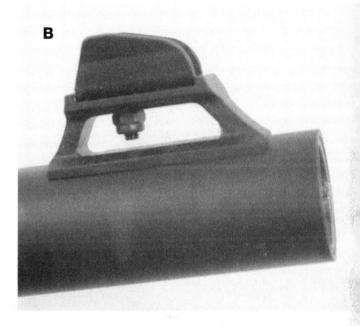

B

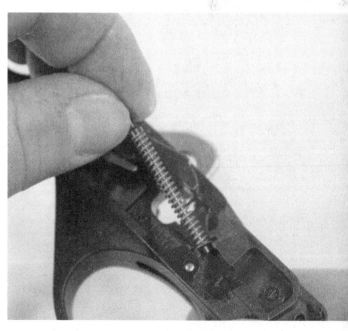

17. Dislodge the carrier arm spring from its position on its arm.

18. Pull the carrier spring and arm from the trigger housing by pulling it slightly to the rear, to the side and forward and out. The back is held by a small thin washer. Don't lose it.

19. With the hammer forward, remove this spring clip and push the hammer bushing out to the right (picture A). As the bushing is removed half way, pull the hammer from the trigger housing. Then remove the hammer spring and plunger (picture B). Then the carrier latch arm will also be freed when the bushing is fully removed (picture C).

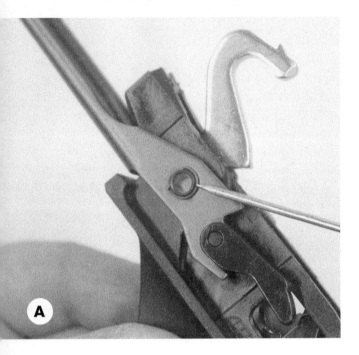

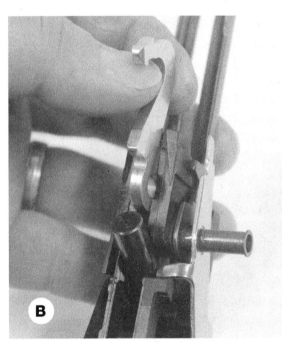

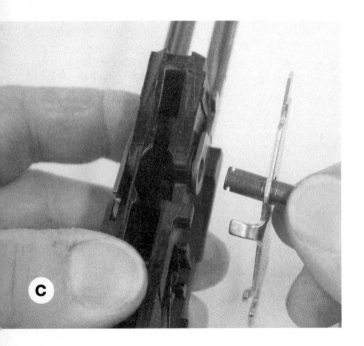

20. Pull the carrier from the front of the trigger housing. The carrier dog and pin are retained by the trigger housing and will easily separate from the carrier.

21. Push out the trigger pin. The trigger spring beneath it will follow, as will the carrier arm spring on the right side of the housing.

22. Leave the disconnector pin in the trigger unless something is broken. The disconnector is retained by this pin, as is the disconnector plunger and spring.

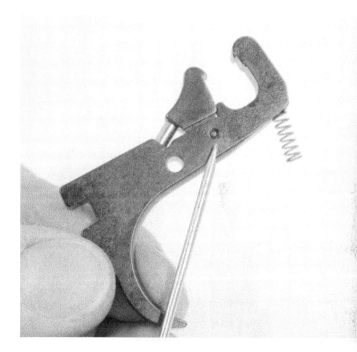

23. This pin is a travel limiter for the trigger and need not be removed

24. This pin retains the safety detent and spring. When these parts are removed, the safety button can be slid out to either side.

Reassembly Tips:

1. When reinstalling the carrier arm spring, emplace it with the trigger pin and then lift the front leg and move it inward to rest on the shelf to the right of the trigger slot. This will ease placing this leg onto the carrier arm itself

2. The little line on the cam pin should be pointing forward or backward or the firing pin will not be able to enter the bolt.

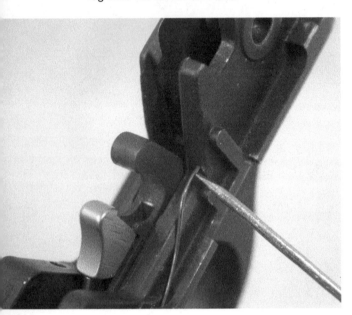

BENELLI M4

Data:	Benelli M4
Origin:	Italy
Manufacturer:	Benelli Armi S.P.A., Urbino
Cartridge:	12 Gauge
Magazine capacity:	5 rounds
Over-all length:	40 inches
Barrel length:	18.5 inches
Weight:	7.8 pounds

The M4, while bearing a resemblance to the inertia-driven Benelli shotguns, is actually gas operated. Designed for tactical/military/LE work, it is used by a great many agencies and armed forces, including the U.S.M.C. Current civilian options are limited to five-round magazines and fixed buttstocks, as these generally Italian manufactured shotguns run up against the 922(r) compliance laws. However, a limited run of fully American manufactured guns, called the H2O, was manufactured with the collapsible stock and full capacity magazine, with a nickeled finish, in 2012.

Disassembly:

1. Unscrew the magazine cap.

2. Lock the bolt to the rear and then pull the barrel assembly from the receiver. The two halves of the forend will be freed to fall from the barrel.

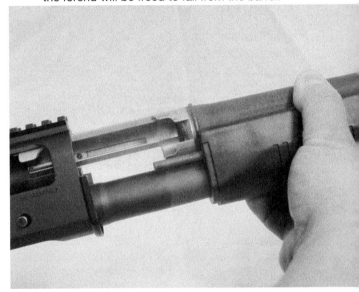

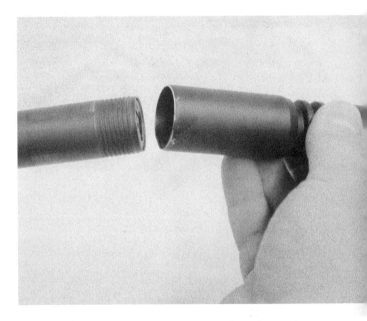

3. The sling loop can be removed by taking this split ring off the barrel lug.

4. Unscrew the magazine extension from the magazine tube.

5. The magazine spring and follower can be removed by first removing this split ring retainer cap with a split ring pliers or by gently prying it from the tube.

6. Unscrew the gas cylinder plugs from the barrel. The plugs need not be disassembled.

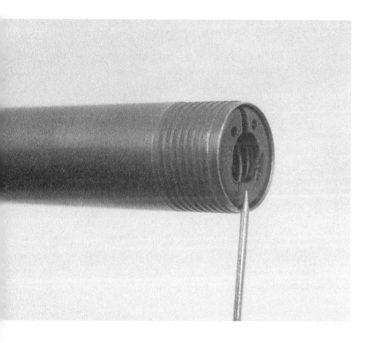

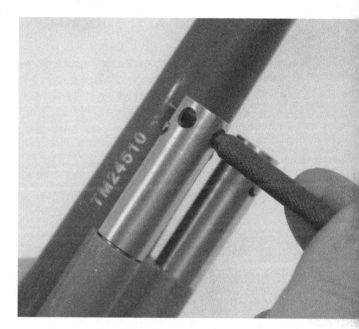

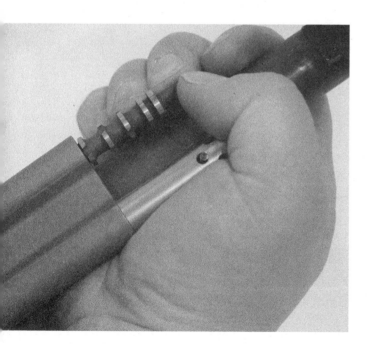

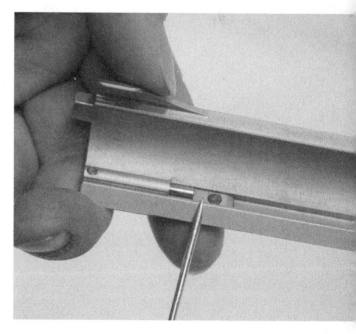

7. Push the pistons forward out of the hole that the gas cylinder plugs previously occupied.

8. The ejector housing is riveted in place and should be left alone unless it needs replacement.

9. Gently allow the bolt to close and pull the charging handle to the side while twisting it slightly to remove it from the bolt carrier.

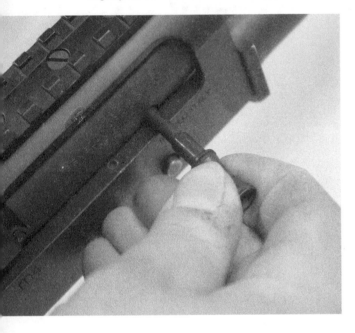

10. Pull the bolt assembly out the front of the receiver. The hammer must be cocked.

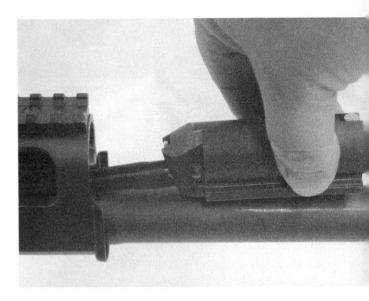

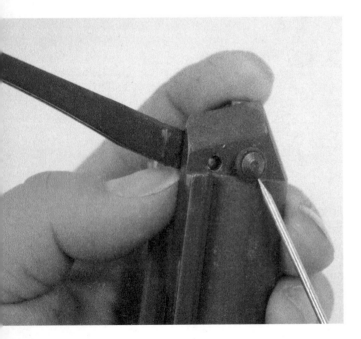

11. Pull out the firing pin retaining pin. Note that the head of the pin incorporates a rubber O-ring. Retain the firing pin with a finger or it will fly forth and be lost with its spring.

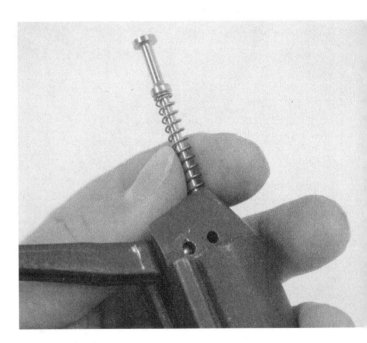

12. Pull the firing pin out of the rear of the bolt carrier. The firing pin spring will follow.

13. Remove the cam pin from the bolt.

14. Remove the bolt from the bolt carrier.

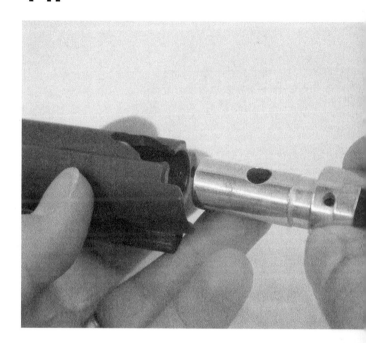

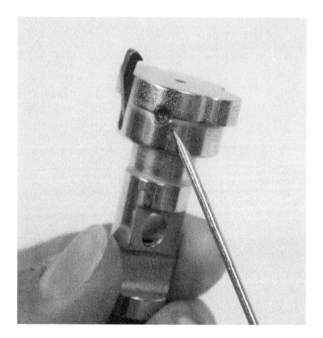

15. The extractor and spring are retained by this pin.

16. The pin that holds the link to the bolt carrier is heavily staked in place and should not be removed without good cause.

17. Push out the trigger guard pin until it stops (picture A). The pin itself is retained by a split ring and should be left in place, barring need for replacement (picture B).

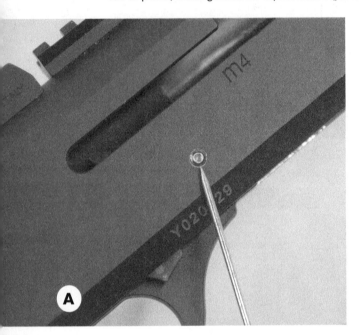

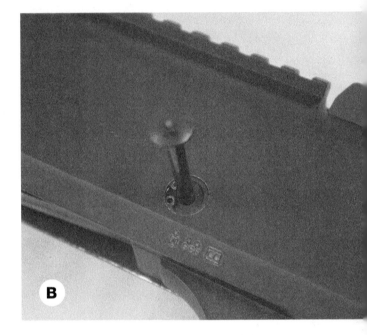

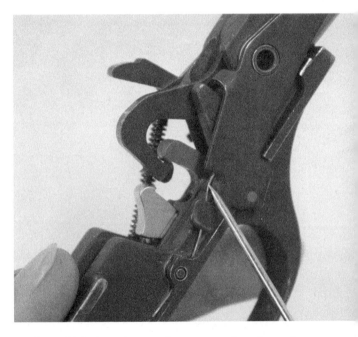

18. Pull the trigger assembly out the bottom of the shotgun by pulling down on the front of the trigger guard, rotating the carrier down, and then pull the trigger assembly forward away from the receiver.

19. Dislodge the carrier arm spring from its position on its arm.

20. Pull the carrier spring and arm from the trigger housing by pulling it slightly to the rear, to the side and forward and out.

22. Pull the carrier from the front of the trigger housing. The carrier dog and pin are retained by the trigger housing and will easily separate from the carrier.

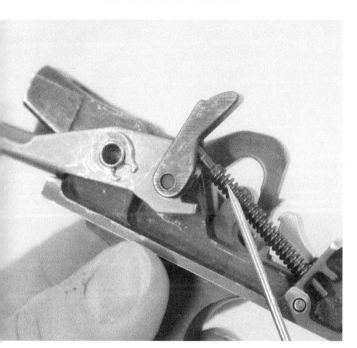

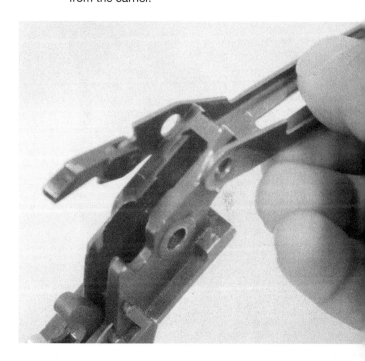

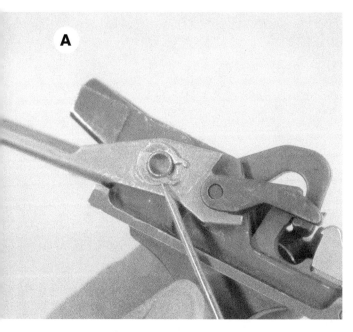

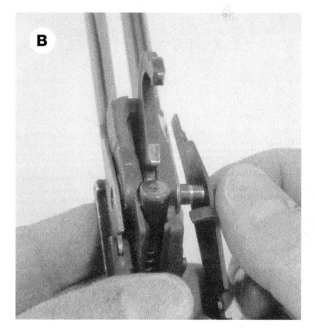

21. The hammer must be forward for this step, with no spring tension on it. Remove this E-clip and push the hammer bushing out to the right (picture A). As the bushing is removed, first the hammer and then the carrier latch arm will also be freed (picture B). Pull the hammer from the trigger housing. Then remove the hammer spring and plunger.

23. Push out the trigger pin. The trigger spring beneath it will follow, as will the carrier arm spring on the right side of the housing.

24. Leave the disconnector pin in the trigger unless something is broken. The disconnector is retained by this pin, as is the disconnector plunger and spring.

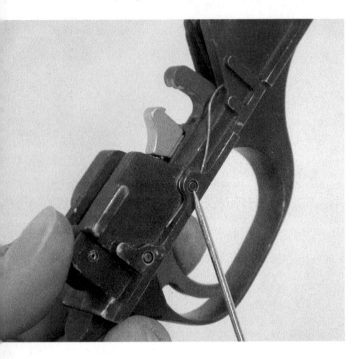

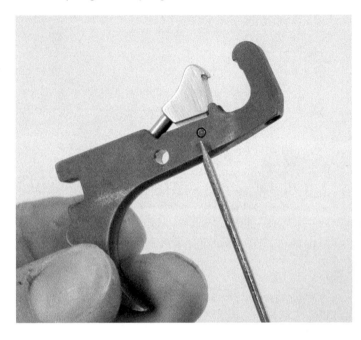

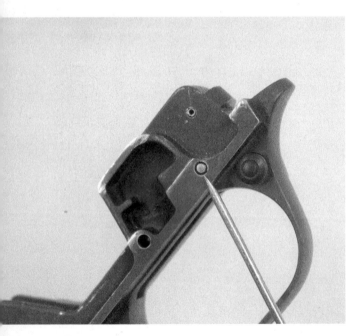

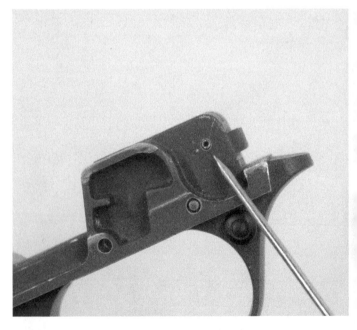

25. This pin is a travel limiter for the trigger and need not be removed.

26. This pin retains the safety detent and spring. When these parts are removed, the safety button can be slid out to either side.

27. The buttstock can be removed by simply unscrewing it from the spring tube inside the stock. The stock is tightly held and may require some careful force to budge it. When fully unscrewed, it will slide off the tube to the rear. The stock sling plate is effectively permanently installed at the factory.

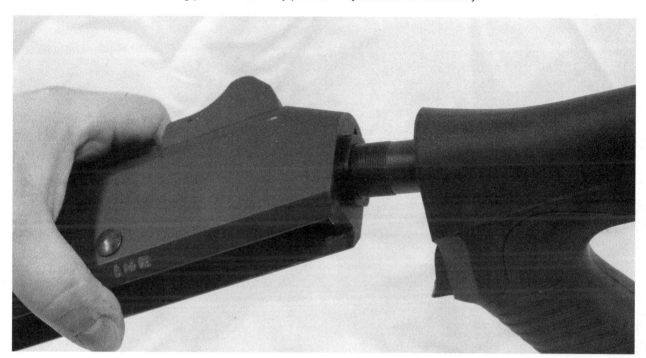

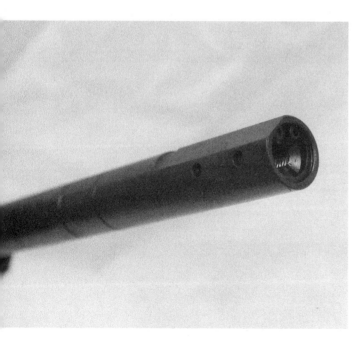

28. The holes in the tube allow cleaning and lubrication of the recoil spring and follower. Any further disassembly, including removing the tube from the receiver, should be reserved for the factory.

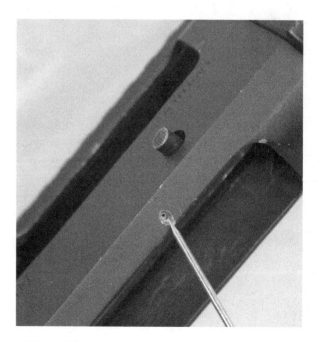

29. The feed latch can be removed by driving out this pin. However, since the receiver and latch can be easily damaged in this process, the pin should be left in place unless the latch or spring needs replacement.

30. The rear sight is held in place by two screws whose heads have been broken to ensure permanence (picture A). The optics rail can be removed by means of the five screws holding it in place. The front sight post is retained in the base by a nut (picture B).

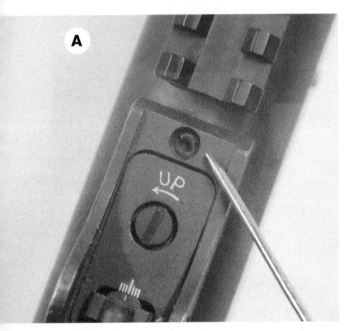

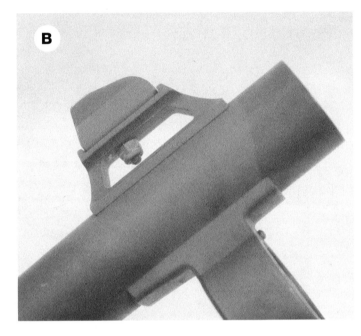

Reassembly Tips:

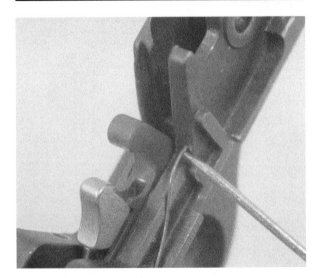

31. The spring in the barrel lug can be removed by displacing one side and then the other, but should generally be left in place.

1. When reinstalling the carrier arm spring, emplace it with the trigger pin and then lift the front leg and move it inward to rest on the shelf to the right of the trigger slot. This will ease placing this leg onto the carrier arm itself.

FNH SLP MK 1

Similar/Identical Pattern Guns

The same basic assembly/disassembly steps used for the FNH SLP Mk 1 also apply to the following guns:

FNH SLP   FNH SLP Tactical

FNH SLP Mk 1 Tactical

Data:	FNH SLP Mk 1
Origin:	Belgium
Manufacturer:	Fabrique National, Herstal
Gauges:	12
Magazine capacity:	8 rounds
Over-all length:	43 inches
Barrel length:	22 inches
Height:	7 inches
Weight:	8.2 pounds

The Self Loading Police shotgun is the FNH entry into the tactical market. The Mk 1 differs from the standard SLP by the addition of standard rifle sights and cantilever optic rail. Other than minor additions such as this rail, or on the tactical models a railed section around the magazine tube, all the SLP models disassemble and function in the same way.

Disassembly:

1. With the bolt locked back and the safety on "safe" remove the magazine cap.

2. Pull the forend with mag tube cover forward off the gun. The cover will easily separate from the forend.

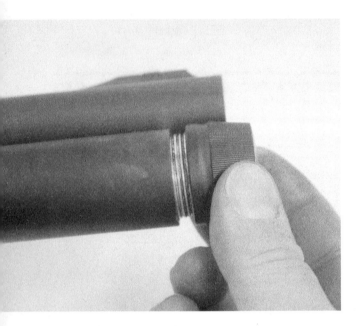

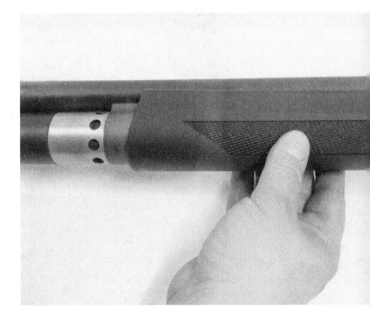

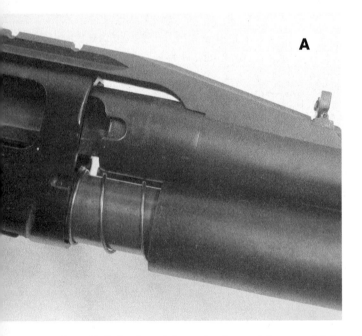

A

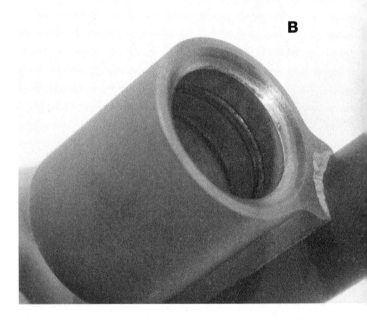

B

3. Pull the barrel from the front of the gun (picture A). There is a synthetic O-ring in the barrel lug (picture B). Do not remove this ring unless it needs to be replaced.

4. Pull the piston, the sleeve assembly, and the piston sleeve spring from the front of the magazine tube.

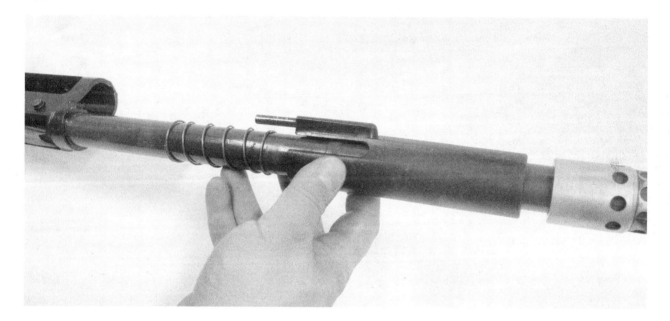

5. The piston assembly can be disassembled by unscrewing the large slotted ring at the rear of the assembly. However, it is best to avoid disassembly unless something needs to be replaced, as it is easily cleaned in assembly.

6. Depress the bolt release and gently allow the bolt to come all the way forward. To remove the operating handle, pull the handle straight out to the right.

7. Remove the bolt assembly by then pulling it out of the front of the receiver. The bolt will easily lift out of the carrier.

8. The firing pin retaining pin is staked in and should be removed only for replacement. Removing this pin will release the firing pin and firing pin spring.

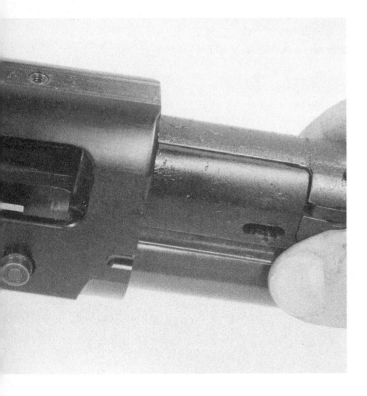

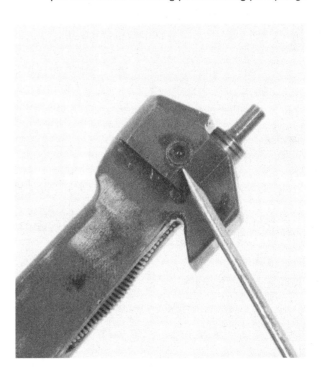

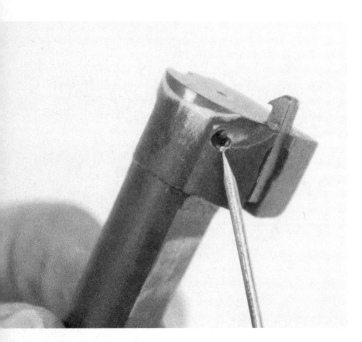

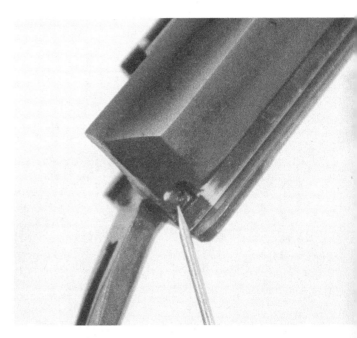

9. Drive out the extractor pin from top to bottom, then remove the extractor and extractor spring.

10. If necessary for repair, the link pin can be driven out from right to left. This will free the link and the detent and spring in front of it.

11. This pin retains the operating handle latch, detent, and spring.

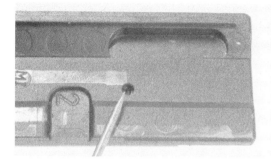

12. Push out these two pins above the trigger guard to remove the fire control group.

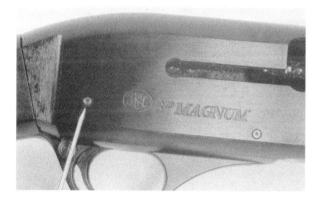

13. To disassemble the fire control group, first remove this cotter pin (picture A), then pull the carrier pivot pin to the left. Remove the carrier forward (picture B). This also frees the rear carrier carrier spring and guides (picture C). Do this carefully to keep control of the spring and multiple parts.

A

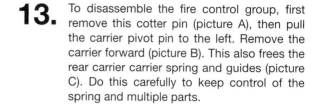

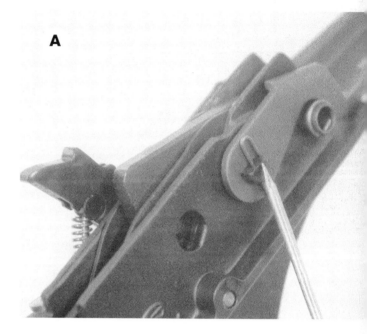

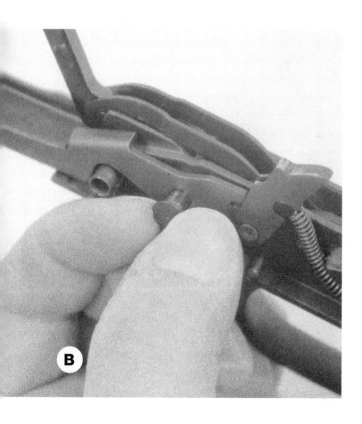

B

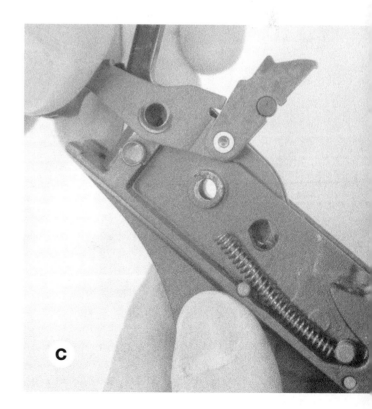

C

14. Unhook the trigger/disconnector spring.

15. Remove this trigger guard bushing.

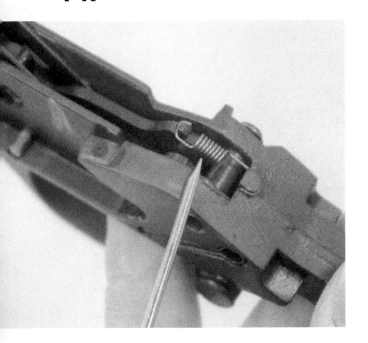

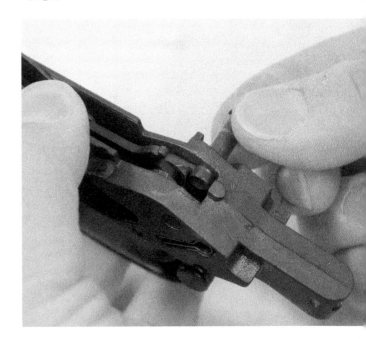

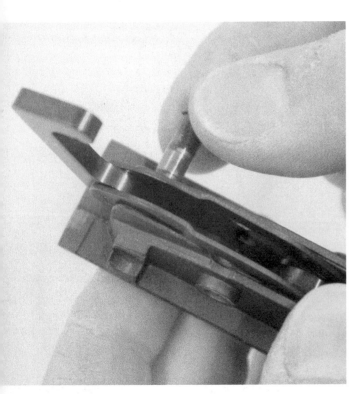

16. Remove the hammer pin bushing and pull the hammer from the housing.

17. Push out the trigger pin. The trigger can now be pulled up and out of the housing.

18. Remove the sear pin and lift the sear and sear spring from the housing.

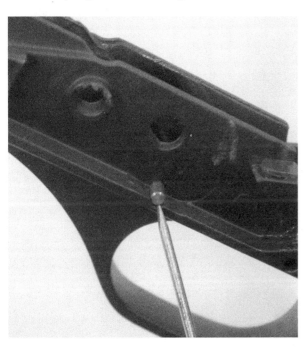

19. Push out this pin to release the hammer spring and detent. Control the spring as it is still compressed.

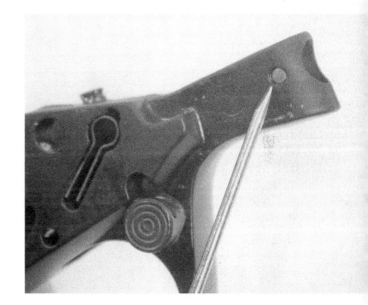

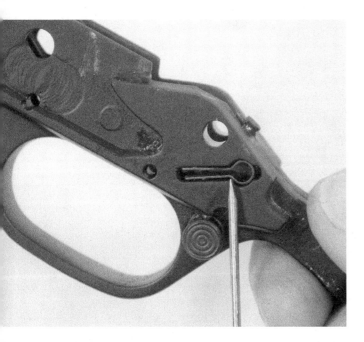

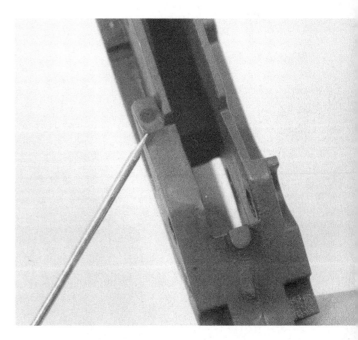

20. Remove this spring to relieve tension on the safety button. Once the spring has been removed, the button can be easily taken out to either side and the safety detent will fall out of the bottom of the housing.

21. There is a synthetic pad on the left side of the housing that should be left unless replacement is needed.

22. This pin retains the shell latch/bolt release. It should be driven out from top to bottom. Control it as its spring is still under some compression. The latch has two halves and a hinge, along with two springs. Do not remove this assembly without need for replacement.

23. Remove the magazine spring retainer by depressing this latch with a screwdriver. Slowly pull the retainer out of the magazine tube. With the retainer removed the magazine spring, limiter and follower can be pulled from the tube. The spring is still very compressed so control it.

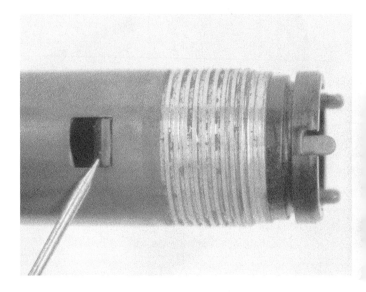

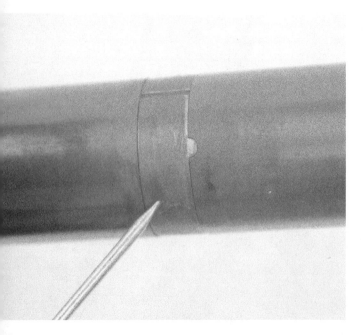

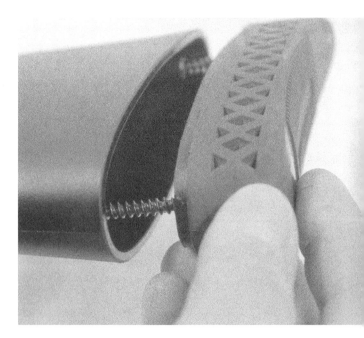

24. There is a seal ring around the magazine tube. Leave it alone unless it is damaged.

25. The buttpad can be removed by unscrewing the two stock screws.

26. Remove the stock bolt nut and spacer. Then remove the action spring support, the plate beneath the nut.

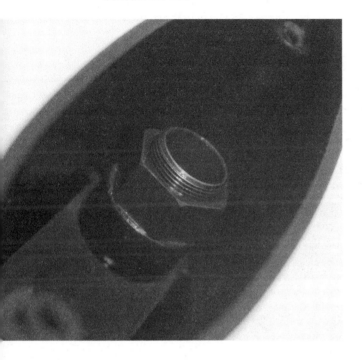

27. Remove the stock.

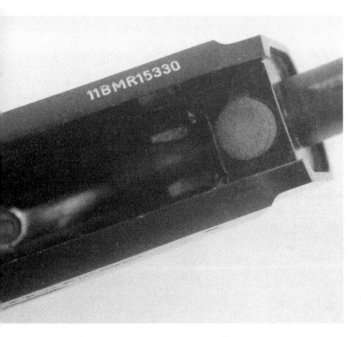

28. The synthetic bolt buffer and the spongy pad beneath the trigger group can be left alone unless they need to be replaced.

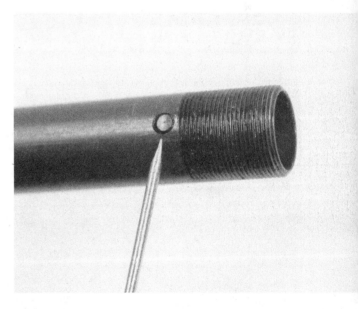

29. This pin retains the action spring retainer. Use a small diameter pin to hold the spring in place, then drive out the pin. Firmly control the retainer when unscrewing the retainer piece as the action spring and detent are under considerable compression. Do not attempt to remove the action tube.

30. The front and rear sights are both dovetailed and can be driven out to the side.

Reassembly Tips:

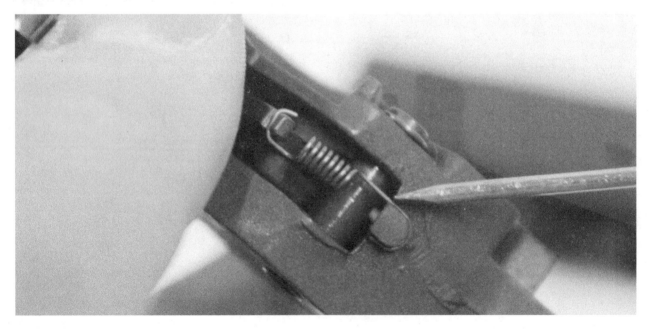

1. Note the orientation of the trigger/disconnector spring. The long leg goes to the rear.

KEL-TEC KSG

Data:	Kel-Tec KSG
Origin:	United States
Manufacturer:	Kel-Tec CNC, Inc., Cocoa, FL
Gauges:	12
Magazine capacity:	14 rounds
Over-all length:	26.1 inches
Barrel length:	18.5 inches
Weight:	6.9 pounds

The Kel-Tec company has a tradition of introducing novel new concepts with their firearms. The Kel-Tec Shotgun is such an example. At the minimum legal length, it is a bullpup style of gun, with the trigger forward of the chamber rather than the traditional design. Two side-by-side magazine tubes are also present with a selector switch to allow feeding from either desired magazine at will. A very well balanced shotgun, it is also short, and thinner than one would think a gun with side-by-side magazines would be.

Disassembly:

1. With the hammer cocked, the magazine selector in the center position, the safety on "safe," and the slide forward, push out the two rear assembly pins. These pins can be stored in the two holes in the pistol grip.

2. Lift the rear of the grip assembly, rotating it forward, and pull the assembly off the receiver.

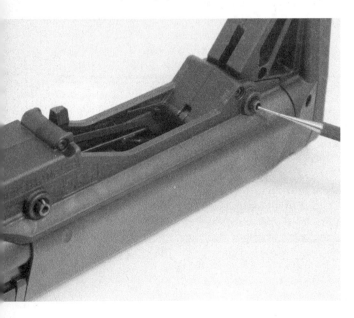

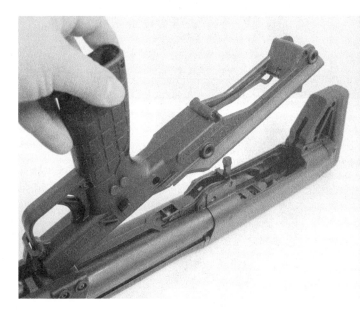

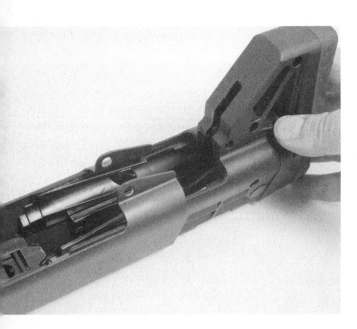

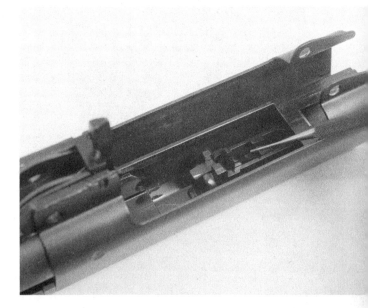

3. Grasp the stock and pull it out to the rear.

4. Holding the KSG upside down, pull the slide to the rear. The bolt assembly will drop into the top of the receiver and can be pulled out.

5. Pull the carrier assembly out to the rear.

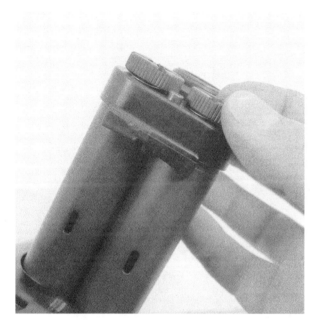

7. The barrel and slide assembly can now be pulled from the receiver and magazine assembly.

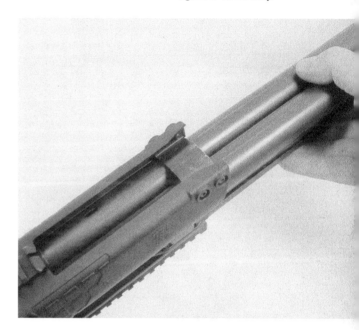

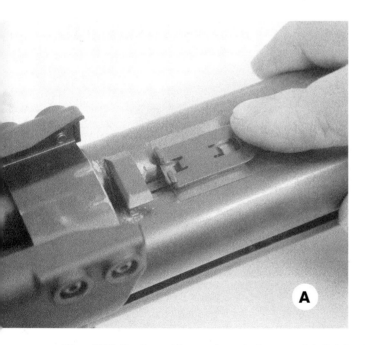

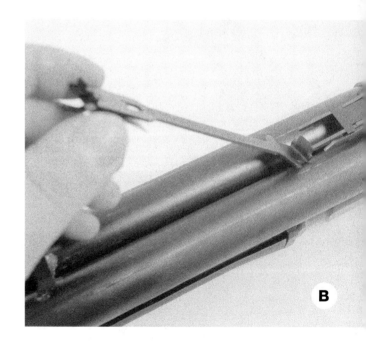

6. With the forend forward, push down on this link to allow the forend to slide over it (picture A). Lift the link out from under the cartridge stops and remove (picture B).

8. There are five socket screws in the stock unit. Remove these screws to access the lifter. The lifter rotates on two lifter axes, these spuds indicated here on the either side of the stock assembly. Unless the lifter needs to be replaced, there should be no need to disassemble the stock assembly.

9. Drift out the lock button's spring pin. The lock button can then be removed from the action lock.

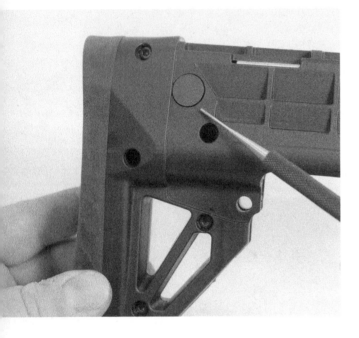

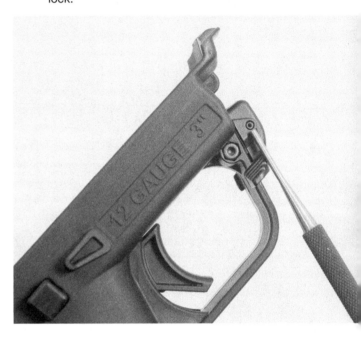

10. Remove the eight socket screws that hold the grip assembly together. Note that the two rearmost screws are of differing lengths than the foremost six screws.

11. Slowly work apart the two halves of the grip assembly. All of the internal parts should stay attached to the left half of the grip assembly.

12. Lift the slide lock off its pin. The slide lock spring is retained by both halves of the grip and will likely fall or spring free when the halves are parted. Control the spring. The slide lock axis pin can also be removed at this time.

13. Lift the hammer from its axis pin at the rear of the grip assembly.

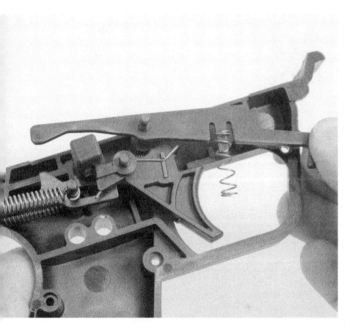

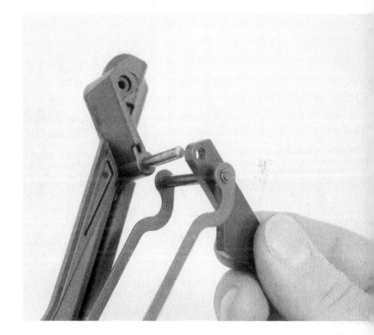

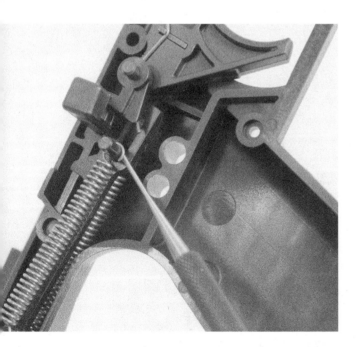

14. Lift the top hammer spring from the sear bar pin to release tension. While not under a great deal of compression when the hammer is down, it should still be controlled.

15. Remove the sear bar pin. It may be necessary to use pliers, since the bottom (left) hammer spring is still pulling on the pin.

16. The hammer and sear bar assembly can now be removed.

17. There is no need to further disassemble the hammer and sear bar assembly unless replacement or repair is warranted. The two hammer bar pins retain the bars with small spring clips. Removing these clips will allow the entire assembly to be taken apart.

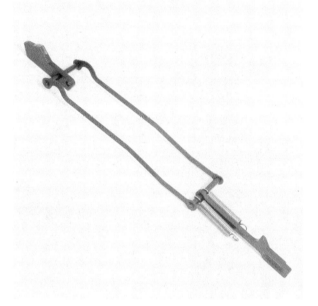

18. The trigger assembly can now be removed in total from the grip.

19. The safety can now be removed from the grip.

20. Remove the safety snap from the trigger axis pin.

21. Push the trigger axis pin left until it is flush with the trigger spring's right side coil. Then remove the trigger spring by lifting the right side coil off the pin. Follow this up by doing the same procedure to the left side coil of the trigger spring.

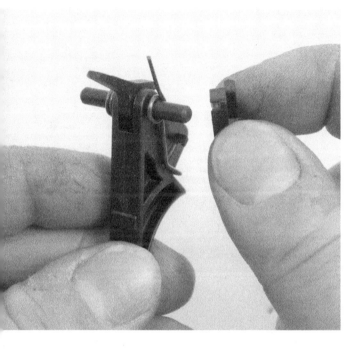

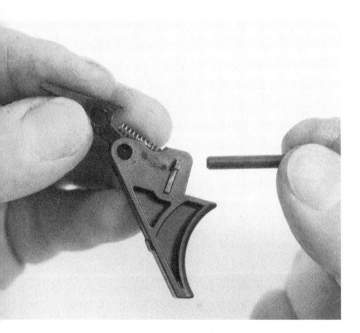

22. Fully remove the trigger axis pin to free the sear. The sear spring is powerful, so control it, and there is a spring guide inside the sear spring which should not be misplaced. The metal sear catch embedded in the top of the trigger should not be removed.

23. If necessary, the magazine springs and followers can be removed by unscrewing the two magazine plugs.

24. Remove this socket screw to release the magazine selector. There is a small brass washer under this screw. Do not lose it.

25. Push out this pin to remove the selector catch.

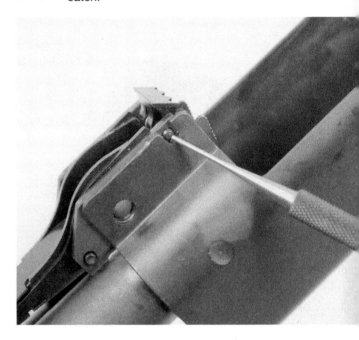

26. Push out the cartridge stop dowel pin to release the stops and spring.

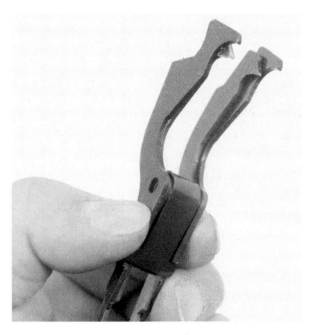

27. This is the cartridge stop assembly, with all four catches and the spring. The four catches are each unique and proper orientation should be observed.

28. If necessary, to remove the Picatinny rail, unscrew the two button head screws on the rail's top. These screws are retained with thread locking compound and are tightly retained. Beneath the rail and rearward of the sight base is the recoil pad.

29. Remove the six socket screws on the handguard forend, three above and three below. The two forend halves can then be spread and pushed around and off the barrel.

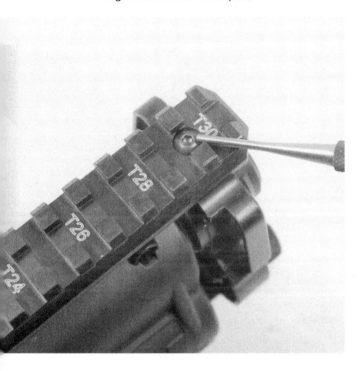

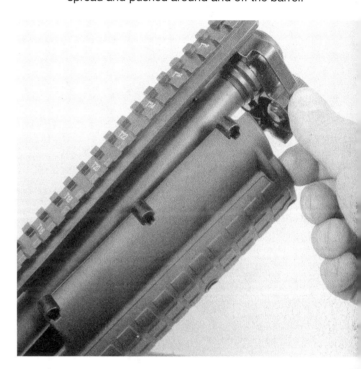

30. The bolt carrier legs can be lifted from the forend here.

31. The socket screw in the muzzle plate retains the pump buffer which rests at the bottom rear of the plate.

32. If necessary, the magazine bolts can be removed using a split-ring pliers to remove the split-rings on the rear side of the muzzle plate. Only do this if replacement is necessary.

33. The sight base and the muzzle plate are held to the barrel by means of three barrel rings. One retains the rear sight base, and two sandwich the muzzle plate. Unless barrel bore work or barrel replacement is to be done, there is no need to remove these rings or the sight base and muzzle plate, as these rings are heavily torqued and are retained with thread locker.

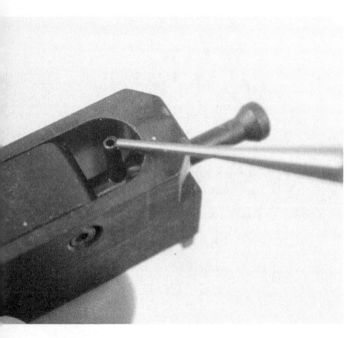

34. Pushing out this pin will free the firing pin which can then be drawn out of the bolt to the rear.

35. Pushing out this pin will free the extractor and extractor spring. Note the spring orientation when removing.

36. Pushing out this large roll pin will release the bolt lock to fall from the bolt.

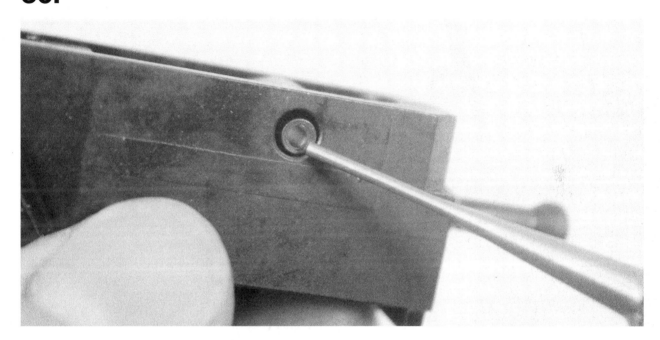

Reassembly Tips:

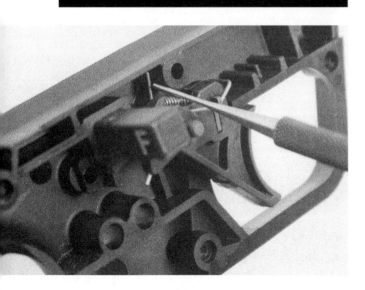

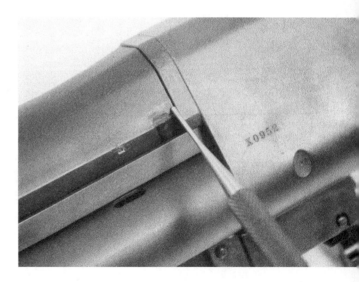

1. When reinstalling the trigger assembly, the left leg of the trigger spring must rest against the back of this boss on the left side grip. Simply place the leg of the spring then compress and insert the trigger axis pin into its hole, then push the entire assembly into the left grip

2. There should be no gap between the barrel extension and the receiver when reassembled.

Remington Model 870R

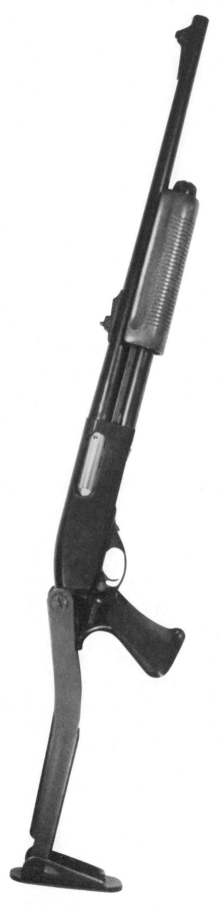

Data: Remington Model 870R
Origin: United States
Manufacturer: Remington Arms Company, Bridgeport, Connecticut
Gauge: 12
Magazine capacity: 4 rounds
Overall length: 40-3/8 inches (stock extended) 29-7/8 inches (stock folded)
Barrel length: 20 inches
Weight: 8 pounds

In police use, the basic Remington 870 will often be found with the factory pistol-grip folding stock, and a short barrel equipped with rifle-type sights. Extended magazine tubes are also available, and sling swivels are often added. Except for the police accessories, the 870R is internally the same as the regular sporting 870, and the instructions can be applied to either gun.

Disassembly:

1. Open the action, and unscrew the magazine endcap. Take off the barrel toward the front.

2. Fold the collapsible stock, and use an Allen wrench or an Allen screwdriver bit to back out the screw at the upper rear of the pistol grip unit.

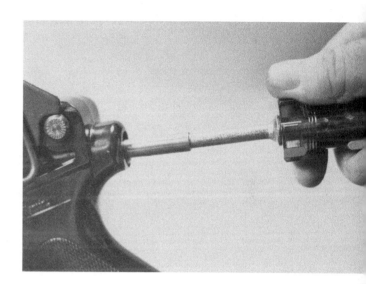

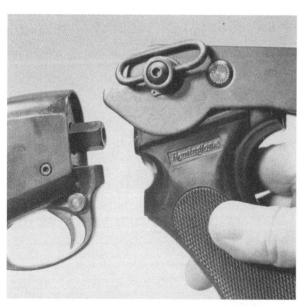

3. Remove the stock unit toward the rear.

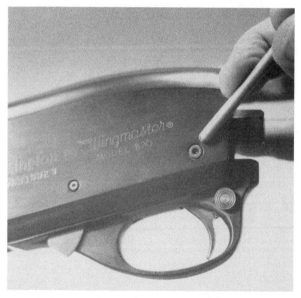

4. Push out the large cross pin at the lower rear of the receiver, and the smaller cross pin at the front of the trigger group.

5. Remove the trigger group downward and toward the rear, tilting it slightly to clear the slide latch on the left.

6. Inside the lower edge of the receiver, depress the left shell stop, and move the action slide and bolt assembly forward out of the receiver. Lift the bolt off the action slide bars, and separate the bolt and slide piece.

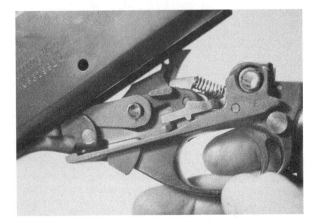

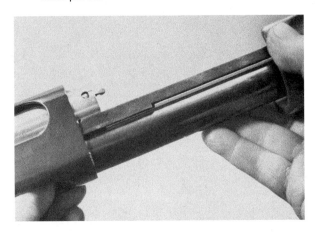

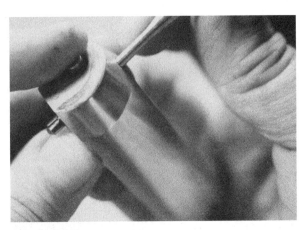

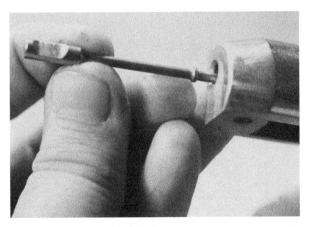

7. Restrain the firing pin, and drift out its vertical retaining pin downward.

8. Remove the firing pin from the rear of the bolt. The spring will be released from the underside of the bolt.

9. Remove the locking block from the underside of the bolt.

10. Insert a small sharp screwdriver between the extractor and its plunger, and depress the plunger toward the rear. Lift the extractor out of its recess in the bolt. **Caution:** *Keep the plunger and spring under control, and ease them out for removal toward the front.*

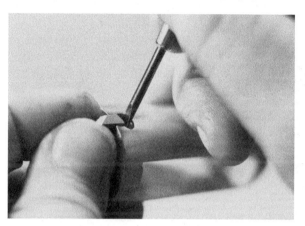

11. Insert a tool into the retainer at the front of the magazine tube, and pry it outward, moving the tool to lift it evenly. **Caution:** *The magazine spring will be released, so control it.* Remove the retainer, spring, and magazine follower. The ejector and its housing are riveted inside the left wall of the receiver, and should be removed only for repair. Replacement requires new rivets and a special tool. The right and left shell stops are staked in place in their recesses at the rear. If removal is necessary for repair, insert a sharp screwdriver to pry them inward, then remove them toward the rear.

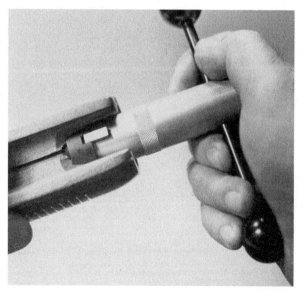

12. Use a B-Square Model 870 forend wrench or a piece of shop steel cut to fit, and unscrew the forend cap nut. Remove the action slide tube and bars toward the rear.

13. Restrain the carrier, and push out the carrier pivot, which is also the front group pin sleeve. Take care not to lose the lock spring at its end.

14. Release the spring tension slowly, and remove the carrier assembly upward and toward the front. Remove the carrier plunger and spring from their well on the right side. The carrier dog and its spacer plate are riveted on the right rear arm of the carrier, and should not be disturbed in normal takedown.

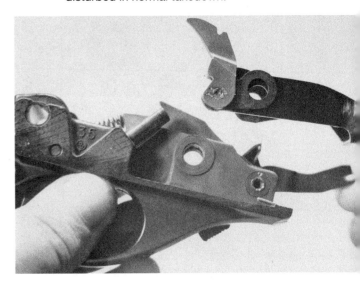

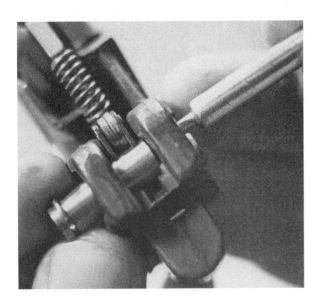

15. Restrain the hammer, pull the trigger, and ease the hammer down to fired position. Push out the rear group cross pin sleeve toward the left, taking care not to lose the lock spring at its end.

16. Removal of the sleeve will allow the top of the trigger to move further toward the rear, relieving the tension of the sear and trigger spring. Detach the front of the spring from its stud on the back of the sear, and remove it upward.

17. Drift out the trigger cross pin toward the left.

18. Remove the trigger assembly upward, turning it slightly to the left to clear the left connector. The two connectors are cross pinned to the top of the trigger, and the pin is riveted. Remove this system only for repair.

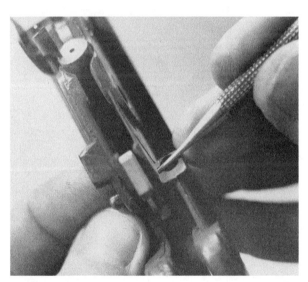

19. The sear cross pin is accessible on the right side inside the carrier spring well. Angle a small drift punch to nudge it out toward the left.

20. Remove the sear upward.

21. The hammer and slide latch are pivoted and retained by the same cross pin at the front of the trigger group, and the pin is riveted on the right side over a washer in a recess. This system should not be removed unless necessary for repair. If it is to be taken out, take care that the slide latch is not deformed during removal of the cross pin, and restrain the hammer, as its plunger and spring will be released as the pin is removed. The slide latch spring will also be freed for removal.

22. Hold a fingertip over the hole at the upper rear of the trigger group, and push out the safety spring cross pin. Remove the safety spring upward. The safety detent ball will probably stay in the well.

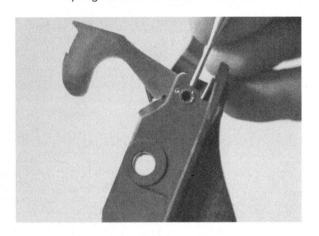

23. Remove the safety toward either side. Insert a tool from the top to push the safety detent ball down into the safety tunnel, and remove it. Take care that this small steel ball is not lost.

Reassembly Tips:

2. When replacing the carrier assembly, be sure the rear step of the carrier dog engages the carrier spring plunger correctly, as shown.

When replacing the firing pin in the bolt, insert the spring through the underside, and be sure the front of the spring enters its recess inside the front of the bolt.

When replacing the bolt and action slide assembly in the receiver, it is necessary to depress the right and left shell stops, in that order, as the assembly is moved back into place.

1. When replacing the trigger assembly, be sure the forward tip of the left connector arm is positioned above the rear tail of the slide latch, as shown.

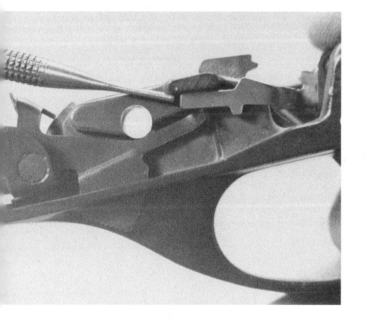

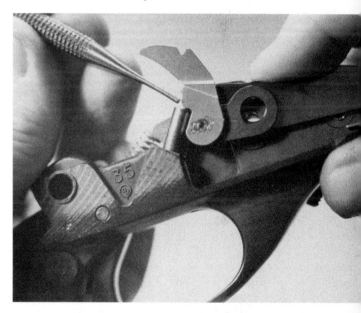

ARMALITE AR-50A1

Similar/Identical Pattern Guns

The same basic assembly/disassembly steps for the Armalite AR-50A1 also apply to the following guns:

Armalite AR-50   Armalite AR-30

Data:	Armalite AR-50A1
Origin:	United States
Manufacturer:	Armalite, Inc., Geneseo, Il.
Cartridge:	.50 BMG
Magazine capacity:	1 rounds
Over-all length:	58.5 inches
Barrel length:	30 inches
Weight:	34 pounds

A big bruiser of a rifle is the AR-50, and beautifully ugly it is. The current A1 edition is a whopping 34 pounds, plus a few for a decent scope and stuff, and firing the .50 BMG, it really needs to be. A huge muzzle brake does wonders for the recoil, and peace of mind is provided by a heavy bolt with huge recoil lugs. It's younger brother, the AR-30 (which fires .300 Win. Mag. or .338 Lapua Mag.) is close enough in design that the takedown here should apply just fine. For what it's worth, leave the muzzle brake on it.

Disassembly:

1. Depress the bolt lock and pull the bolt assembly from the rear of the receiver.

2. Loosen the set screw locking the bipod to the rail under the chassis. Slide the bipod assembly forward off the chassis. The sling stud can also be removed by unscrewing the stud and sliding the stud assembly forward off the chassis. Do not attempt to disassemble the bipod as it is permanently assembled.

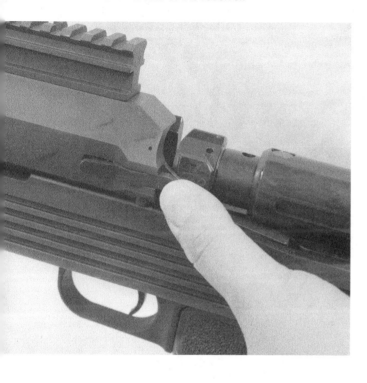

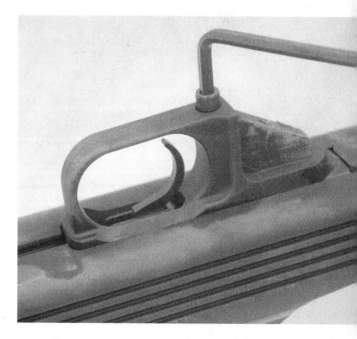

3. Remove the pistol grip by unscrewing the screw within and lifting the grip from the chassis.

4. Remove the trigger guard by unscrewing this bolt.

5. The rifle is held to the chassis by three bolts. Two are beneath the front receiver ring and one is beneath the trigger guard. Remove these to free the barreled action from the chassis. The front bolt is different, so remember their orientations.

6. Lift the chassis from the barreled action. There is a small block (bedding wedge) that will fall out from in front of the receiver. Keep track of it.

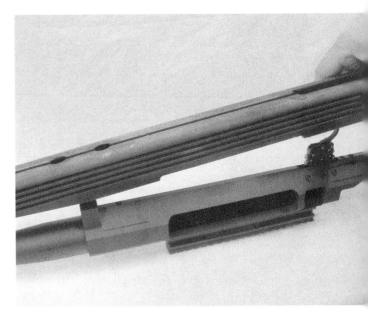

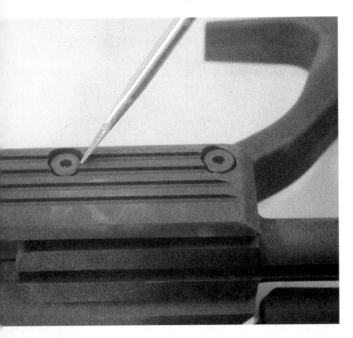

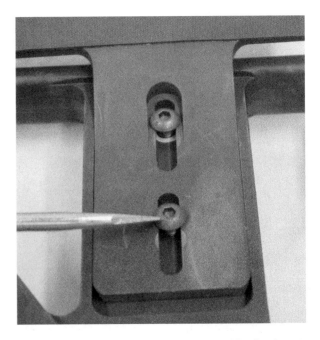

7. These two bolts retain the buttstock to the chassis. Remove them to slide the stock rearward out of the chassis.

8. These two bolts retain the adjustable cheek rest. Remove them and the cheek rest will fall off the left side of the stock. The nuts on the opposite side should not be misplaced.

9. These two bolts retain the adjustable butt plate. Remove them to release the butt plate.

10. Use a small punch to push the bolt stop pin down out of the receiver.

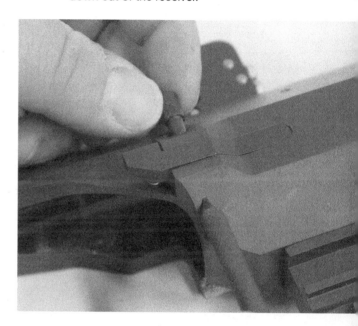

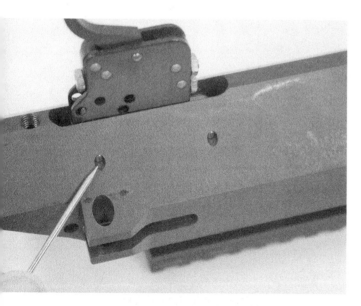

11. The trigger assembly is held to the receiver by these two pins. Push them out to remove it.

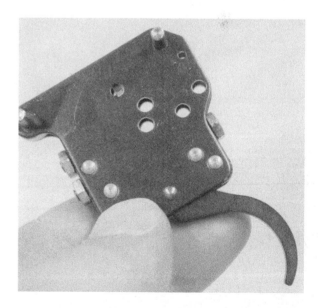

12. The trigger should not be disassembled. It is riveted together. The sear itself will be freed as the trigger retaining pins are removed, as will its spring. The three adjustments can also be removed if necessary, but the housing and trigger itself should be left intact or the assembly should be replaced as a whole.

13. The immense muzzle brake can be removed from the barrel if necessary by unscrewing it from the barrel.

14. The scope rail is held to the receiver by four bolts.

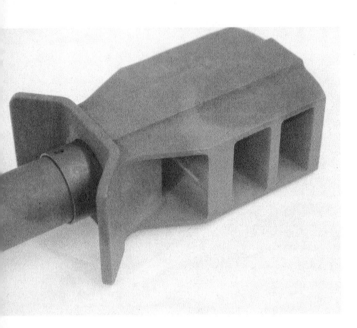

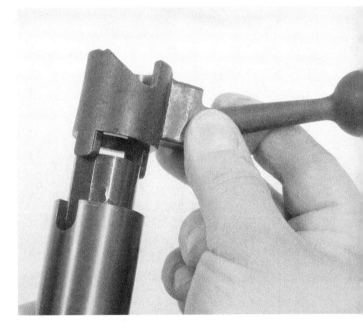

15. Place a spacer (in this case a wide screwdriver bit) beneath the safety lever. Then unscrew the firing pin assembly from the bolt and pull it out the rear of the bolt body.

16. Remove the bolt handle.

17. Push out the bolt head pin.

18. Pull the bolt head from the bolt body.

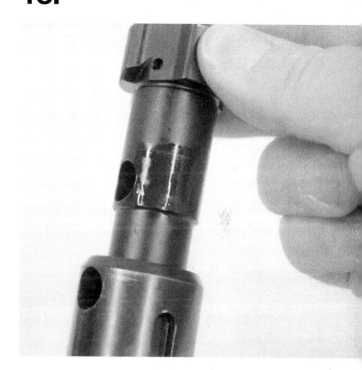

19. Pull back the extractor plunger to free the extractor for removal.

20. Push out this pin to remove the ejector.

21. The firing pin can be disassembled by pushing out this pin. As the spring is still compressed, do this with care.

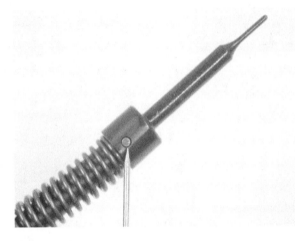

22. With the firing pin tip and spring removed, the firing pin body and safety can be withdrawn from the shroud to the rear.

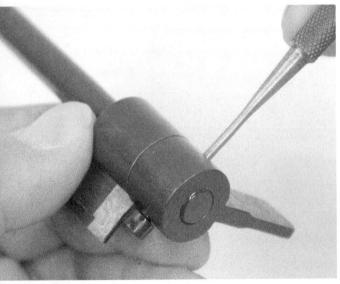

23. The safety arm and cocking piece are removed by pushing out this pin.

Reassembly Tips:

1. The bedding wedge has an angle on it. When reinstalling it, the angle should be forward and down to match the angle in the chassis

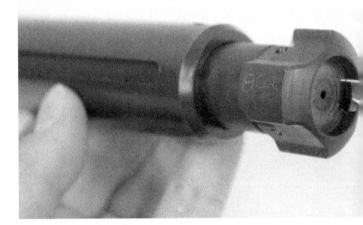

2. The bolt can be installed upside down. The extractor should be located opposite the groove in the bolt body.

ARMALITE AR-180

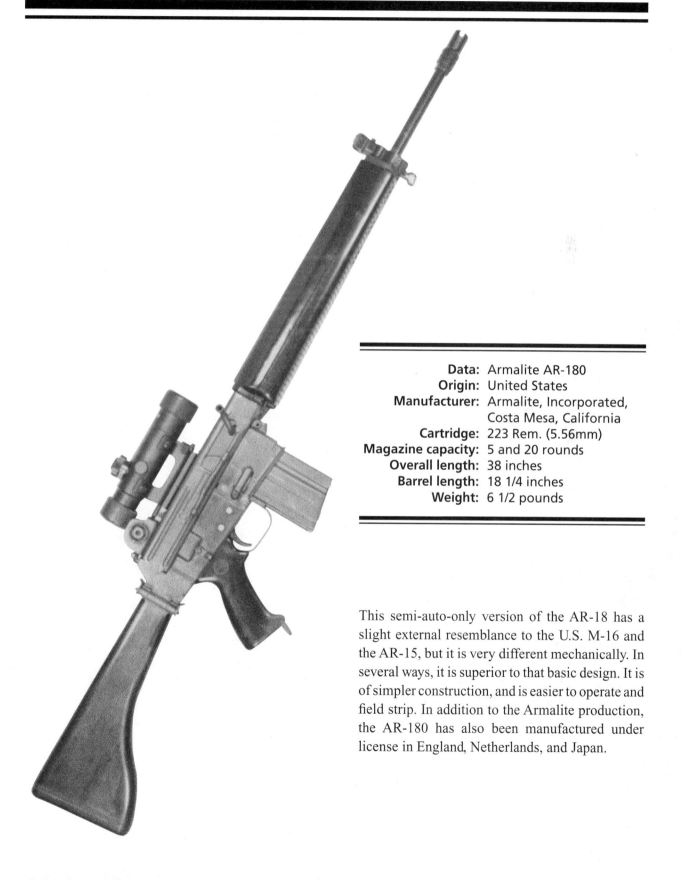

Data:	Armalite AR-180
Origin:	United States
Manufacturer:	Armalite, Incorporated, Costa Mesa, California
Cartridge:	223 Rem. (5.56mm)
Magazine capacity:	5 and 20 rounds
Overall length:	38 inches
Barrel length:	18 1/4 inches
Weight:	6 1/2 pounds

This semi-auto-only version of the AR-18 has a slight external resemblance to the U.S. M-16 and the AR-15, but it is very different mechanically. In several ways, it is superior to that basic design. It is of simpler construction, and is easier to operate and field strip. In addition to the Armalite production, the AR-180 has also been manufactured under license in England, Netherlands, and Japan.

Disassembly:

1. If the gun has an Armalite telescopic sight, push the scope base latch toward the left, and move the scope and base toward the rear until it stops. A spring inside the base will be compressd.

2. Move the scope and base straight upward, and when the base has cleared its track on top of the receiver, the scope assembly will be forced off toward the front.

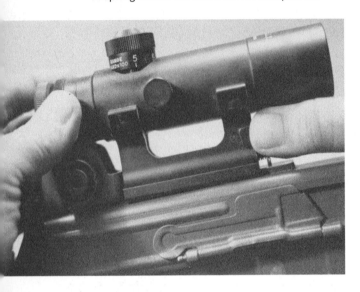

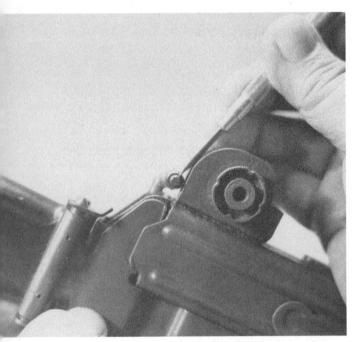

3. Remove the magazine, and cycle the action to cock the internal hammer. Set the safety in the on-safe position. Depress the receiver latch plunger, and push the receiver latch forward. Its upper projection will enter the rear sight mount.

4. Keeping the latch depressed, tilt the rear of the receiver upward. **Caution:** *Keep a firm grip on the latch, as it is the rear base of the compressed recoil spring assembly.*

5. Slowly release the spring tension, and remove the recoil spring assembly from the rear of the receiver.

6. Move the bolt back to align the bolt handle with the larger opening at the end of its track, and remove the bolt handle toward the right.

7. Remove the bolt assembly toward the rear.

8. Depress and hold the firing pin, and push the firing-pin-retaining cross pin out toward the left and remove it.

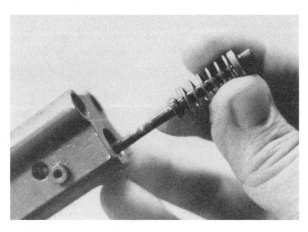

9. Remove the firing pin and its spring toward the rear.

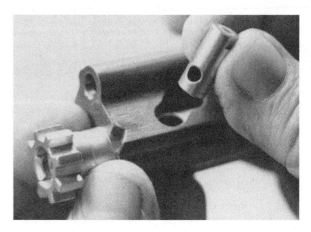

10. Remove the bolt cam pin toward the left.

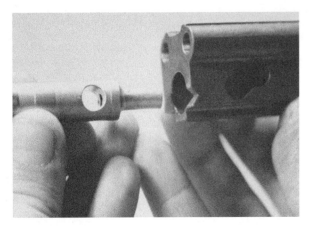

11. Remove the bolt from the front of the carrier.

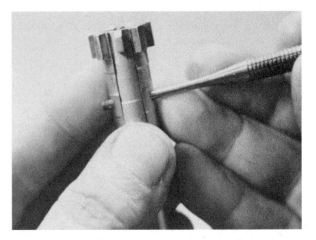

12. Restrain the extractor, and push out the extractor cross pin toward either side.

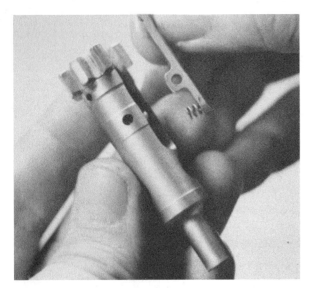

13. Remove the extractor and its spring from the bolt.

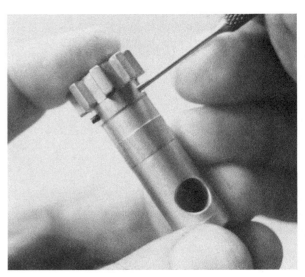

14. The ejector is retained by a small roll pin at the front of the bolt. Restrain the ejector against the tension of its spring, and drift out the roll pin. Remove the ejector and its spring toward the front.

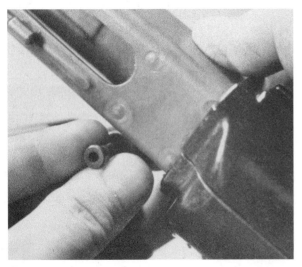

15. Push out the hinge pin at the front of the receiver toward the right, and separate the grip frame and buttstock unit from the receiver.

16. Removal of the recoil spring unit will have released the upper handguard. Tip it upward at the rear, and remove it.

17. Move the gas piston rod toward the rear, fully compressing its spring, and remove the connector toward the rear, tilting it toward the side.

18. Slowly release the spring tension, moving the gas piston rod forward and tilting it toward the side for removal, along with its spring.

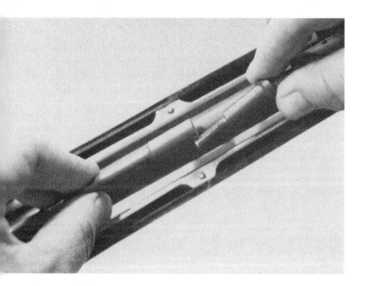

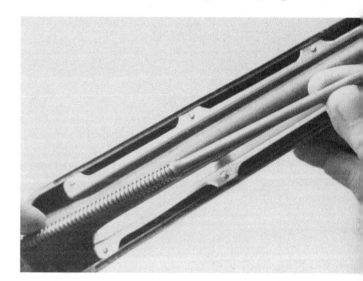

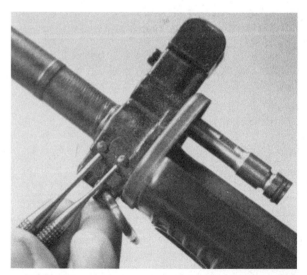

19. Remove the gas piston toward the rear. The gas piston tube can be unscrewed from the rear sight base, but in normal takedown it is best left in place.

20. Drifting out the two cross-pins in the front sight unit will allow the unit to be moved forward. This will release the lower handguard for removal forward and downward. The handguard plate can then be removed toward the rear.

21. The flash hider can be unscrewed from the muzzle by using a wrench of the proper size. The front sight unit can then be taken off toward the front.

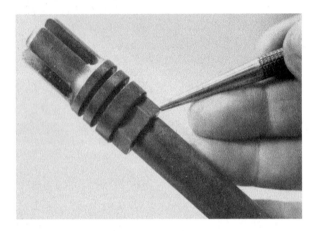

22. The ejection port cover hinge has a grooved tip at the rear for engagement of a tool to nudge it out rearward, releasing the cover and its spring. The hinge pin is often tightly fitted, and unless necessary for repair, it is best left in place. The cover latch plunger and spring are retained by a roll pin.

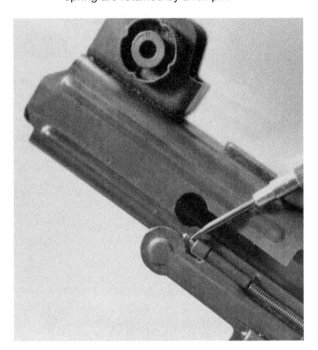

23. Swing the bolt latch up to the vertical position. Release the safety, restrain the hammer, and pull the trigger, lowering the hammer to the fired position.

24. Remove the C-clip that retains the bolt latch pivot, and push the latch pivot inward for removal.

25. Remove the bolt latch upward. A plunger and spring are retained in the front of the latch by a roll cross-pin. Take out the plug, spring, and plunger downward.

26. Remove the C-clip from the tip of the safety cross-piece on the right side of the frame.

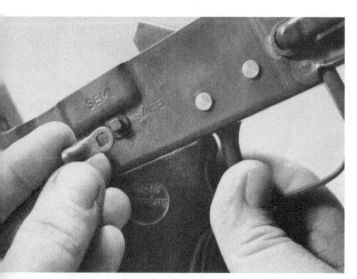

27. Remove the safety indicator lever toward the right. Return the hammer to the cocked position.

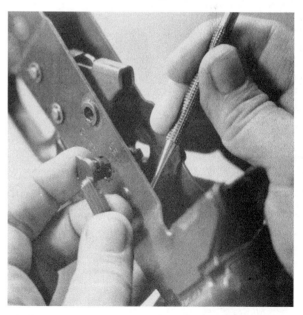

28. Insert a tool from the top to engage the hole in the safety spring yoke, and depress the yoke and spring toward the rear. While holding them there, remove the safety toward the left.

29. Slowly release the spring tension, and remove the safety yoke and spring upward.

30. Restrain the hammer, pull the trigger, and lower the hammer to the fired position. Remove the C-clip from the left tip of the hammer pivot, restrain the hammer, and push out the pivot toward the right.

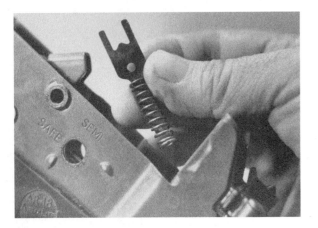

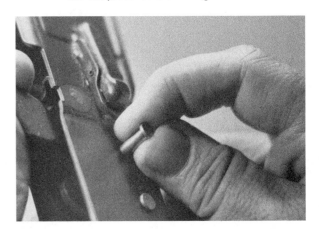

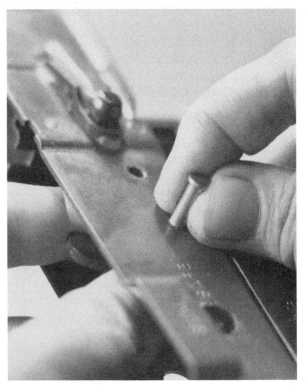

31. Remove the hammer and its spring forward and upward.

32. Remove the C-clip from the left tip of the trigger pivot. Restrain the trigger and sear, and push out the trigger cross-pin toward the right.

33. Remove the trigger assembly upward. Pushing out the pivot sleeve will release the trigger spring for removal, and will also release the secondary sear, or disconnector, for removal. If the sleeve is to be removed, use a large roll-pin punch to avoid deforming it.

34. The magazine catch and its spring are retained by a vertical roll pin, which is drifted out upward, and the catch and spring are taken off toward the right.

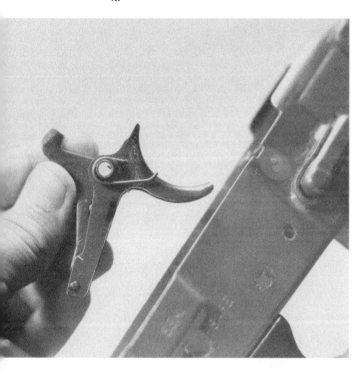

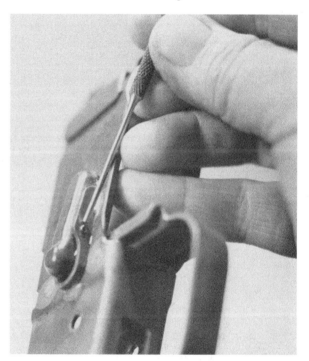

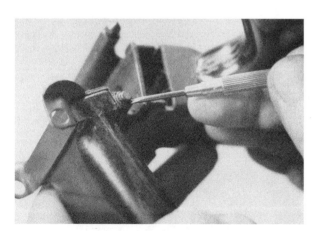

35. The buttstock hinge pin is retained by a C-clip in a groove at its lower tip, and the hinge pin is taken out upward. The buttstock can then be removed.

36. . The upper and lower stock latch plungers and their common spring are retained by two roll pins. Drifting out one of the pins will allow removal of one plunger and the spring.

37. The pistol grip is retained by a screw accessible from below, and the grip is taken off downward. The buttstock is retained on its hinge plate by a long screw accessible at the center of the buttplate.

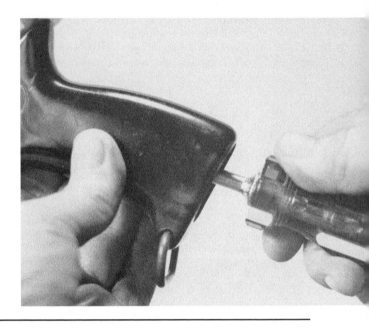

Reassembly Tips:

1. Note that the cam pin hole in the bolt is staked on one side, to prevent the bolt from being reinstalled in the bolt carrier backwards. When replacing the bolt in the carrier, be sure the extractor is on the right.

2. When replacing the cam pin, note that the crosshole in the pin must be oriented lengthwise for passage of the firing pin.

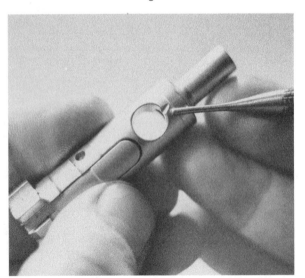

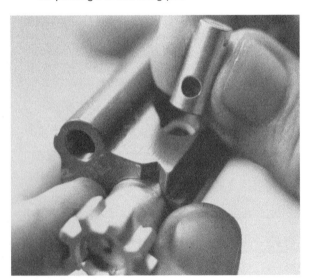

BARRETT MRAD

Similar/Identical Pattern Guns

The same basic assembly/disassembly steps for the Barrett MRAD also apply to the following gun:

Barrett Model 98B

Data:	Barrett MRAD
Origin:	United States
Manufacturer:	Barrett Firearms, Murfreesboro, TN
Cartridge:	.338 Lapua Magnum
Magazine capacity:	10 rounds
Over-all length:	46.9 inches
Barrel length:	24 inches
Weight:	14.28 pounds

The MRAD is the second incarnation of Barrett's .338 Lapua Magnum tactical bolt rifle. Very similar to the first rifle the M98B, the MRAD is distinguished mostly by the rapidly interchangeable barrel and folding adjustable stock. The 98B has a fixed stock and barrel. Differences in takedown procedures are otherwise inconsequential.

Disassembly:

1. To begin disassembly open the bolt so that it is in an open position rather than locked.

2. Depress the receiver latch and lift the rear of the upper receiver assembly from the lower receiver assembly.

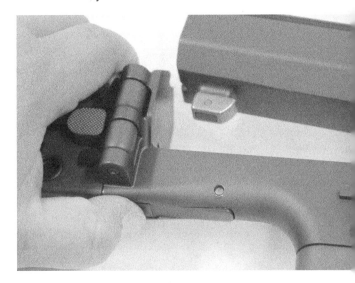

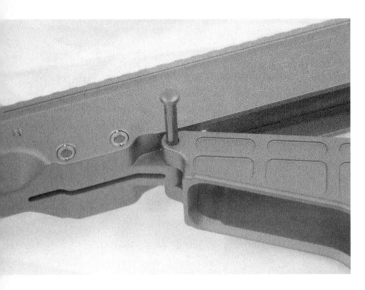

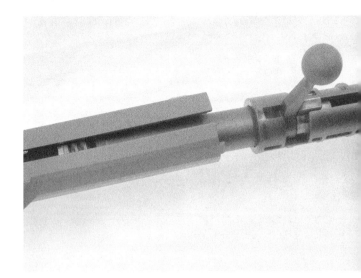

3. Push out the assembly pin and fully separate the two receiver assemblies.

4. Pull the bolt and bolt and rear bolt guide from the rear of the upper receiver. Pull the bolt assembly out from the back of the rear bolt guide.

5. Displace the front bolt guide and remove it out the back of the upper receiver.

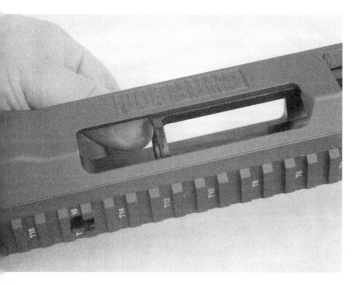

6. To remove the barrel, remove the two cross bolts just in front of and below the ejection port. Pull the barrel from the receiver.

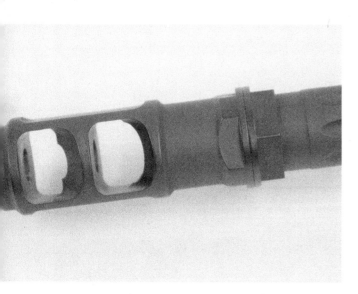

7. The muzzle brake need not be removed unless necessity requires it. It is retained by a jam nut.

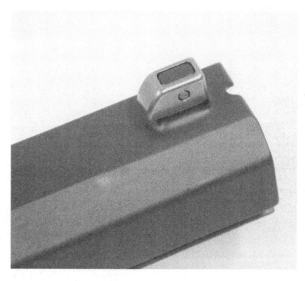

8. The upper receiver's lug is pinned to the receiver and removal is not necessary unless it needs to be replaced.

9. Absent the factory supplied bolt disassembly tool, disassemble the bolt assembly by pushing the cocking piece back until the slots on either side are exposed. Place an appropriately-sized tool into the slot and release the tension (picture A). Rotate the cocking piece about 120 degrees until its internal lugs clear and pull it from the rear of the bolt body (picture B).

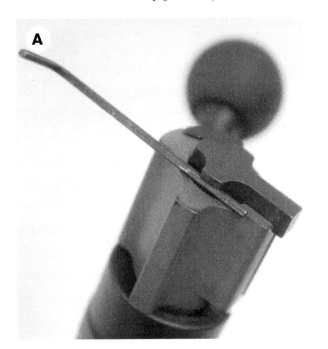

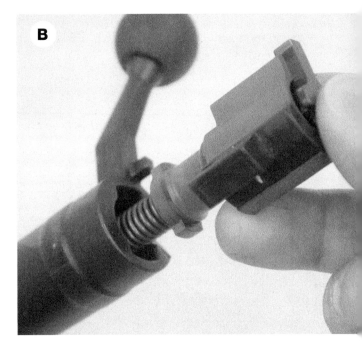

10. Push out the bolt pin and pull the bolt head from the bolt body. The pin will only exit the "top" of the bolt carrier and not in the reverse, "down" toward the bottom of the rifle.

11. The extractor spring tail wraps partially around the bolt. Lift up the tail (picture A) and pull the head of the spring out of the bolt head; this frees the extractor for removal (picture B).

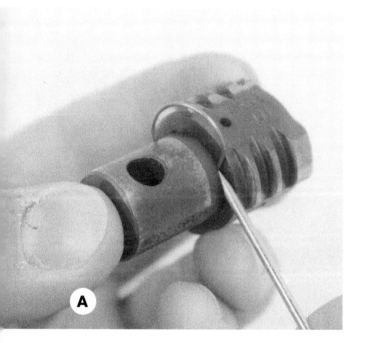

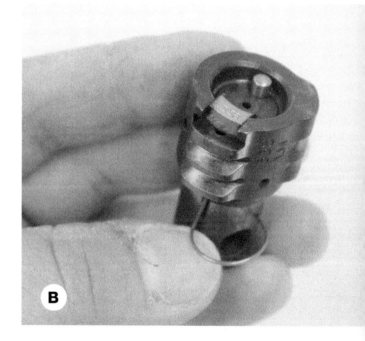

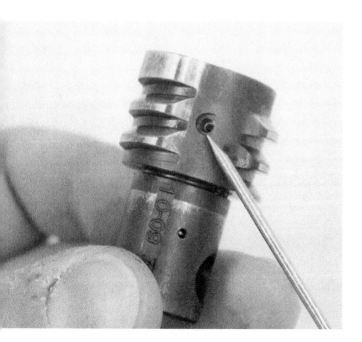

12. The ejector and spring can be removed by driving out this pin.

13. The bolt stop can be removed by driving out this pin.

14. The firing pin assembly can be disassembled by pushing the cocking piece out to expose this pin. Move the tool so that it sits below the cocking piece. Pushing out this pin will separate the cocking piece from the firing pin. Keep tension on the firing pin to ease pin removal and to control the whole assembly.

15. Unscrew the pistol grip screw (inside the grip). The safety lever is retained by a detent and spring which are held in place by the pistol grip. With the detent and spring removed, the safety can be pulled out of the receiver to the left.

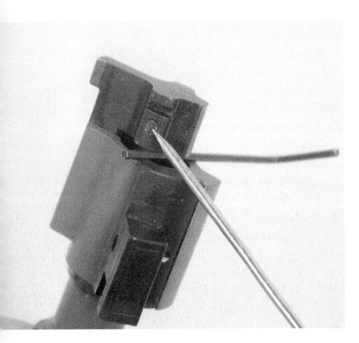

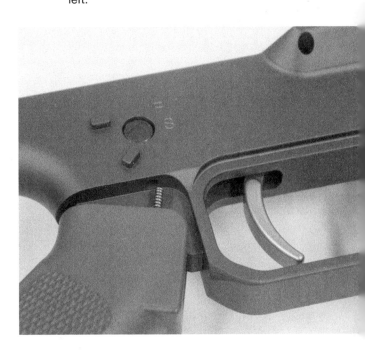

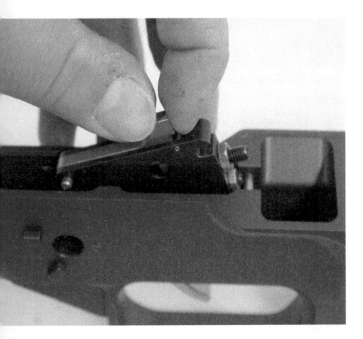

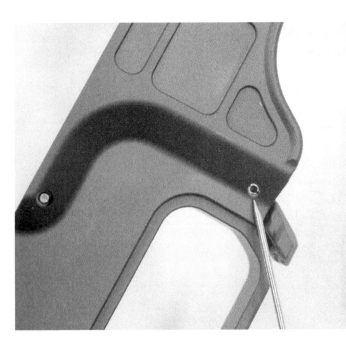

16. Pull the trigger housing back and then up out of the receiver. The pin that holds the front of the housing in the receiver need not be removed.

17. If necessary, the magazine catch and spring can be removed by driving out this pin.

18. If necessary, the receiver latch, the receiver safety latch (large piece above it that prevents disassembly with a closed bolt) and spring can be removed by driving out this pin.

19. The receiver assembly pin can be removed, along with its detent and spring, by inserting a small tool into this hole, and depressing the detent enough to allow the pin to rotate, so the pin can be pulled from the receiver.

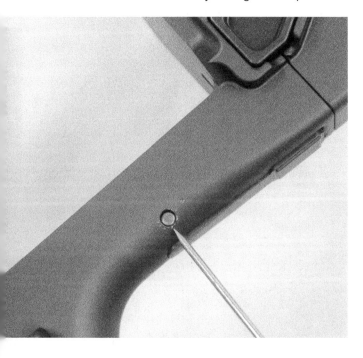

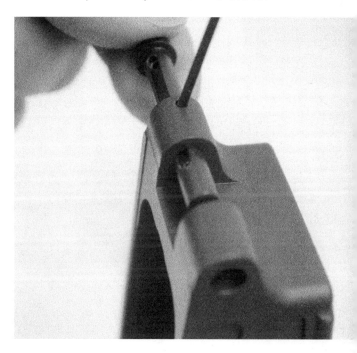

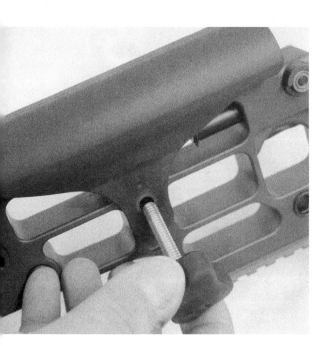

20. Completely unscrewing the cheekpiece locking knob/screw will allow the cheekpiece to be removed from the stock by pulling it straight up.

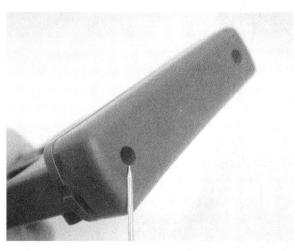

21. Further disassembly of the highly robust stock should only be necessary to repair great damage, as the stock pivot pin, the adjustable stock base pad assembly, and the folding stock latch assembly can be considered semi-permanently installed, due to the very high spring tension in the latches and the tight fit of the pivot pin. The butt pad is held to the adjustable folding stock by two screws and can be changed by removing these screws.

22. stock pad base can be removed from the stock by removing the adjustment button. The button should be fully depressed and the latch unscrewed (picture A). A snap ring also retains the base's upper guide rod (picture B).

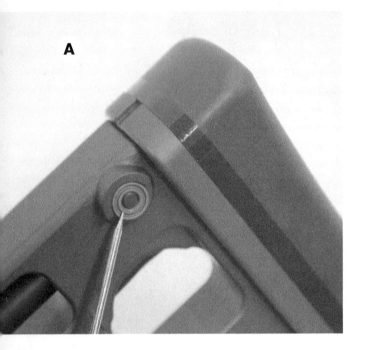

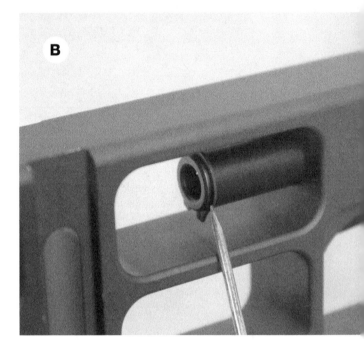

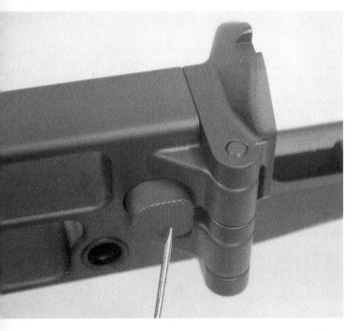

23. The stock is held to the lower receiver by a large press fit pivot pin. The stock latch disassembles in a similar way to the stock adjustment screw.

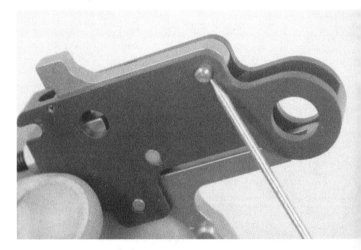

24. The trigger assembly can be disassembled for cleaning by first removing the sear pin. The sear spring will be loose beneath the sear. The small roll pin that retains and limits sear movement need not be removed.

25. The trigger pivot pin is staked in place and, if removed, should be secured in a similar fashion when replaced.

26. There are three adjustment screws. The top forward screw has spring tip in it and is used to adjust trigger pull weight. The lower front screw is an overtravel screw. Both can be adjusted or removed if necessary by simply unscrewing them from the housing.

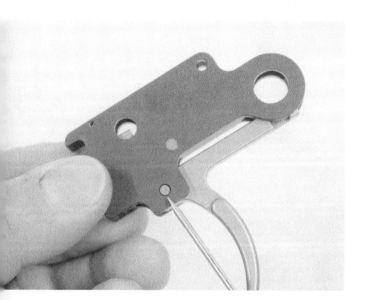

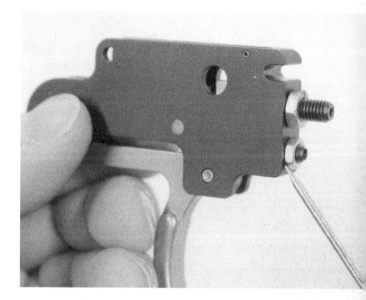

27. A hole is drilled in this slot that contains the sear engagement set screw. Removal of this screw will require a full resetting of the trigger adjustments.

28. Do not remove this plastic insert.

29. The magazine can be disassembled for cleaning by pinching the bottom of the mag body, just above the floorplate, depressing the button in the floorplate, and pushing the floorplate forward off the body.

30. The magazine body, floor plate, follower, spring, and spring base.

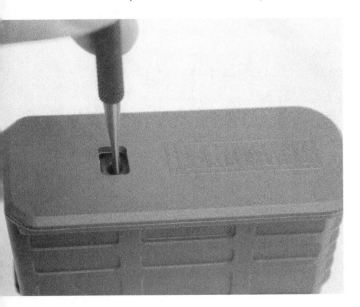

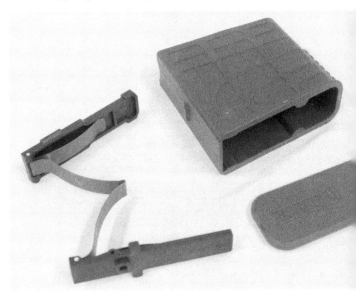

Reassembly Tips:

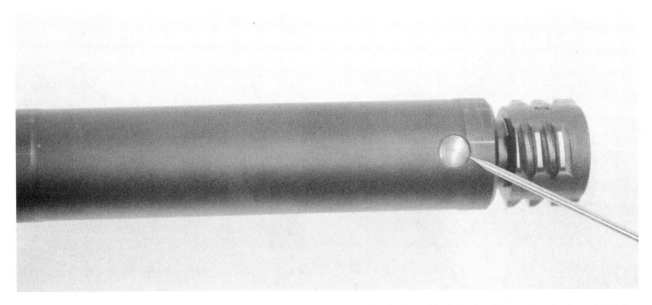

1. Note that the bolt pin can only be inserted one way through the bolt and bolt body. Attempting to do so with the bolt head rotated 180 degrees out of alignment may result in damage to the various parts of this assembly. The large end of the pin is at the "top" of the bolt body.

BENELLI MR1

Data:	Benelli MR1
Origin:	Italy
Manufacturer:	Benelli Armi S.P.A., Urbino
Cartridge:	5.56x45 mm
Magazine capacity:	30 rounds
Over-all length:	37.1 inches
Barrel length:	16 inches
Weight:	7.9 pounds

Benelli's .223 rifle is based on the R1 semi auto hunting rifle. However it has significant differences. LE and military models feature a collapsible stock that is replaced on the civilian legal versions with either a fixed pistol grip stock or a Benelli ComforTech recoil management stock of traditional design. It feeds from the common AR-15 magazines, and features the same gas system as seen on the M4 shotgun. The Beretta RX4 is identical and was the marketed name of the MR1 when the rifle was first introduced. The RX4 designation is still used outside of the USA.

Disassembly:

1. Unscrew the forend cap from the forend and remove.

2. Slide the forend from the barrel.

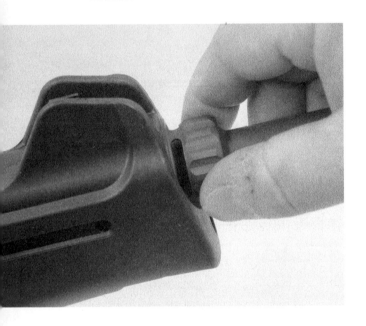

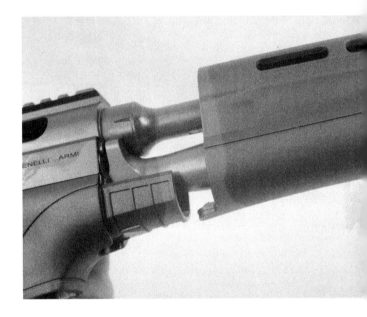

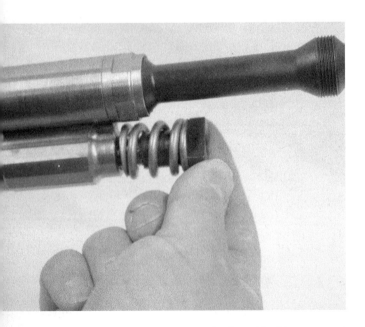

3. Unscrew and remove the barrel locking cap and spring.

4. With the bolt closed, grasp the top receiver and barrel assembly and pull gently and slowly forward. This will disengage the upper receiver from the lower receiver and clear the gas block from the piston assembly. Lift the entire barrel assembly with bolt from the lower.

5. The piston extension can be pulled from the front of the piston guide rod.

6. Pull the piston from the piston guide rod.

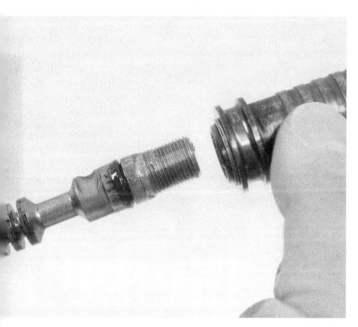

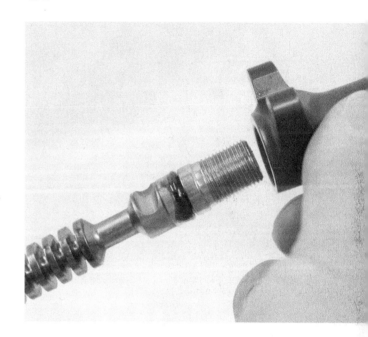

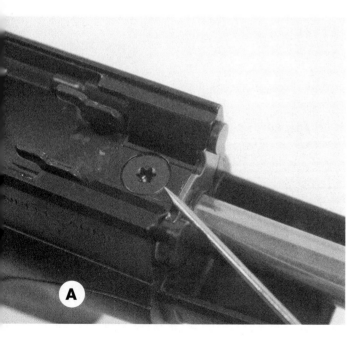

7. If the cylinder plunger pin (piston guide rod) needs to be replaced it can be removed by unscrewing this large screw, the cylinder plunger pin screw (picture A). The bolt follower pins (tappets) are retained by the shoulder plate that is held to the guide rod by a spring clip (picture B). As a rule these parts should be considered semi-permanent assemblies and left in place for general maintenance.

8. Push out this pin, just behind the magazine catch (picture A). Remove this screw from just in front of the magazine well in the bottom of the rifle (picture B).

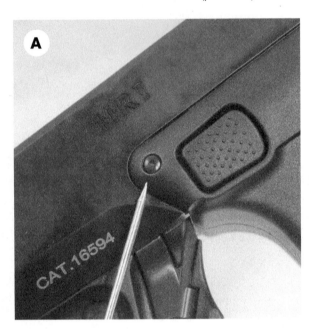

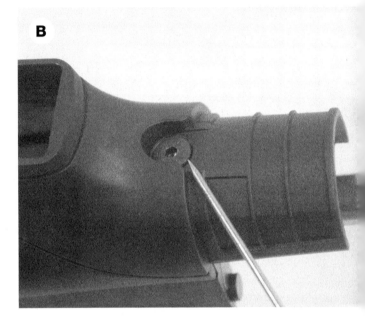

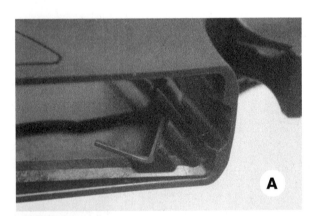

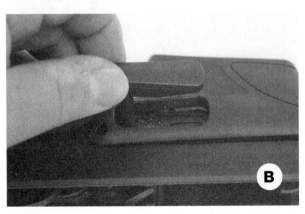

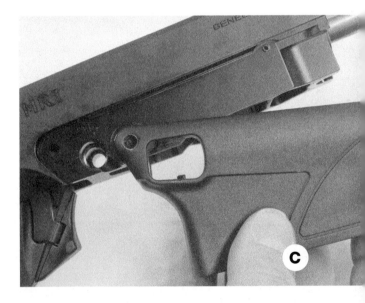

9. There is a small set screw, deep in the right rear corner of the inside of the magazine well (picture A). Remove this set screw to free the right mag catch button. The button and mag catch spring will fall out as this set screw is removed. The magazine catch can then be removed from the left side of the mag well (picture B). Remove the mag well (picture C).

10. This pin can be driven out to remove the mag plate position arms that sit next to the bolt follower pins (tappets).

11. Remove the recoil pad (pulls off) and unscrew the stock bolt from the recoil spring tube.

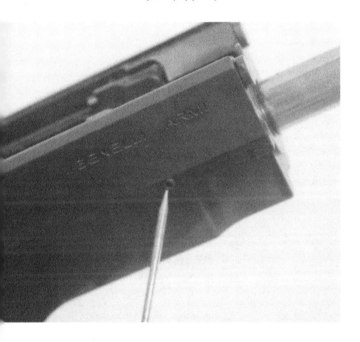

12. Removing this spring clip and unscrewing the stock retaining screw will free the recoil spring and plunger from the tube. However, it is recommended that these parts not be removed unless detailed cleaning of the tube is required, and the tube itself should not be removed except by the factory.

13. Push out this pin to remove the trigger guard assembly (picture A). Lift the assembly up and out of the receiver (picture B).

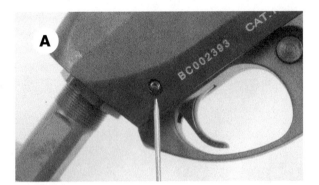

14. Remove this small spring clip and push the hammer pin bushing out to the right of the housing.

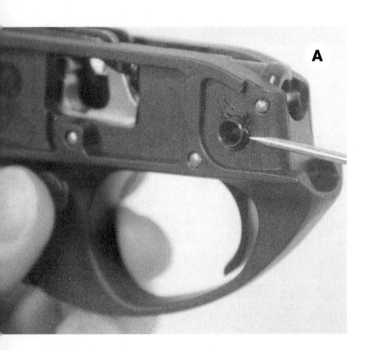

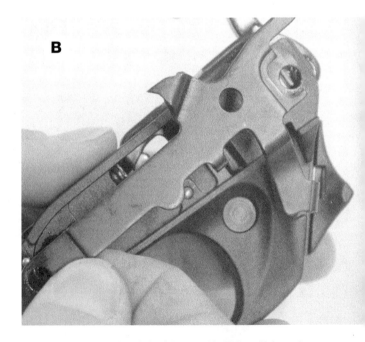

15. Remove this small spring clip and push the trigger pin bushing out to the right (picture A). This will free the bolt catch arm. Pull the arm straight out to the right and out of the bolt catch button (picture B). The spring lies behind the arm and should be contained as the arm is removed. The bolt catch button will be freed from its slot at this time as well.

16. Push out this pin that retains the hammer spring cap. Then withdraw the cap and spring from the rear.

17. Remove the hammer and strut by lifting it straight up and out of the housing.

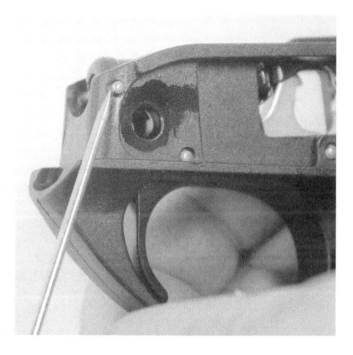

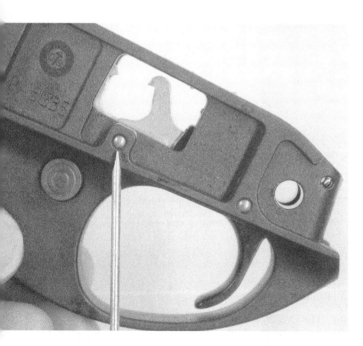

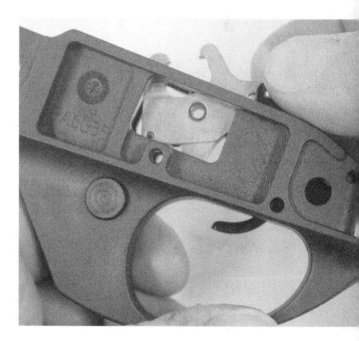

18. Push out both the trigger pin and sear pin.

19. Lift the sear assembly from the trigger housing. The sear bushing, if removed, will allow the sear and disconnector to be separated, along with the spring. Then lift the trigger assembly from the housing.

20. The sear engagement pin and trigger return spring and plunger can be easily removed from the trigger.

21. The safety plunger must be depressed to allow the safety to be removed. Place the safety button in the "fire" position, and use a long thing screwdriver to depress the plunger. Turning the housing onto its side while depressing the plunger will allow the button to fall out.

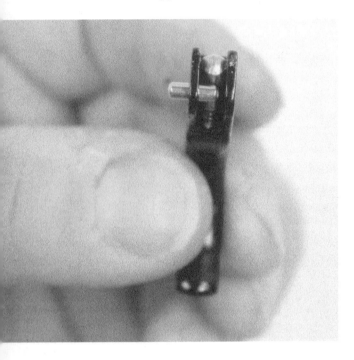

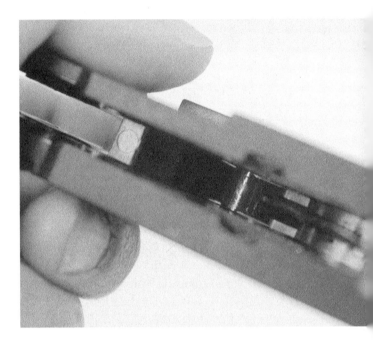

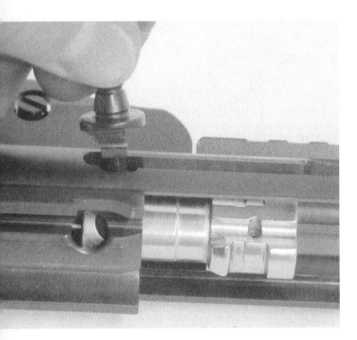

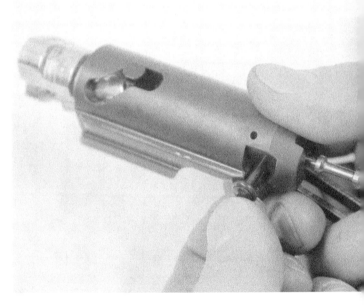

22. To remove the bolt handle, withdraw the bolt assembly all the way to the rear of its slot and pull the handle straight out to the right. With the bolt handle removed, the bolt assembly can be removed out the back of the upper receiver.

23. Pull out the firing pin retaining pin. This will free the firing pin and spring as well.

24. Remove the cam pin from the bolt by aligning the bottom head of the pin with the hole in the bottom of the bolt carrier and pushing it down out of the carrier.

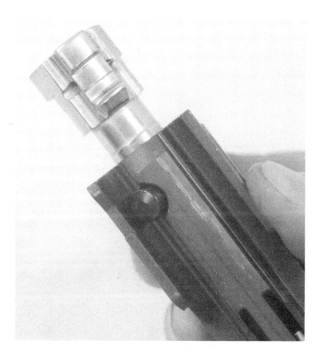

25. Remove the bolt from the carrier.

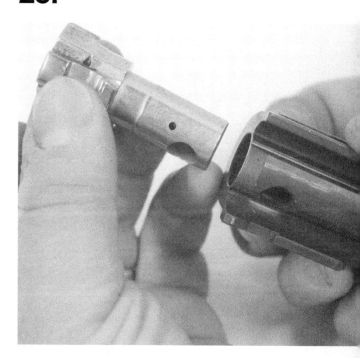

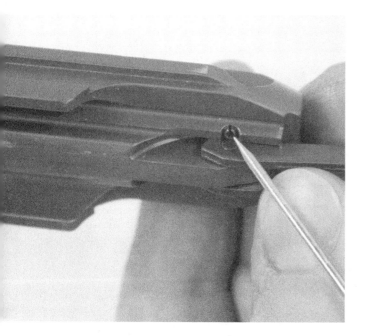

26. This roll pin retains the link pin. There is no need to remove either pin unless the link is damaged and needs replacement.

27. The optic rail and rear sight are retained by torx screws.

28. The hole below the front of the front sight contains a set screw that holds the sight in place.

29. The piston extension assembly is held together by this spring clip. Disassembly of this unit is not necessary during normal maintenance

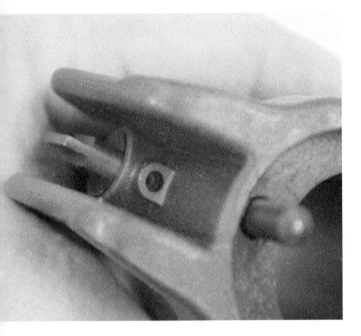

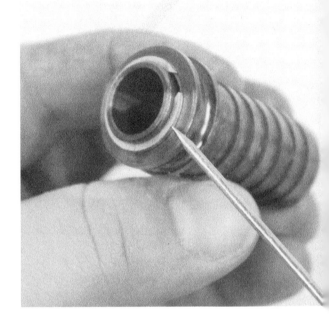

Reassembly Tips:

1. Note that the hammer spring cap's notch should be down, not up.

2. To ease reassembly, reinstall the trigger housing with the rear housing pin prior to reinstallation of the buttstock.

Beretta Cx4 Storm

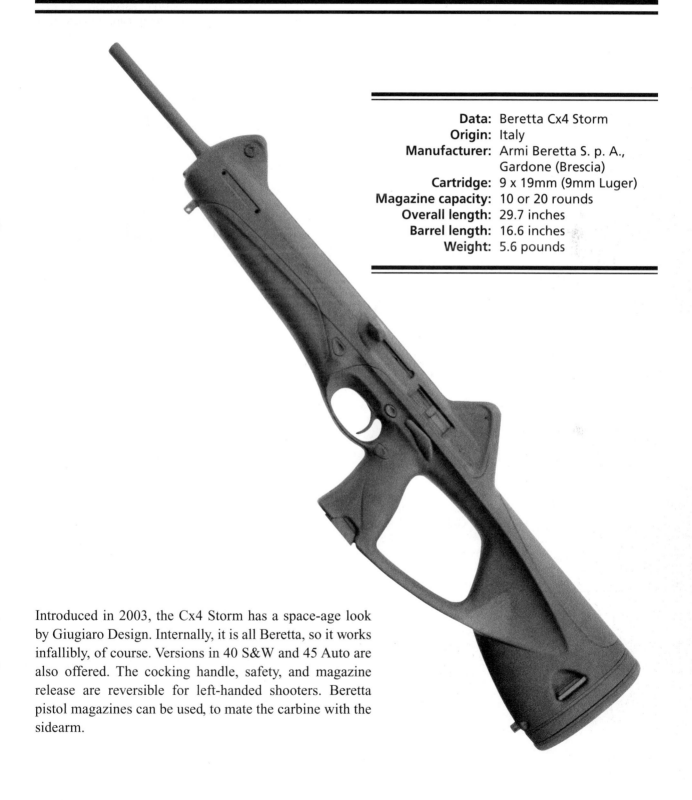

Data:	Beretta Cx4 Storm
Origin:	Italy
Manufacturer:	Armi Beretta S. p. A., Gardone (Brescia)
Cartridge:	9 x 19mm (9mm Luger)
Magazine capacity:	10 or 20 rounds
Overall length:	29.7 inches
Barrel length:	16.6 inches
Weight:	5.6 pounds

Introduced in 2003, the Cx4 Storm has a space-age look by Giugiaro Design. Internally, it is all Beretta, so it works infallibly, of course. Versions in 40 S&W and 45 Auto are also offered. The cocking handle, safety, and magazine release are reversible for left-handed shooters. Beretta pistol magazines can be used, to mate the carbine with the sidearm.

Detail Strip:

1. Remove the magazine, and cycle the action to cock the internal hammer. Set the manual safety in onsafe position. Push out the disassembly latch.

2. Move the barrel and bolt assembly forward off the grip frame/buttstock.

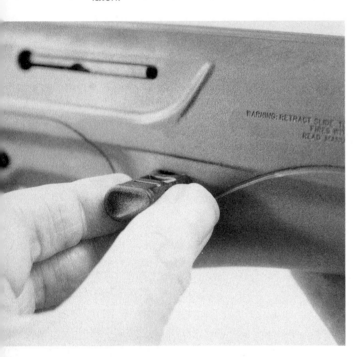

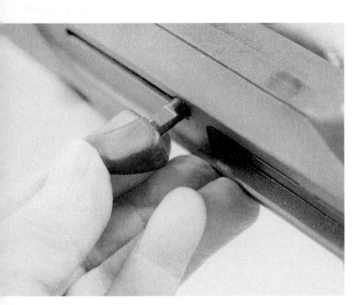

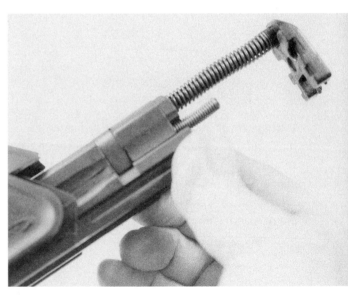

3. Move the bolt assembly rearward until the cocking handle aligns with its circular exit track, and remove the handle.

4. Remove the bolt assembly.

5. The ejection port cover is removed inward, using a small tool in the access recesses at the top.

6. Use a wide tool to nudge the retainer off upward.

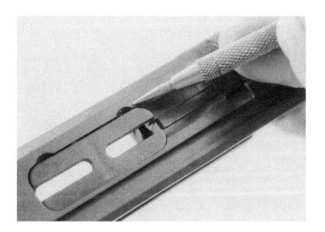

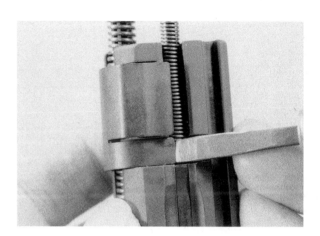

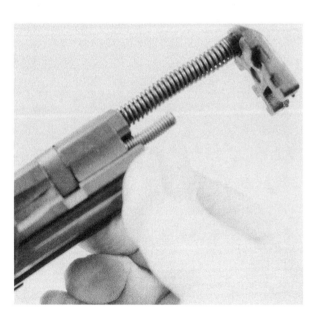

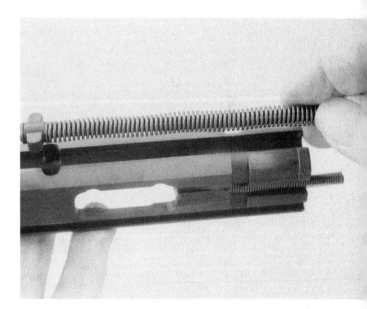

7. Remove the extractor.

8. Remove the recoil spring assembly.

9. The recoil spring unit is dismountable, by retracting the spring, moving the endpiece forward, and turning it. CAUTION: Control the compressed spring.

10. Remove the ejector assembly. This unit is not routinely dismountable.

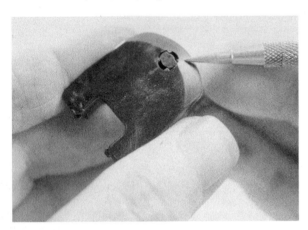

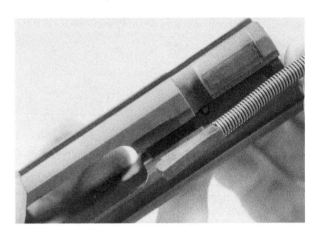

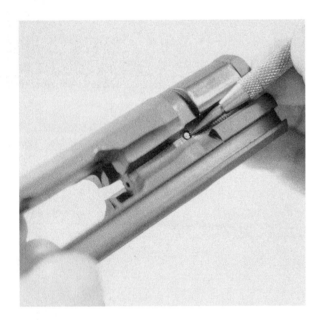

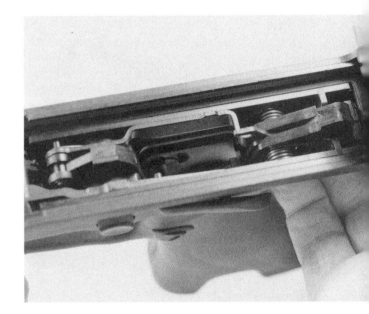

11. Pushing out this cross pin will release the firing pin and its return spring, and the firing pin safety block and its spring, in that order. Control the parts.

12. While it is possible to remove the sub-frame containing the firing system parts, this requires prior removal of the manual safety, detachment of the bolt latch handle, and other operations. It would be best to have this done by an authorized Beretta repair facility.

13. Removal of the barrel requires a special long-reach wrench, and the advice in number 12 applies.

14. What appears to be a simple cross pin retaining the rear sight is not. Actually, the apertures access twin plungers and springs that are detects for the two sight positions. This unit should not be routinely disassembled.

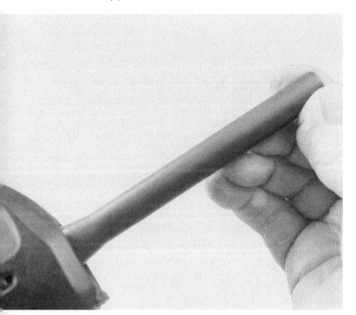

15. The front sight is another unit that should not be disassembled.

Reassembly Tips: None. The Cx4 cannot be mis-assembled.

BUSHMASTER ACR

Data:	Bushmaster ACR
Origin:	United States
Manufacturer:	Bushmaster Firearms, Inc.
Cartridge:	5.56x45 mm,
	6.8mm Rem. SPC
Magazine capacity:	30 rounds
Over-all length:	31.5 inches
Barrel length:	20 inches
Weight:	9 pounds

The Adaptive Combat Rifle from Bushmaster started its evolution as the MagPul Masada. The rifle has the ability to quickly change barrels (and therefore chamberings) and several other items giving it a highly modular nature. Several factory variants are available including smooth or railed handguards, and fixed or folding and adjustable stocks.

Disassembly:

1. Push out the rear takedown pin (picture A) and the front pivot pin (picture B). Separate the upper and lower receivers.

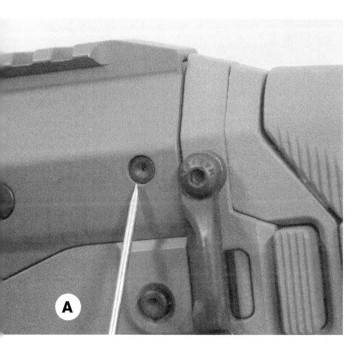

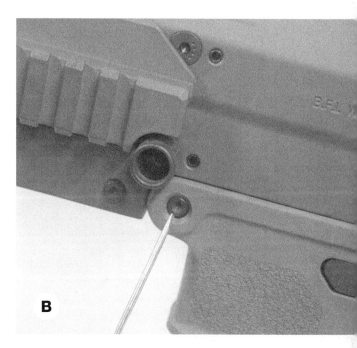

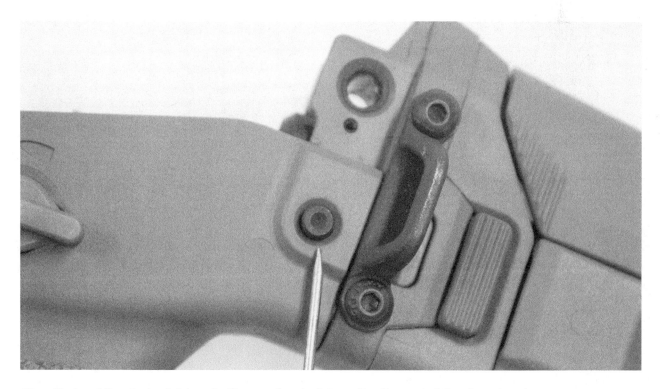

2. Push out the stock retaining pin. Remove the stock by pulling it up out of the trigger housing.

3. With the bolt fully closed, press forward on the charging handle until an audible and tactile click occurs (picture A). This dislatches the charging handle from the operating rod. Pull the bolt assembly out from the rear of the receiver (picture B).

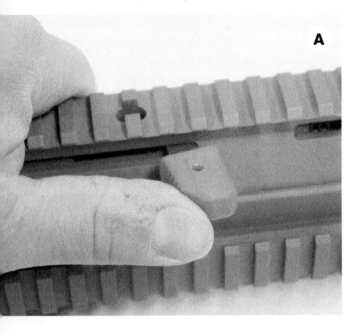

A

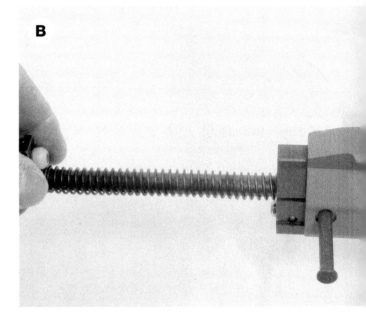

B

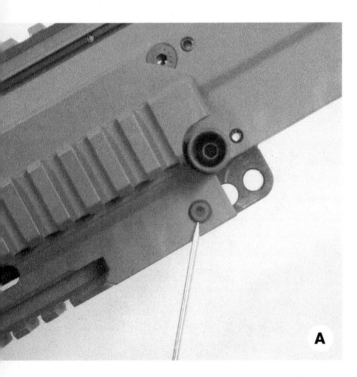

A

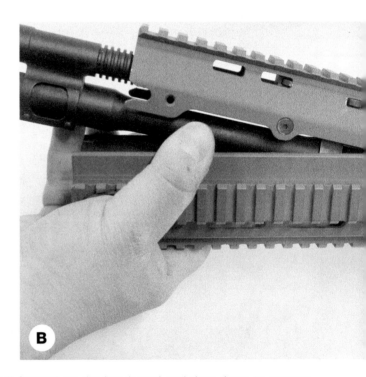

B

4. Push out the handguard retaining pin (picture A). Pull forward on the handguard and then down to remove (picture B).

5. The action spring assembly must be rotated clockwise to remove it from the bolt carrier (picture A). Push the guide rod forward slightly, then rotate counterclockwise until the prongs align with the slots in the carrier (picture B). Pull the action spring assembly out to the rear.

A

B

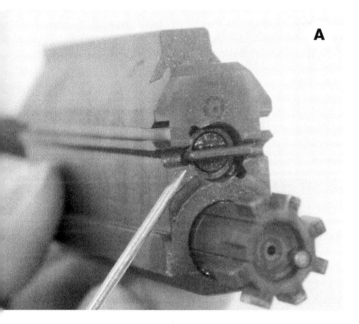
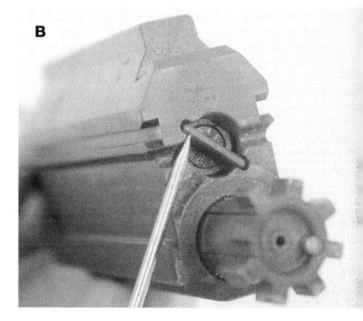

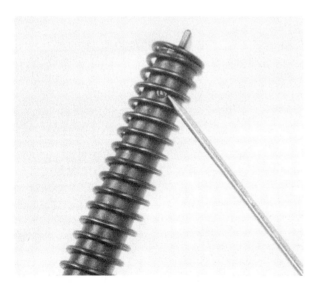

6. The action spring assembly can be taken down by driving out the front roll pin that holds the pronged end to the tube. The spring must be retracted to gain proper access to this pin. A similar pin on the opposite end of the assembly retains the buffer plate. Furthermore the buffer is held to the plate by a third roll pin. Leave this assembly together unless it requires repair.

7. Push out the firing pin retaining pin which frees the firing pin and spring to be pulled from the rear of the bolt carrier.

8. Pull the bolt cam pin. Then pull the bolt from the front of the receiver.

9. Push out this pin in remove the extractor and spring.

10. Push out this pin to remove the ejector and spring.

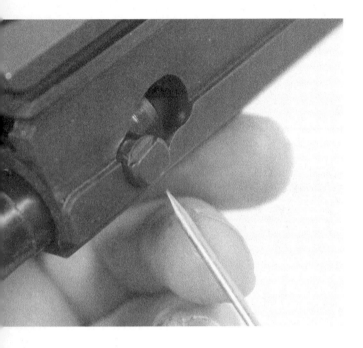

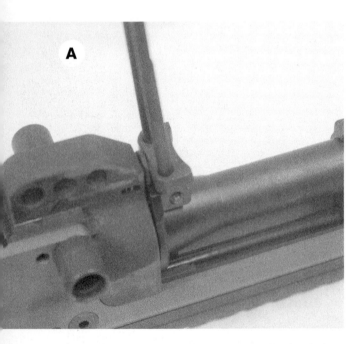

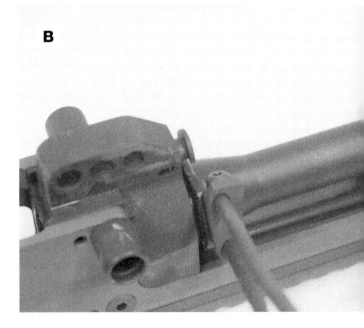

11. Lower the barrel locking lever so that it depresses the small button behind it (picture A). Rotate the locking lever to the left to unlock the barrel (picture B).

12. Pull the barrel forward off the trunnion.

13. Depress the plunger in the regulator and rotate the gas regulator so that the "S" marking is facing to the right side of the barrel. Pull the regulator out.

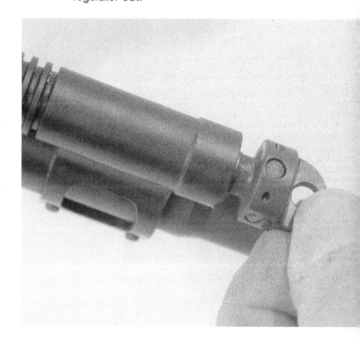

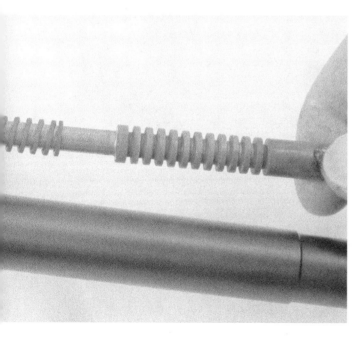

14. Remove the operating rod and spring by pushing them forward through and out the front of the gas block.

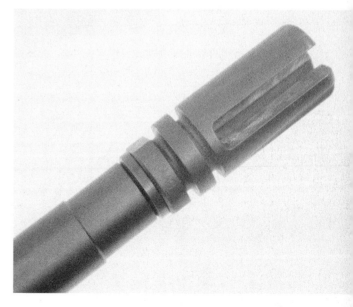

15. The muzzle attachment can be easily unscrewed and removed from the barrel. The rest of the barrel attachments, while removable, should be left in place for routine maintenance. These include the gas block, op rod guide, locking lever assembly, and barrel extension bushing.

16. To remove the charging handle, lock the handle in its forward position. Then push the release button, located in the witness hole in the top rail, back while pulling the charging handle out to the side.

18. Drive out this pin to remove the bolt carrier latch and spring from the rear of the operating slide.

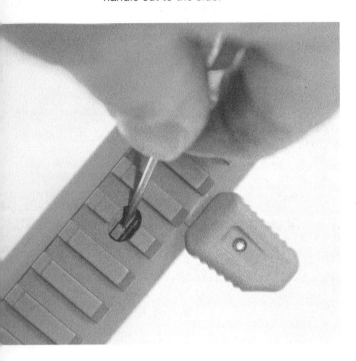

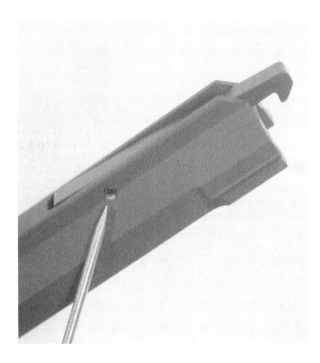

A

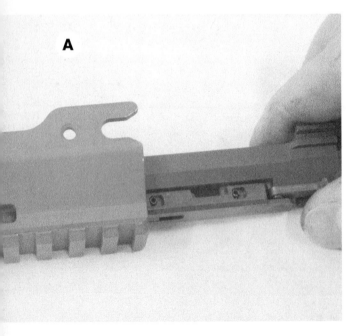

B

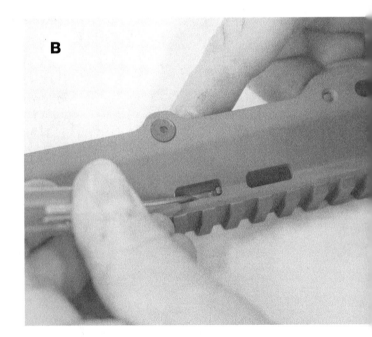

17. Pull the operating slide forward out of the receiver (picture A). It will be necessary to use a small tool to depress the hook to clear the slots on the receiver (picture B).

19. Drive out the two roll pins, bracketing the charging handle slot, to disassemble the charging handle latch apparatus. The cover will lift off, freeing the latch and spring and the latch pin.

21. All the pivot and take down pins can be removed by using a small punch to depress the detent enough to pull the pin out to the side. The detent and spring will then drop from their hole.

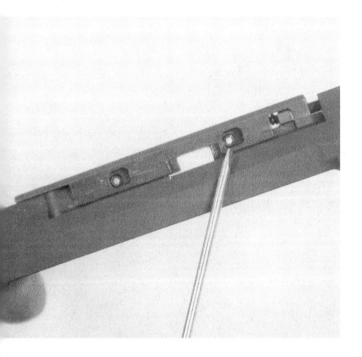

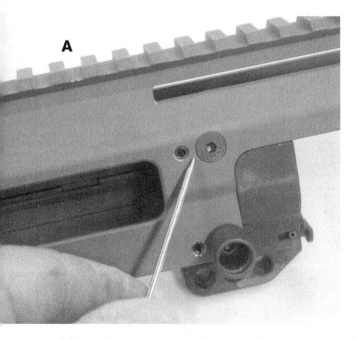

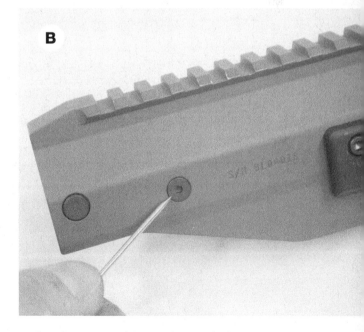

20. The barrel trunnion is retained by two large roll pins as well as four screws (picture A), two of which also serve as attachment points for quick detach sling swivel anchors. The internal receiver rails are retained by six similar screws (picture B), one of which also holds the brass deflector to the receiver. The rails and the trunnion should not be removed outside of the factory.

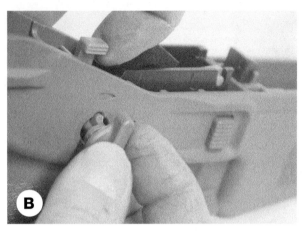

22. Lift the long safety locking lever on the right side of the trigger pack and rotate the safety lever so that it is pointing down (picture A). While holding the long lever up, pull the right side safety lever straight out of the receiver (picture B). The left side safety lever, along with the drum itself, can now be pulled out to the left.

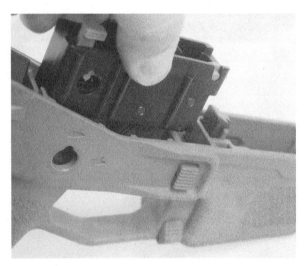
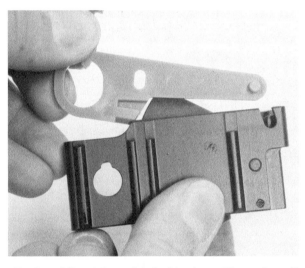

23. Lift out the trigger pack from the trigger housing.

24. Lift out the safety locking lever. The spring will audibly snap as the lever is pulled out

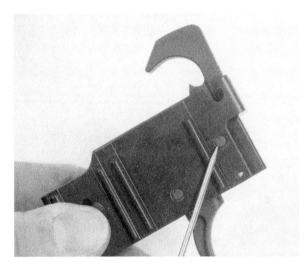

25. Push out this pin to free the hammer and spring.

26. Push out this pin to free the trigger, disconnector and spring, and trigger spring.

27. This pin is a seat for the trigger spring and does not need to be removed.

28. With the trigger pack removed, press in on the mag catch button from the left and it will dislodge from the catch and can be removed from the right side of the housing.

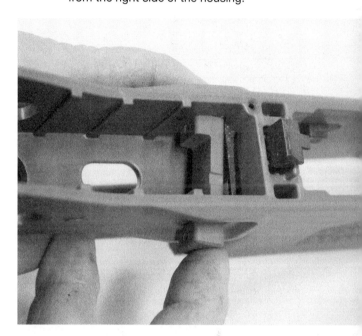

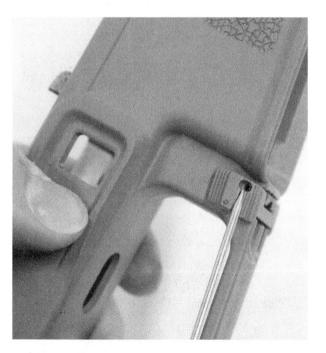

29. Drive out this pin to remove the bolt catch. The button and spring will exit the bottom and the catch out the top.

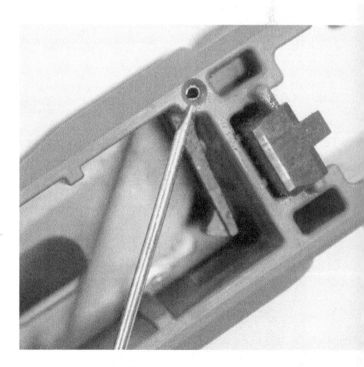

30. Drive out this pin to remove the mag catch and spring.

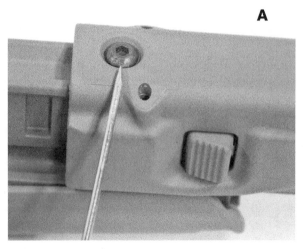

A

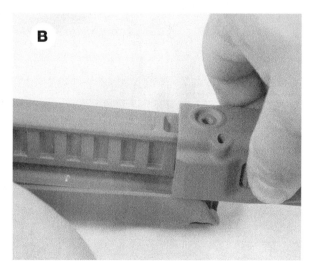

B

31. Remove this screw on the bottom of the adjustable stock assembly (picture A) to free the sliding stock section. Pinch the two lock buttons on either side, as if to adjust the stock, and pull the sliding stock off the cheek piece section (picture B).

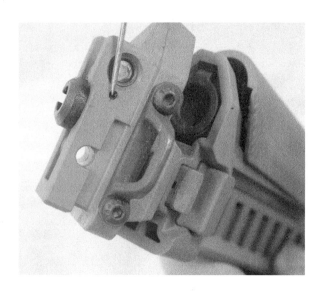

32. The bolt recoil buffer can be removed for replacement by driving out this pin. Just behind that is a sling swivel loop that can be removed by the two hex screws. On the stock base piece, the adjustable cheek rest is permanently installed, as is the folding stock lock button. The storage compartment cover that rests under the cheek piece can be replaced by opening the compartment and firmly pulling the cover forward. While the stock hinge pin can be removed, it is not recommended that it be done.

Reassembly Tips:

33. The sliding lock buttons can be removed, along with their springs, by driving out this pin and its counterpart on the other side.

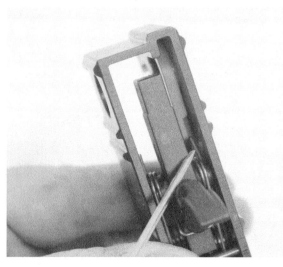

1. Reinsert the safety locking lever. Then push the hammer spring leg up from the bottom so that is snaps into place along the side of the lever.

Colt AR-15

Similar/Identical Pattern Guns

The same basic assembly/disassembly steps for the Colt AR-15 also apply to the following guns:

Colt AR-15A2 Sporter II
Colt AR-15A2 Delta HBAR
Colt AR-15 Delta HBAR Match
Colt AR-15A2
  Government Model Carbine
Colt Sporter Target Model
Colt Sporter Match HBAR
Olympic Arms AR-15 Heavy Match
Olympic Arms CAR-15
Colt AR-15 Collapsible Stock Model
Colt AR-15A2 Carbine
Colt AR-15A2 HBAR
Colt AR-15A2
  Government Model Target

Colt Sporter Lightweight Rifle
Colt Sporter Match Delta HBAR
Eagle Arms EA-15
Olympic Arms AR-15 Service Match
Bushmaster XM-15
DPMS A-15
DPMS LR-308
Armalite AR-15
Armalite AR-10
Rock River Arms LAR-15
JP Enterprises JP-15
JP Enterprises CTR-02
Remington R-15

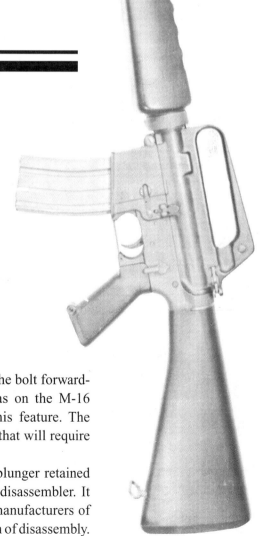

Data: Colt AR-15
Origin: United States
Manufacturer: Colt Firearms
Hartford, Connecticut
Cartridge: 223 Remington (5.56mm)
Magazine capacity: 5 and 20 rounds
Overall length: 38 3/8 inches
Barrel length: 20 inches
Weight: 7 1/4 pounds

The original AR-15A1, made from 1963 to 1984, did not have the bolt forward-assist plunger and spring on the right side of the receiver, as on the M-16 military gun. All AR-15A2 rifles, up to the present, have this feature. The plunger is retained by a pin, and removal is a simple operation that will require no additional instructions.

Furthermore, the vast majority of AR-15 clones use standard plunger retained takedown and pivot pins. These should offer no issues to the disassembler. It should be particularly noted that there are literally dozens of manufacturers of AR-15 clones, too many to list. All follow the same overall pattern of disassembly. Generally speaking, if it looks closely like an AR-15, it probably is.

Disassembly:

1. Remove the magazine, and cycle the action to cock the hammer. Push out the takedown pin, located at the upper rear of the grip frame, toward the right.

2. With the takedown pin stopped in pulled-out position, tip the barrel and receiver assembly upward at the rear.

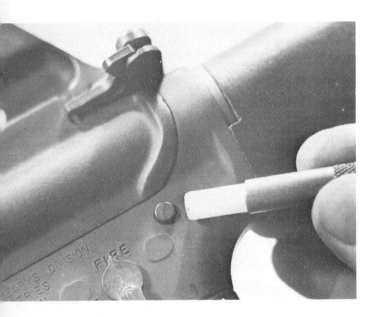

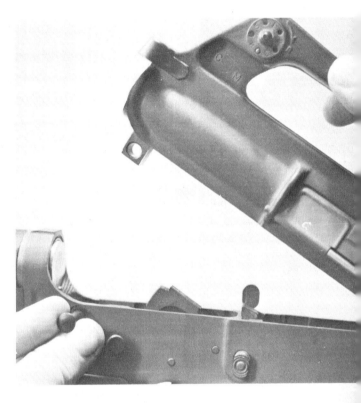

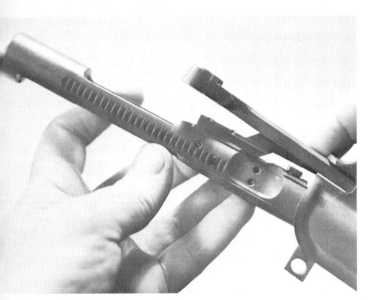

3. Use the charging handle to start the bolt assembly toward the rear, and remove the assembly from the rear of the receiver.

4. Move the charging handle to the rear until it stops, then move it out the rear of the receiver.

5. The charging handle latch and its spring are retained in the handle by the vertical roll pin. In normal takedown, it is best left in place.

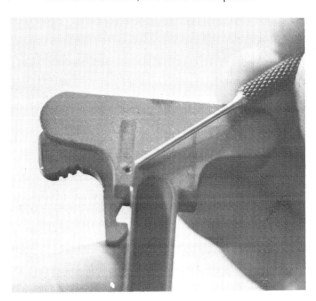

6. Use a small tool to pull out the cotter pin on the left side of the bolt carrier, to free the firing pin.

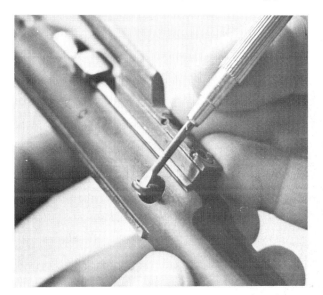

7. Remove the firing pin toward the rear.

8. Rotate the bolt cam pin to clear its flange from beneath the edge of the overhang, and remove the bolt cam pin upward.

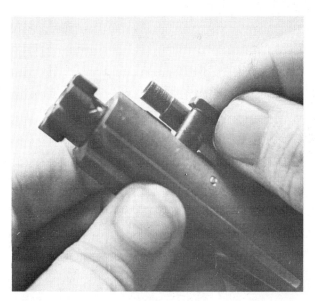

9. Remove the bolt from the front of the bolt carrier. The three gas seal rings at the rear of the bolt should not be removed unless they need to be replaced.

10. The extractor and its coil spring are retained in the bolt by a cross pin which is easily pushed out in either direction.

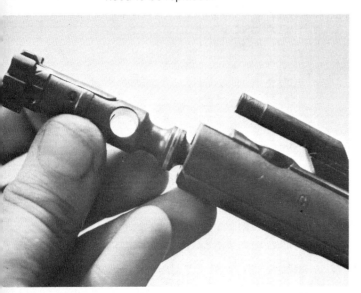

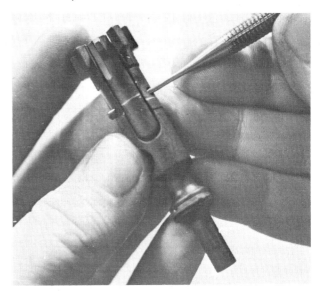

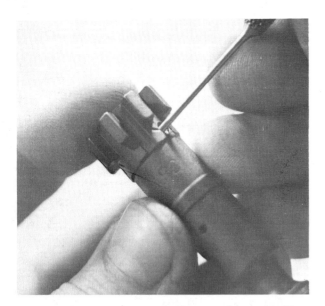

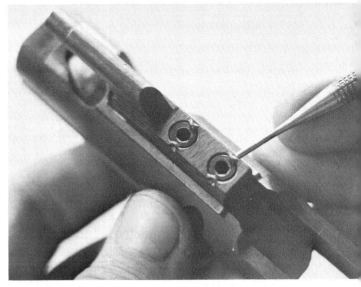

11. The ejector and its spring are also retained by a pin, a small roll pin that crosses the front of the bolt. The ejector spring is quite strong, so restrain the ejector during removal.

12. The gas cylinder is retained by two Allen screws on top of the bolt carrier, and these are heavily staked in place. **CAUTION:** *This unit should be removed only if repair or replacement is necessary.*

13. Remove the cap screw at the left end of the receiver pivot. It will be necessary to stabilize the screw-slotted head of the pivot with another large screwdriver on the right side during removal.

14. Use a slim drift punch that will not damage the interior threads to nudge the receiver pivot out toward the right, and separate the barrel and receiver unit from the stock and grip frame assembly.

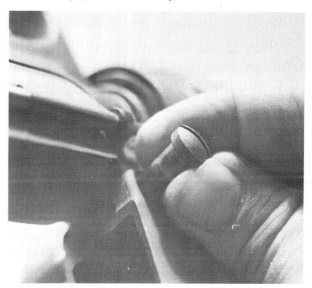

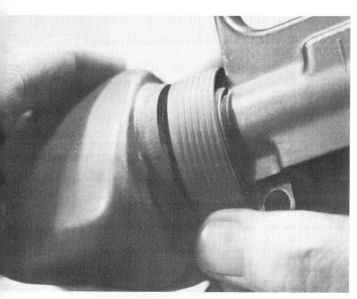

15. Pull back on the grooved slip ring right at the rear of the handguard units, and alternately tip each unit outward at the rear, then remove them rearward.

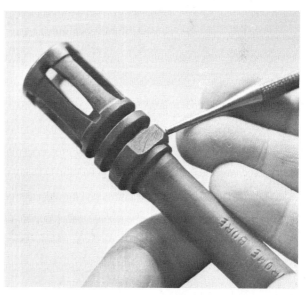

16. With a wrench of the proper size, unscrew the flash hider from the end of the barrel, and take care not to lose the lock washer behind it.

17. The combination front sight base, gas port unit, and bayonet mount is retained on the barrel by two large cross pins. When these are drifted out toward the right, the unit can be nudged forward off the barrel. During removal, take care that the gas transfer tube is not damaged.

18. The gas conduit is retained in the sight unit by a roll cross pin. In normal takedown, this should not be disturbed.

 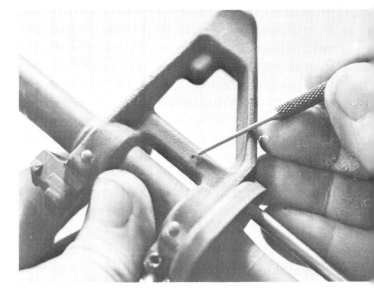

 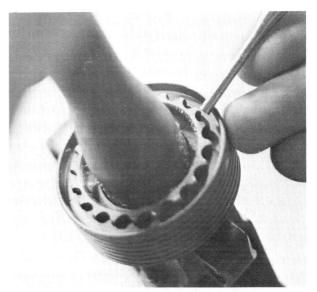

19. Insert a small tool in one of the holes at the top of the large clip-ring at the front of the receiver, and gently pry the ring out of its channel. Moving it rearward will relieve the tension of the circular spring assembly that powers the handguard slip-ring.

20. Move the slip-ring to the rear to give access to the toothed barrel retaining nut, and unscrew the nut counter-clockwise (front view). Take off the retaining nut, slip-ring, spring, and clip-ring toward the front.

21. The long pin which forms the hinge for the ejection port cover is retained by a C-clip in a groove near its forward end. Take off the C-clip, and move the hinge pin out toward the rear. **Caution:** *The cover spring will be released as the pin is cleared, so restrain it. Take care that the very small C-clip is not lost.*

22. Restrain the hammer and pull the trigger to lower the hammer to fired position. Push out the hammer pivot pin toward either side, controlling the hammer against its spring tension.

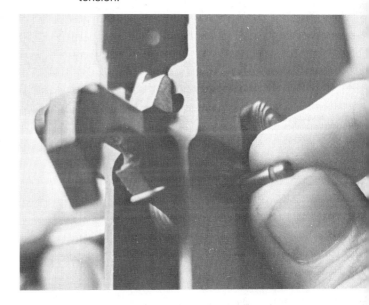

23. Remove the hammer and its spring upward. The spring is easily detached from the hammer.

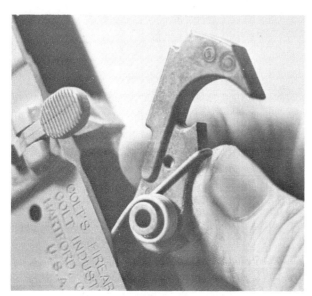

24. Push the trigger pin just far enough toward the right that the disconnector is cleared, and remove the disconnector from the top of the grip frame.

25. The pistol grip is removed by backing out the screw accessible through the bottom of the grip. Note that this will also release the safety plunger and its spring for removal downward (picture A). With the grip, plunger, and spring removed, the safety can be removed from the receiver out to the left (picture B).

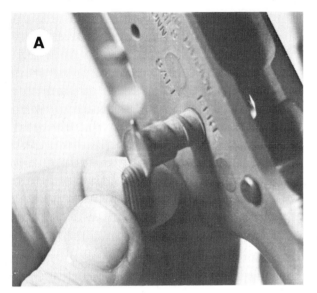

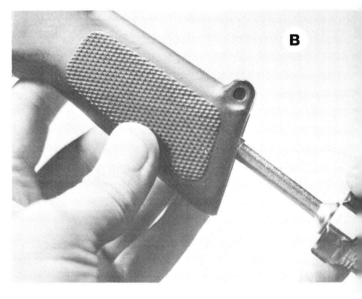

26. Remove the trigger pin, and take out the trigger assembly upward. The trigger spring and disconnector spring are easily detached from the trigger.

27. The magazine catch is removed by pushing it toward the left beyond its normal magazine release point, then unscrewing the catch piece from the button. The button and spring are then take off toward the right, and the catch piece toward the left. The catch piece is unscrewed counter-clockwise, left-side view.

28. The hold open device and its spring are retained on the left side of the grip frame by a roll pin, and after removal of the pin they are taken off toward the left.

29. Restrain the recoil buffer against the tension of the recoil spring, and depress the buffer stop plunger. Caution: The spring is strong, so take care to keep it under control.

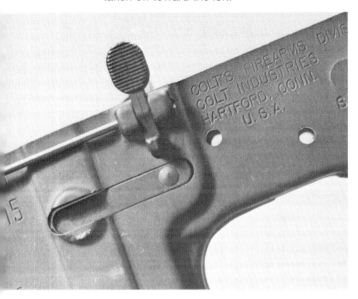

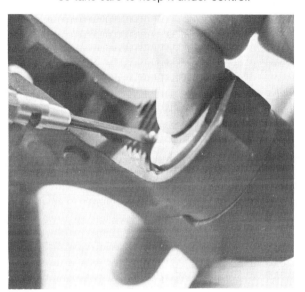

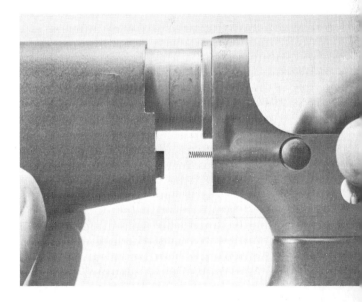

30. Slowly release the tension of the spring, and remove the buffer and spring toward the front.

31. Remove the upper screw in the buttplate and remove the buttstock toward the rear. Take care not to lose the takedown pin retaining plunger and its spring at the rear of the grip frame. Removal of the lower screw in the buttplate will give access to the mechanism of the storage compartment cover and its latch.

32. Remove the takedown pin spring and plunger from the rear of the grip frame. The takedown pin can then be removed toward the right.

33. The rear of the trigger guard is retained by a roll pin, and the front by a pin backed by a spring. Depressing the forward pin will allow the trigger guard front to be pulled down and folded back to rest against the pistol grip. The ears holding the rear of the trigger guard and roll pin can be broken easily and this pin should be left in place unless the trigger guard is being replaced.

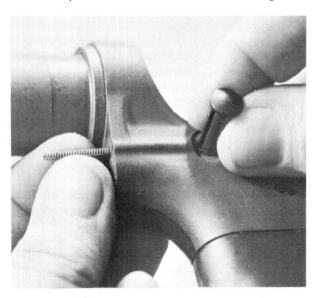

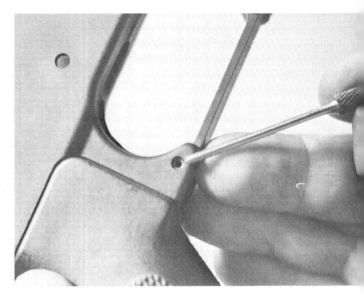

Reassembly Tips:

1. The trigger must be installed prior to the installation of the safety. First install the trigger and disconnector, then the safety, then the hammer.

3. When replacing the bolt in the bolt carrier, note that the extractor must be oriented to the upper right, and the ejector to the lower left. Also, remember to turn the bolt cam pin so its flange is beneath the edge of the gas cylinder.

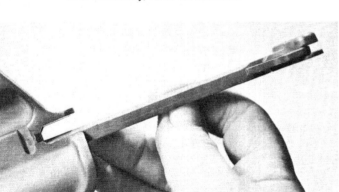

2. When replacing the cocking handle, remember that its forward end must be inserted into the receiver and then moved upward into its track.

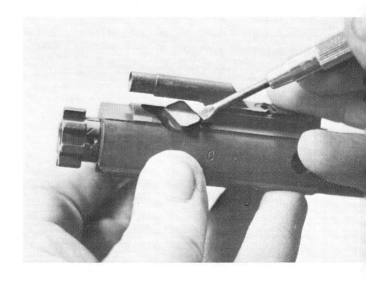

DAEWOO DT 200

Data:	Daewoo DT 200
Origin:	Korea
Manufacturer:	Daewoo Precision Industries Co., Ltd.
Cartridge:	.223 Rem.
Magazine capacity:	30 rounds
Over-all length:	**38.5 inches**
Barrel length:	**18.3 inches**
Weight:	7.2 pounds

The DT 200 is the civilian legal version of the South Korean main infantry rifle, called the K2. It was imported in limited numbers by Kimber and is usually found with a thumbhole stock and other post-ban features. This is an interesting meld of AR-15 and AK-47 concepts, topped off with South Korean designed features to make it a rather unique firearm.

Disassembly:

1. Rotate the takedown lever latch until the latch points to the rear. This unlocks the lever and allows it to move forward far enough to activate.

2. Push the latch forward until it stops and lift the rear of the upper receiver.

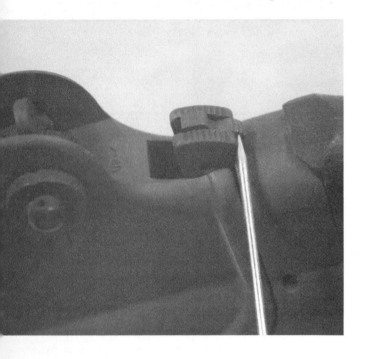

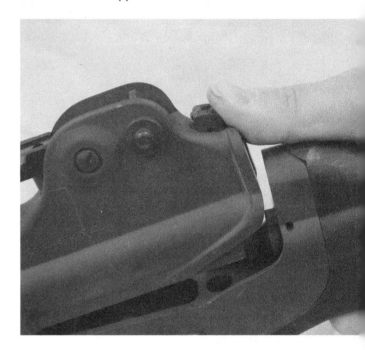

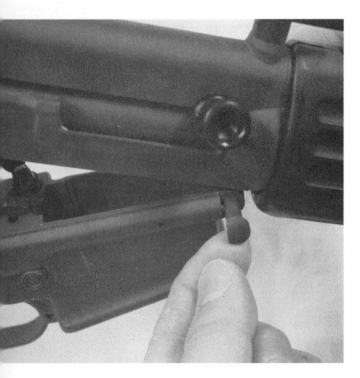

3. Push out the front pivot pin until it stops. Remove the upper receiver assembly from the lower assembly.

4. The front pivot pin can be removed by using a small punch or pin, inserting it through the small hole in the front of the pin, depressing the detent and then rotating the entire pin. The pin can then be pulled out to the right, out of the receiver. The detent and spring can exit with speed, so control should be used.

5. Drive out this small pin to detach the magazine catch button from the catch. The button and spring will be removed from the right side. Again, control the spring.

6. Driving out this pin will free the ejector, the ejector sleeve, and its spring, and the bolt catch and its spring.

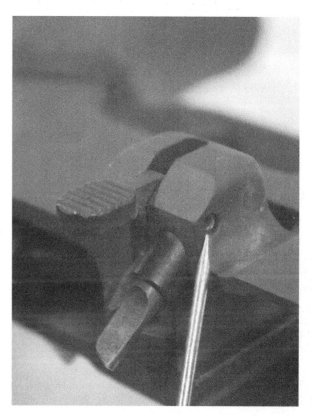

7. Drive out this pin to free the hammer and its spring.

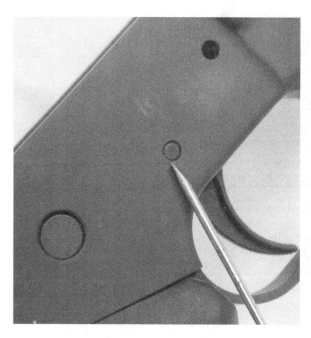

8. Drive out this pin to free the trigger, trigger spring, disconnector, and disconnector spring. Rotate the safety lever so it points up to provide clearance for the removal of the trigger.

9. Drive out this pin to remove the bolt buffer and spring.

11. Remove this set screw. Below it are the safety detent and spring. When these are removed, the safety lever can be pulled from the left side of the receiver.

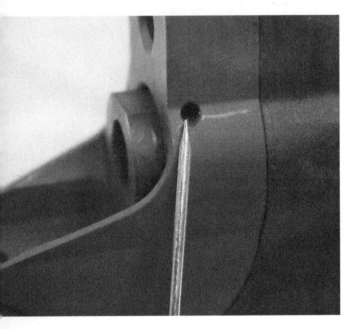

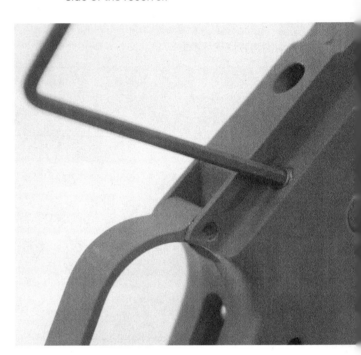

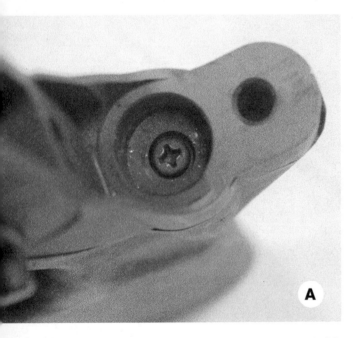

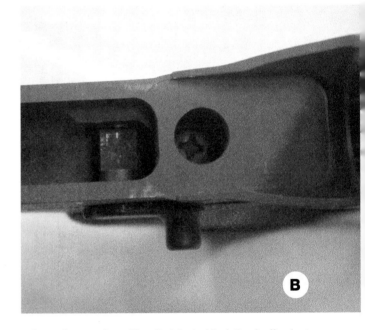

10. Remove the two Phillips head screws holding the stock to the receiver. The first is behind the buffer just removed (picture A), and the other goes down into the pistol grip (picture B). When removed, the thumbhole stock will separate from the receiver.

12. Depress this pin and pull the trigger guard down. The trigger guard can be removed by driving out the rear pin.

13. Pull the recoil spring assembly from the rear of the upper receiver.

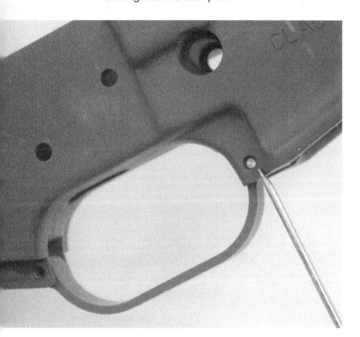

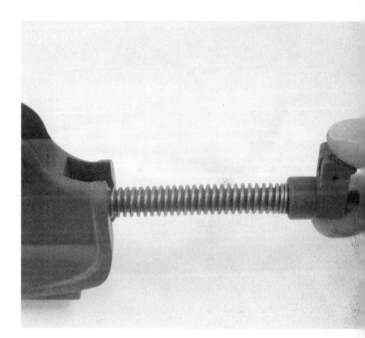

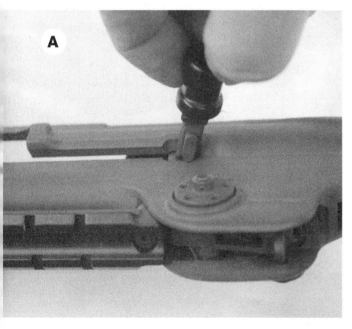

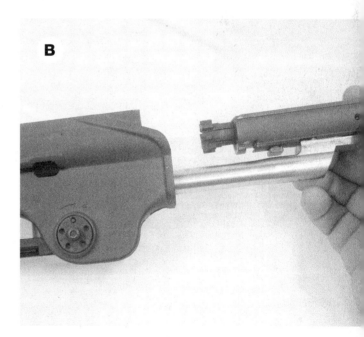

14. Pull the bolt all the way to the rear until the bolt handle stops rearward movement. At this point the bolt handle can be pulled out to the right (Picture A). Pull the bolt assembly out to the rear of the receiver (Picture A). The chrome plated operating rod will immediately separate from the bolt carrier.

15. Pull this retaining pin to free the firing pin, which will drop out from the rear of the carrier.

17. The extractor and extractor spring can be removed by driving out this pin.

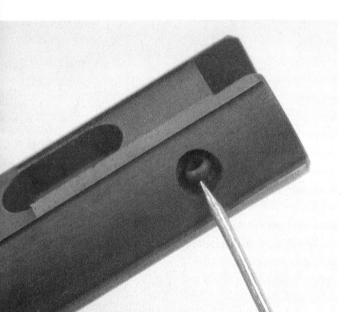

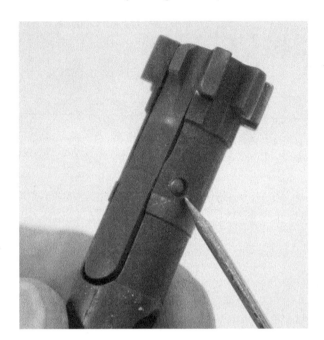

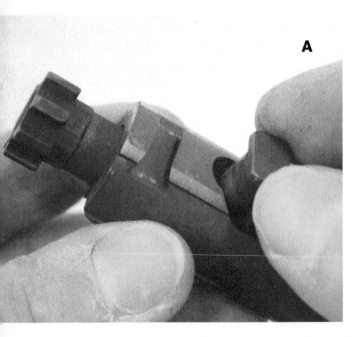

A

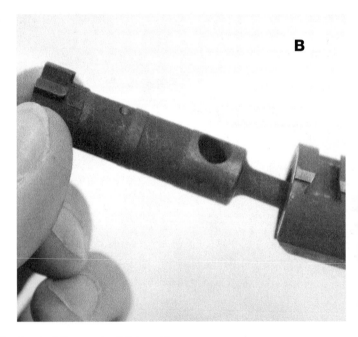

B

16. Pull the cam pin (Picture A) and then the bolt from the front of the carrier (Picture B).

18. The recoil spring/takedown latch assembly can be disassembled by slightly compressing the spring and sliding out the spring seat at the front of the assembly. The latch should left assembled unless it is broken and needs repair.

19. Remove this screw and then pull the handguard forward. When pulled forward, the two handguard halves will separate and can be fully removed from the barrel.

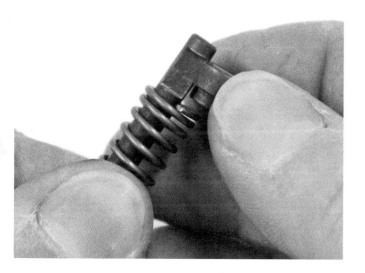

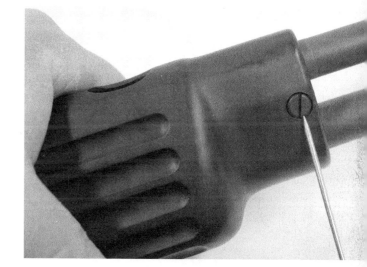

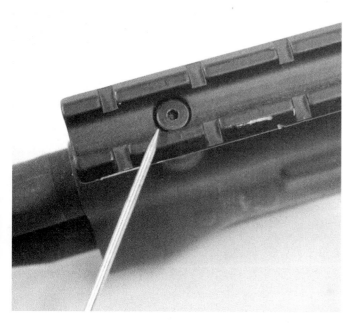

20. If necessary, the optics mount can be removed by taking out these two screws.

21. The rear sight can be removed by first driving out this pin. The windage drum, its spring and detent, and tension washer can be pulled from the right side of the sight housing. The sight axis can then be unscrewed from the left side and the rear sight aperture then lifted up out of the housing. Beneath the sight is a spring for the sight.

22. This E-clip is removed to free the elevation axis. Below is the elevation turret that can be unscrewed and removed from the receiver.

23. Turn the gas valve until the button is pointing up, then pull the valve assembly from the front of the rifle. The valve assembly should not be disassembled without need.

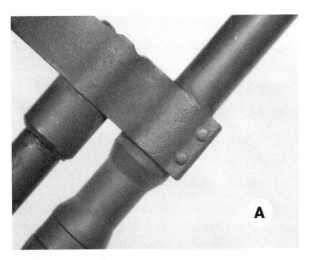

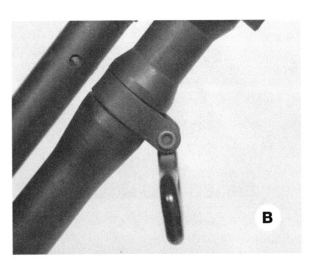

24. Further disassembly is generally contraindicated. Furthermore, the muzzle attachment is likely brazed onto the barrel, which will prevent further disassembly anyway. The gas block is held to the barrel by two cross pins (picture A). The sling swivel pin is riveted in place (picture B).

Reassembly Tips:

1. When reinserting the safety detent, spring, and set screw, the screw can be overtightened, causing the safety to lock up. Be sure to turn the screw in only far enough for sufficient tension that allows freedom of movement of the safety. This may mean leaving the screw slightly proud of the receiver.

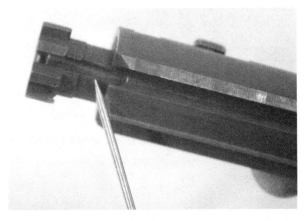

2. When reassembling the bolt carrier assembly, be sure the ejector groove in the bolt lines up with the similar groove in the bottom left of the bolt carrier.

FN-FAL

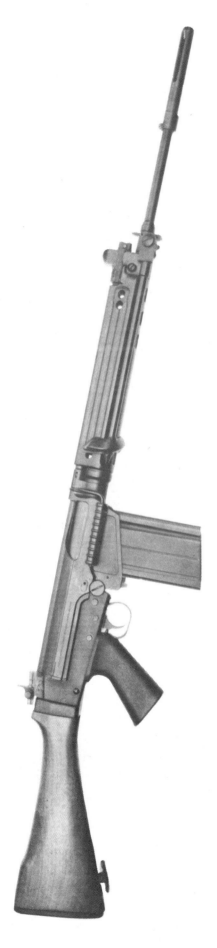

Similar/Identical Pattern Guns

The same basic assembly/disassembly steps for the FN-FAL also apply to the following guns:

Springfield Armory SAR 48
Springfield Armory SAR 4800
Springfield Armory SAR 48 Bush Rifle
Springfield Armory SAR Para Model
DS Arms SA58
German G1
Austrian StG 58
British L1A1

Data:	FN/FAL
Origin:	Belgium
Manufacturer:	Fabrique Nationale, Herstal (Liege)
Cartridge:	7.62mm NATO (.308 Win.)
Magazine capacity:	20 rounds
Overall length:	41.50 inches
Barrel length:	21 inches
Weight:	9 pounds 8 ounces

Some elements of the FN Model 1949 were used in the design of the Fusil Automatique Leger (FAL), but it is a true assault rifle in the modern sense. It was first made around 1950, and by the middle of that decade it was the standard military rifle of so many countries that a list would fill too much space here. Among these contract versions, there are some small differences in various features, but nothing that would cause difficulty in takedown. This gun has been marketed in the U.S. by Springfield Armory of Geneseo, Illinois, in a number of civilian-legal styles. They are essentially exact copies of the original FAL in semi-automatic only, and these instructions apply to all. The gun shown here is an original Belgian version.

Disassembly:

1. Remove the magazine, and cycle the action to cock the hammer. Move the latch lever toward the rear and tip the barrel and upper receiver upward at the rear.

2. Grasp the spring rod at the rear of the bolt carrier and remove the bolt and carrier assembly toward the rear.

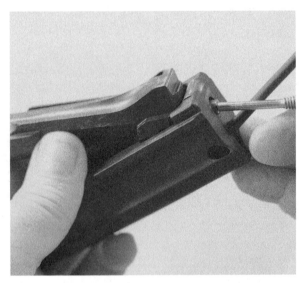

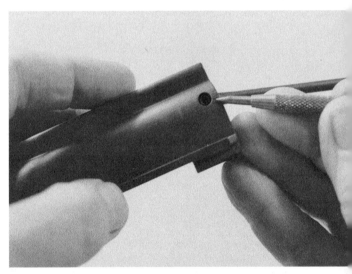

4. The bolt spring rod and its positioning spring can be removed by drifting out its cross pin toward the right. This pin is riveted on the left side, and in normal takedown it is best left in place.

3. Move the bolt to the rear of the carrier and lift it at the front. Use a tool to depress the firing pin head, and remove the bolt from the carrier.

5. Restrain the firing pin, and push out the retaining cross pin toward the left. The return spring is powerful, so control the firing pin.

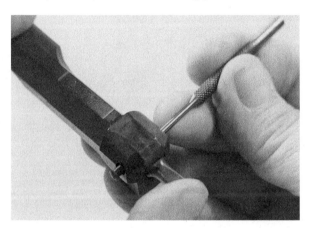

6. Remove the firing pin and its return spring toward the rear.

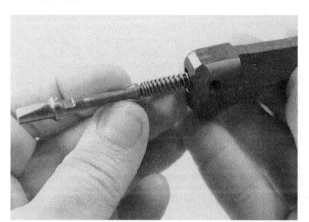

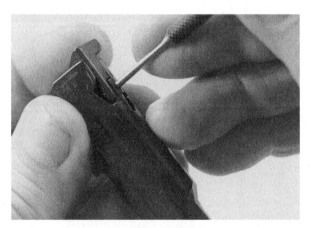

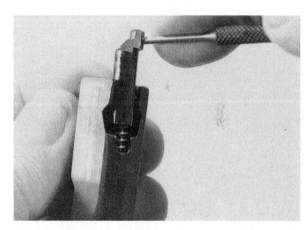

7. Insert a drift punch into the hole in the extractor plunger, and draw the plunger rearward until the extractor can be tipped out toward the front. Again, this is a very strong spring, so control it.

8. After the extractor is removed, ease the plunger and spring forward and take them out.

9. Slide the cover rearward off the receiver.

10. A tool with a hollow end is used to compress the locking split-end of the hinge cross screw, and push it level with the side.

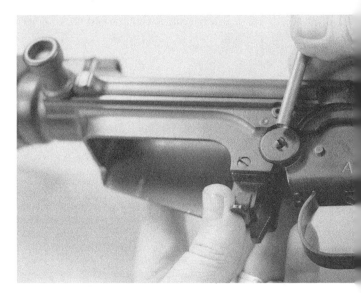

11. After the tip is unlocked, use a coin to unscrew the hinge cross screw on the right side.

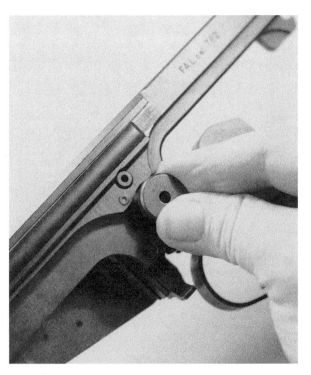

12. After the cross screw is removed, push out the hinge-piece toward the left, and separate the barrel and upper receiver from the action and buttstock unit.

13. Ease the hammer down to fired position, and pry the hammer spring housing upward at the rear, as shown. **Caution:** *Keep the housing and spring under control.*

15. Inside the action on the right side is the pin lock-plate. Turn it over toward the front, and in the position shown, it can be taken out upward.

14. Turn the safety-lever up past the on-safe position to vertical, and remove it toward the left.

16. Depress the trigger, push out the hammer pivot toward the right, and remove the hammer.

17. Restrain the sear on the inside, and push out the trigger cross pin toward the right.

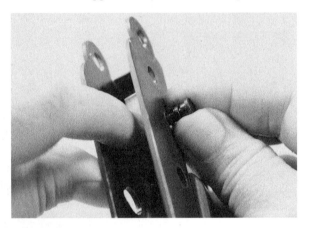

18. Remove the trigger and sear assembly upward. The sear and the sear plunger and spring are free for removal from the trigger.

19. Spring the wire latch out of its locking recess in the pistol grip, and turn it outward.

20. Remove the combination oiler and cleaning kit from the pistol grip.

21. Use a large screwdriver with a wide blade to unscrew the retaining nut inside the pistol grip.

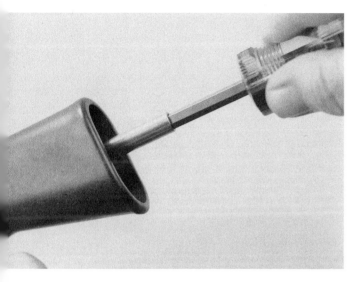

22. Remove the pistol grip downward.

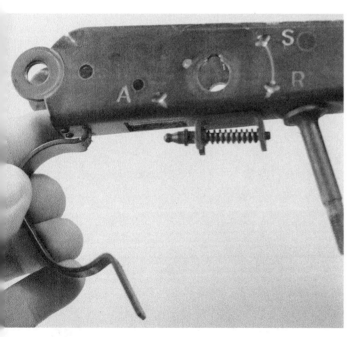

23. Turn the trigger guard forward to the position shown, and take it off downward.

24. To remove the trigger spring and its plunger, tip the plunger downward out of its slot in the mount.

25. Use a screwdriver with a wide, thin blade to remove the buttplate screw, and take off the buttplate. Take care that the lock washer on the screw isn't lost.

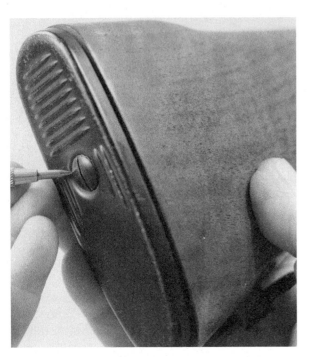

26. Use a large screwdriver with a wide blade to remove the buttstock retaining nut. **Caution:** *As the nut clears its threads, the bolt spring will be released, and it is powerful. Control it.*

27. Remove the concentric recoil springs and the follower toward the rear.

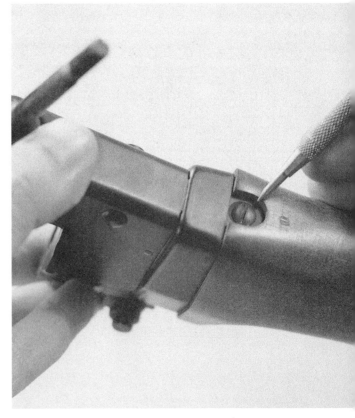

28. Remove the retaining screw on the underside at the forward edge of the stock.

29. Take off the buttstock toward the rear.

30. If removal of the receiver latch is necessary, drift out this cross pin. **Caution:** *The spring will be released rearward. Ease out the spring.*

31. Removal of this small screw will allow the latch lever to be taken off toward the left, and the latch bolt can then be taken out rearward.

32. The rear sight can be removed by backing out the adjustment screws on each side.

33. The magazine catch and the bolt hold-open, and their attendant springs, can be removed by taking out a single cross screw. Note that this screw is usually staked in place, and it should be removed only for repair purposes.

34. The ejector is retained by a cross pin which is heavily riveted on both sides, and again, removal should be only for repair.

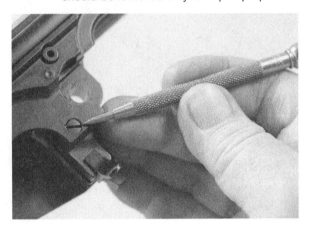

35. A small vertical pin retains the stop piece in the cocking handle assembly. After removal of the pin, the stop piece can be pushed out toward the left, and the cocking handle slide can be moved out of its track toward the rear. When this unit is out, another small vertical pin can be drifted out to free the handle and its spring and plunger.

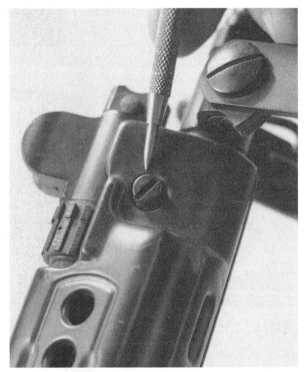

36. A cross screw on the right side retains the forend plates. Removal of the large screws on each side of the bipod will allow the bipod to be taken off, but in normal takedown this unit is best left in place.

37. Tip the forend plates outward, then remove them toward the front. The cross screw is captive in the right plate.

38. If the flash hider, sling swivel, and bipod have been removed, and the gas piston assembly is to be removed for repair, it is retained by this cross pin.

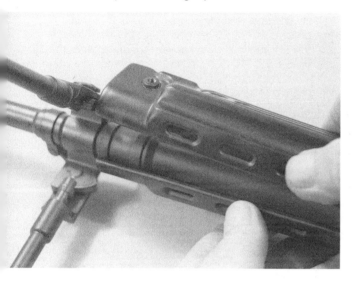

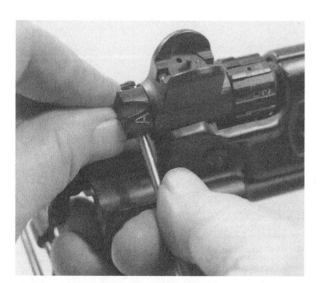

39. For access to the gas system, use a bullet tip or a tool to depress the latch button, and turn the gas cylinder plug clockwise, front view, about a quarter turn. When it is clear, the piston spring will push it out, so control it.

40. Remove the gas cylinder plug, and take out the piston and its spring toward the front.

Reassembly Tips:

1. When replacing the gas cylinder plug, be sure the large letter "A" is on top when the plug is locked, as shown. If the plug is installed the other way, the gas system will be blocked. This is a feature for grenade launching. Note that the gas adjustment sleeve, to the rear of the sight, is designed to work with a special wrench. However, it can be turned with tools, if care is taken to avoid marring.

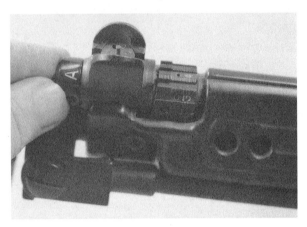

2. When replacing the trigger and sear assembly, be sure the sear is inserted with the large recess toward the rear, as shown, to mate with the plunger.

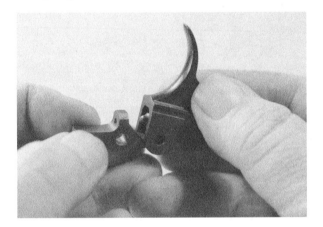

3. When reinstalling the hammer spring and its housing, seat the follower in the hammer recess, place the housing on top of the lower receiver, and push it forward and downward to lock in place.

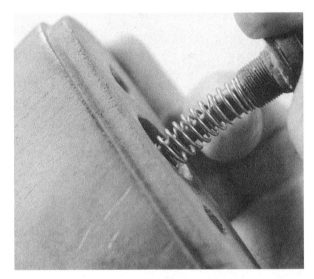

4. To replace the recoil spring in the buttstock, use a rod small enough to pass through the hole in the retainer, to guide the spring, and use a screwdriver on each side in the slot to start the retainer into its threads. Avoid cross-threading.

FNH FS2000

Similar/Identical Pattern Guns

The same basic assembly/disassembly steps for the FNH FS2000 also apply to the following guns

FNH F2000   **FNH FS2000 CQB**

Data:	FNH FS2000
Origin:	Belgium
Manufacturer:	Fabrique National, Herstal
Cartridge:	.223
Magazine capacity:	30 rounds
Over-all length:	29.3 inches
Barrel length:	17.4 inches
Weight:	7.58 pounds

The now standard-issue rifle of the Belgian military the F2000 has been marketed to the American public in the form of the FS2000. A very well-balanced rifle (because it's a bullpup, obviously), it is also labor intensive to manufacture (lots and lots of little parts), resulting in a rather steep price tag. However, it field strips for the user very easily and can use the now ubiquitous AR-15 magazine. A CQB version is available that differs from the standard model by the use of a railed forend in place of the standard smooth version, and is otherwise identical. An earlier model sold that used the military issue optic has since been replaced with the current standard models using a Picatinny optic rail in lieu of the provided scope.

Disassembly:

1. Pull out on the toe of the soft plastic buttplate and slide the buttplate up and off the heel of the stock.

2. Reach into the buttstock and pull out the trigger pack, straight to the rear.

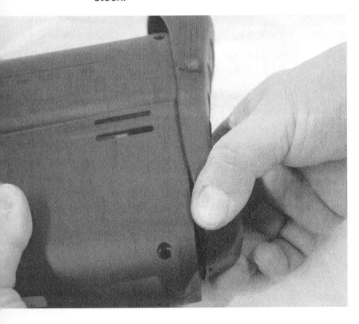

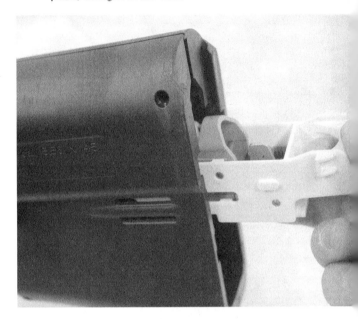

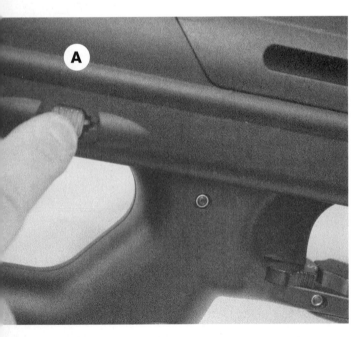

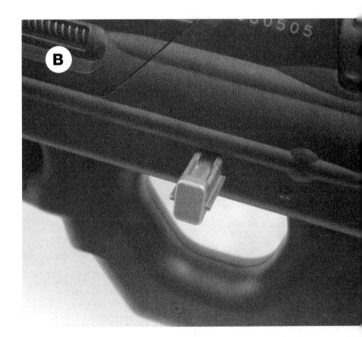

3. There is a square button above the thumbhole on the right side of the rifle (picture A). Press this button through the rifle to the left until it stops (picture B).

5. The bolt carrier assembly can be pulled forward and then up out of the frame.

4. Pull the barreled receiver forward off the frame.

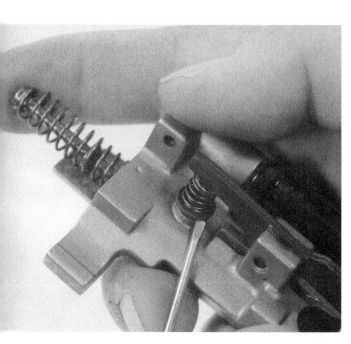

6. Using a small flat device, lift up slightly on the firing pin retaining plunger to free the firing pin and spring from the rear of the bolt carrier.

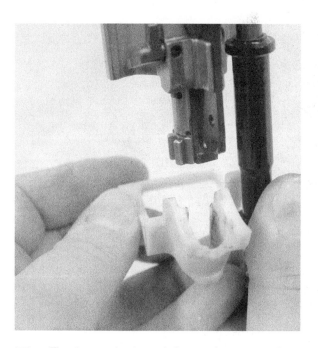

7. The large plastic switch can be removed by pulling the long spring seat forward to allow clearance for the switch.

8. Lift this long bolt lock lever up while pushing the bolt all the way to the rear. The cam pin can then be lifted out of the bolt carrier. The bolt and bolt spring are now free to be removed from the front of the carrier.

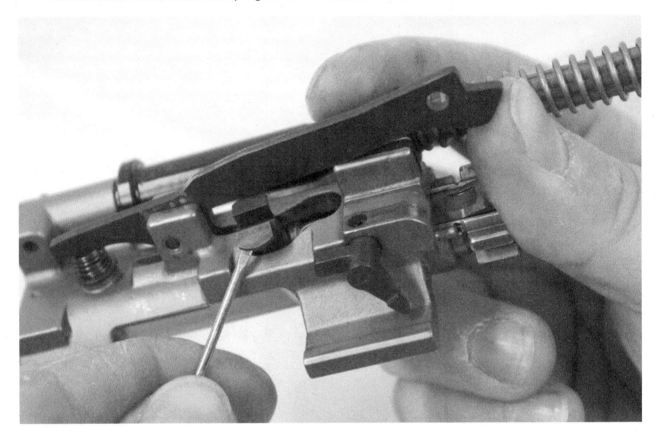

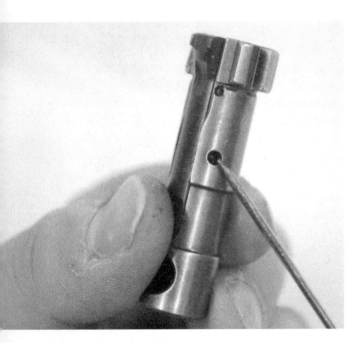

9. Push out this pin to release the extractor and spring.

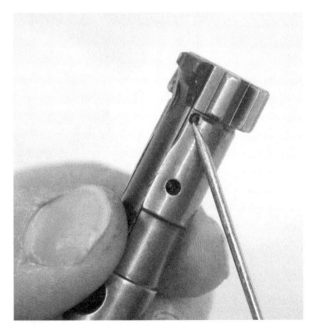

10. Drive out this pin to free the ejector and spring.

11. Displace the small ring spring at the front of the operating rod. This will free the washer behind it, the spring, and spring seat (picture A). The operating rod can be removed by driving out this pin (picture B) and unscrewing it from the carrier, but should not be unless the rod needs replacement.

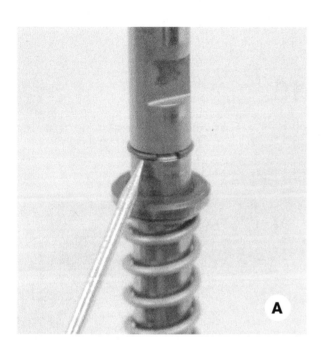

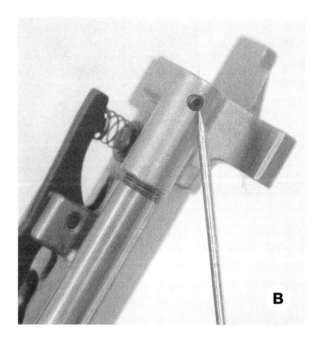

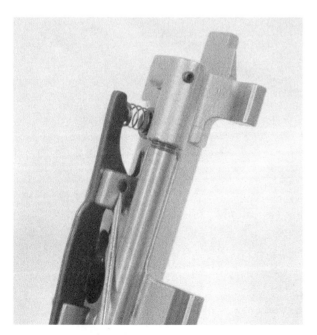

12. The bolt lock lever can be removed by driving out this pin. However, it is staked in place and should only be removed if completely necessary.

13. This bolt locking arm can be removed by inserting a probe into the small hole in its body (through the witness hole in the carrier), depressing the internal detent, and sliding the lever to the right. The detent will exit with great speed.

14. To separate the halves of the barrel receiver pieces, remove the six hex head socket screws, four below the barrel, and two above. Note that on the other side these screws are held in place by nuts. Do not lose the nuts.

15. Remove the left side piece first by gently working it straight to the left and then bring the rear out and slightly forward to clear the gas regulator. Then remove the right side piece in a similar manner to the right.

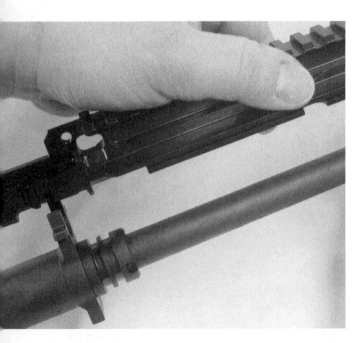

16. The optics rail can be lifted from the barrel assembly.

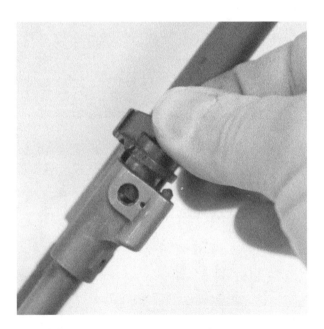

17. Remove the gas plug by turning it so that the finger flange points to the left of the barrel. Depress the plunger with a small tool. Then continue rotating to the left until it stops (pointing down). Pull the plug from the piston tube.

18. The piston can be removed forward out of the piston tube.

20. The plungers on either receiver half can be removed by depressing this tab, allowing the plunger and spring to separate from the frame piece.

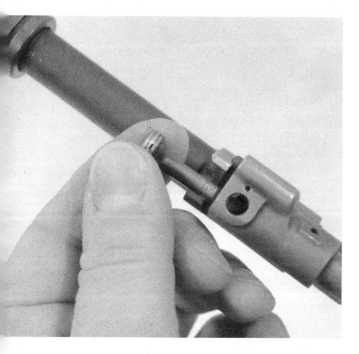

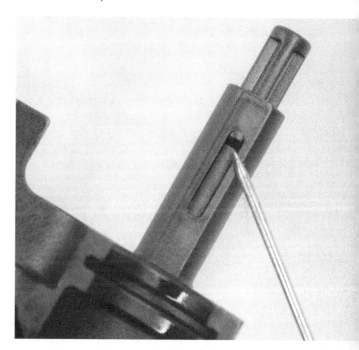

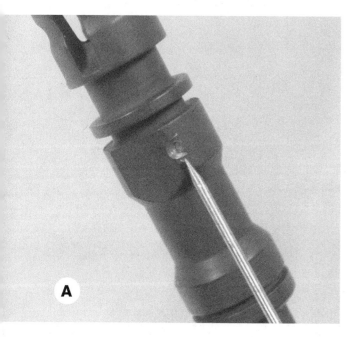

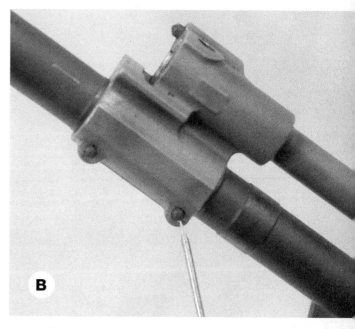

19. The muzzle attachment (picture A) is likely retained by a blind pin which prevents detachment from the barrel. As a result, the regulator/gas block assembly should be left in place (picture B), though it can be removed by driving out the two solid retaining pins (following removal of the muzzle attachment), and the plug detent and spring removed by means of the small spring pin just behind the exposed detent.

21. The ejection port door can be removed by pulling this pin back and out of the door assembly. This will free the door and spring.

22. It is adviseable to leave the charging handle in place. Removal requires the drifting out of the three roll pins seen in the handle. This will disassemble the entire assembly, including the steel loop on the inside.

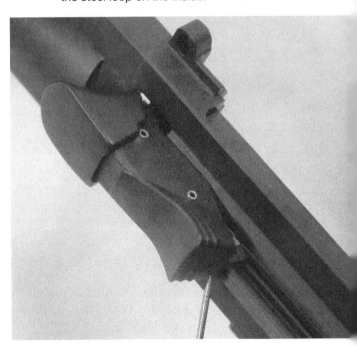

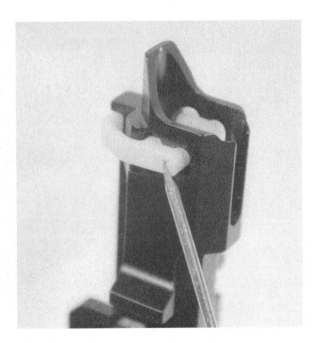

23. Unless the ejection tube gate is damaged, leave it in place.

24. The forend can be pulled straight down and off the frame.

25. Separation of the frame pieces first requires the removal of the inspection door. Drive out this pin to remove the door (picture A). Then the spring legs should be displaced from the cover (picture B). The cover will now fall off and the spring can be removed from its seat.

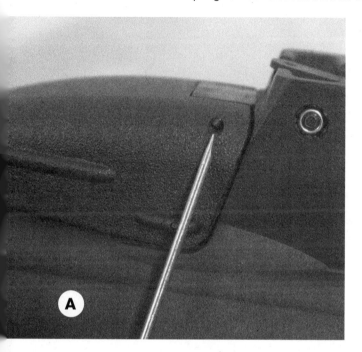

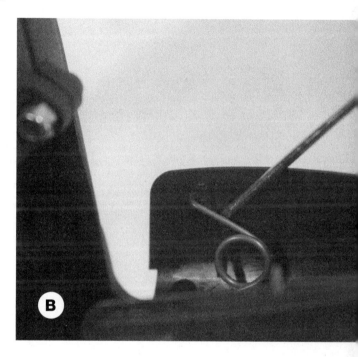

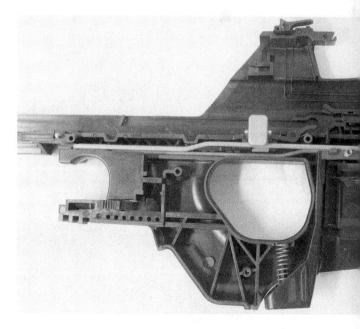

26. Remove the twelve screws holding the frame halves together. There are four different length screws. Note the lengths and corresponding locations.

27. Place the frame on the bench so that it is lying on its right side, and then carefully remove the left frame half. All the parts should remain in the right half. The latch that locks the disassembly button may fall out, as might the magazine catch button.

28. Remove the mag catch button by lifting up and out. The spring is quite energetic.

29. Remove the magazine catch by lifting up.

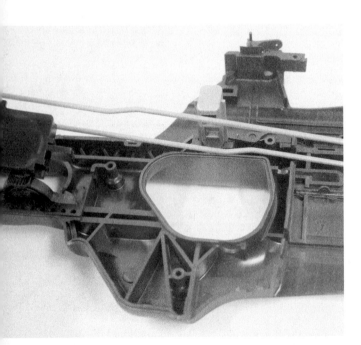

30. Remove the trigger and trigger bar assembly.

31. Remove the takedown button latch. Note the orientation of the latch and spring. Then pull out the takedown button. There is a detent on the front wall of the button which can be pulled out if necessary.

32. Remove the safety wheel by rotating past the fire position and then lifting up. A double-ended detent and spring lies beneath.

33. There are five location pins, three behind the inspection port along the top of the frame, and two at the front of the frame above the forend area. These pins are loose and will fall out of the frame. Also there is a support arch at the very rear of the frame at the heel area of the stock that can also be easily lifted from its position.

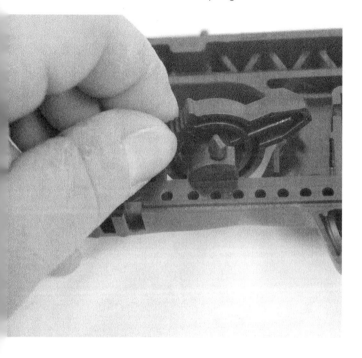

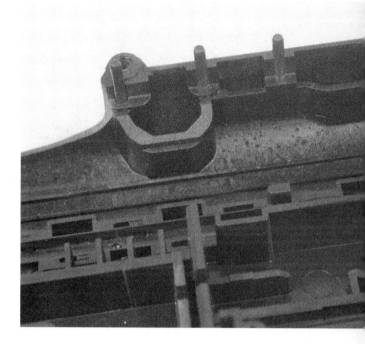

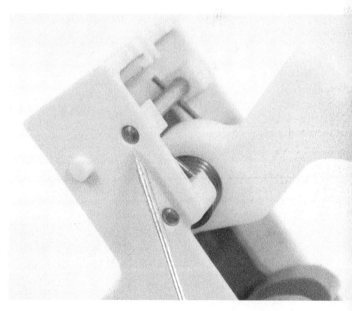

34. The rear sight can simply be pulled out of its seat in the frame. Note that the curved "flat" spring beneath it is placed with its bend facing up.

35. Drive out this pin which acts as a spring seat for the hammer spring. All the pins in the fire control group/trigger housing are splined on the right side and should be driven out in that direction. Take care not to damage the plastic housing.

36. Drive out the hammer pin and remove the hammer and springs.

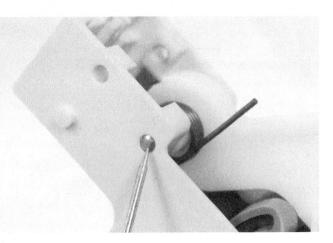

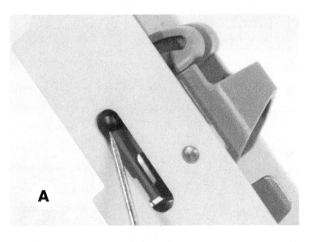

37. This pin which holds the disconnector to the hammer (picture A) and also holds the small disconnector spring in the underside. However, the pin is held into the disconnector by means of a small pin inserted in to a blind hole (picture B). This prevents further disassembly, which will damage the disconnector when the pin is driven out. Any further disassembly should only be done if a replacement trigger pack is unavailable.

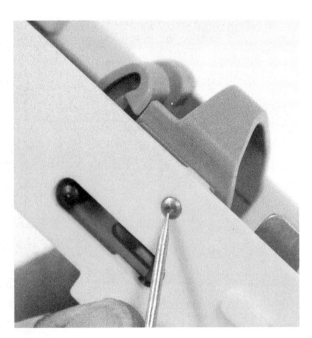

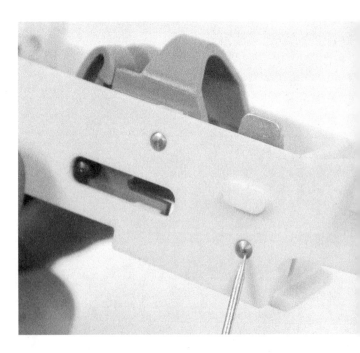

38. Drive out this pin which holds the sear assembly. When removed the sear will be pushed forward by its two springs which bear on the inner rear wall of the housing. Control the assembly to prevent loss of the springs.

39. Drive out this pin to remove the drop safety. This is the tall somewhat triangular piece at the rear left corner of the housing. Its spring is just below it and removal of the safety also frees the spring.

Reassembly Tips:

1. When reinstalling the return spring seat, be sure that the skinny section is forward.

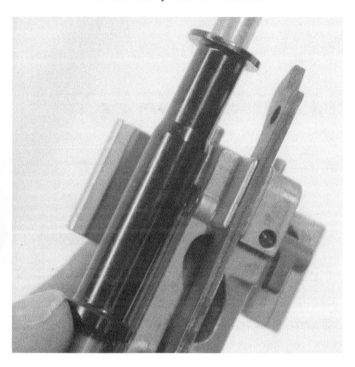

2. When recombining the two barrel frame halves, this positioning plate will cause trouble if not located in this location correctly.

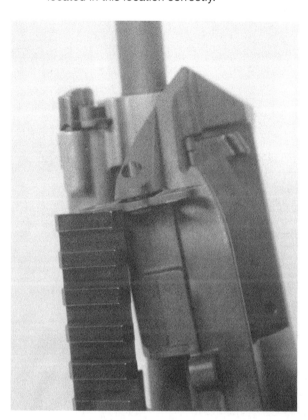

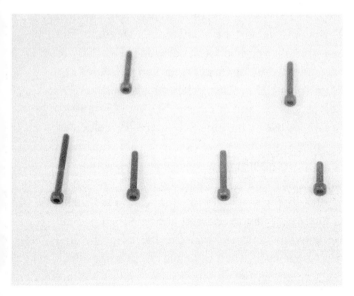

3. Viewed from the left, the six barrel frame screws are arranged here. The muzzle end is to the left. Note that there are three different sized screws.

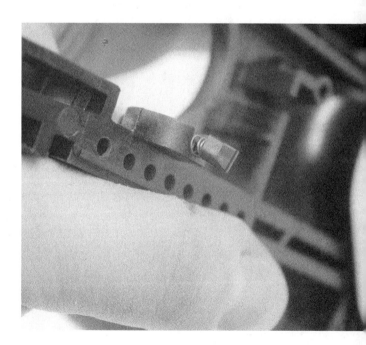

4. The safety detents have a flat side and a round side. The flat side goes up and the round down in order to replace the safety wheel.

FNH PS90

Similar/Identical Pattern Guns

The same basic assembly/disassembly steps for the FNH PS90 also apply to the following guns:

FNH P90

Data:	FNH PS90
Origin:	Belgium
Manufacturer:	Fabrique National, Herstal
Cartridge:	5.7x28mm
Magazine capacity:	50 rounds
Over-all length:	26.3 inches
Barrel length:	16.1 inches
Weight:	6.61 pounds

One of the coolest and most unique guns ever, the P90/PS90 is a fun little lightweight carbine. The ammo is sort of a super .22 Magnum, but has since proven itself as a cartridge. The P90 has been adopted by many agencies and militaries as a PDW (personal defense weapon), such as the U.S. Secret Service, and of course, Stargate Command. In fact, its use by the elite SG-1 team has cemented its place in American society. FN borrowed heavily from the Steyr AUG when designing the trigger pack for the P90 and the F2000, so owners of this firearm will enjoy the very easy basic maintenance involved with the PS90. It should be noted in advance that the barrel group and just about everything attached to it is, however, not something that should be taken apart without very good reason, and that has been noted in the takedown steps here. Some owners have elected to replace the longer PS90 barrel with a shorter standard P90 model (following NFA regulations) but the vast majority have not, and guns that are taken in for service will almost always be the PS90 with the standard longer barrel.

Disassembly:

1. The PS90 must be cocked to begin. There is a square button in the magazine tray area. (picture A). Press this button down pull the barrel assembly forward of the stock (picture B).

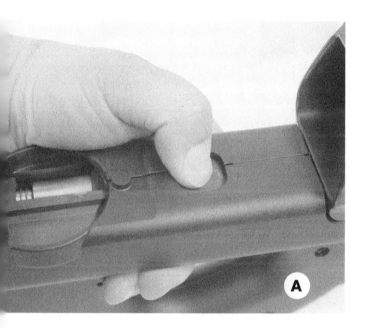

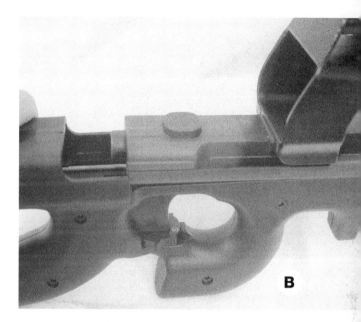

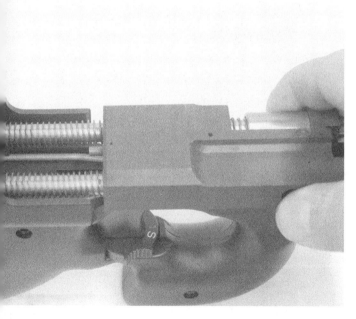

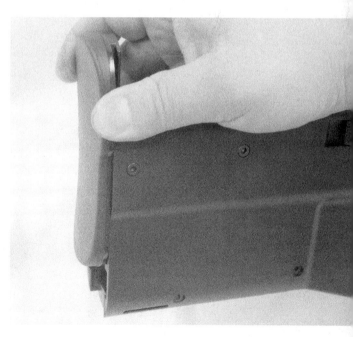

2. The bolt carrier assembly can be pulled forward out of the stock assembly.

3. Slide the buttplate up out of the stock.

5. To disassemble the bolt assembly, the two spring clips on the guide rods must be removed. Gently, slightly spread the spring apart to fit over the groove shoulder and slide the spring forward off the guide rod. The bolt springs are under a great deal of compression, so control over this assembly is vital.

4. Reach into the buttstock, lift the black lever on the lower right corner of the trigger pack and pull out the trigger pack, straight to the rear.

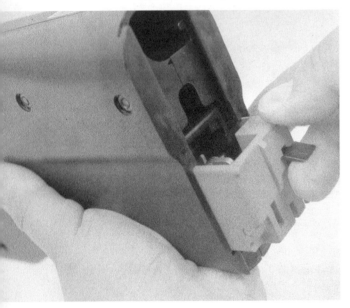

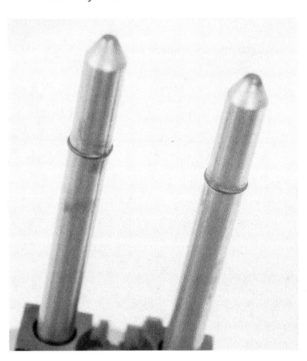

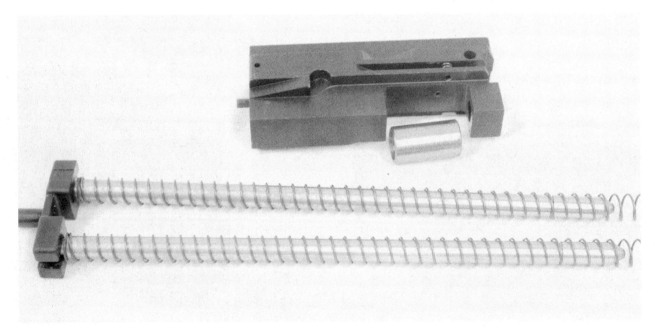

6. Separated, the moving parts group consists of the bolt, a cylindrical buffer, the two springs, two guide rods and a base. The plastic base need not be removed from the guide rods.

7. Drive out this pin to free the ejector and spring. It is best if driven out from bottom to top.

8. Push out this pin to release the extractor spring.

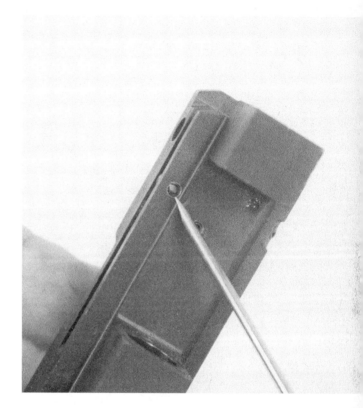

9. Push out this pin to release the extractor

10. Drive out this pin to release the firing pin and spring.

11. Dislodge both hammer spring legs (picture A). Drive out this pin which holds the safety sear (picture B). Take care not to damage the plastic housing.

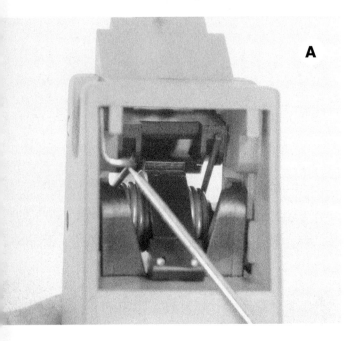

A

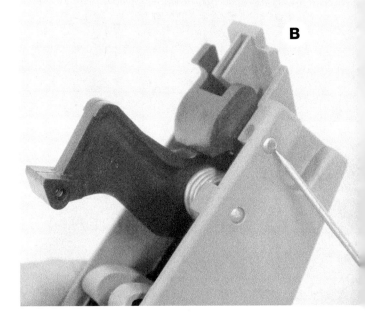

B

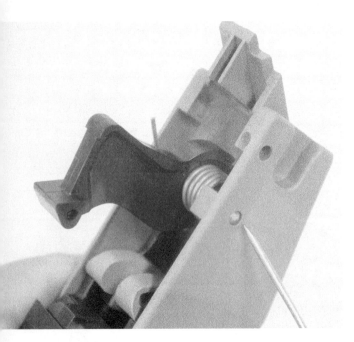

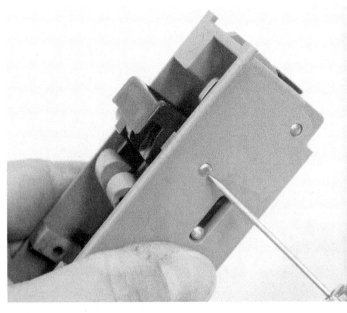

12. Push out the hammer pin and remove the hammer and springs.

13. Push out this pin which holds the sear assembly. It also holds the trigger/disconnector spring.

14. This pin holds the disconnector to the sear (picture A). However, the pin is held into the disconnector by means of a small pin inserted in to a blind hole (picture B). This prevents further disassembly, which will damage the disconnector when the pin is driven out. Any further disassembly should only be done if a replacement trigger pack is unavailable.

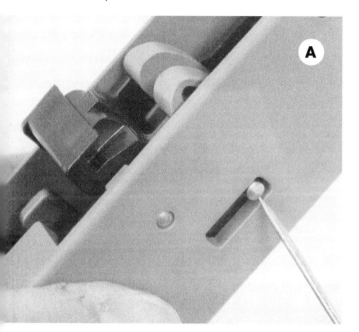

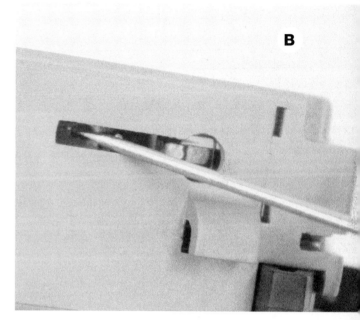

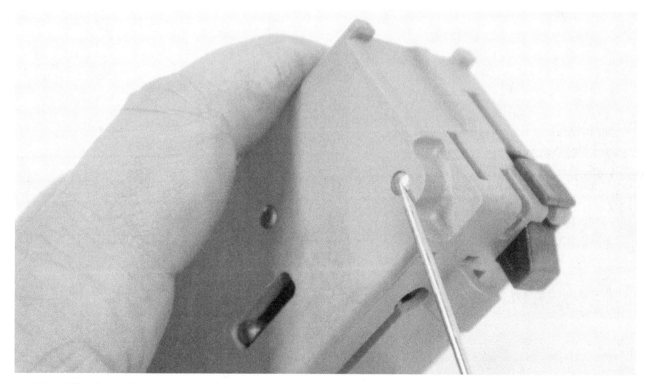

15. This pin retains the housing latch and spring, as well as the drop safety. With the drop safety (roughly triangular piece) removed, the spring will come with it.

16. Disassembly of the receiver is best left to the factory. There is a blind pin fitted to the barrel just behind the flash suppressor (picture A). This pin prevents the barrel from being unscrewed from the barrel sleeve (flash suppressor and extension). The barrel retains the takedown button and spring and the charging handle assembly, as the barrel passes through both assemblies. Disassembly of the optic rail and interface should be left to the factory as well (picture B). The accessory rails can be unscrewed from the receiver (picture C).

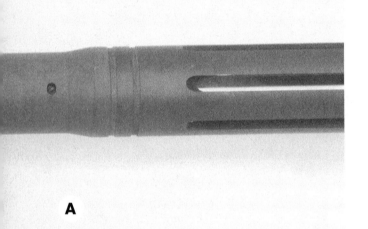

A

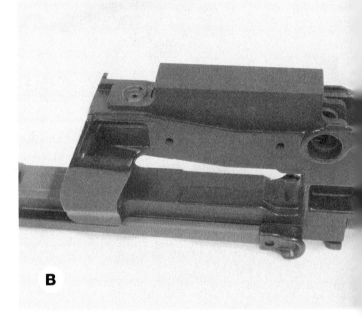

B

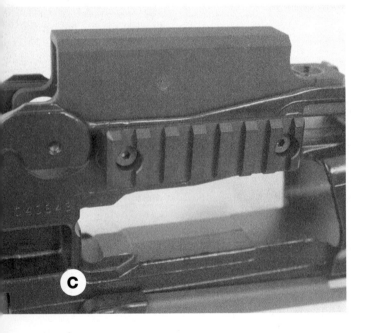

C

17. To separate the halves of the stock, remove the ten hex head socket screws. Note that on the other side these screws are held in place by nuts. Do not lose the nuts. Remove the left side piece first by gently working it straight to the left and then bring the rear out and slightly forward.

18. The ejection port door can be removed by pulling this pin back and out of the door assembly. This will free the door and spring.

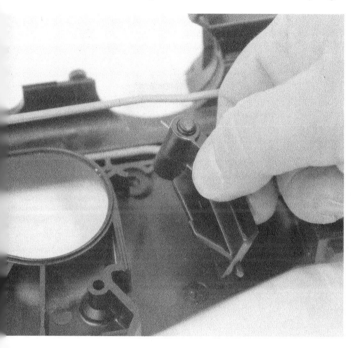

19. The trigger and trigger bars can then be lifted out. The bar is snapped in place on the trigger and need be removed only for replacement.

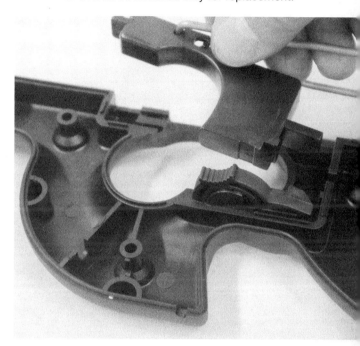

20. The magazine catch can be removed by depressing the hook in the bottom into the catch and rotating the catch forward to clear the stock.

21. The safety can be removed by rotating past the fire position and then lifting up. Note the detents and spring beneath. Control them to prevent loss as the safety is removed.

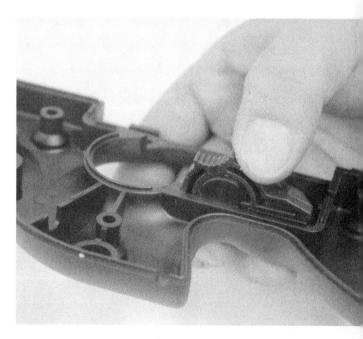

22. The magazine can be disassembled by depressing the catch button on the "bottom" and slide the plate off the body (picture A). The disassembled magazine consists of the body, spring, catch plate, floor plate, follower wedge, and the two rollers that act as followers.

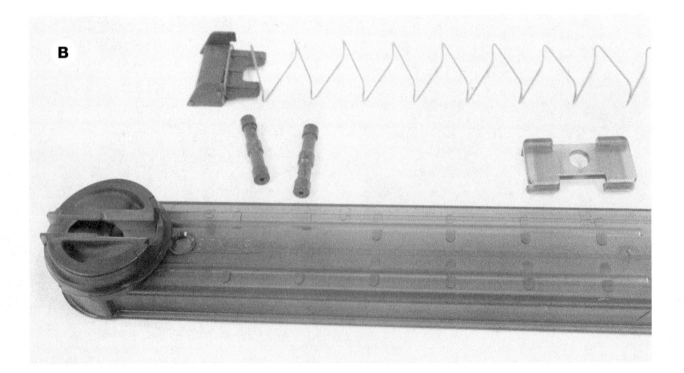

Reassembly Tips:

1. When reinstalling the stock screws, note that there are three sizes. The two longest are the two rearmost. Next are the middle length. The remaining six are all the same size and are all forward of the ejection port.

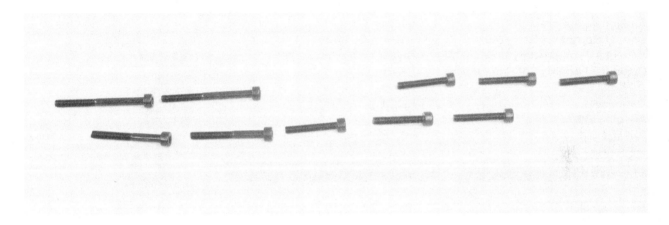

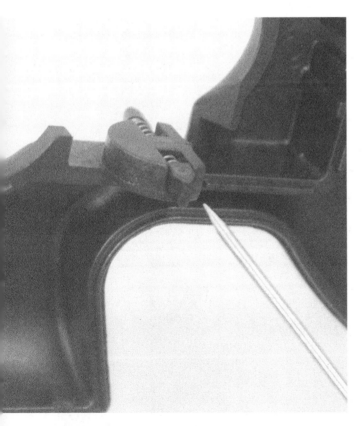

2. The safety detents have a flat side and a round side. The flat side goes up and the round down in order to replace the safety wheel.

3. As the ejection port cover spring seat is against the left side stock half, reassembly of this part should be done in the left side first, placing the right side stock containing the majority of the internal parts onto the left.

HECKLER & KOCH HK 91

Similar/Identical Pattern Guns

The same basic assembly/disassembly steps for the
Heckler & Koch HK 91 also apply to the following guns:

Springfield Armory SAR 48   German G3
Springfield Armory SAR 4800   Spanish CETME
Springfield Armory SAR 48 Bush Rifle   HK 33
Springfield Armory SAR Para Model   HK 41
DS Arms SA58   HK 53
German G1   HK 93
Austrian StG 58   PSG-1
British L1A1

Data: Heckler & Koch HK 91
Origin: Germany
Manufacturer: Heckler & Koch GmbH,
Oberndorf/Neckar
Cartridge: 308 Winchester
(7.62 x 51mm)
Magazine capacity: 5 and 20 rounds
Overall length: 40-1/4 inches
Barrel length: 19 inches
Weight: 10.3 pounds

The HK 91 is the semi-auto version of the
selective-fire G3, the standard German military
rifle. Except for the full-auto system, the two guns
are mechanically very similar, and most of the
instructions will apply. There is also a version in
223, the HK 33, and all three guns are available in
retractable-stock models.

The HK91/G3 is itself an upgraded version of
the Spanish CETME rifle. While there are some
differences, the basic steps for the HK91 can be
used for the CETME as well.

Disassembly:

1. Remove the magazine, and cycle the action to cock the internal hammer. Push out the two locking cross pins at the lower rear of the receiver. Cross-holes are provided in the buttstock for storage of the pins during disassembly.

2. Remove the buttstock and back plate assembly toward the rear. The recoil spring and its guide and the buffer assembly can be taken out of the stock, if necessary, by removal of two slotted screws inside the front of the buttstock. Control the springs during this operation.

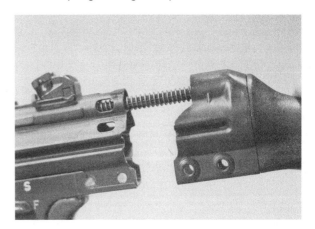

3. Tip the grip frame down at the rear, and remove it downward.

4. Turn the safety lever up to vertical position, and remove it toward the left. The hammer should be in the fired position for this operation.

5. Remove the sub-frame from the pistol-grip unit. If it is very tight, it may be necessary to pry it gently at the front to start it.

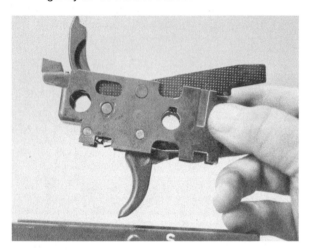

6. Restrain the ejector, and push the ejector pivot out toward the left.

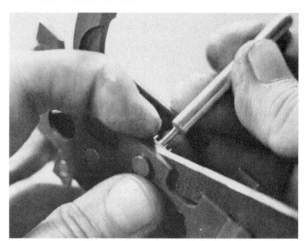

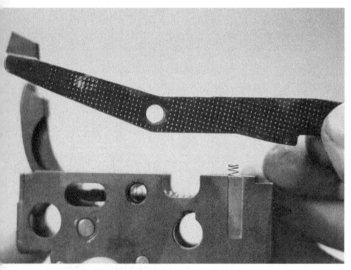

7. Remove the ejector upward, and take out its vertical spring at the rear.

8. Restrain the hammer spring and its guide at the top, and insert a tool through the side opening to lift the forward end of the guide out of its engagement with the hammer.

9. Remove the hammer spring and guide upward and toward the front.

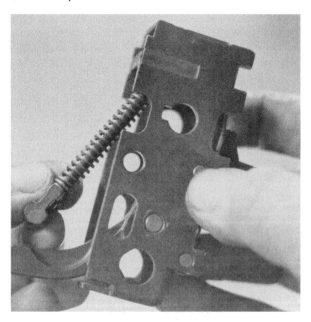

10. Remove the hammer pivot toward either side.

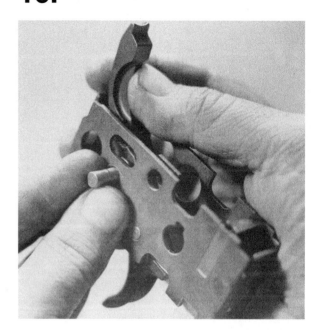

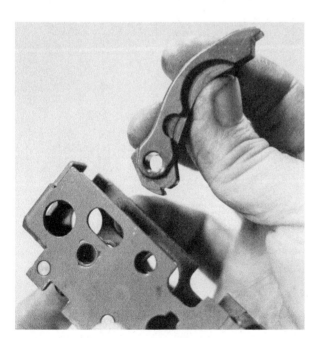

11. Remove the hammer upward.

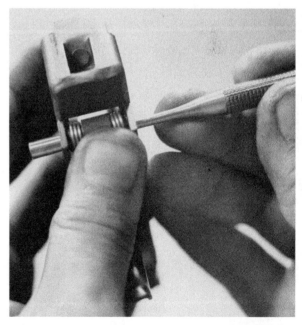

12. Restrain the sear spring and its roller at the front, and push out the sear cross pin toward either side.

13. Remove the sear spring and its roller, or mounting sleeve, downward.

14. Unhook the trigger spring from its shelf on the trigger, on the left side at the rear, and move the spring arm downward and forward, relieving its tension. Caution: Keep fingertips clear, as the released spring can cause injury.

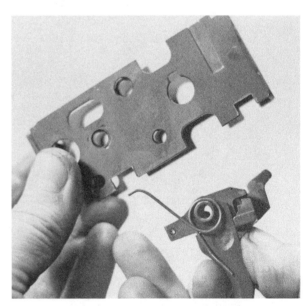

15. Push out the trigger pivot pin toward either side.

16. Remove the trigger assembly downward. The sear is easily lifted out from the trigger top, and the trigger spring from the left side of the trigger.

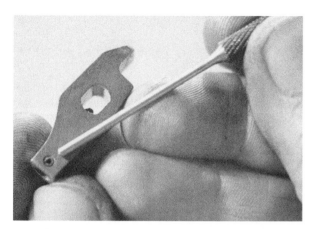

17. A roll pin at the front of the sear retains an internal plunger and spring. If this is to be removed, control the plunger and spring, and ease them out.

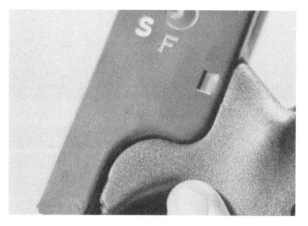

18. A single screw on the right side retains the pistol-grip handle on the grip frame. After the screw is removed, the handle is taken off downward.

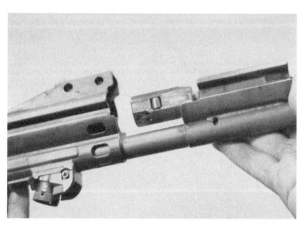

19. Remove the bolt assembly from the rear of the receiver.

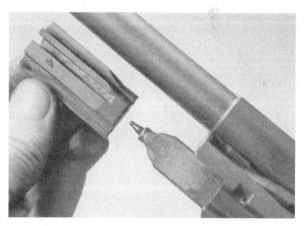

20. Turn the bolt head 90 degrees toward the right, and remove the bolt head toward the front.

21. Insert a small screwdriver in the loop of the extractor spring on the bolt head, and lift it just enough to clear its shoulder on the extractor, then pull the spring out toward the front.

22. After removal of the spring, the extractor can be lifted out of its recess in the bolt head. The locking rollers are retained by an inner bracket, which is held by a roll pin. The pin can be drifted down into the bolt head, and the bracket and rollers moved out toward the side. In normal takedown, this unit is best left in place.

23. Rotate the locking piece one-half turn in either direction, and remove it toward the front.

24. Remove the firing pin toward the front, along with its spring.

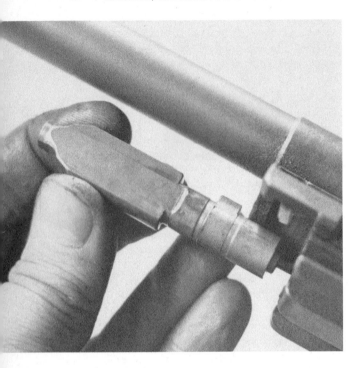

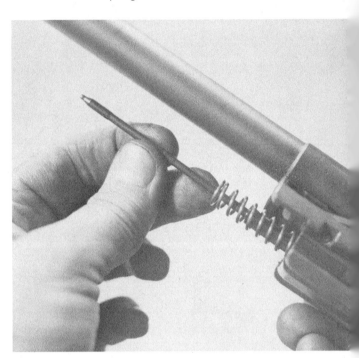

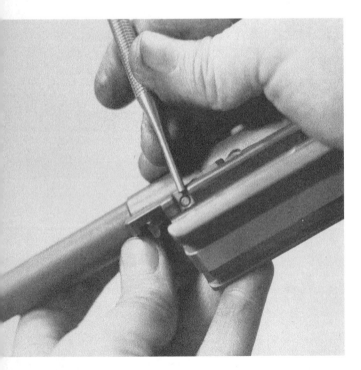

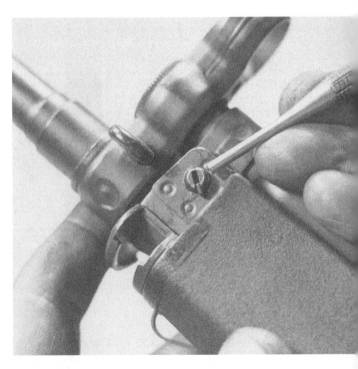

25. The bolt head locking lever and its spring are retained on the bolt carrier by a cross pin. If these parts are to be removed, keep them under control, as the spring is very strong.

26. Push out the locking pin at the front of the handguard.

27. Tip the handguard down at the front, then remove it toward the front and downward.

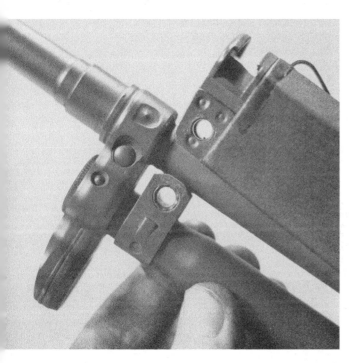

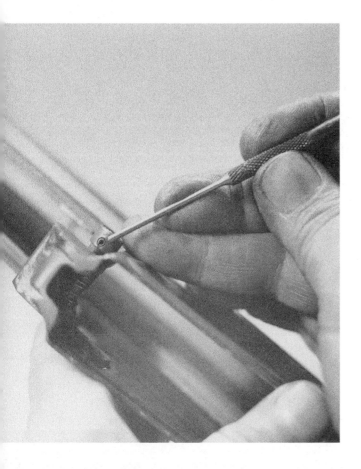

28. It is possible to remove the cocking handle assembly by aligning its cross pin with the access holes in the sleeve and drifting out the pin. The handle and spring are then removed outward, and the internal rod is moved out toward the rear. In normal takedown, this unit is best left in place.

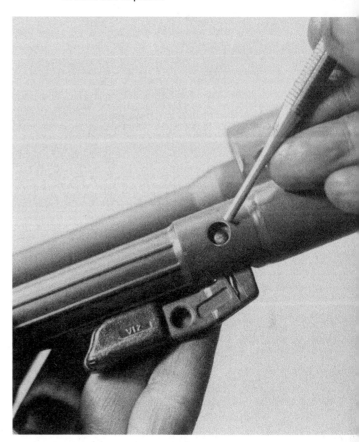

29. The magazine catch button is retained on the cross-piece by a vertical roll pin. When the pin is drifted out, the button and spring are released toward the right, and the catch piece is taken off toward the left.

30. The cap at the front is retained by a plunger and spring. Depress the plunger, and take off the cap toward the front.

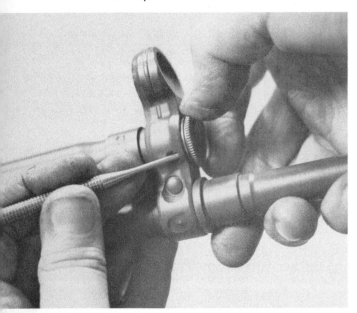

31. Engage a tool or a piece of bar stock with the opposed notches in the front of the flash hider, and unscrew it from the end of the barrel. Take care not to lose the retaining spring.

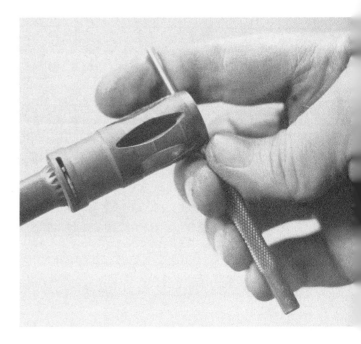

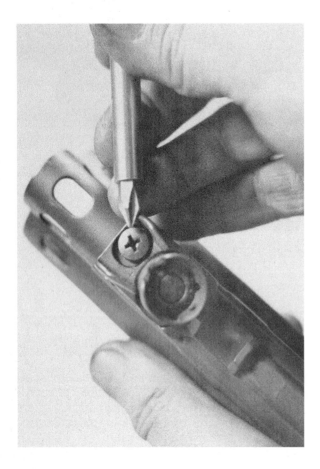

32. The rear sight is both horizontally adjusted and retained by a large Phillips screw on top. If this is removed, take care that the lock washer and the flat spring plate are not lost. The turret locking ball and spring will also be released on the underside of the sight, so keep these small parts under control. Unless repair is necessary, the sight should be left in place.

Reassembly Tips:

1. When replacing the bolt head in the carrier, it will be necessary to depress the rear of the locking lever or lift its front beak to engage with its track on the bolt head.

2. When reassembling the trigger group, install the sear spring assembly first, being sure that its upper arms are in front of the hammer pivot projections inside. Lift the lower portion of the spring, and insert one of the major retaining pins, as shown, to hold the spring during installation of the sear and trigger assembly. When the parts are installed, remove the pin, and be sure the small roller at the rear tip of the spring engages the underside of the sear.

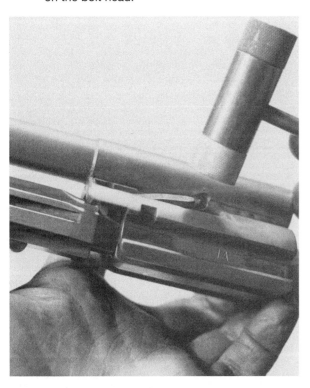

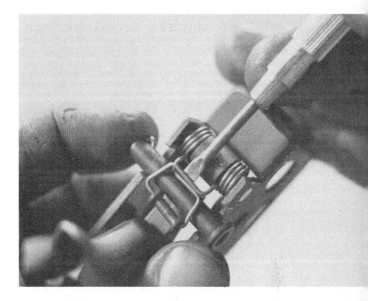

3. Before replacing the bolt and bolt carrier in the receiver, the bolt head must be moved forward slightly in the carrier, as shown, to retract the locking rollers.

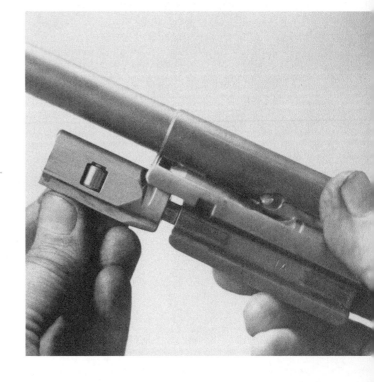

IWI TAVOR

Data:	IWI Tavor
Origin:	United States
Manufacturer:	IWI US, Harrisburg, PA.
Cartridge:	5.56x45 mm, 9x19mm, 5.45x39mm
Magazine capacity:	30 rounds
Over-all length:	26.1 inches
Barrel length:	16.5 inches
Weight:	8.5 pounds

Formerly the small arms division of Israel Military Industries, Israel Weapons Industries has a long (or perhaps short, depending on your perspective) history of manufacturing innovative firearms and other weapons. The Tavor is the newest model to be sold in the United States. Manufactured in this country, it features all the goodies one would expect from a rifle derived from a military firearm, plus it is a modular system built in the bullpup style. The Tavor has become the standard issue IDF rifle. Also of note, the rifle can be readily converted to other chamberings with the off the shelf conversion kits sold by IWI.

Disassembly:

1. With the bolt closed and the magazine absent, push out this pin (picture A) at the stock heel and open the buttstock. Pull out the bolt and recoil mechanism assembly (picture B).

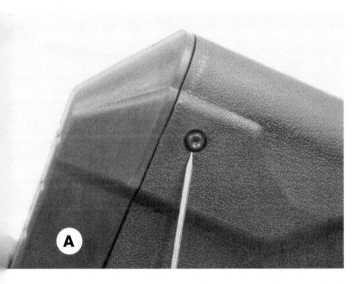

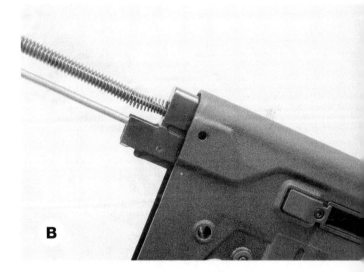

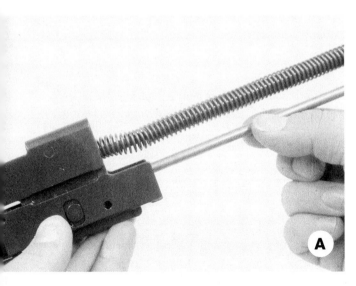

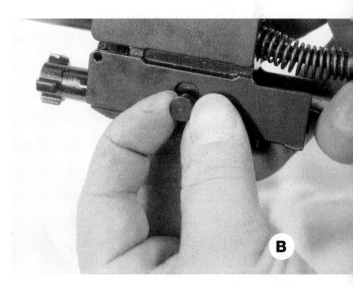

2. Pull the rotation control bar (no spring) all the way to the rear (picture A). Then push out the cam pin from the right (picture B).

3. Pull the bolt from the carrier. The firing pin and spring will follow behind it.

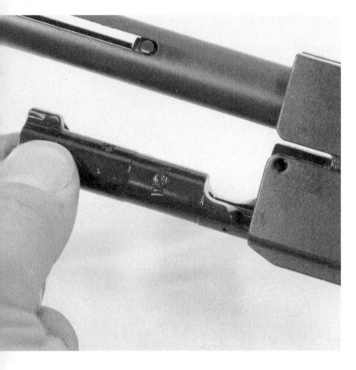

4. Push out this pin to remove the extractor. A conical synthetic bumper takes the place of the spring.

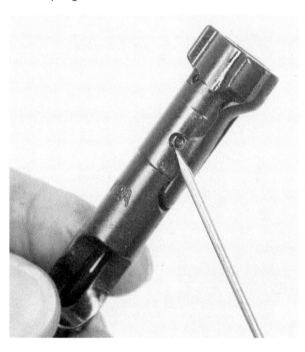

5. Drive out this pin to remove the ejector and spring.

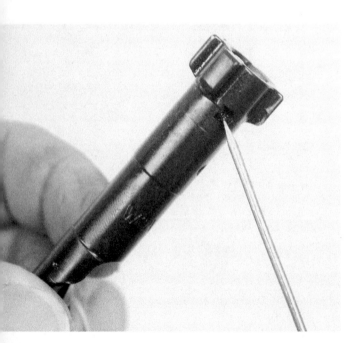

6. Further disassembly of the bolt carrier and recoil assembly group should be reserved for the factory. Remaining pins, such as this one holding in the recoil spring housing, are heavily staked in place.

7. To remove the sear assembly, push out the two pins just above the bolt carrier stop (picture A). Then rotate fully downward and pull the sear assembly from the stock (picture B).

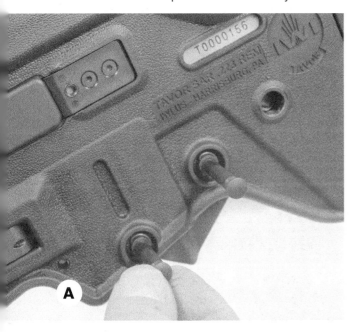

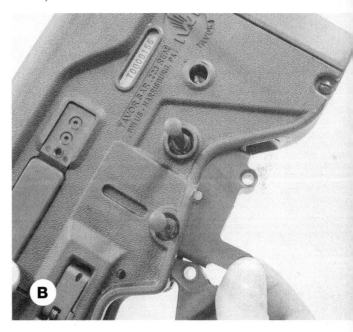

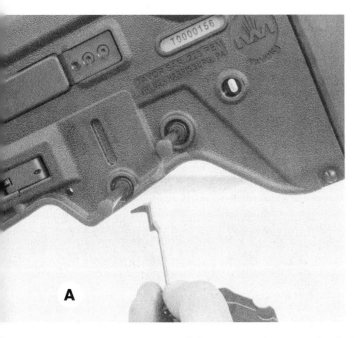

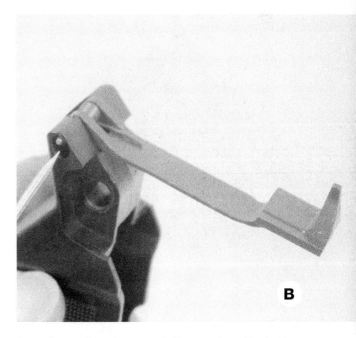

8. With the bolt stop fully open, push up to unlatch the stop from the stock and remove it down and out the bottom (picture A). The bolt carrier stop can be disassembled by pushing out this pin to separate the large button, the pin, the spring, and the stop itself (picture B).

9. There is a small roll pin in the center of the hammer here. Tap this pin out, and then push the hammer pin out to one side. Remove the hammer and spring.

10. Unhook this small coil spring from its perch on the trigger bar.

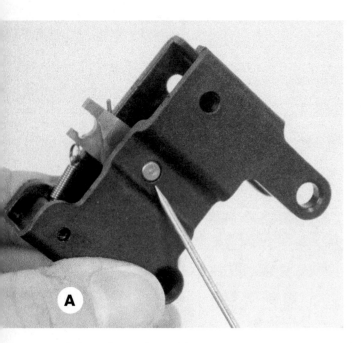

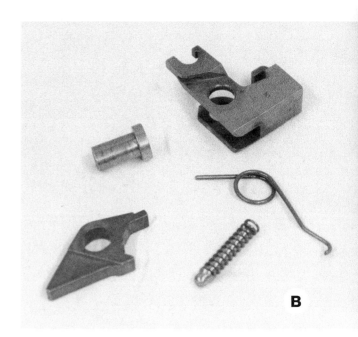

11. Push out this pin to remove the sear assembly (picture A). The sear assembly can be separated by pulling the bushing out to the right (picture B).

12. Removing this roll pin will allow the small coil spring to be removed.

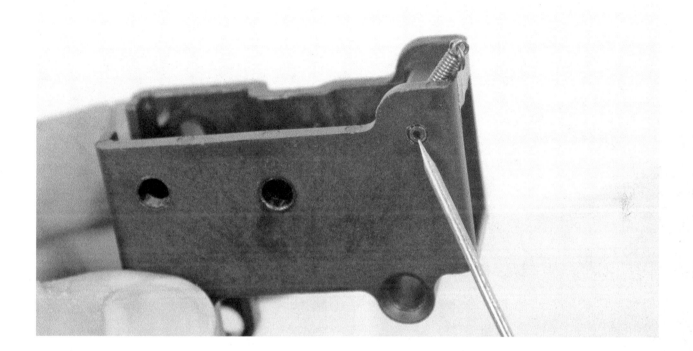

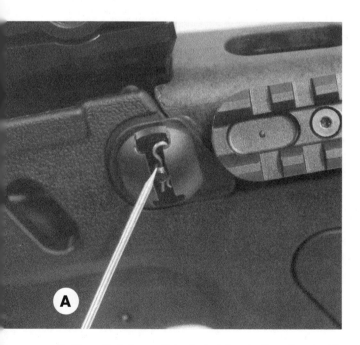

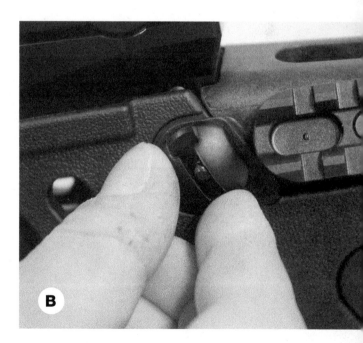

13. Pull the cotter pin holding in the sling locking screw and sling sleeve (picture A). Unscrew the plastic lock entirely from the pin (picture B). Then push out the threaded pin and the sleeve to the left

14. Unscrew and remove the foregrip fastening screws from either side of the foregrip (picture A). Then pull the foregrip forward and down off the stock body (picture B).

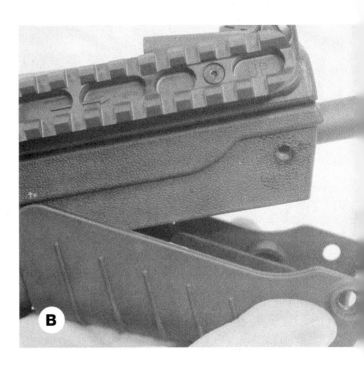

15. Remove the flash hider. It is retained by means of a jam nut. Loosen the nut and then remove both the flash hider and nut.

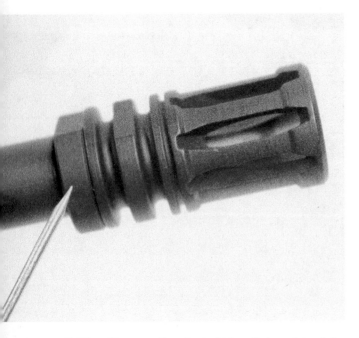

16. With the cocking lever unlocked, pull the cocking group forward off the stock. It will be necessary to pull the stock halves apart slightly to allow the cocking handle to clear the barrel flanges.

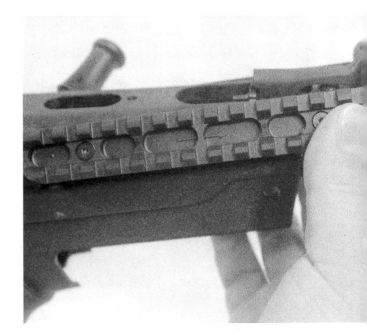

17. The cocking handle can be removed by driving out this pin (picture A). The operating rod can be separated from the charging handle assembly by driving out this pin (picture B). The charging handle piece can be separated from the handle latch by removing this pin (picture C). The spring can then be removed from the handle piece.

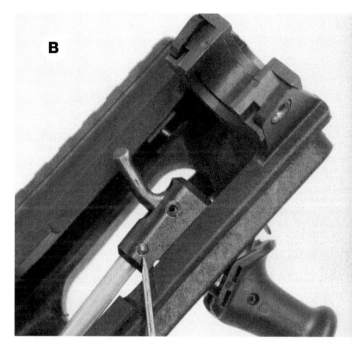

18. The accessory rail can be removed by first removing these two screws (picture A). Then the rail clamps must be squeezed and pushed out with a needle nosed pliers (picture B).

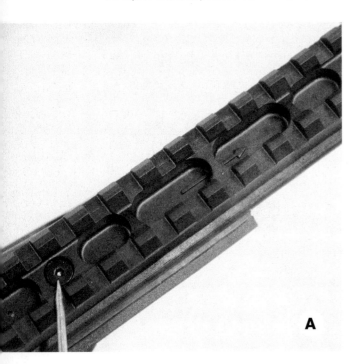

A

B

19. The front sight can be removed by aligning this pin with the slot and driving it out. Then the adjustment screw on the right side should be fully removed to free the sight arm. With the arm removed, the spring plate and spring beneath it will also be freed. The front sight post, detent, and spring should be left in place, but can be unscrewed fully out of the sight arm.

20. With a punch unlock the blocking plate for the barrel lock pivot (picture A). While the plate is being depressed, rotate the pivot pin so that the white mark is pointing forward (picture B). If the proprietary wrench is unavailable, a 5/32 hex wrench will work.

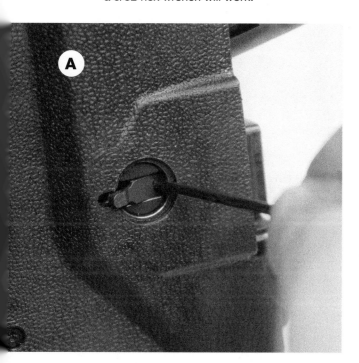
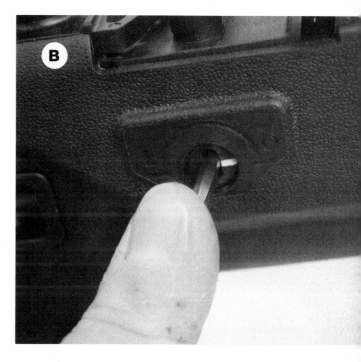

21. Pull the barrel assembly forward out of the stock.

22. Pull the gas cylinder forward and then up out of the stock (picture A). The dust plate can be removed from the front (picture B). The rear sight is removed from the cylinder assembly by removing this spring clip (picture C). Push out the pin and the sight will come out the right side. The flat sight spring can also be removed.

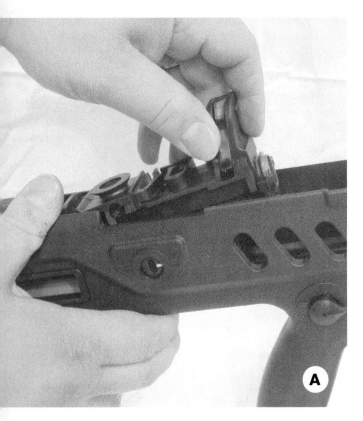

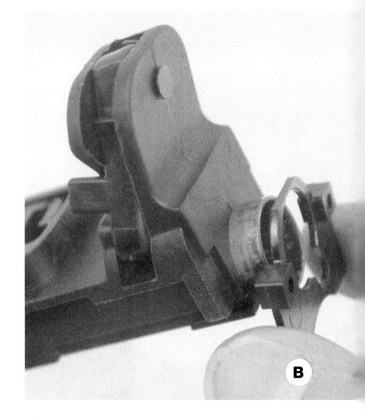

23. The reflex optic can be removed by unscrewing these nuts. Beneath the sight is a pair of Picatinny style rails. This optic mounting platform and the flange further up the barrel are retained by staked in pins and should not be removed.

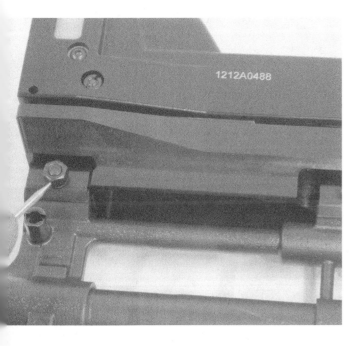

24. If necessary, the brass deflector can be removed by removing this screw. The deflector frame will then also lift out.

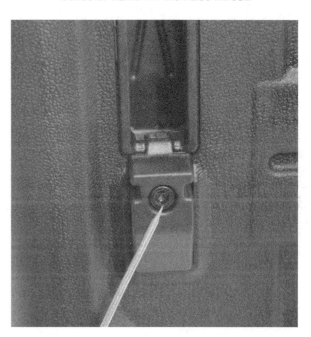

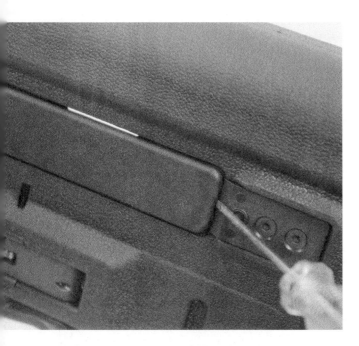

25. If necessary, usea flat thin screwdriver to pry up the ejection port cover for removal. The cover base beneath it can also be removed.

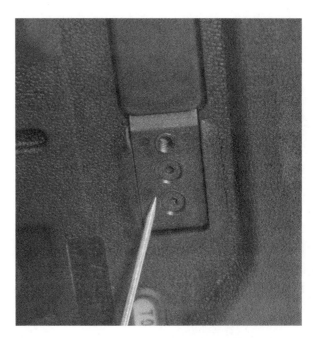

26. The filler block can be removed via these two screws.

27. To remove the magazine catch and spring, drive out this pin from top to bottom (picture A). The drive out this pin from left to right (picture B). Remove the catch cover and double hooked catch arm by sliding them forward out of the stock (picture C). Drive out this pin to remove the magazine catch button and spring (picture D).

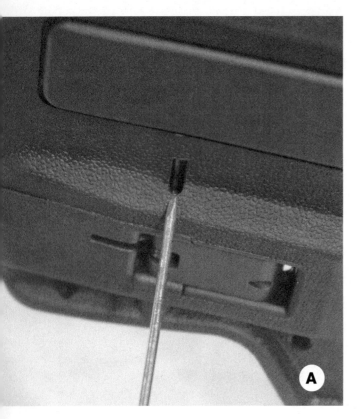

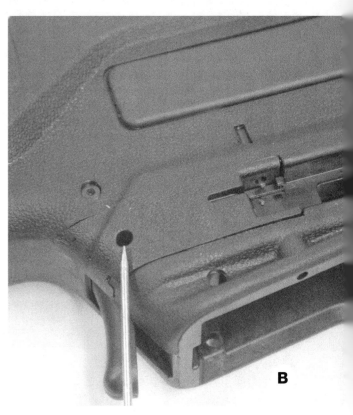

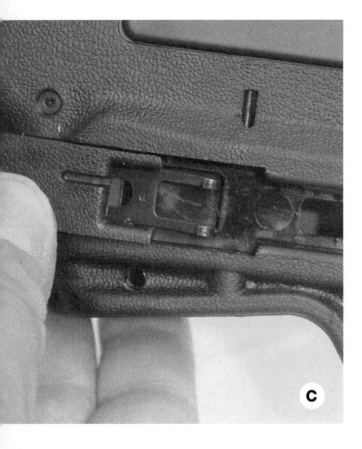

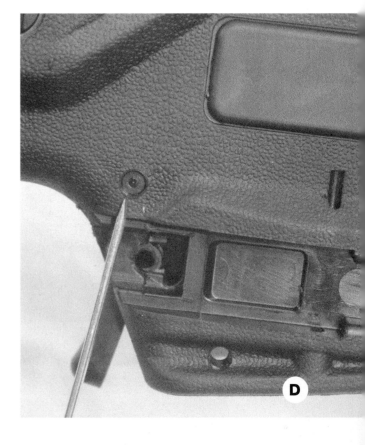

28. If necessary for replacement, the sear retaining pins can be removed by displacing these spring clips.

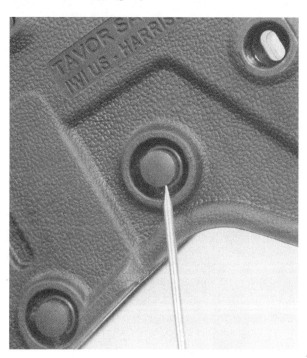

29. Should it be necessary to remove the butt plate/cover the screws on either side of the stock toe can be removed to release the cover from the stock.

30. If necessary for replacement, the butt locking pin can be removed by first pulling this spring out of its seats.

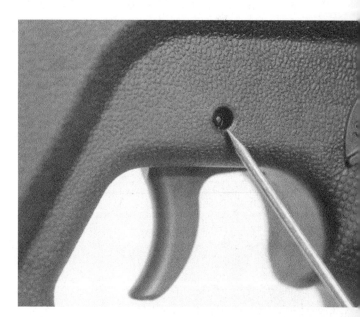

31. The trigger pin, while removable, should be left in place. In order to remove the trigger bar and trigger itself, the receiver must first be removed. The barrel locking pivot partially retains the receiver inside the stock and both should be left in place and removed only by the factory.

32. To switch the safety lever to the opposite side of the stock, depress this small pin in the center of the lever and slide the lever down (with the lever oriented in this way). The cover on the opposite side can be removed in an identical fashion.

Reassembly Tips:

1. The flat on the firing pin head must be facing straight up when the bolt is being reassembled or the cam pin will not fit back into the carrier.

2. When reassembling the sear housing, use a screwdriver in the hammer pin slot to align the retaining pin hole in the hammer with the hole in the hammer pin.

KEL-TEC RFB

Data:	Kel-Tec RFB
Origin:	United States
Manufacturer:	Kel-Tec CNC, Inc., Cocoa, FL
Cartridge:	7.62 mm NATO
Magazine capacity:	20 rounds
Over-all length:	27.5 inches
Barrel length:	18 inches
Weight:	8.6 pounds

The Rifle, Forward ejecting, Bullpup design from Kel-Tec is an interesting companion to their highly sought after KSG shotgun. Like the KSG, the RFB is built in a bullpup pattern, with the magazine, action, and chamber placed to the rear of the pistol grip and trigger. As with other examples of this type of longarm, this allows a full length rifle barrel to be placed into a system that has an overall length shorter than most carbines. The usual trade-off, a horrible trigger pull, has been avoided with the Kel-Tec guns. Another unique feature, the receiver section over the chamber (shooter's cheek) is heavily reinforced. The RFB is available with longer barrel lengths to produce ballistics comparable with magnum cartridges.

Disassembly:

1. With the hammer cocked, push out the two assembly pins above the magazine well.

3. Pull the charging handle all the way to the rear so that it aligns with its clearance slot, then pull the handle out of the gun to the side.

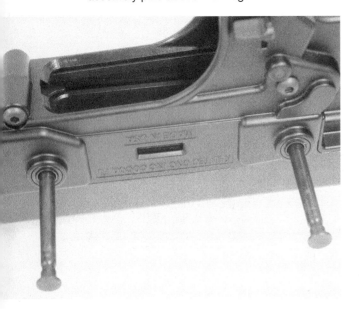

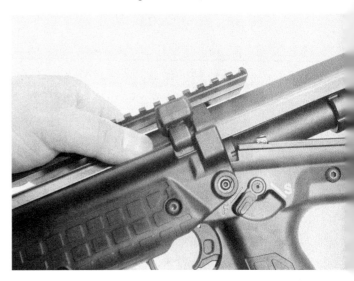

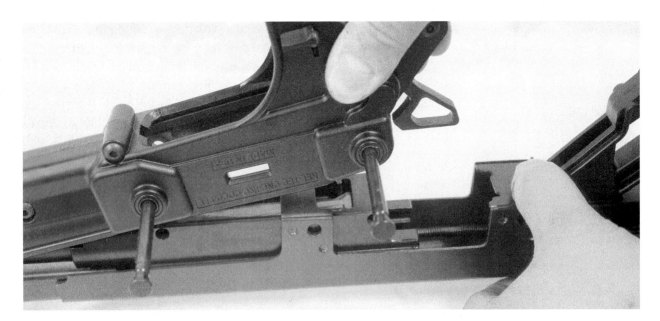

2. Lift the grip away from the buttstock and pull the buttstock out to the rear.

6. The recoil spring guides are held in place, front and rear, by staked-on nuts. These should not be removed outside of the factory.

4. Pull the carrier assembly out to the rear.

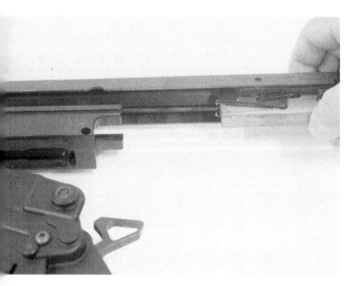

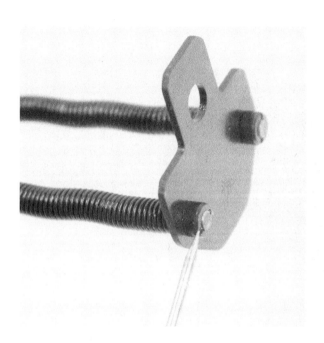

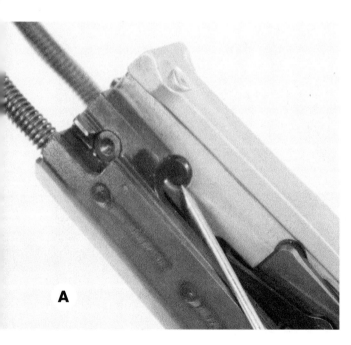

A

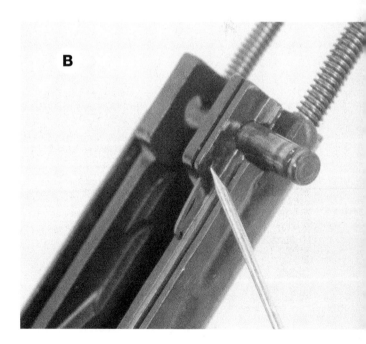

B

5. Push out this pin from left to right to free the bolt from the carrier (picture A). This roll pin retains the spring which locks the bolt cam pin and should be left in place for routine maintenance.

7. Push out this pin to free the firing pin and spring. Place the striker end of the bolt assembly against a firm surface, otherwise the firing pin will shoot across the room.

9. Remove the piston.

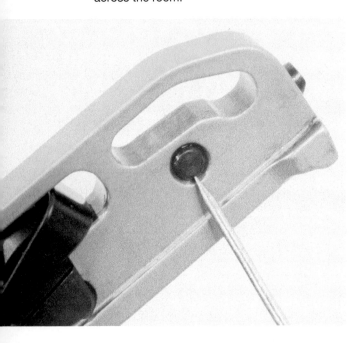

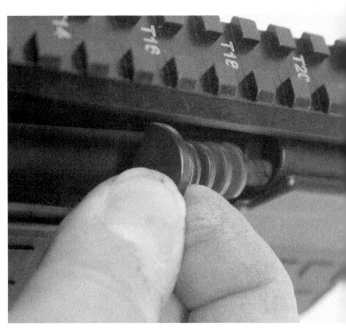

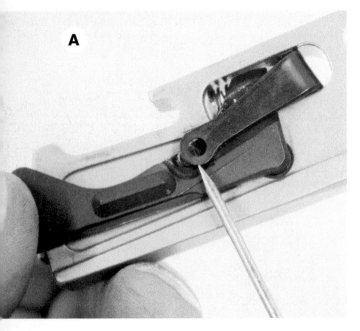

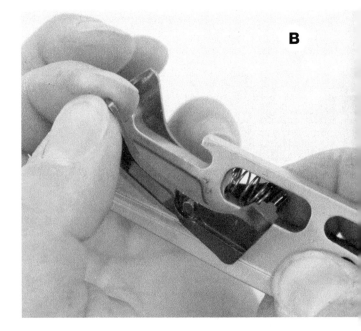

8. The extractor is removed by first displacing the extractor clamp spring from its pegs on the extractor (picture A), and then removing it from the bolt. The extractor (two pieces) can then be separated and removed, as well as the coil spring (picture B). It is best to leave the extractor fully assembled unless some part of it needs repair or replacement.

10. Push out the forward assembly pin at the front of the handguard, and the central assembly pin just forward of the safety lever.

12. Displace the ejection chute to the left until the front clears the barrel assembly, and pull the chute forward out of the action.

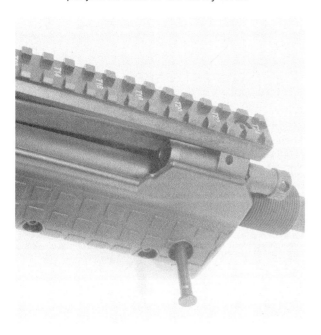

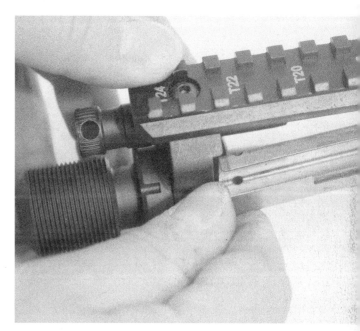

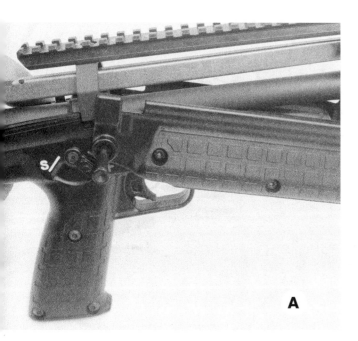

A

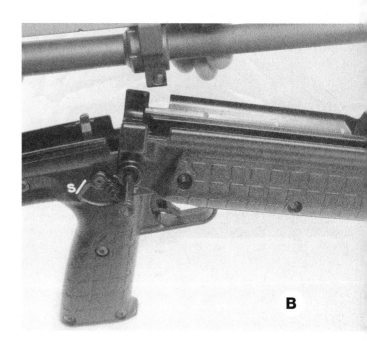

B

11. Rotate the front of the handguard down (picture A), then lift the barreled action from the stock (picture B).

13. The gas adjust can be fully removed by unscrewing it. The valve plunger (gas adjust detent) and spring above the gas adjust can be pulled forward out of their hole. The gas block itself, while retained by a large spring pin, should be left in place. Beware of the detent ejecting from its position, as it is under spring tension.

14. The flash hider can be removed by first loosening the jam nut and then unscrewing both from the barrel. Further disassembly of the barreled receiver should be done only in the factory.

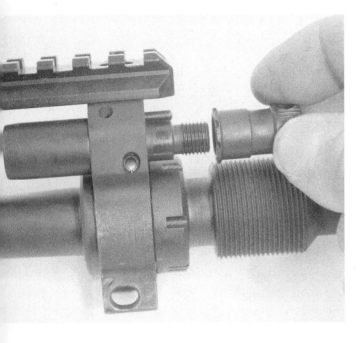

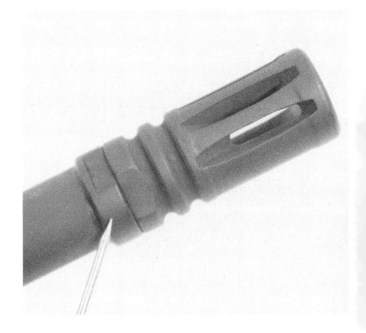

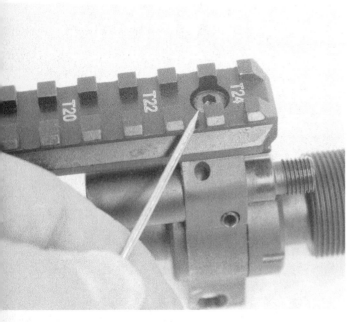

15. The optics rail can be removed, if necessary, by the removal of the two screws holding it to the barrel.

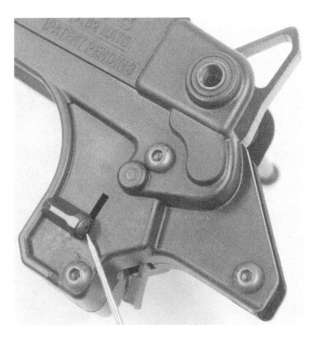

16. Remove the left side bolt catch button by removing this screw. Do the same on the right.

17. Take this screw out to remove the left side safety lever. Do the same on the right.

19. Remove the nine large screws from the left half of the grip frame. Then separate the grip frame halves.

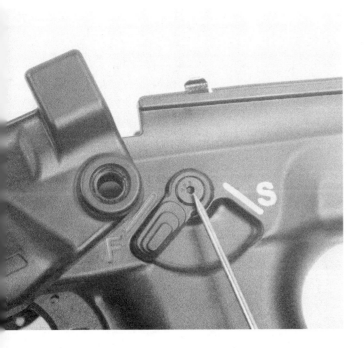

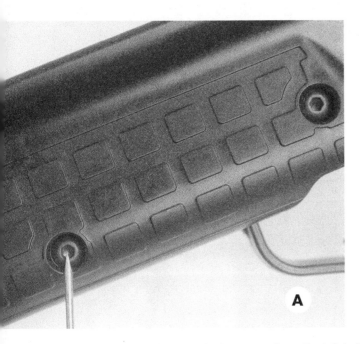

A

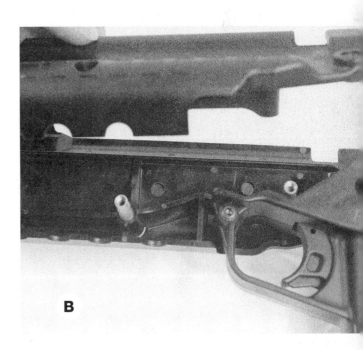

B

18. Remove the three large screws from the left half of the handguard (picture A). Lift the left side handguard off the right side. It is not necessary to remove the crosspins from the handguard.

20. Lift out the disconnector arm.

21. Lift out the sear trip and spring.

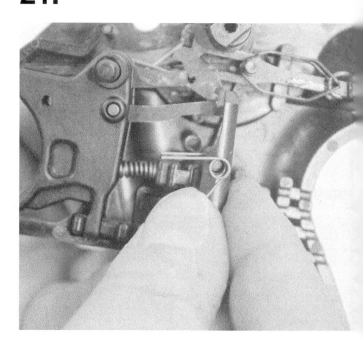

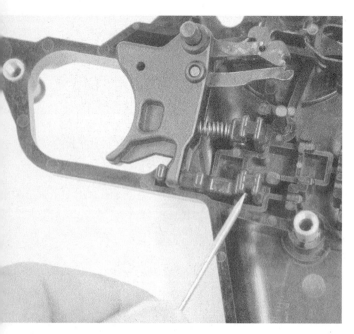

22. Remove the trigger stop and spring seat (and spring) from behind the trigger.

23. Pull out the trigger assembly.

24. The trigger bar and spring can be removed by pushing out this pin.

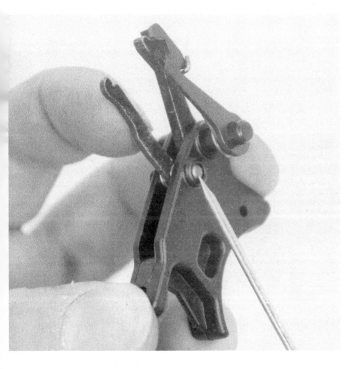

25. The sear and safety snap can be removed by pushing the trigger axis pin fully out of the trigger.

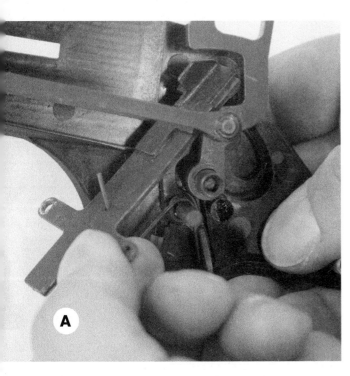

A

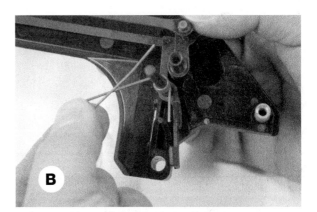

B

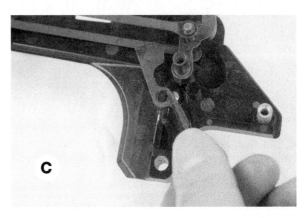

C

26. The bolt catch can be removed (picture A), and then the bolt catch spring with the pin (picture B), and the magazine catch (picture C).

27. Lift the entire hammer assembly out. The safety will now fall out of the remaining pistol grip frame. Disassembly of the hammer and bar assembly is not necessary for routine maintenance.

28. While not necessary for routine maintenance, the takedown pins can be removed from their bushings by first displacing this spring clip.

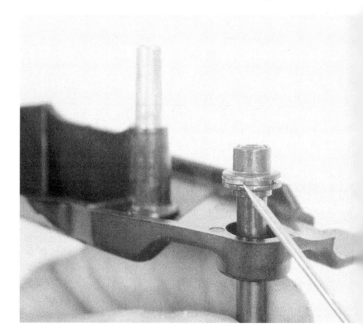

Reassembly Tips:

1. Reassembly of the grip frame is simplified by installing the internal parts first into the left side, as several pieces' spring seats are located on the left grip frame.

Kel-Tec SUB-2000

Data:	Kel-Tec SUB-2000
Origin:	United States
Manufacturer:	Kel-Tec CNC Industries, Cocoa, Florida
Cartridge:	9 x 19mm (9mm Luger)
Magazine capacity:	10, 15, or 20 rounds
Overall length:	30 inches
Barrel length:	16 inches
Weight:	4 pounds

The SUB-2000 arrived in 2001, and replaced the SUB-9 in the Kel-Tec line. The labor-intensive SUB-9 was quite pricey, and the SUB-2000 more affordable. Like the SUB-9, the SUB-2000 is "foldable," reducing the overall length to just sixteen inches. A version in 40 S&W chambering is also offered.

Detail Strip:

1. Remove the magazine, and cycle the action to cock the internal hammer. With the manual safety in on-safe position and the bolt closed, push out the large cross pin at the rear until it stops.

2. Move the bolt assembly all the way to the rear, and remove the buffer/endpiece.

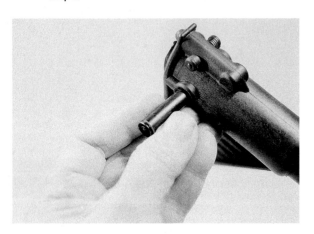

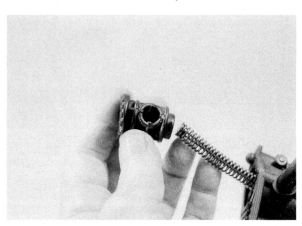

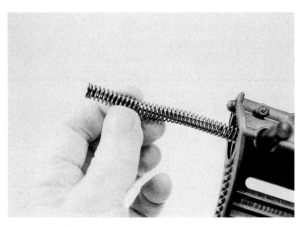

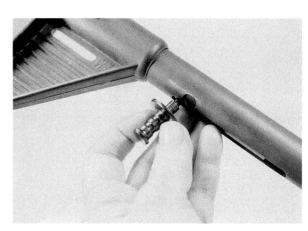

3. Remove the recoil spring assembly.

4. Remove the bolt handle.

5. Remove the bolt and bolt tube assembly.

6. Separate the bolt head from the bolt tube.

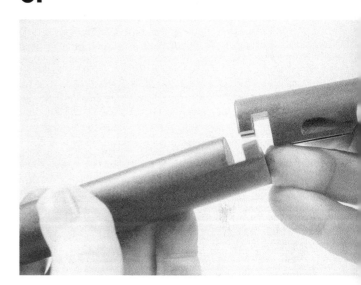

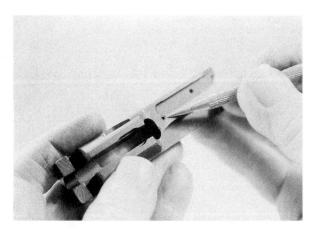

7. The firing pin and its return spring are retained by a vertical roll-type pin. CAUTION: The return spring is strong. Control the parts.

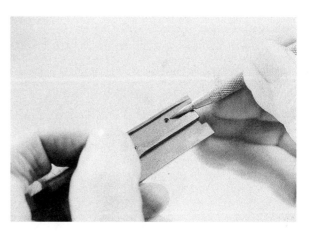

8. The extractor and its coil spring are retained by a vertical roll-pin.

9. If extensive cleaning makes it necessary to take off the two sides of the fore-grip, there are six screws on each side, twelve in all, and six internal spacer-nuts. Obviously, this should be done only in an instance of mud immersion.

10. The receiver can be disassembled, but the factory warns against doing this, and so do I. There is an inter-dependence of springs and parts, no through-pins, and other considerations. In the unlikely event that there is a problem, send it to Kel-Tec.

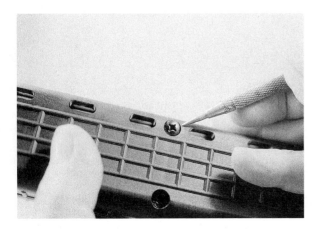

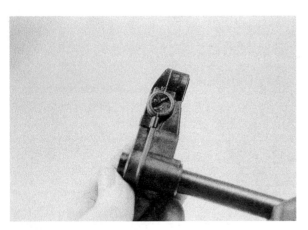

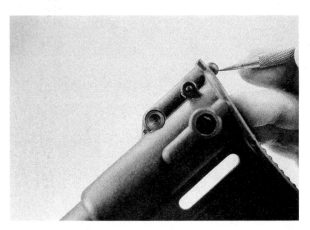

11. This advice also applies to the front sight unit.

12. The safety lock and the stock snap unit are not routinely removable.

13. If necessary for repair, the takedown cross pin can be taken out by depressing its lockspring.

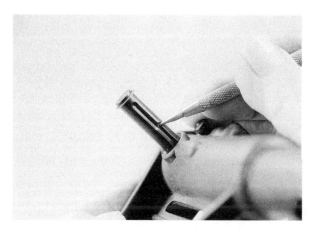

Reassembly Tips:

1. In some SUB-2000 guns, the cocked hammer may stop the bolt as it is re-inserted. If so, use a tool, through the ejection port, to slightly depress the hammer as the bolt is moved forward.

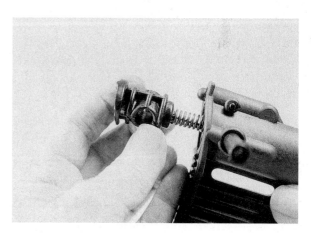

2. When installing the recoil spring and buffer, be sure the rear tip of the spring assembly is seated properly in its recess in the buffer.

Kel-Tec SU-16

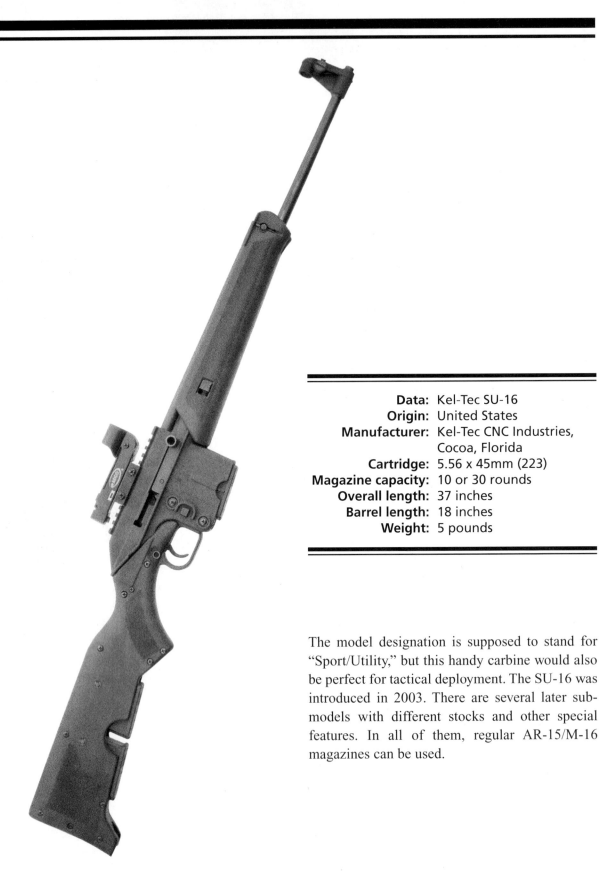

Data:	Kel-Tec SU-16
Origin:	United States
Manufacturer:	Kel-Tec CNC Industries, Cocoa, Florida
Cartridge:	5.56 x 45mm (223)
Magazine capacity:	10 or 30 rounds
Overall length:	37 inches
Barrel length:	18 inches
Weight:	5 pounds

The model designation is supposed to stand for "Sport/Utility," but this handy carbine would also be perfect for tactical deployment. The SU-16 was introduced in 2003. There are several later sub-models with different stocks and other special features. In all of them, regular AR-15/M-16 magazines can be used.

Detail Strip:

1. Remove the magazine, cycle the action to cock the internal hammer, and set the manual safety in on-safe position. Push the opposed fore-grip latches rearward and allow the combination fore-grip and bipod to swing down and forward.

2. Push out the assembly pin, and turn the buttstock unit down and toward the front.

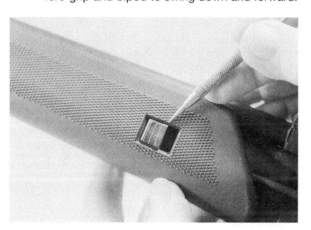

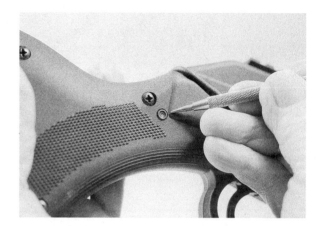

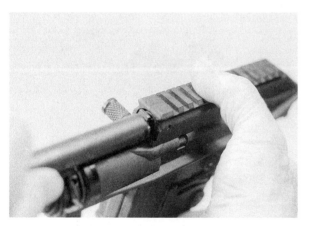

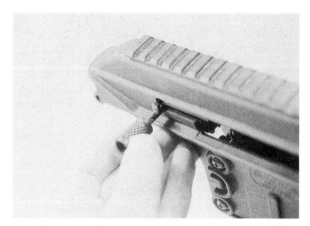

3. Pull the recoil spring tube forward, and turn it to bring the locking lug to the top, as shown. When eased back, the tube will enter the receiver to a depth of about a quarter-inch.

4. Move the tube and bolt assembly all the way to the rear, and move the rear part slightly downward to align the bolt handle with its exit track. Remove the bolt handle.

5. Tip the bolt and tube assembly downward at the rear, and take the unit out of the receiver.

6. Push out the firing pin retainer.

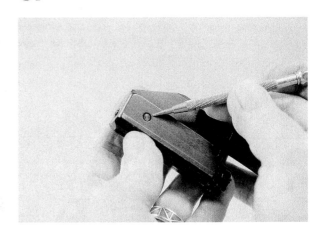

7. Remove the firing pin.

8. Remove the bolt cam piece.

9. Remove the bolt from the carrier.

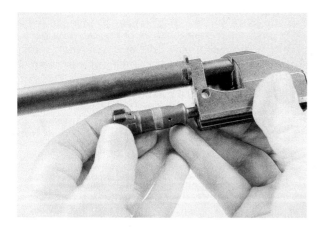

10. If the extractor needs to be removed for repair purposes, drifting out this pin will release the extractor, its coil spring, and a small buffer.

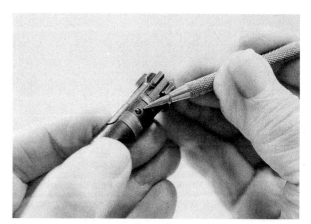

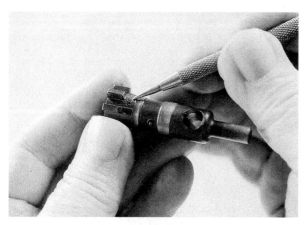

11. The ejector and its coil spring are retained by this roll-type pin. CAUTION: This strong spring is compressed, so take care to control the parts.

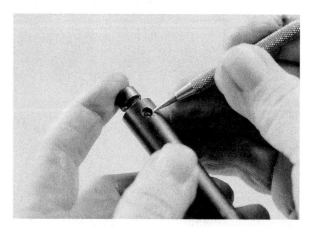

12. Turn the tube to align the hole with the pin that retains the piston head. CAUTION: When this pin is pushed out, the piston head and the powerful recoil spring will be released. Control the piston, and keep the unit pointed away from you.

13. Ease out the piston and spring, and remove the tube.

14. The buttstock unit, which contains the trigger and hammer system, is composed of two sides that are held together by 18 opposed Phillips screws. There are also several internal spacers, and the pivot pins for the parts are not through-pins. It is, of course, possible to disassemble this unit, but reassembly would be quite a challenge. If there is a problem, it would be best to return it to Kel-Tec. This also applies, for the same reason, to the receiver.

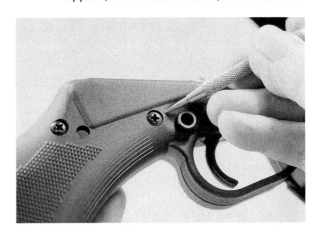

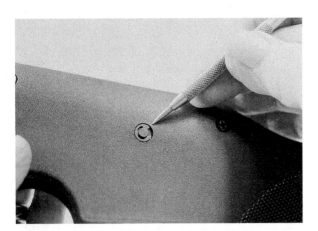

15. If the magazine retainers in the buttstock need to be replaced, prying out the C-clips will release them for removal inward, along with their circular springs. Note that the front and rear "snap-pins" are of different lengths.

16. If the fore-grip/bipod sides have to be removed, first detach the torsion spring from its recesses.

17. With one of the fore-grip pieces in the position shown, flex it slightly to clear the lower tip of the lock pin from its recess, and use a sharp tool to nudge the pin out downward. The head of the cross-piece is ball-shaped, and after the pin is removed the side can be snapped off. This will free the cross-piece and the opposite fore-grip.

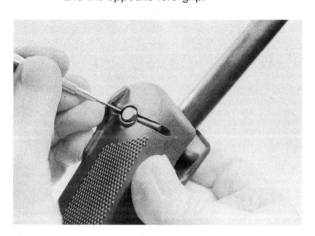

18. The gas piston head is retained by a roll-pin, and the head is removed toward the rear. Removal should be for repair only. The large roll-pin below retains the housing on the barrel, and this unit is not removed in normal takedown.

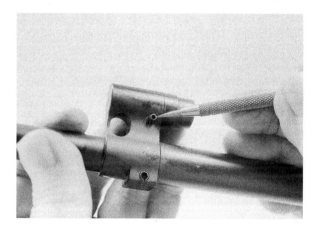

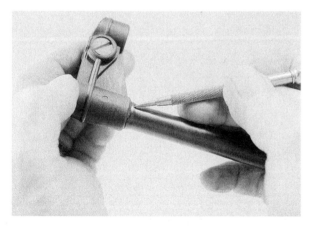

19. The front sight unit is a press-lock fit on the barrel, and it is removed toward the front. Some damage to the polymer is inevitable, and this should be done only for repair purposes.

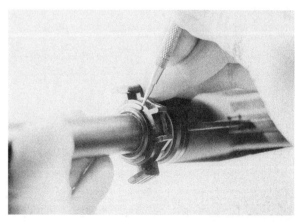

20. If the fore-grip latch or its spring have to be replaced, these parts are retained by a large C-clip. However, removal would require that the piston housing and the front sight are first taken off.

Reassembly Tips:

1. When the piston and recoil spring unit is reassembled, use a tapered drift to align all of the holes for reinsertion of the pin. CAUTION: Control the spring.

2. When the piston and bolt unit is put back into the receiver, be sure the locking lug is on top, as shown. Also, the bolt must be forward in the carrier, to clear its side lug.

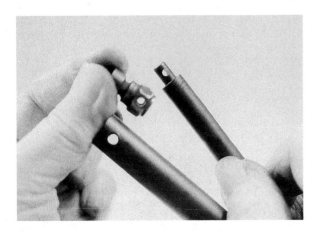
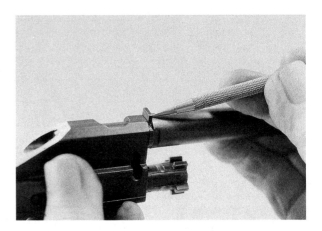

Marlin Model 9

Similar/Identical Pattern Guns

The same basic assembly/disassembly steps for the Marlin Model 9 also apply to the following gun:

Marlin Model 45

Data:	Marlin Model 9
Origin:	United States
Manufacturer:	Marlin Firearms
	North Haven, Connecticut
Cartridge:	9mm Parabellum
Magazine capacity:	12 rounds
Overall length:	35-1/2 inches
Barrel length:	16-1/2 inches
Weight:	6-3/4 pounds

This handy "Camp Carbine" was introduced in 1985, and the following year the Marlin company brought out a version in 45 ACP, that one having a seven-round single-row magazine. Except for the dimensional differences to accommodate the larger round, the 45 version is essentially the same as the 9mm, and the instructions will apply.

Disassembly:

1. Remove the magazine. Back out the screws at the front and rear of the magazine housing/trigger guard unit. These are captive screws.

2. Remove the action from the stock

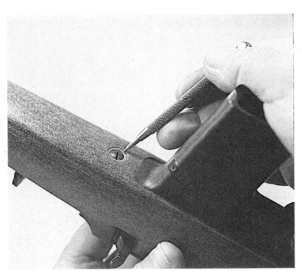

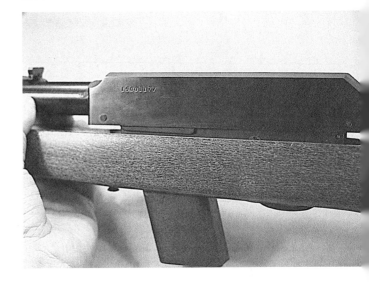

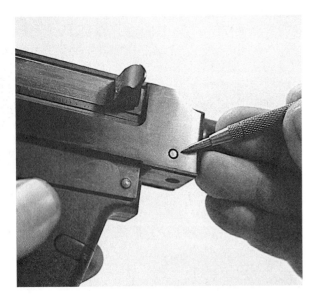

3. Drift out the cross pins at front and rear, at the lower edge of the receiver. The forward cross pin must be pushed out toward the left.

4. Remove the trigger guard/magazine housing downward. Note that the bolt hold open latch will also be released on the left side at the lower edge of the receiver.

5. Remove the hold open latch spring from its recess in the lower edge of the receiver.

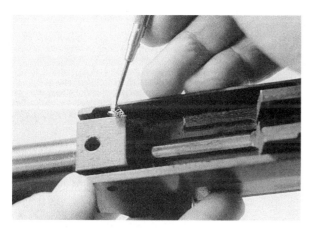

6. Move the bolt slightly to the rear, lift it at the front, and remove the cocking handle

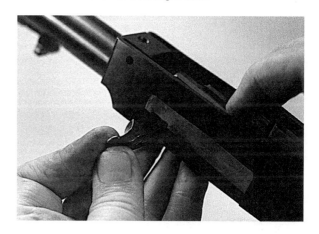

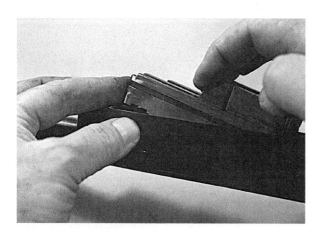

7. Continue lifting the bolt at the front until it will clear, and ease it out toward the front. Control the recoil spring tension.

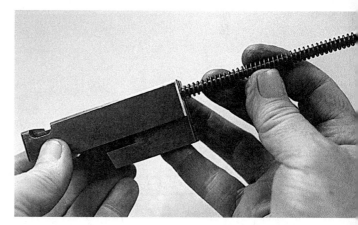

8. Remove the recoil spring and its guide from the rear of the bolt.

9. The firing pin and its return spring are retained in the bolt by a vertical pin, which is driven out upward.

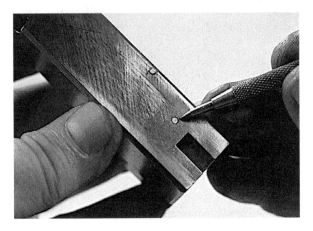

10. The extractor is pivoted and retained by a vertical pin, which is driven out upward.

11. Remove the extractor toward the right, and take out the coil extractor spring from it recess.

12. The loaded chamber indicator and its coil spring are also retained and pivoted by a vertical pin which is driven out upward.

13. If it is necessary to remove the polymer recoil buffer for replacement, it is pried out of its recess toward the front. On the barrel, the rear sight is dovetail-mounted, and the front sight is retained by two vertical screws.

14. Insert a small drift or a paper clip into the hole at the rear of the hammer spring strut, and ease the hammer down to fired position. This will trap the spring on the strut. Note that you will have to temporarily reinsert the magazine to lower the hammer.

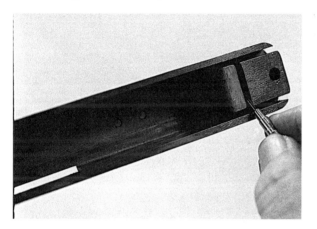

15. Remove the C-clip on the left tip of the hammer pivot.

16. Remove the sideplate.

17. Remove the trapped hammer spring, the strut, and spring base plate. If this unit is taken apart, use caution, as the spring is compressed.

18. Restrain the sear, and push on the hammer pivot to move the right sideplate off.

19. Remove the cartridge guide and its spring.

20. Remove the hammer.

21. Remove the sear from the to of the trigger, along with its spring.

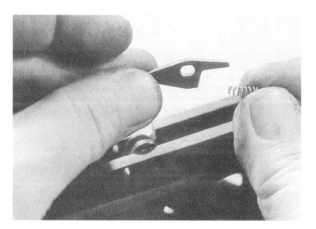

22. Tip the trigger upward at the front, moving it from under its spring at the rear, and remove it.

23. Push the safety out upward for removal. Keep a fingertip over the hole indicated, to arrest the safety positioning ball and spring.

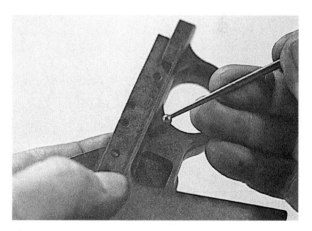

24. Use a magnetized tool to remove the safety ball and spring.

25. Depress the magazine safety at the front, and take out the trigger block lever.

26. The magazine safety and its spring are retained by the forward cross pin of the two ejector mounting pins. In normal takedown, this system is best left in place.

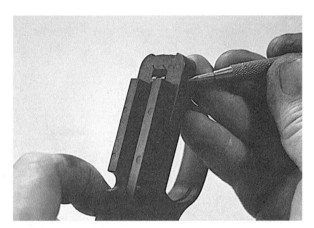

27. The trigger spring can be removed by drifting out the cross pin.

28. The magazine catch can be removed by unscrewing its slotted button. The button is then taken off toward the left with the spring, and the catch is taken off toward the right.

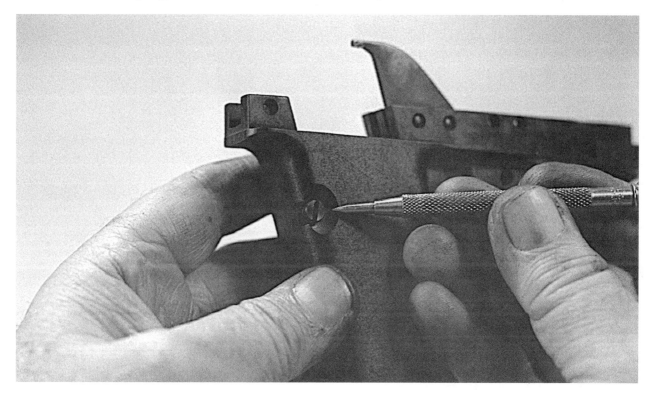

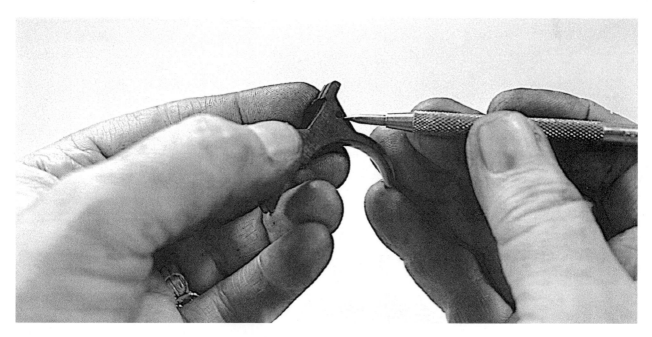

29. The sear/disconnector trip in the trigger, and its coil spring, can be removed by drifting out a small cross pin.

Reassembly Tips:

1. When reinstalling the safety, it will be necessary to insert a tool to depress the positioning ball and spring as the safety-lever is moved down into place.

2. When reinstalling the trigger, use a tool at the rear to lift the spring onto the rear of the trigger.

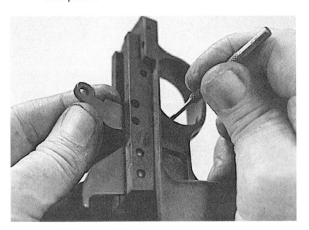

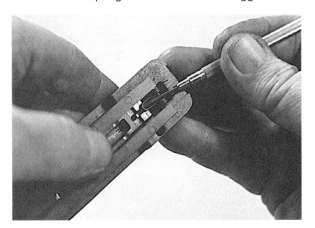

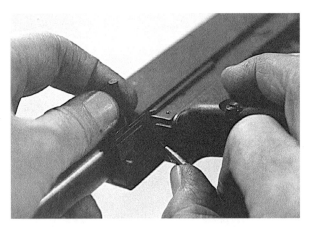

3. Remember that the bolt hold open and its spring must be installed before the lower housing is put back on the receiver.

4. As the trigger and magazine unit is put into place, the cartridge guide must be flexed slightly rearward to clear the edge of the receiver

When reassembling the trigger unit, the use of slave pins may be a help. However, with patience, it can be done without them.

When replacing the firing pin, extractor, and loaded chamber indicator on the bolt, remember that they are retained by splined pins that are drive in downward.

Ruger Mini-14

Similar/Identical Pattern Guns

The same basic assembly/disassembly steps for the Ruger Mini-14 also apply to the following guns:

Ruger Mini-14 Ranch Rifle
Ruger Mini Thirty

Data:	Ruger Mini-14
Origin:	United States
Manufacturer:	Sturm, Ruger & Company
	Southport, Connecticut
Cartridge:	223 Remington (5.56mm)
Magazine capacity:	5 rounds
Overall length:	37-1/4 inches
Barrel length:	18-1/2 inches
Weight:	6.4 pounds

While externally it may appear to be a miniature of the U.S. M-14 rifle, the Mini-14 is all Ruger on the inside. Introduced in 1973, this neat little carbine has gained wide acceptance both as a sporting gun and in police and guard applications. There has been one small change in the original design—a bolt hold-open button was added on the top left side of the receiver, and all guns of more recent manufacture will have this feature. The Ruger Mini Thirty in 7.62x39 and the Ruger Ranch Rifle are mechanically the same.

Disassembly:

1. Remove the magazine, and cycle the action to cock the internal hammer. Push the safety back to the on-safe position, and insert a on-marring tool through the hole at the rear of the trigger guard to spring the guard downward at the rear. Swing the guard toward the front until it s tops.

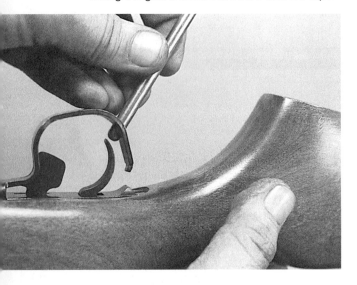

2. Remove the trigger housing downward.

3. Tip the rear of the action upward out of the stock, and remove it toward the front.

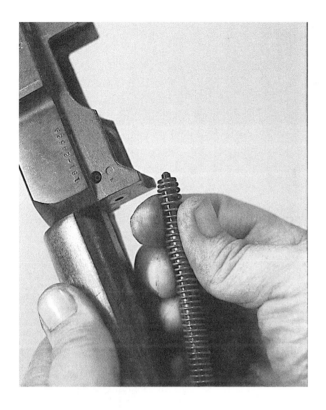

4. Grasp the recoil spring firmly at the rear, where it joins the receiver, and lift the tip of the guide out of its hole in the front of the receiver. **Caution:** *This is a strong spring, so keep it under control.* Tilt the spring and guide upward, slowly release the tension, and remove the spring and guide toward the rear.

5. Move the slide assembly toward the rear until its rear lug aligns with the exit cut in the slide track, and move the operating handle upward and toward the right. Remove the slide assembly.

6. Move the bolt forward to the position shown, and remove it upward and toward the right. The bolt must be turned to align the underlug of the firing pin with the exit cut in the bottom of the bolt track.

7. In normal takedown, the gas block assembly should not be removed. If it is necessary, use an Allen wrench to remove the four vertical screws, separating the upper and lower sections of the gas block. The gas port bushing will be freed with removal of the lower block, so take care that it isn't lost.

8. Slide the bolt hold-open cover downward out of its slots in the receiver and remove it.

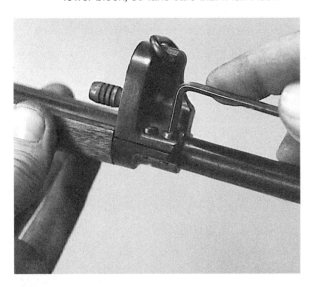

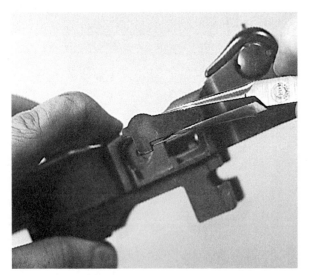

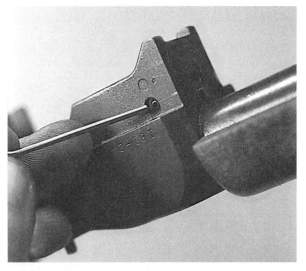

9. Depress the bolt latch plunger on top of the left receiver rail, and lift the bolt lock out of its recess toward the left. **Caution:** *The bolt latch retains the plunger, so control the plunger and ease it out upward, along with its spring.*

10. The front magazine catch, located in the front of the receiver below the barrel, is retained by a roll cross pin, accessible through holes on each side. Drift out the cross pin, and remove the catch toward the front.

11. Insert a small screwdriver beside the extractor plunger, and turn and tip the screwdriver to depress the plunger. Move the extractor upward out of its recess. **Caution:** *As the extractor post clears the ejector it will be released, so restrain the ejector and ease it out toward the front. Also take care to keep the extractor plunger under control, and ease it out.* Removal of the extractor will also free the firing pin to be taken out toward the rear.

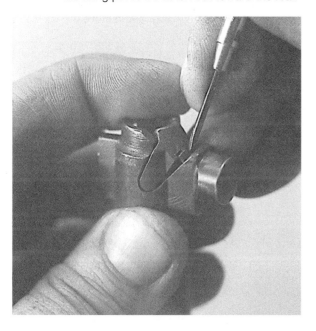

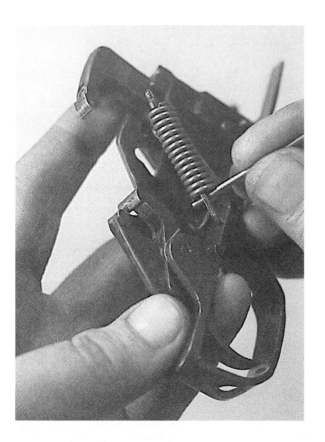

12. Close and latch the trigger guard, and insert a piece of rod or a drift punch through the hole in the rear tip of the hammer spring guide.

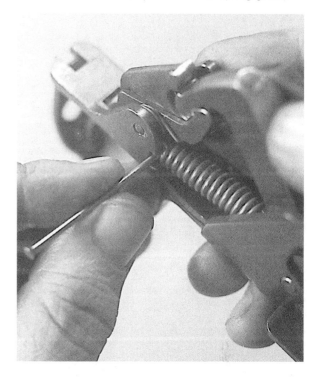

13. Restrain the hammer, move the safety to the off-safe position, and pull the trigger to release the hammer. The rod will trap the hammer spring on the guide. Tip the front of the guide upward, out of its recess at the rear of the hammer, and remove the guide assembly toward the right. If the spring is to be taken off the guide, proceed with care, as the spring is fully compressed.

14. Push out the hammer pivot, and remove the hammer upward and toward the right.

15. Move the safety back to the on-safe position, and take off the trigger guard downward and toward the rear.

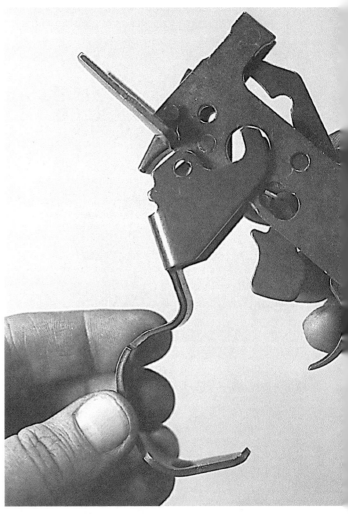

16. Drift out the safety spring pin toward the left, ease the spring tension slowly, and move the spring toward the rear, unhooking it from the safety. Remove the spring toward the right rear.

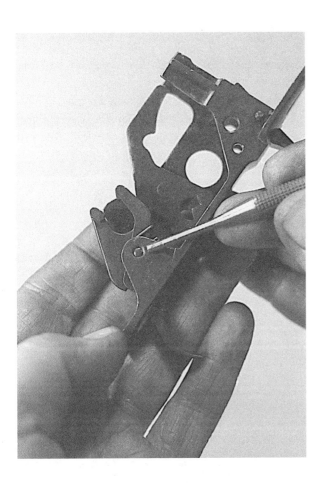

17. Restrain the trigger and sear assembly, and drift out the trigger cross pin.

18. Remove the trigger and sear assembly upward.

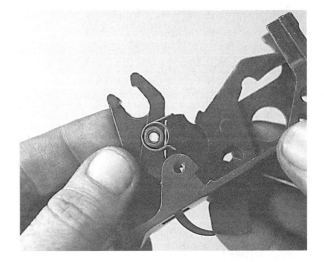

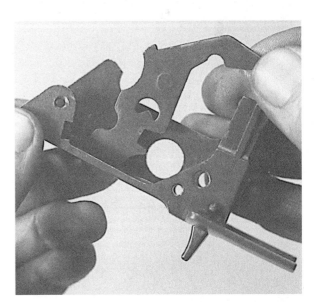

19. The trigger spring is easily detached from the trigger and the pivot bushing can be drifted out to free the secondary sear and its coil spring from the top of the trigger. **Caution:** *Use a roll pin punch to avoid damaging the bushing, and take care to restrain the sear against the tension of its spring.*

20. Tip the upper portion of the safety catch toward the right, moving its pivot stud out of its hole in the trigger housing, and remove the safety upward.

21. The main magazine catch is retained by a cross pin at the front of the trigger housing, and the pin must be drifted out toward the left. **Caution:** *The strong magazine catch spring will also be released when the pin is removed, so insert a shop cloth into the housing behind the spring to catch it.* This spring is rather difficult to reinstall, so if removal is not necessary for repair, the catch is best left in place.

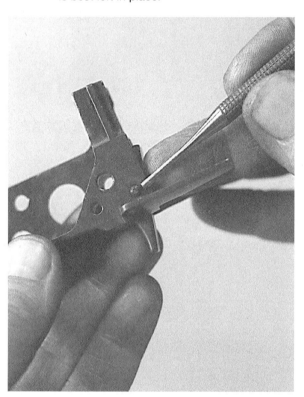

Reassembly Tips:

1. When installing the trigger and sear assembly, tilt the assembly forward, and be sure the front hooks of the trigger spring engage the top of the cross piece in the housing. Push the assembly downward and toward the rear until the cross pin can be inserted.

When replacing the safety spring, be sure that its front arm goes on the right side of the rear arm of the magazine catch spring. Otherwise, the safety spring pin cannot be fully inserted.

Russian AK-47

Similar/Identical Pattern Guns

The same basic assembly/disassembly steps for the Russian AK-47 also apply to the following guns:

American Arms AKY-39	**American Arms AKF-39**
American Arms AKC-47	**Egyptian Maadi AK-47**
Mitchell Arms AK-47	**Mitchell Arms AK-47 Heavy Barrel**
Norinco Type 84S AK	**Poly Tech AKS-47S**
Poly Tech AKS-762	**Valmet Model 62**
Valmet Model 71	**Valmet Model 78**

Data:	Russian AK-47
Origin:	U.S.S.R.
Manufacturer:	Russian arsenals, and factories in China, Egypt, Yugoslavia, and other satellite nations.
Cartridge:	7.62x39 Russian
Magazine capacity:	30 rounds
Overall length:	34.65 inches
Barrel length:	16.34 inches
Weight:	9.40 pounds

The Avtomat Kalashnikov was adopted in 1947 as the standard Russian military rifle. It has also been produced in large quantities by various Eastern-bloc nations, as well as in civilian versions in other countries. While there are slight variations in some of the non-Russian versions, there are no major mechanical differences that would affect the takedown. The gun shown here was made by the Maadi factory in Egypt.

Disassembly:

1. Remove the magazine. Cycle the action to cock the internal hammer. Push in the takedown latch at the rear of the receiver cover, and left the cover at the rear. Take off the cover toward the rear.

2. Keeping the spring under control, push the guide forward out of its mount in the receiver, lift it up slightly, and remove the guide and spring toward the rear. The captive recoil spring and its linked internal guide are not routinely dismountable.

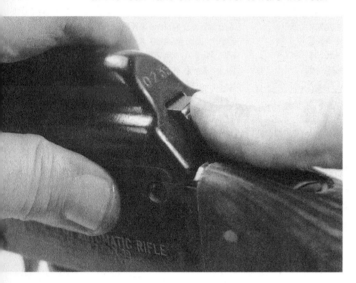

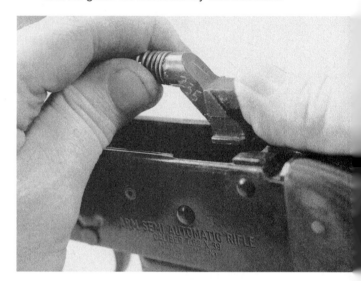

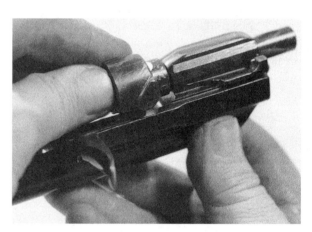

3. Pull the bolt assembly all the way to the rear. It will be forced upward, out of its exit cuts, by the hammer spring tension. Remove the bolt assembly upward and toward the rear.

4. Note that the gas piston is attached to the bolt carrier by a large cross pin. In Normal takedown this is best left in place. Move the bolt all the way to the rear in the carrier, and turn it counterclockwise, front view, until its cam lug is clear of its track in the carrier, as shown.

5. Remove the bolt toward the front.

6. Drift out the retaining cross pin, and remove the firing pin toward the rear.

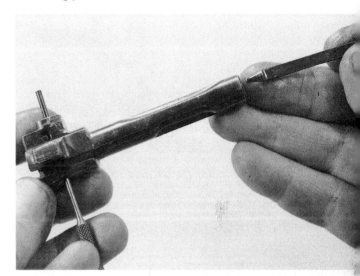

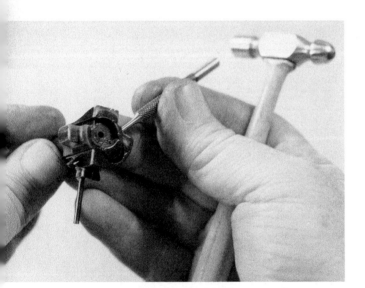

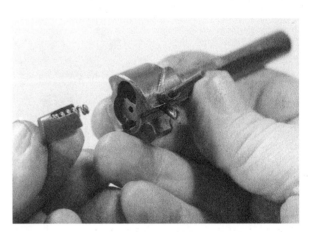

7. Drift out the extractor retaining pin in the direction of the cam lug. Note that this can be done only after removal of the firing pin retaining pin, as it crosses the beveled head of the extractor pin.

8. Remove the extractor and its spring.

9. Turn the gas tube latch up to the position shown.

10. Lift the gas tube assembly at the rear, and take it off rearward. In normal takedown, the tube and handguard are not separated.

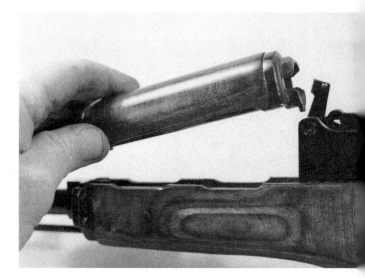

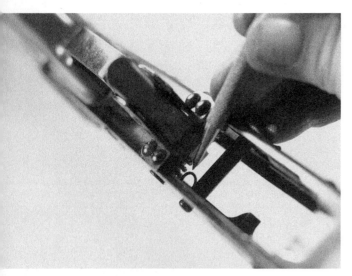

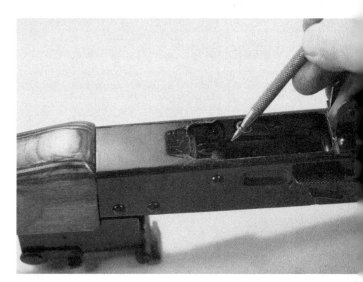

11. Inside the magazine opening on the left side is the loop of the pin retaining spring. This spring arches over a groove in the hammer pin, and goes under a groove in the trigger pin.

12. Insert a tool in the loop, and pull the spring out toward the front.

13. Push out the trigger pin toward the left.

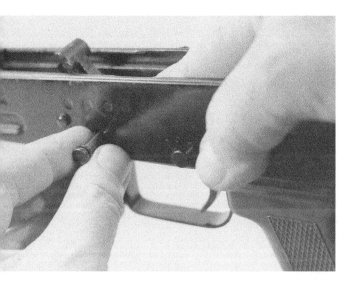

14. Move the trigger forward, past the ends of the hammer spring, and remove the assembly upward.

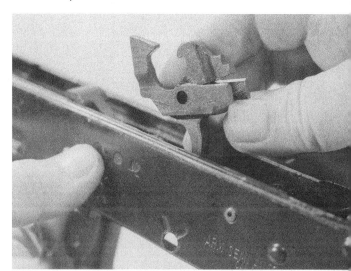

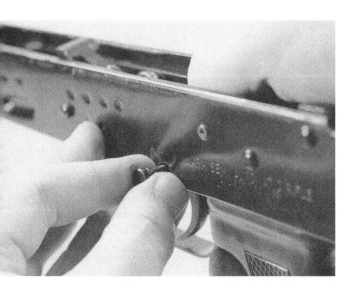

15. Push out the hammer pin toward the left. Control the hammer and its spring. Turn the hammer and spring assembly in either direction, and remove it upward. The hammer must be moved rearward during this operation, to clear the side rails inside the receiver.

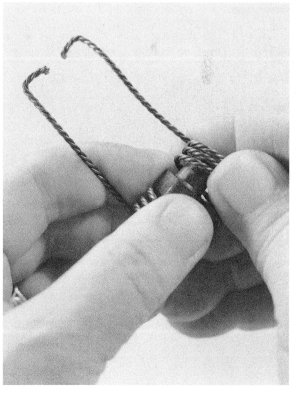

16. If necessary for repair, the hammer spring can be sprung off the side posts for removal.

17. Turn the safety-lever up to vertical position, as shown, and remove it toward the right.

18. The magazine catch and its torsion spring are retained by a cross pin. The pin is heavily riveted and removal should be only for repair.

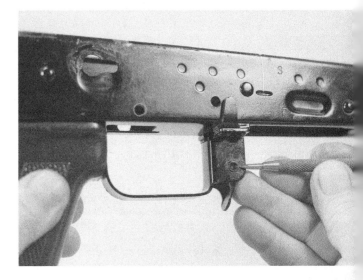

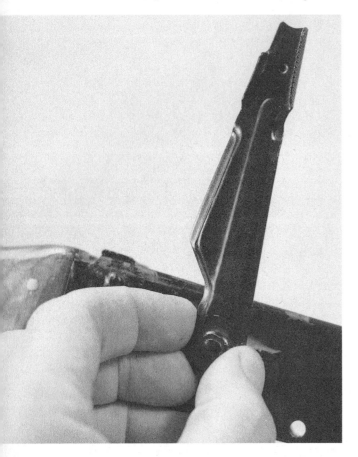

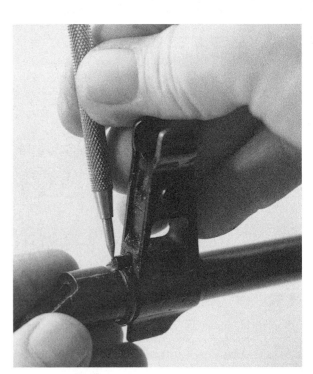

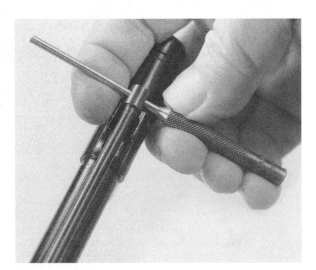

20. If removal of the muzzlebrake is necessary, depress the plunger and unscrew the muzzlebrake clockwise, front view (a reverse thread). If the front sight and its base are to be removed they are retained by two cross pins.

19. Insert a tool in the hole in the read of the cleaning rod, lift it out of its recess, and remove it toward the front.

21. Turn the forend latch over to the position shown, and move the forend cap forward until it clears the wood. If it is tight, it may be necessary to nudge it with a non-marring tool.

22. Move the forend forward, and take it off downward.

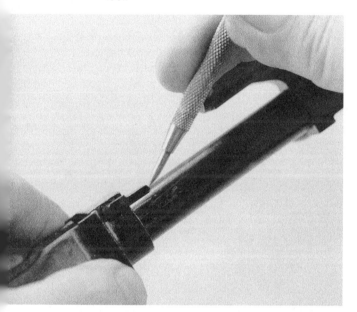

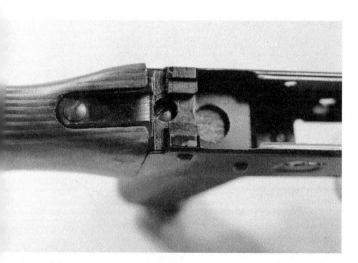

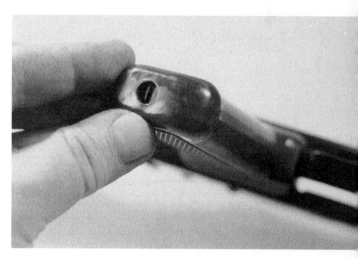

23. The buttstock assembly is retained by two vertical screws at the rear of the receiver.

24. The pistol grip is retained by a single through-bolt.

25. A spring-powered trap door in the buttplate is pushed inward to release a container of cleaning equipment. The buttplate is retained by two screws.

Reassembly Tips:

When the hammer and trigger are reinstalled, be sure the rear tips of the hammer spring are hooked into the top of the trigger.

When replacing the pin lock spring, be sure its small arched area goes over the hammer pin, and its rear tip goes under the trigger pin, engaging the grooves in the pins.

1. When reassembling the bolt, remember that the extractor pin must be oriented so its beveled head will allow passage of the firing pin retaining pin.

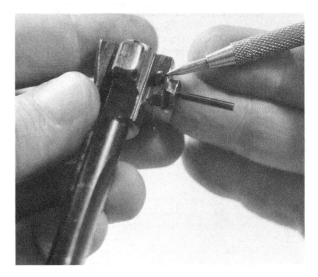

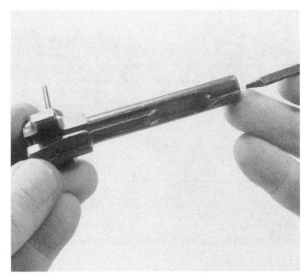

2. When reinstalling the firing pin, note that it has a sloped area near the front, and also a more vertical step on the opposite side. The vertical cut, nearer the tip, must align with the retaining cross pin.

Russian SKS (Simonov)

Similar/Identical Pattern Guns

The same basic assembly/disassembly steps for the Russian SKS (Simonov) also apply to the following guns.

Chinese Type 56   **Yugoslavian Model 59/66**

Data:	Russian SKS (Simonov)
Origin:	Russia
Manufacturer:	Russian arsenals, and factories in China and other satellite nations
Cartridge:	7.62x39mm Russian
Magazine capacity:	10 rounds
Overall length:	40.2 inches
Barrel length:	20.47 inches
Weight:	8.5 pounds

Introduced in 1945, the Samozaryadnyi Karabin Simonova (SKS) was the first rifle chambered for the then-new 7.62mm "short" cartridge. The gun was made in large quantity, and it has been used at some time by every communist country in the world. Versions of it have been made in China, Yugoslavia, and elsewhere. While some of these variations may be different in small details, the mechanism is the same, and the instructions will apply.

Disassembly:

1. Cycle the action to cock the internal hammer. Turn the takedown latch up to vertical position, and pull it out toward the right until it stops. Take off the receiver cover toward the rear.

2. Move the bolt and recoil spring assembly back until it stops, and lift it off the receiver.

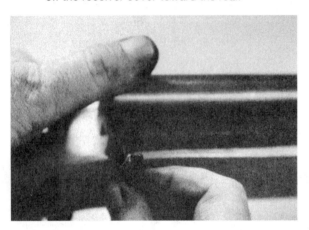

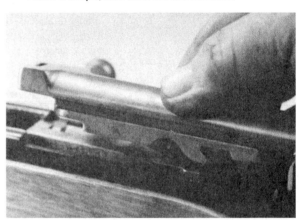

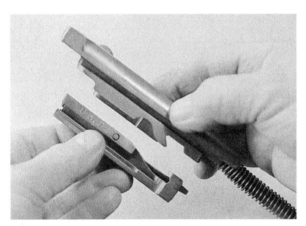

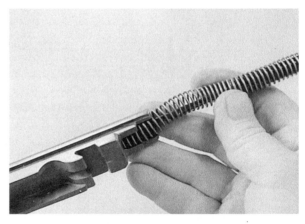

3. The bolt will probably be left in the receiver when the carrier and recoil spring unit are removed. If not, the bolt is simply lifted out of the carrier.

4. The captive recoil spring assembly is removed from the bolt carrier toward the rear.

5. If it is necessary to dismantle the spring assembly, rest the rear tip on a firm surface, pull back the spring at the front, and move the collar downward until it clears the button and take it off to the side. **Caution:** *Control the spring.*

6. Push out the firing pin retainer toward the right.

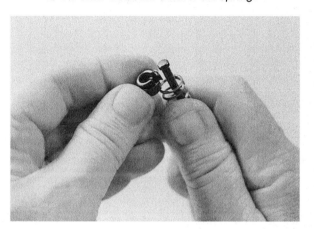

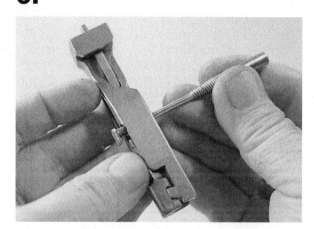

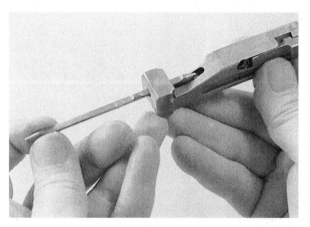

7. Remove the firing pin toward the rear.

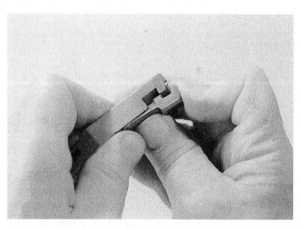

8. Push the extractor toward the rear, and tip it out toward the right for removal. The spring is mounted inside the rear of the extractor, and it will come off with it.

9. The takedown latch is retained by an internal cross pin. In normal takedown, it is best left in place. To get the latch out of the way for the remainder of takedown, push it back into its locked position.

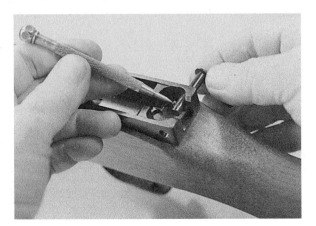

10. Insert a drift through the hole in the head of the cleaning rod. Lift it out of its locking recess, and remove it toward the front.

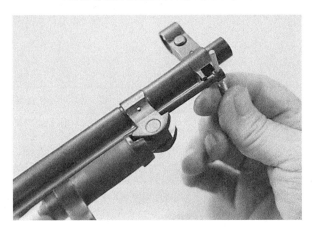

11. The bayonet hinge is often riveted in place. If removal is not necessary for repair, it is best left in place.

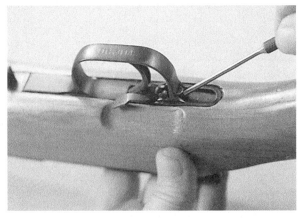

12. Be sure the internal hammer is in cocked position, and set the manual safety in on-safe position. Use a bullet rip or a suitable tool to push the guard latch forward.

13. When the latch releases, the guard will jump out slightly. Tip the guard away from the stock, move it toward the rear, and remove the guard unit.

14. Release the safety. Depress the disconnector, at the front of the hammer, about half way. Control the hammer, and pull the trigger. Ease the hammer down to fired position. Caution: The hammer spring is powerful.

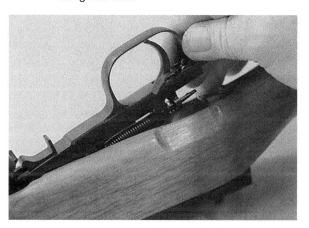

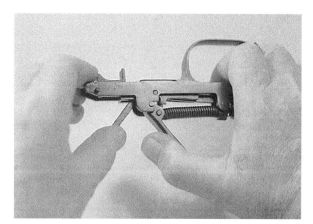

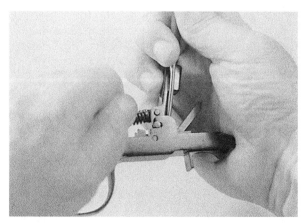

15. Insert a sturdy drift in front of the hammer, and lever it toward the rear until its pivot studs are clear of the hooks on the unit. **Caution:** *Keep a good grip on the hammer.* When it is clear, take off the hammer and its spring and guide. Another method is to grip the unit in a padded vise and use a bar of metal to apply pressure to the front of the hammer.

16. The trigger spring can be removed by gripping a forward coil with sharp-nosed pliers and compressing it slightly rearward, then tipping it out.

17. Pushing out the cross pin will free the disconnector for removal upward.

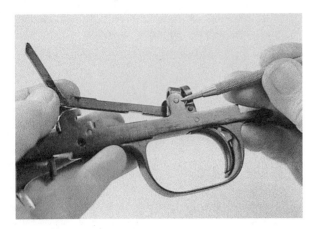

18. Removal of this cross pin will allow the rebound disconnector to be taken out.

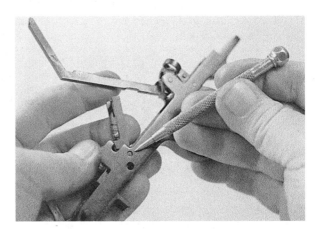

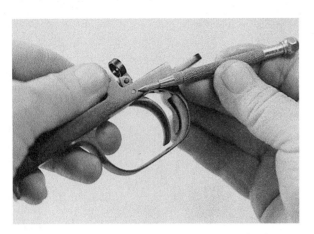

19. Drift out the trigger cross pin, and take out the trigger upward. The safety spring will also be freed for removal.

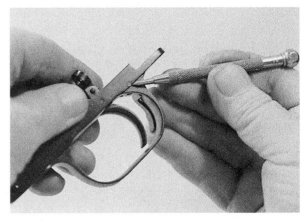

20. Drift out the safety-lever pin, and remove the safety.

21. This cross pin at the front of the trigger guard assembly retains the magazine catch, the combination spring , and the sear.

22. The trigger guard spring can be lifted out of its well in the stock.

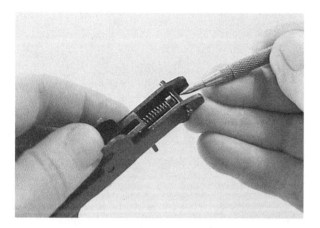

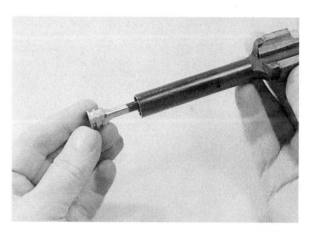

23. With a bullet tip or a non-marring tool, turn the handguard latch upward until it is stopped by its lower stud in the track. Lift the handguard and gas cylinder assembly at the rear, and remove it.

24. Remove the gas piston from the cylinder.

25. The gas port unit is retained on the barrel by a cross pin. In normal takedown, it is left in place.

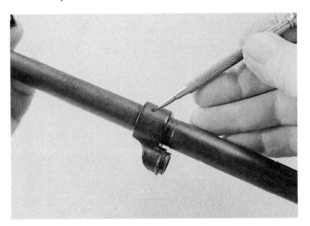

26. Drift out the stock end cap cross pin. Use a non-marring tool to nudge the end cap slightly forward.

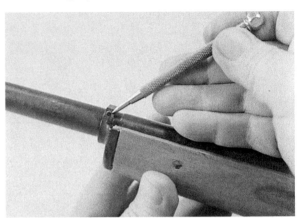

27. Grip the magazine assembly, and pull it rearward and downward for removal.

28. Remove the action from the stock.

29. The rear sight assembly is retained on the barrel by a cross pin, and is driven off toward the front. In normal takedown, the unit is left in place.

30. Drifting out this cross pin will allow removal of the bolt hold-open latch and its coil spring downward.

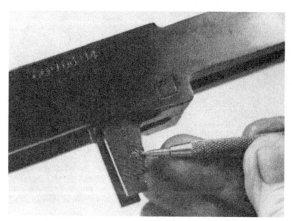

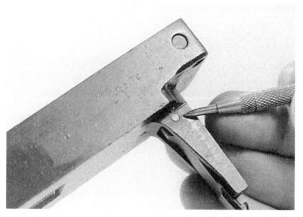

31. The trigger guard latch, which is its own spring, is retained by a cross pin. After removal of the pin, the latch is driven out downward.

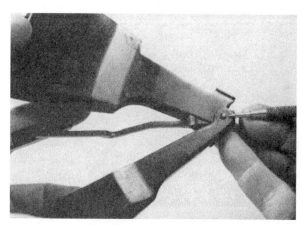

32. The magazine, the follower and its spring, and the magazine cover are joined by a cross pin at the front. The pin is riveted on both sides, and removal should be only for repair.

Reassembly Tips:

1. When the stock end piece has been nudged back into position, insert a drift to align the hole with the barrel groove.

2. For those who have disassembled the trigger group, here is a view of that unit with all of the parts properly installed.

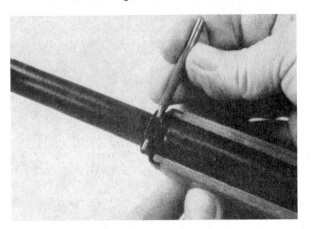

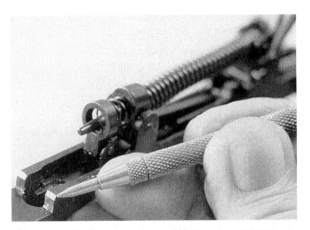

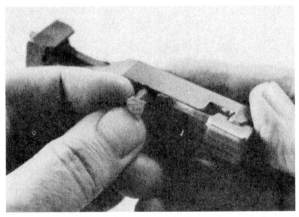

3. When replacing the trigger group in the gun, extremely sharp shoulders at the rear of the sub-frame may cause a seating problem. These can be easily beveled, as shown, with a file. Note: For installation of the trigger group, the manual safety must be in on-safe position. Rest the top of the receiver on a firm surface as the guard unit is pressed into place.

4. When replacing the firing pin in the bolt, be sure the retaining shoulder is on top. Also, be sure the retainer is oriented to fit into its recess on the right side.

SIG SAUER 551 A1

Similar/Identical Pattern Guns

The same basic assembly/disassembly steps for the SIG SAUER 551 A1 also apply to the following guns:

SIG 550

SIG 551

SIG 552

SIG 553

SIG SAUER 556

Data:	SIG SAUER 551 A1
Origin:	United States
Manufacturer:	SIG SAUER, Inc., Exeter, NH
Cartridge:	5.56x45 mm
Magazine capacity:	30 rounds
Over-all length:	36.1 inches
Barrel length:	16 inches
Weight:	7 pounds

The Sig 551 A1 is an almost direct copy of the Sig 550 series of rifles in service with the Swiss military. The main differences from the parent design are a Picatinny style optic rail mounted to the top of the receiver, the lack of a folding bipod, and of course, the lack of fully automatic functionality. Otherwise it is the same rifle and takedown procedures will be very similar. The 556 models will also closely follow the pattern, however the 556 series uses AR-15 magazines where the 551 uses the 550 series of translucent plastic magazines. The 550 series was never largely present in the US until the 556 series and 551 A1 began production domestically, however the rest of the 550 series may occasionally be encountered with police agencies.

Disassembly:

1. Push out the takedown pin from left to right (picture A). Push out the pivot pin from left to right (picture B). Lift the upper receiver from the lower receiver/trigger housing.

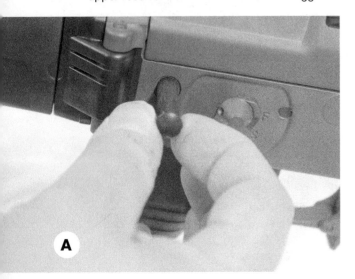

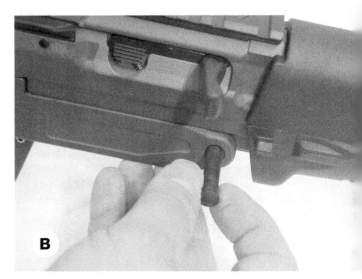

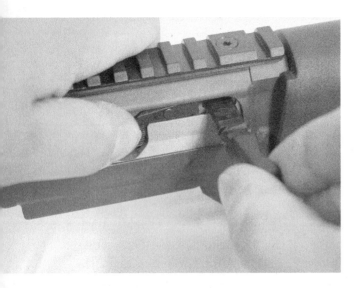

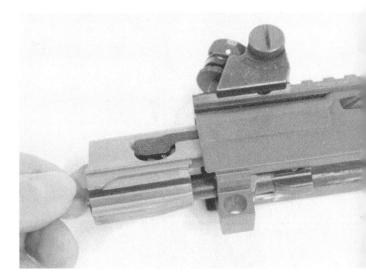

2. Depress the charging handle latch and pull the handle straight out to the right.

3. Pull the bolt carrier assembly out of the upper receiver.

5. Push out this pin to remove the firing pin and spring.

4. Push the bolt back into the carrier and rotate it to the right so that the camming lug clears the carrier. Then pull the bolt forward out of the carrier.

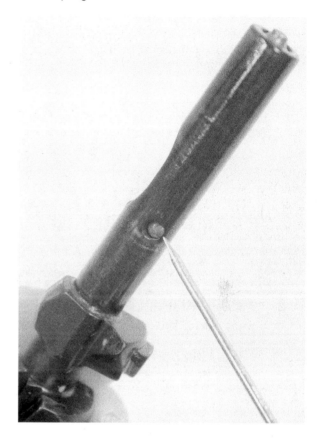

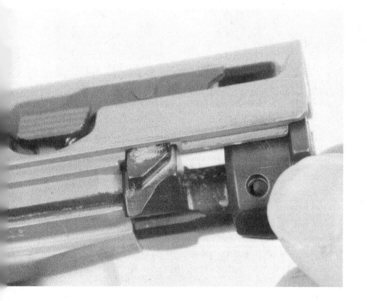

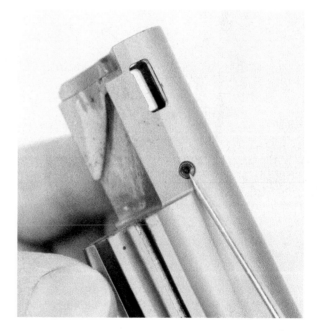

6. Push out this pin to remove the extractor and spring. However, the pin is heavily staked and should be left in place unless repair is necessary.

7. This pin retains the charging handle latch and is heavily staked. The latch and spring should be left in place for general maintenance.

8. Pull the bottom handguard piece to the rear and then down off the barrel. The upper piece will now also be free to be removed from the barrel.

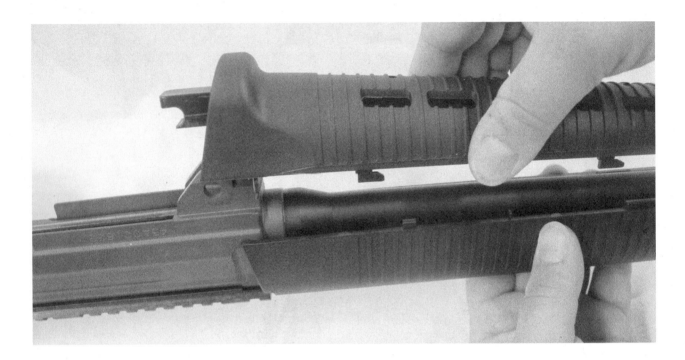

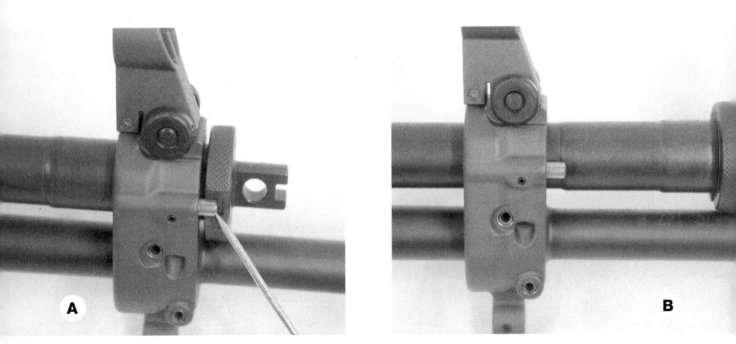

A   **B**

9. Depress this plunger and rotate the gas cylinder assembly 90 degrees so that the cut radius is toward the barrel (picture A). Pull the assembly forward out of the upper receiver (picture B).

10. Rotate the gas valve so that its flanges align with the slots in the gas cylinder, and pull the valve out. The operating rod assembly will follow.

11. Removing this roll pin will allow the operating rod/piston to be separated from its spring. Do not lose the washer/spring seat.

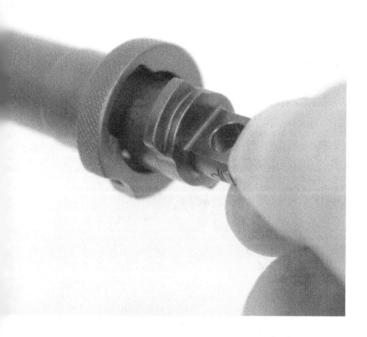

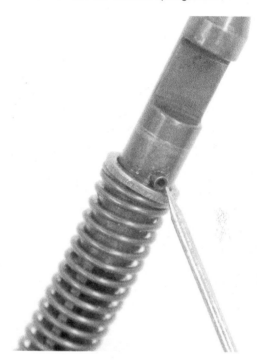

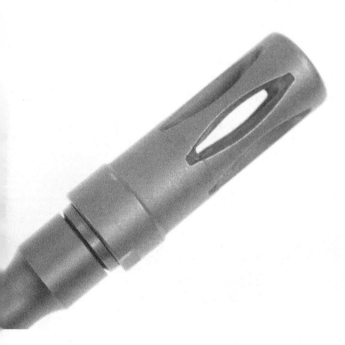

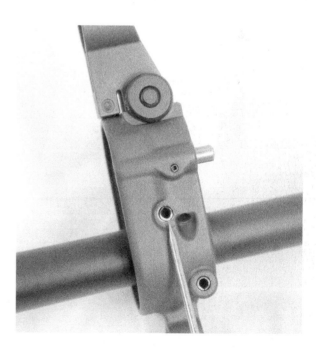

12. The flash hider can be removed by unscrewing it from the barrel

13. The gas block assembly is held in place by two pins and should not be removed for normal maintenance. The gas cylinder retaining plunger, retained by a small roll pin, should also be left in assembly.

14. The front sight assembly can be removed by first driving out this pin, and then unscrewing the adjustment screw from the nut on the opposite side.

15. The rear sight is held in place by a nut and clamp. The optic rail upon which the rear sight rests can be removed, if necessary, by the removal of the three large hex screws holding it to the receiver. Disassembly of the rear sight assembly should be done by the factory.

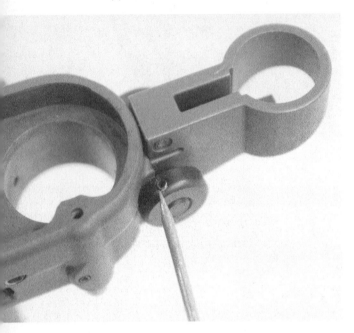

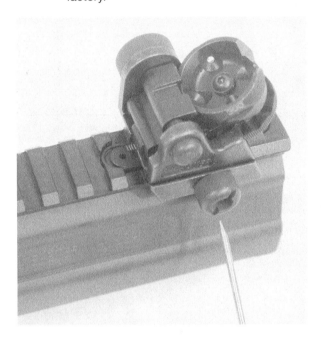

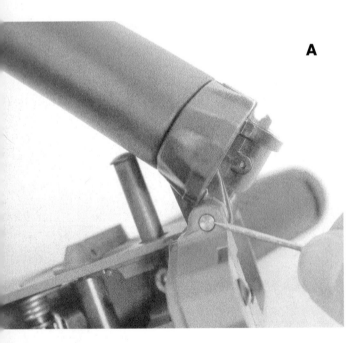

A

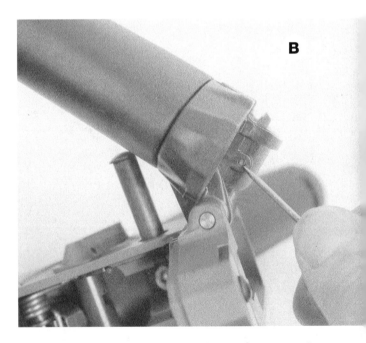

B

16. The buttstock can be removed by driving out this hinge pin (picture A). The button and spring can be removed by driving out this small pin (picture B). Leave these in assembly unless the stock is being replaced.

17. The pistol grip is retained by means of this large screw (picture A) and a mating nut inside the pistol grip. As the grip is removed, a spring and detent that operates the takedown pin will fall from the lower receiver (picture B).

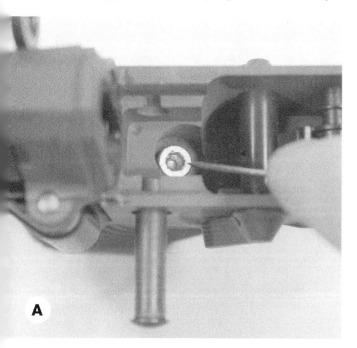

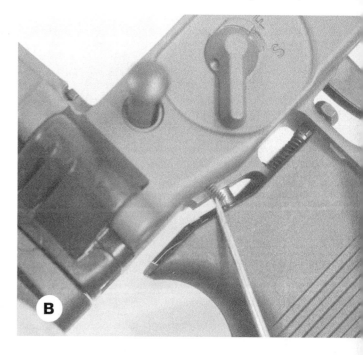

18. Drive out this roll pin and the corresponding pin on the opposite side of the lower receiver to remove the safety levers.

19. Hold up the tail of this long spring and push out the safety. There will still be considerable tension placed on the safety by the trigger spring wrapping around the bottom.

20. The safety spring can then be dislodged from the hammer pin and lifted from the receiver.

21. Push out this pin to remove the hammer and spring.

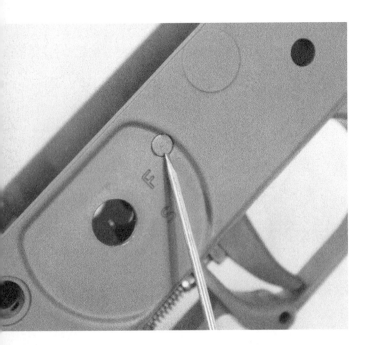

22. Push out this pin to remove the trigger assembly.

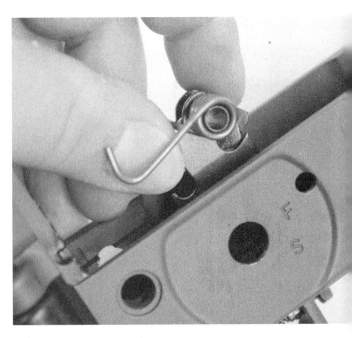

23. Lift the trigger assembly from the lower receiver.

24. Remove the trigger bushing to separate the trigger assembly into the trigger itself, the sear, the connector, and sear spring.

25. The pressure point screw assembly (2nd trigger stage) should be left in place for normal maintenance.

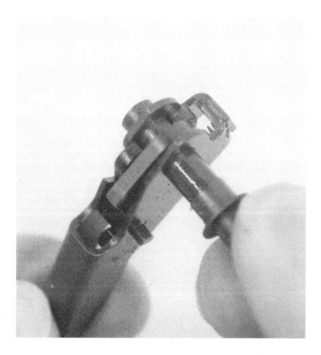

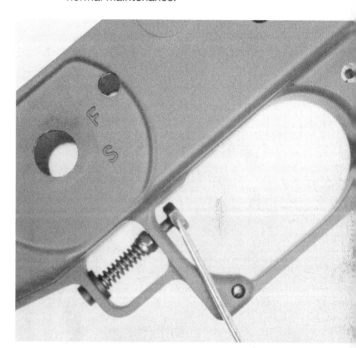

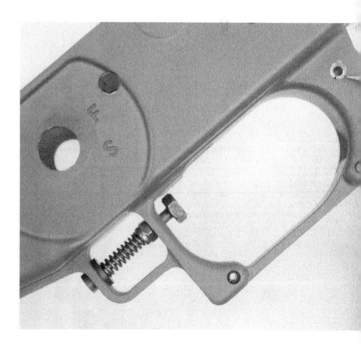

26. The trigger guard can be removed by driving out this pin. The front guard axis is a pin that can be pushed into the trigger guard and the guard can then be pulled out. The trigger guard front axis pin should not be disassembled.

27. The magazine catch and spring can be removed by driving out this pin.

28. The bolt catch and spring are retained by this split ended pin. If necessary, the bolt catch can be removed by pinching the end of this pin and pushing it forward into the magazine well.

29. The pivot pin can be removed by inserting a punch into this hole to depress the detent. While depressed, the pin can be pulled out to the left. Contain the detent and spring.

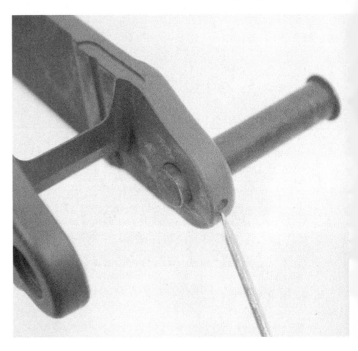

30. The bolt stop plate and its shoe can be tapped out from the rear of the lower receiver. The sling plate can be removed by simply unscrewing the retaining screw.

Reassembly Tips:

1. Ensure that the hammer spring legs are placed into their seating slots on the bottom of the lower receiver..

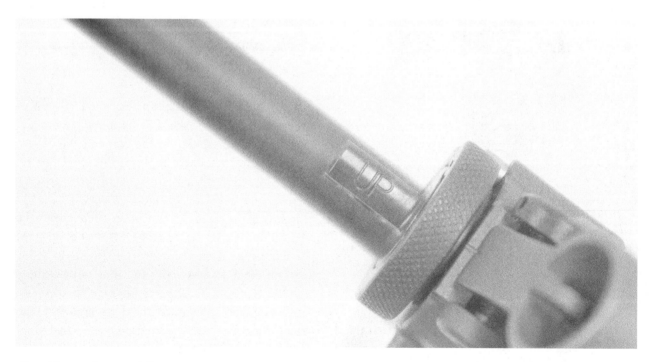

2. Ensure that the "UP" side of the gas valve is actually up when reassembled.

SPRINGFIELD SOCOM 16

Similar/Identical Pattern Guns

The same basic assembly/disassembly steps for the Springfield M1A also apply to the following guns:

Springfield SOCOM II   **Springfield M21 Tactical**
Springfield M1A   **U.S. M-14**
Springfield M1A Scout   **Polytech M14S**

Data:	Springfield Armory SOCOM 16
Origin:	United States
Manufacturer:	Springfield Armory, Geneseo, IL
Cartridge:	.308 Win.
Magazine capacity:	20 rounds
Over-all length:	37.25 inches
Barrel length:	16.25 inches
Weight:	8.8 pounds

The SOCOM 16 is s shorter-barreled version of Springfield's M1A, itself being a semiautomatic, civilian legal version of the military M-14. An effective muzzle brake replaces the longer barrel and familiar flash suppressor, and this assembly causes the SOCOM 16 and SOCOM II to differ slightly in the takedown procedures concerning the barrel. Furthermore, the SOCOM-16 and SOCOM II feature modern accessory rails; a scout scope rail on the SOCOM and a full four rail assembly on the SOCOM II. These variations should pose no particular difficulty for the disassembler. Other than this, all of the existing copies of the M-14 will should follow these steps with little or no deviation. National match rifles are also available.

Disassembly:

1. Pull the rear of the triggerguard back and then down (picture A). This will rotate the entire triggerguard to unlock the trigger housing. Pull the trigger housing down and out of the receiver (picture B). Pull the receiver up and then back to separate the action from the stock (picture C).

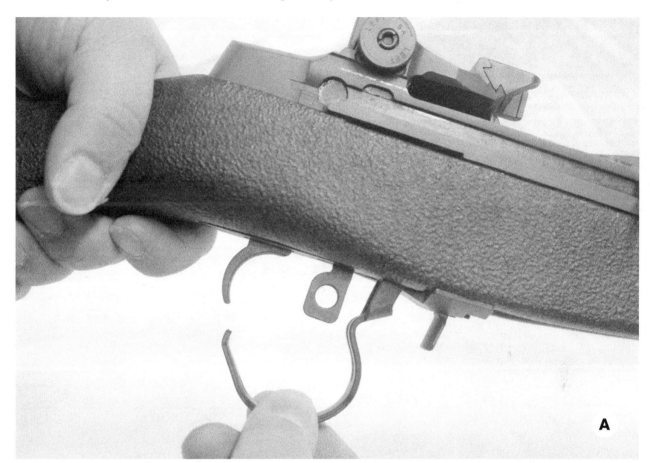

A

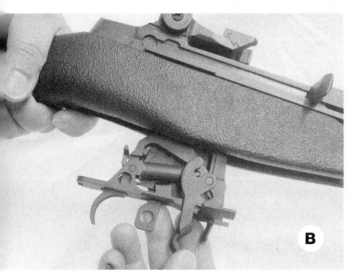

B

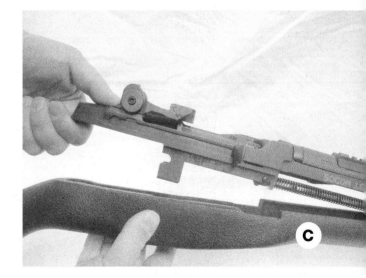

C

2. The buttplate assembly can be removed by taking out these two screws. The rear sling swivel is retained by the bottom screw and will fall out when that screw is removed.

3. If elements of the buttplate assembly need to be replaced, removal of two pins will remove or disassemble the door. Indicated is the small spring pin that contains the latch. The hinge pin is to the left and can be driven out to remove the door (picture A). The pivoting plate can be removed by driving out this large roll pin (picture B). Visible between the pivoting plate and the buttplate is the detent ball bearing, beneath which is the spring.

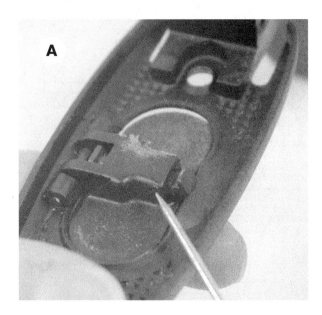

4. With the hammer forward, push out the trigger pin (picture A). In a controlled fashion, release the disconnector and hammer spring and plunger tube so that they can be removed up and to the rear (picture B).

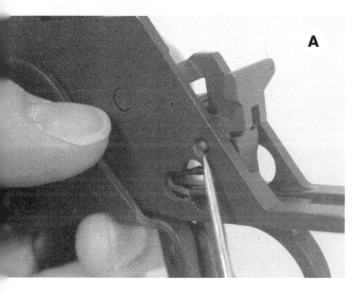

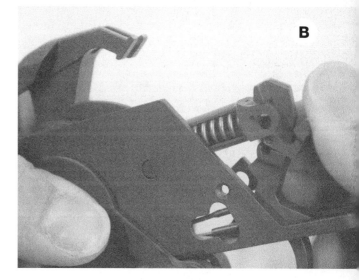

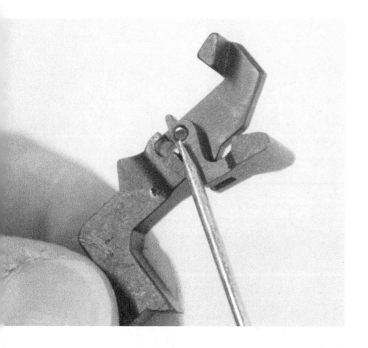

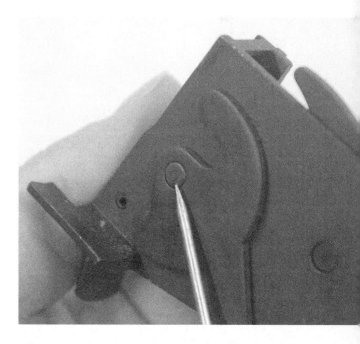

5. The disconnector can be removed from the trigger by driving out this pin. However, the pin is staked and the disconnector should not be removed unless it needs to be replaced.

6. Tap out the hammer pin from left to right. Remove the hammer. The trigger guard will be loose but cannot be removed until the safety lever is removed first.

7. Tip the top of the safety bar to the right to dislodge its pin from the hole in the housing and lift it up out of the housing. The safety spring will also be loose and can be removed at this time.

8. Remove the trigger guard by rotating it down and then the guard section to the right, to fit the pin portion around the beveled section at the bottom of the housing.

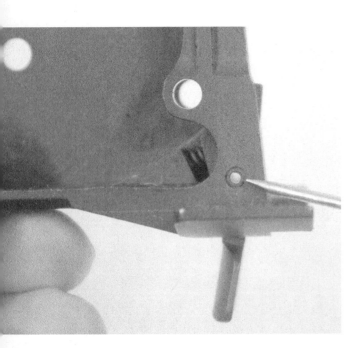

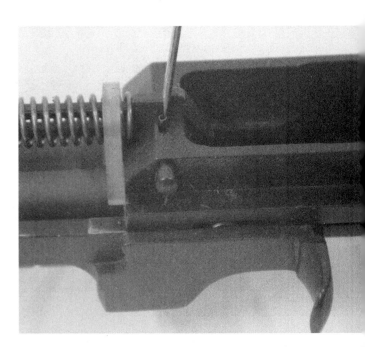

9. The magazine catch pin can be driven out to free the magazine catch and spring. It may be heavily staked and, if so, should not be removed unless repair is necessary. The pin should be re-staked upon reassembly.

10. Pull the small roll pin adjacent to the recoil spring guide rod to the side of the receiver. This pulls the rod's retaining pin out of the rod.

11. Lift the guide rod up and then back and pull the rod and spring from the operating handle's spring guide tube. The guide rod and buffer can be easily removed from the spring.

12. This pin must be pulled out of the cross pin for the cross pin to be removed. Unless there is damage, this is not required. If the pin is removed, it will need to be replaced with a new one.

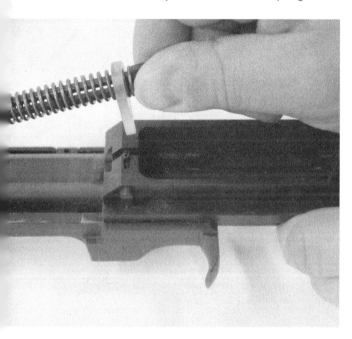

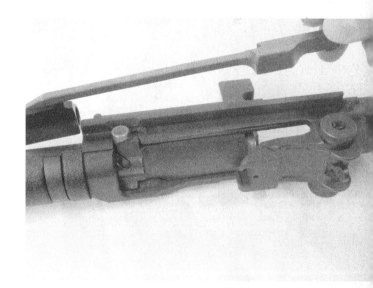

13. The very rear of the operating handle has a tab that interacts with this step in the slot. Align the tab with the step and rotate the charging handle slightly while pulling it out. This will dislodge the operating handle from the slot and the bolt from the handle.

14. Pull the operating handle all the way to the back and then angle it out to the right to remove it from the action.

15. Pull the bolt assembly forward and angle it so that the roller is angling up. Then tilt it out to the right so that the firing pin tail clears the lower bridge of the receiver and the bolt can be removed from the receiver.

16. The bolt roller can be replaced usually by simply popping or prying it off the bolt (many cannot and must be ground to be removed). There is a small ring-type spring inside of it. **DO NOT** attempt this unless replacement is required as the lug underneath can be damaged easily, particularly if the roller is stubborn.

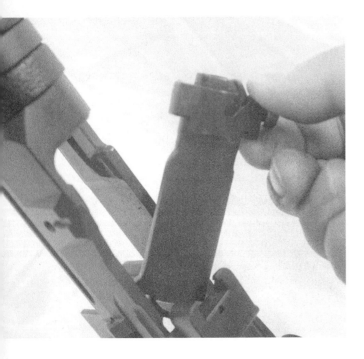

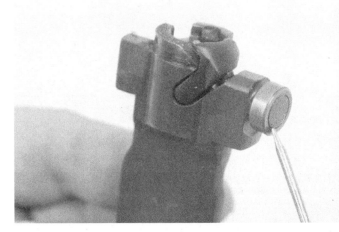

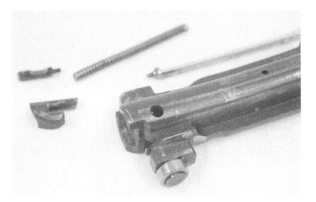

18. The parts of the bolt assembly are shown here. The extractor detent and spring are still contained in their hole.

17. Disassembly of the bolt is easier accomplished with the special tool available from multiple sources. This pin (which is part of the extractor) must be pushed out. This will free the extractor and its detent and spring, as well as the ejector and spring. The ejector spring is quite powerful and care should be taken to control the ejector as it is removed.

19. The bolt stop and spring can be removed by driving out this pin toward the rear.

20. The handguard can be removed by prying this clip out of its slot and pulling the rear of the handguard upward. The handguard then can be pulled back slightly to clear the front handguard ring and removed.

21. The front sight can be removed by removing this screw and drifting the sight off the dovetail.

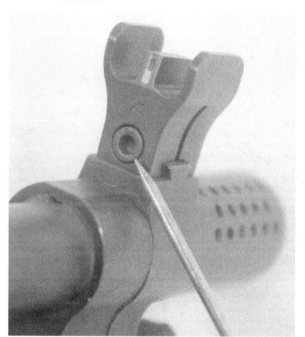

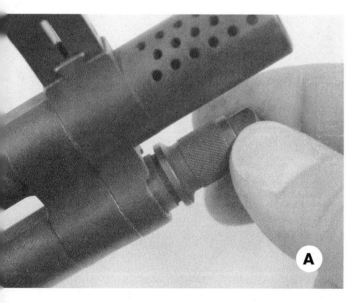

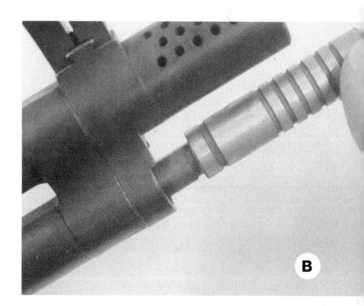

22. Unscrew and remove the gas plug (picture A) and then the piston can be removed from the piston cylinder (picture B).

23. The front sight base and compensator can now be unscrewed and removed from the barrel.

24. Only if necessary to replace the barrel should steps 24 – 26 be undertaken. To remove the spindle valve, drive out this pin. The valve and spring will be removed from the other side of the gas cylinder.

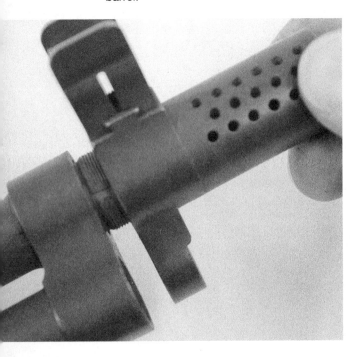

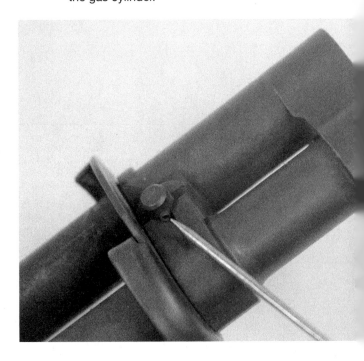

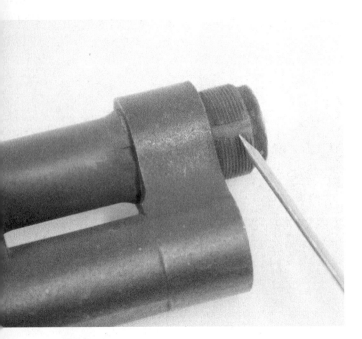

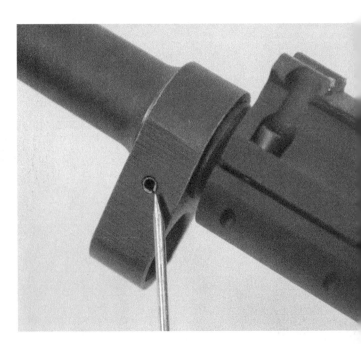

25. The gas cylinder assembly can now be gently tapped forward off the barrel. This unit also rides on these three splines cut into the barrel. Fouling can make this assembly very tight.

26. The operating rod guide can be removed by driving out this pin and tapping it forward and over the muzzle.

27. If necessary for cleaning or repair, the scout scope mount can be removed at this time. The two pieces are retained by six socket screws.

28. To disassemble the rear sight, push in on the left side (elevation) screw while unscrewing the screw in the face of the right side (windage) knob until it is fully loose.

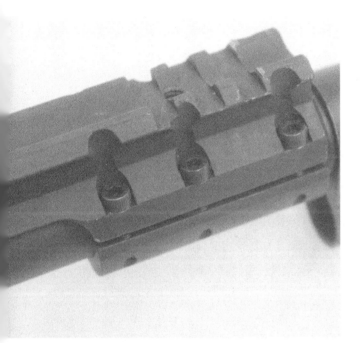

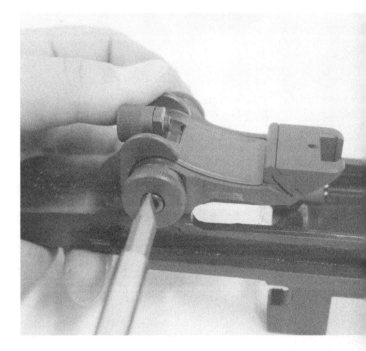

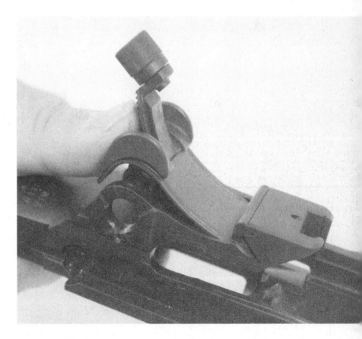

29. Pull the left side knob from the assembly. Then unscrew and remove the right side knob from the sight base. Beneath the right side knob is a detent ball and spring. Do not lose them. Do not remove the screws from either of the side knobs. There is also a split ring spring clip in the left side knob that should also be left installed.

30. Pull the rear sight aperture most of the way up and then push forward and up on the rear of the assembly below the aperture to pop it out of position.

31. The sight assembly parts, disassembled.

32. The magazine is disassembled by lifting up the rear of the floorplate and pulling it to the rear and out of its slot in the magazine body.

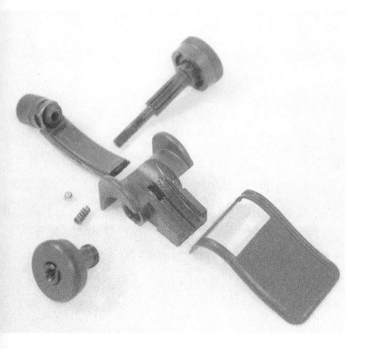

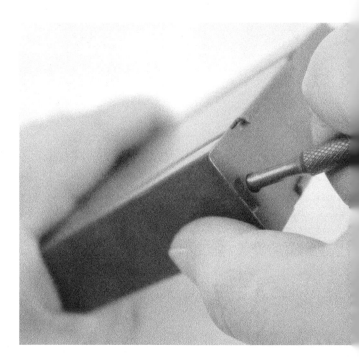

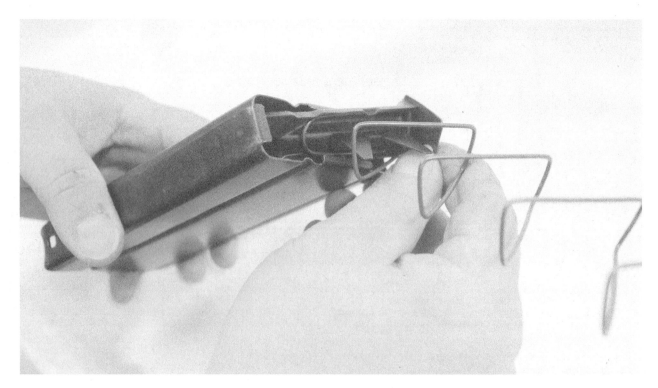

33. The follower should be tilted to clear the floorplate tabs on the body to remove it and the spring.

Reassembly Tips:

1. The pin projection on the inside of the right trigger guard arm should be behind the tab on the bottom of the hammer. This pin cocks the hammer when the trigger guard is pulled down.

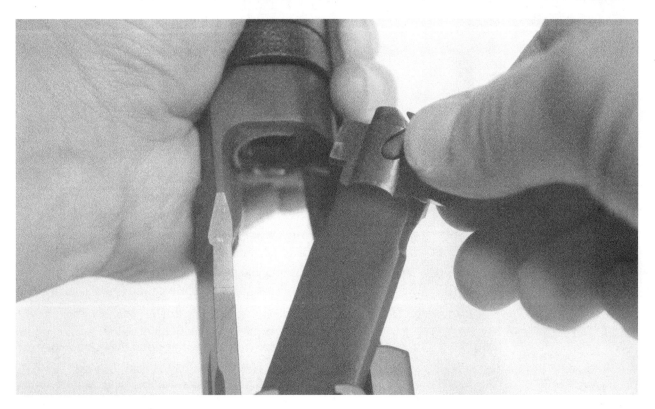

2. When reinstalling the bolt, angle it in such a fashion to that the left lug will slide down into its slot and the rear of the bolt clears the lower receiver lug.

STEYR AUG

Similar/Identical Pattern Guns

The same basic assembly/disassembly steps for the Steyr AUG also apply to the following guns:

MSAR STG-556   **MSAR STG-E4**

Data:	Steyr AUG
Origin:	Austria
Manufacturer:	Steyr Mannlicher GmbH.
Cartridge:	5.56x45 mm
Magazine capacity:	30 rounds
Over-all length:	31.5 inches
Barrel length:	20 inches
Weight:	9 pounds

The AUG (Armee Universal Gewehr) is one of the first massively successful bullpup style rifles manufactured, and was adopted by many countries and agencies worldwide. It is a very easy gun to field strip, is readily convertible to left or right handed use, uses a great deal of plastic in its construction (notably in the fire control mechanism), and was an early modular design. Barrels of various lengths could be swapped in only a few seconds, and the rifle had alternate stock housings for using original Steyr magazines and also for using M-16 magazines. The original models came with a 1.5x scope integral with the receiver (which should not be disassembled), while newer models, such as the much more recent civilian AUG/A3 SA, simply have a Picatinny optics mounting rail instead. Other than the fixed optic/Picatinny rail differences, and the usual deviations typical of a civilian legal rifle derived from a military rifle, the versions of the AUG available to the American public are essentially the same. A well made clone is also provided by MSAR.

Disassembly:

1. With the bolt locked to the rear, depress the barrel lock button (picture A), rotate the barrel up to the left until it stops (picture B), then pull the barrel assembly forward out of the receiver (picture C).

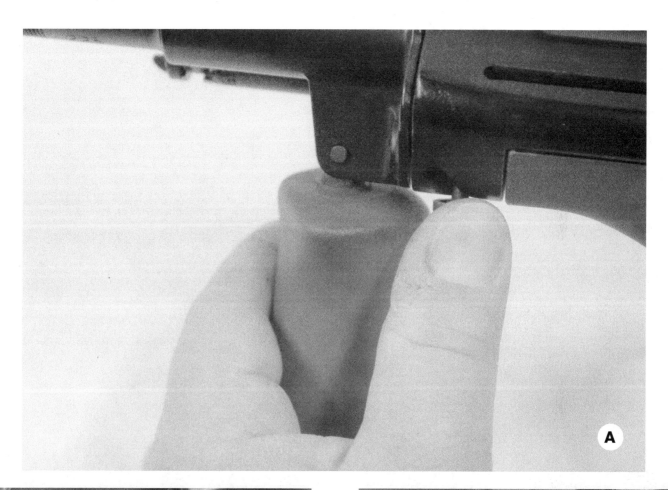

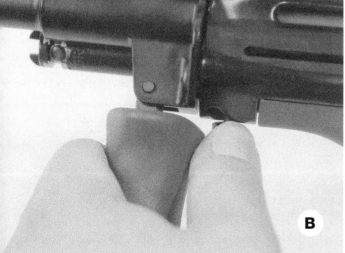

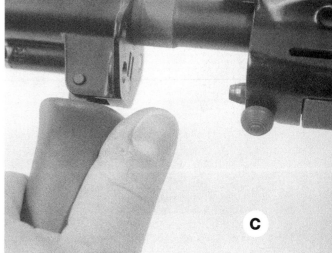

2. Rotate the gas regulator to this intermediate position and pull it out of its housing. The locking tab should align with the small vent port (picture A). The pin in the regulator assembly is staked and disassembly of the regulator should be left to the factory. Remove the piston and spring from the barrel (picture B).

A

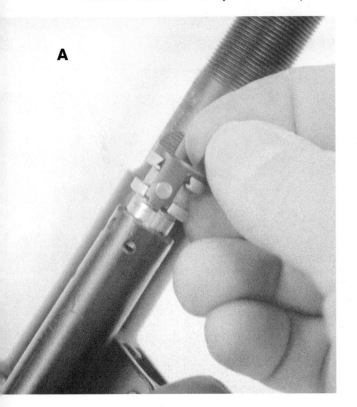

B

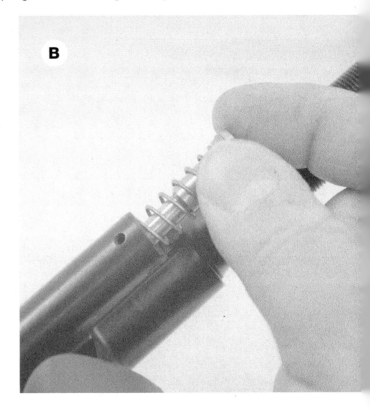

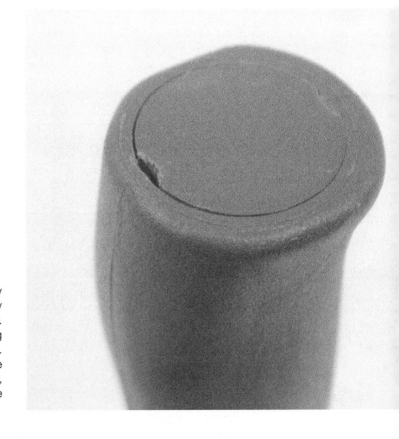

3. Further disassembly of the barrel assembly should be avoided. The forward grip assembly should not be removed without need of repair. Its base is retained by the same long spring that supplies tension to the locking mechanism. Unhooking the spring from the plate will free it for its pivot pin to be removed. If necessary, the flash hider or other muzzle device can be removed by unscrewing it from the barrel.

4. Depress the indented area of the buttstock while simultaneously pulling the stock swivel pin out to remove the pin (picture A). Pull the top tip of the stock plate out and unhook the bottom from the stock toe to remove the stock plate (picture B).

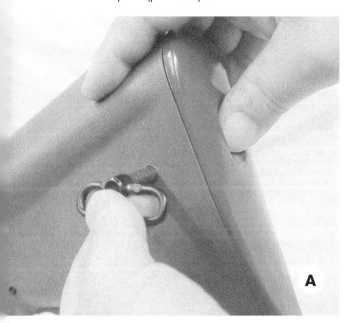

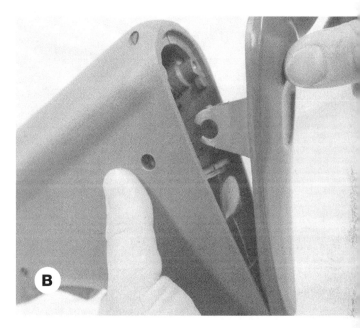

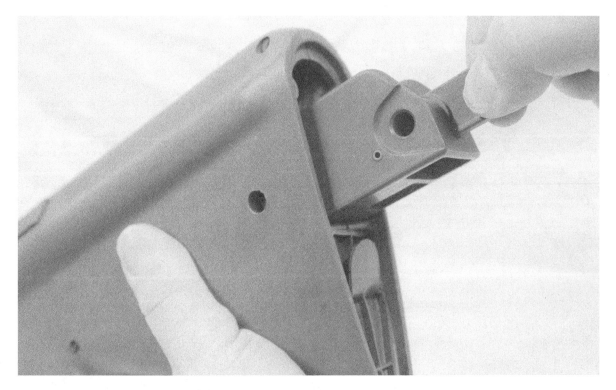

5. Reach into the buttstock and pull out the trigger pack, straight to the rear.

6. There is a squarish button above and forward of the magazine well on the left side of the rifle (picture A). Press this button through the rifle to the right until it stops (picture B). Pull the barreled receiver forward out of the stock (picture C).

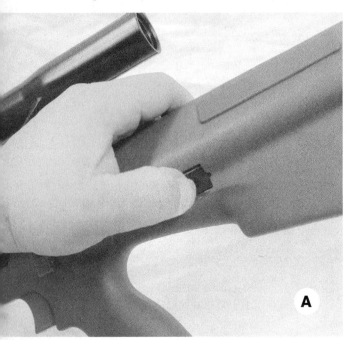

A

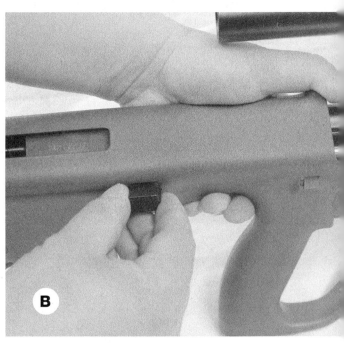

B

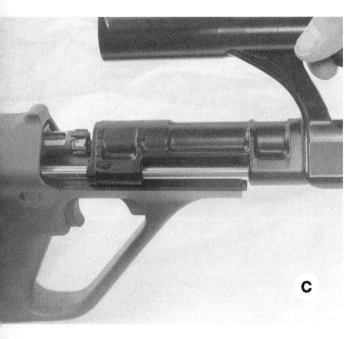

C

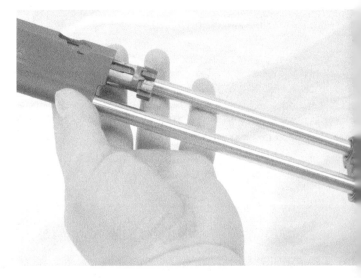

7. The bolt carrier assembly can be pulled back and out of the receiver. Disassembly of the rest of the receiver should be left to the factory. The charging handle must be completely disassembled for removal from the receiver and will need replacement pins to be reassembled to the receiver. The barrel lock and optics are likewise factory-only maintenance items.

8. Rotate the firing pin 90 degrees counter clockwise to free it from the bolt. Pull it from the rear of the bolt assembly.

9. Push down on the control bolt (cam pin) so that it is wholly inside the bolt (picture A), and then pull the bolt assembly forward out of the carrier (picture B). At this point the cocking piece will fall out of the back of the carrier (picture C). There is a roller bearing at the top rear corner of the carrier. Do not remove this bearing or the two heavy guide rods from the carrier.

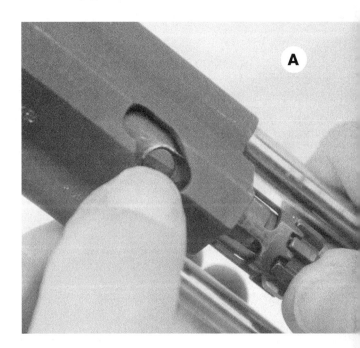

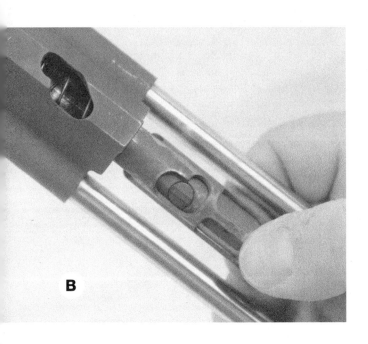

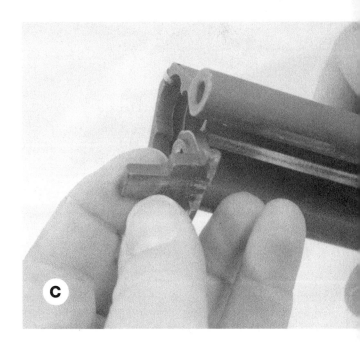

10. The locking piece, spring, and locking sleeve can remain together, or replaced individually as necessary

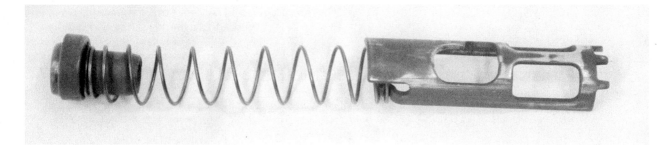

11. Push out this pin to release the extractor and spring.

12. Drive out this pin to free the ejector and spring.

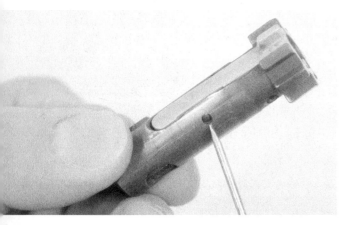

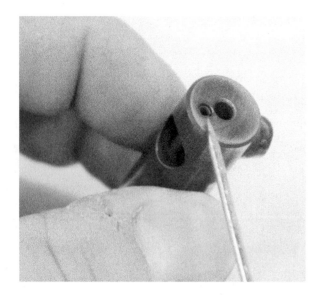

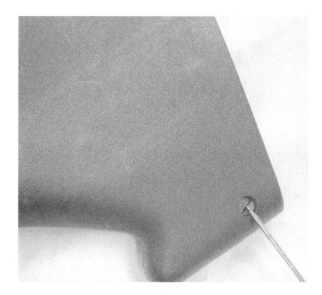

13. Push out this pin to remove the control bolt. It is a semi-permanently installed pin, so don't do it unless the control bolt needs replacement.

14. The two stock halves, while having three assembly screws, are welded together to prevent disassembly. Therefore, removal of the trigger and trigger bars, magazine catch, safety, and disassembly latch should be left to the factory.

15. The cleaning kit compartment and its contents are in the toe of the stock.

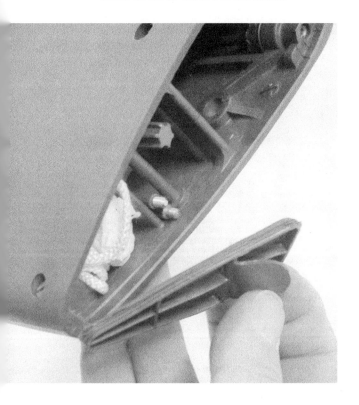

16. The bolt catch is retained by this pin. Pull it forward to remove the pin and the catch and its spring can then be removed.

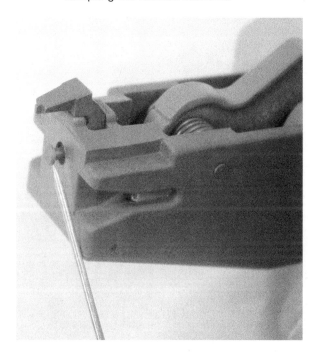

17. Dislodge the hammer spring legs from their seats in front of and to each side of the hammer. Then push out this pivot pin to remove the hammer and springs

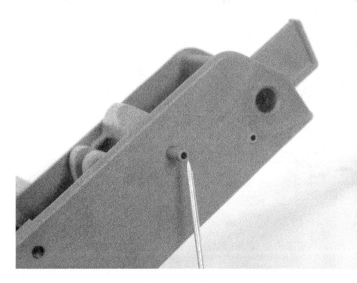

18. Push out this sear pin. There is a spring encircling the pin inside the sear. This tensions both the sear and the bolt retaining lock (takedown button).

19. Lift the sear assembly from the housing. This will also free the spring.

20. This pin holds the disconnector to the sear.

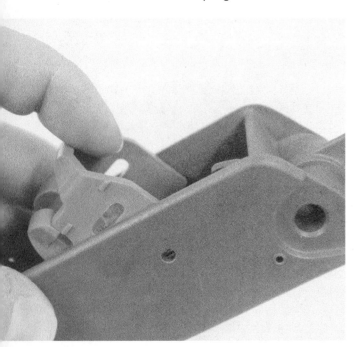

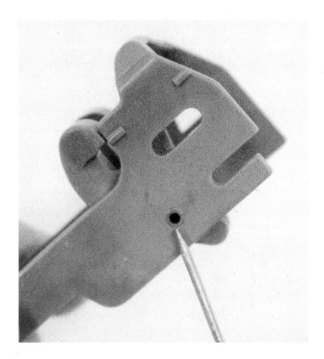

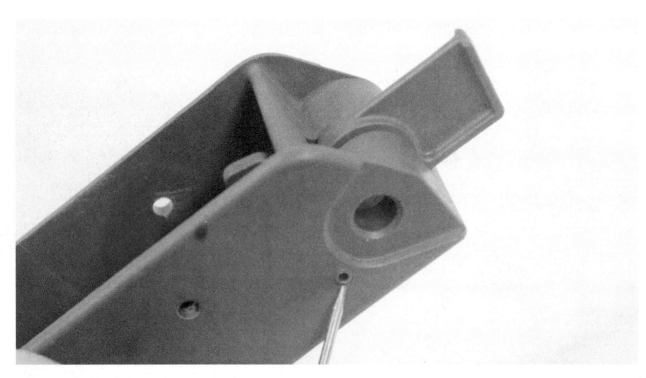

21. Drive out this pin to remove the drop safety, the tall, somewhat triangular piece at the rear left corner of the housing. Its spring is just below it and removal of the safety also frees the spring. Removal of this pin will allow the bolt retaining lock to be removed as well.

22. The magazine can be disassembled by depressing the lock button in the base plate and pushing the base plate forward of the base of the magazine (picture A). The magazine body, base plate, spring follower, and spring seat (picture B).

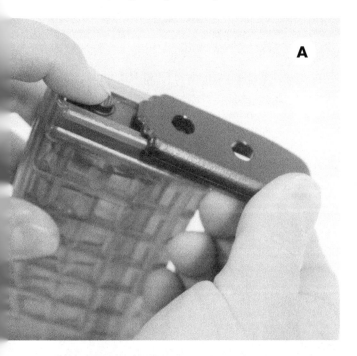

A

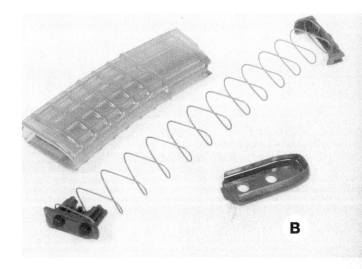

B

Reassembly Tips:

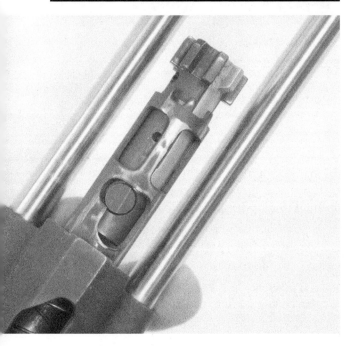

1. When reinstalling the bolt, the parts should be arranged in this fashion when inserting them into the bolt carrier.

2. Replace the sear spring with its pin and the sear assembly into the housing. Then reinsert the bolt retaining lock, compressing the spring. Then push in the lock's pin to complete the reassembly of the housing.

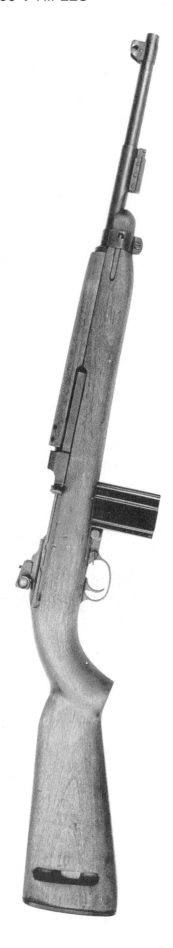

U.S. 30 M-1 Carbine

Similar/Identical Pattern Guns

The same basic assembly/disassembly steps for the U.S. 30 M-1 Carbine also apply to the following guns:

Iver Johnson M-1 Carbine   **Plainfield M-1 Carbine**
Universal M-1 Carbine   **U.S. 30 M1A1**

Data:	U.S. 30 M-1 Carbine
Origin:	United States
Manufacturer:	Winchester, IBM, General Motors, and several other contractors
Cartridge:	30 Carbine
Magazine capacity:	15 or 30 rounds
Overall length:	35.6 inches
Barrel length:	18 inches
Weight:	5 1/2 pounds

Designed by an engineering group at Winchester, the Carbine was adopted as a U.S. military arm in 1941. Several sub-models were developed later, such as the M1A1 with folding stock, and M2 selective fire version. With the exception of the parts that pertain to their special features, the instructions for the standard M1, given here, can be applied to the others. Early and late Carbines will have some small differences, such as the change from a flat-topped bolt to a round one, different rear sight, etc., but none of the changes affect the takedown to any great degree. This can also be said of the post-war commercial versions.

Disassembly:

1. Remove the magazine, and cycle the action to cock the internal hammer. Loosen the cross screw in the lower flanges of the barrel band. It should be noted that if a screwdriver is not available, the rim of a cartridge case can be used to turn the specially-shaped screw head.

2. Depress the barrel band latch, located on the right side, and slide the band and bayonet mount unit toward the front. Move the upper handguard wood forward, and lift it off. Tip the action upward at the front, unhooking its rear lug, and lift it out of the stock.

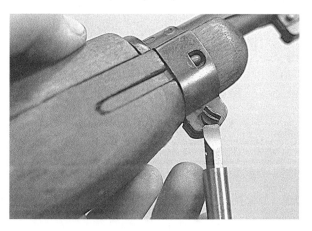

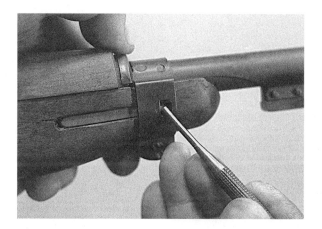

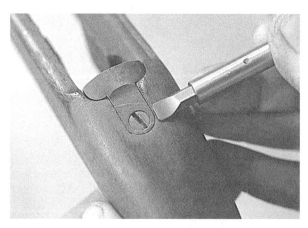

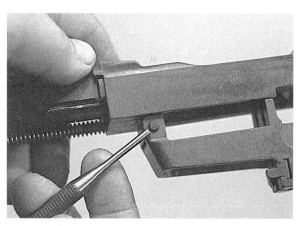

3. The barrel band latch can be removed by drifting its cross post toward the right, using the small access hole on the left side of the stock. Backing out the vertical screw in the tail of the recoil plate will allow removal of the plate upward.

4. Push out the cross pin at the front of the trigger housing, move the housing forward, out of its slots at the rear, and remove it downward.

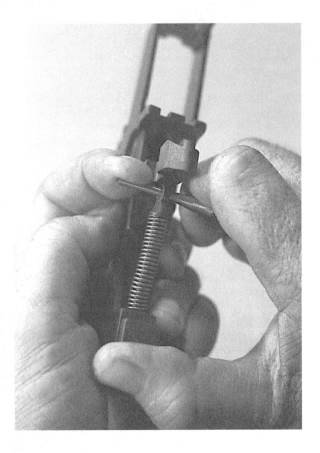

5. Restrain the hammer, pull the trigger, and ease the hammer down to the fired position. Insert a drift punch through the hole in the front of the hammer spring rod, move the rod toward the rear, and lift its head out of its seat in the back of the hammer. **Caution:** *The spring is under heavy tension, so control it as the rod and spring are eased out upward, and toward the left for removal.*

6. Take out the hammer pivot pin, and remove the hammer upward.

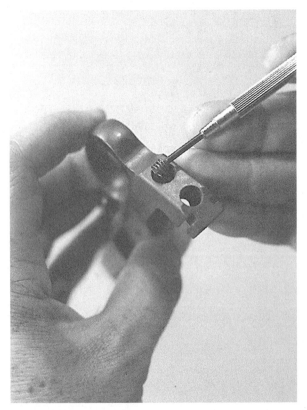

7. Insert a small tool at the rear of the trigger housing, and pull the trigger spring toward the rear until it stops, about as far as shown.

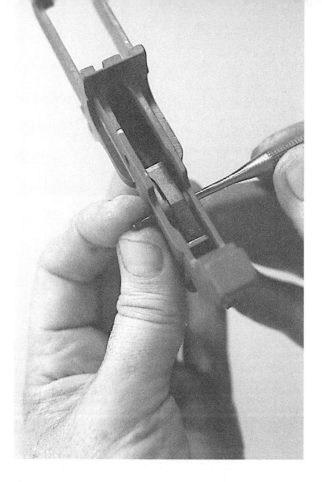

8. Restrain the sear, inside the trigger housing, and push out the trigger pin toward either side.

9. Remove the sear, sear spring, and trigger upward.

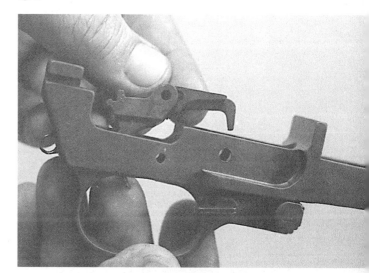

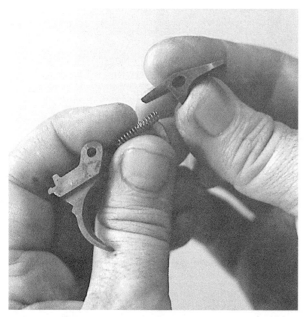

10. The sear and its spring are easily detached from the top of the trigger. After the trigger is removed, the trigger spring can be moved forward out of its well at the rear of the housing and taken out.

11. Insert a small screwdriver into the hole on the underside of the trigger housing, below, below the magazine catch, and push the catch retaining plunger toward the rear, holding it there while moving the catch out toward the right, along with its spring and plunger.

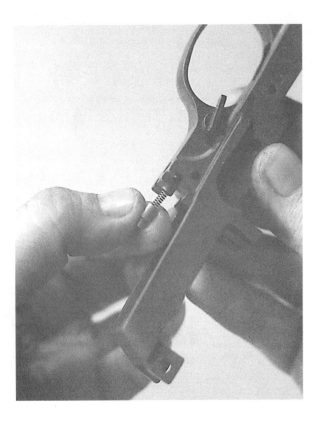

12. Remove the magazine catch retaining plunger toward the front, slowly releasing the tension of its spring. Remove the spring, and the rear plunger which positions the safety. The two plungers are identical, and need not be kept separated.

13. Remove the safety-catch toward the right.

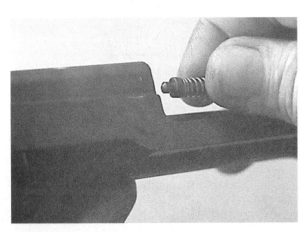

14. Grip the action slide spring and its guide rod firmly, just behind its front tip, and move it just far enough toward the rear to disengage its front stud from the recess on the back of the action slide. Tip the rod and spring away from the slide, and slowly ease the tension, removing them toward the front.

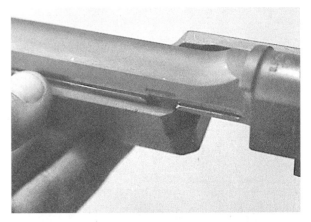

15. Move the action slide toward the rear until its inner projection on the left side is aligned with the exit cut in the barrel groove. Turn the slide toward the left and downward, disengaging the inner projection from the groove. At the same time, the rear lug of the cocking handle will be aligned with its exit cut in the receiver track, and the action slide can be removed.

16. Move the bolt to the position shown, and lift its right lug upward and toward the right. Rotate the bolt, and remove it upward and forward.

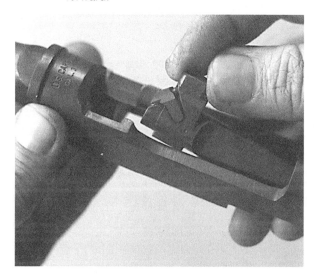

17. Disassembly of the bolt is much easier if the special military tool is used. The knurled knob of the screw is turned to back it out, the bolt is laid in the tool, and the knob tightened, pushing the disassembly nose on the rotary piece against the extractor plunger. At the same time, the ejector is depressed by a post in the front of the tool. With these two parts held in place, the extractor is easily lifted out, the screw backed off, and the other parts removed. In the photo, the tool is shown with the screw tightened, ready for removal of the extractor. It is possible, without the tool, to use a small screwdriver to depress the extractor plunger. If this method is used, be sure to restrain the ejector, as it will be released when the extractor shaft clears its retaining cut.

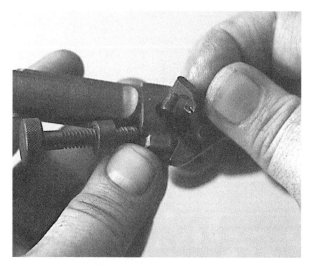

18. A hole is provided in the underside of the tool for pushing out the extractor, and it is removed upward.

19. After the extractor is removed, the screw on the tool is backed off, and the ejector and its spring are removed toward the front. The extractor plunger and its spring can be taken out of their hole at the base of the lug, and the firing pin can be removed from the rear of the bolt.

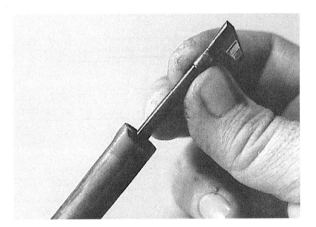

20. To remove the gas piston, it is best to use the standard military wrench designed for this. The retaining nut is simply unscrewed, and the piston is taken out toward the rear. It is possible to remove the nut without the wrench, with pliers, for example, but the nut is sure to be damaged.

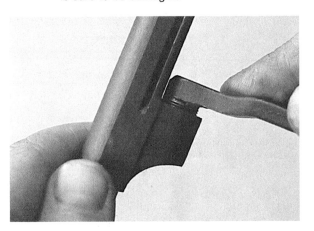

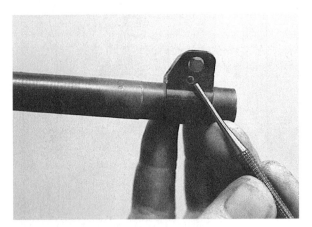

21. The front sight can be removed by drifting out its cross pin, and using a non-marring punch to nudge it off toward the front. When the sight is taken off, be sure the small key inside it is not lost. The barrel band unit can be taken off after the sight is removed.

Reassembly Tips:

1. When replacing the ejector in the bolt, be sure the ejector is oriented as shown for proper engagement with the extractor post.

2. When replacing the tiny extractor plunger, be sure the notch on the plunger is oriented downward, as this surface locks the extractor in place,

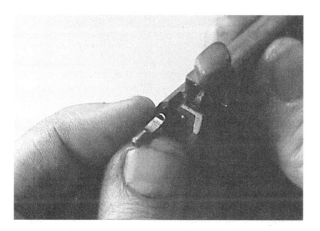

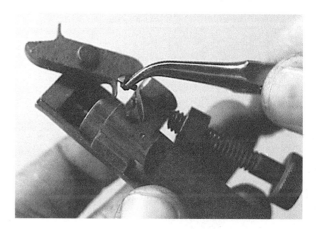

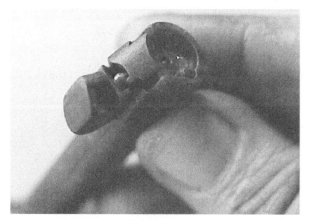

3. When property assembled, the extractor and its plunger will be engaged as shown.

4. During replacement of the action slide, position the bolt as shown, then bring the slide onto the bolt lug and move it into place in its track.

Insert the trigger spring from the front, and push it back to the temporary rear position, just as in disassembly. After the trigger/sear system is installed, move the spring back toward the front, lifting its forward end to drop into the groove at the upper rear of the trigger.

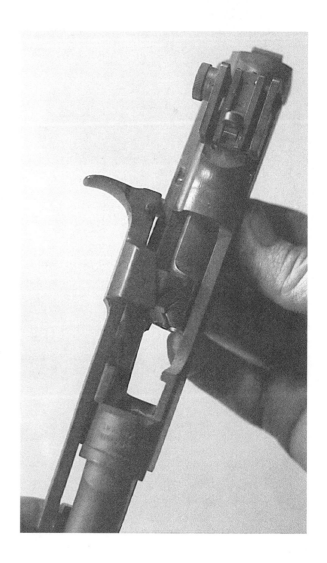

VALMET 76FS

Data: Valmet 76 ГS
Origin: Finland
Manufacturer: Valmet Oy, Helsinki
Cartridge: 223 Rem. (5.56mm)
Magazine capacity: 15 and 30 rounds
Overall length: 36-5/8 inches
Barrel length: 16-5/8 inches
Weight: 8-3/4 pounds

Imported for a time by Interarms in several models, the Valmet is essentially a modified semi-auto version of the Russian AK-series of guns. The Valmet was offered in two chamberings, the 223 and the 7.62x39mm, and the models were the 62/S, 62/FS, 71/S, and 76/FS. The last folding-stock model, the M76/FS, is the gun shown here. They are all mechanically similar, but not identical.

Disassembly:

1. Remove the magazine, and cycle the action to cock the internal hammer. Set the safety in the off-safe position. Depress the receiver cover latch, and lift the rear of the cover upward.

2. Detach the receiver cover and remove it upward and toward the rear.

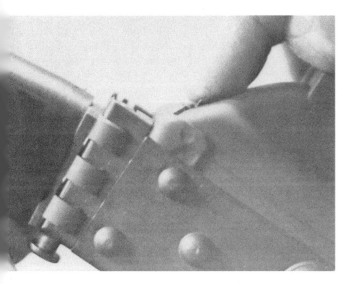

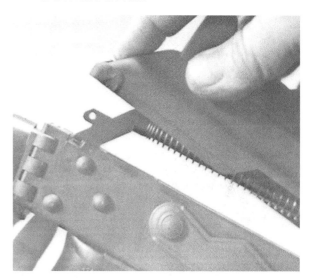

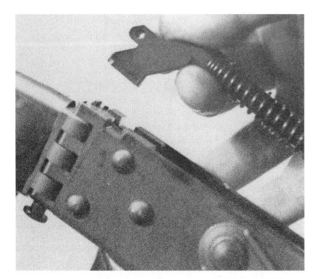

3. Move the rear base of the recoil spring guide forward to detach it from its seat in the receiver, lift it upward, and remove the guide and spring toward the rear.

4. Move the bolt carrier assembly toward the rear until the piston is clear of its sleeve at the front. Lift the rear of the carrier as it is moved toward the rear, and remove the assembly.

5. Move the bolt rearward in the carrier until it stops, turn it to the left (counter-clockwise, front view) until its lug clears, then remove the bolt toward the front.

6. If the gas piston is damaged and requires replacement, drifting out this roll pin will release it for removal toward the front. Otherwise, don't disturb it.

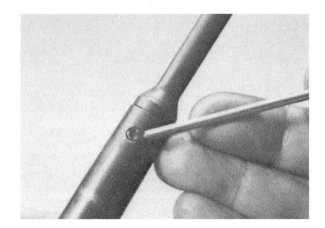

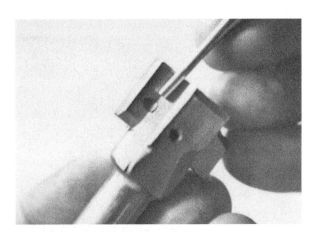

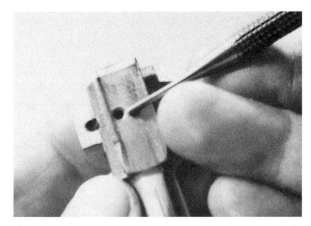

7. The extractor and its spring are retained by the larger of the two pins that cross the front of the bolt. The pin is drifted out toward the right. Restrain the extractor and spring, and ease them out.

8. The smaller of the two pins in the bolt retains the firing pin and its spring. Restrain the firing pin at the rear, drift out the pin upward, and remove the firing pin and spring toward the rear.

9. Move the gas tube toward the rear, lift it slightly to clear its lower edges, and remove it rearward.

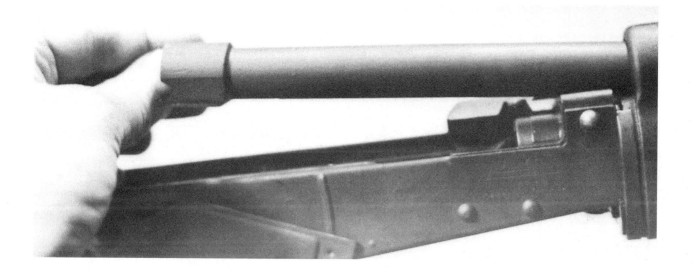

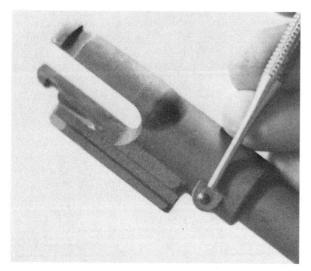

10. The flash hider is retained on the end of the barrel by a cross pin which is driven out toward the right.

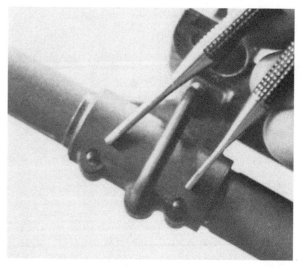

11. The combination front sight base and gas port unit is retained by two cross pins. After the pins are drifted out toward the right, the unit can be nudged forward off the barrel.

12. The handguard is retained by a threaded nut-plate at the front, and the plate has spanner-holes for the use of a special wrench. In the absence of this tool, use a nylon drift punch set in one of the holes to free the nut, then unscrew it, counter-clockwise (front view). Take off the nut-plate, washer, and the second nut, then remove the handguard toward the front. The rear handguard plate will also be freed for removal. The barrel and the bolt cam plate are cross-pinned and riveted in place, and routine removal is neither practical nor advisable. The ejector is also riveted in place on the left inner wall of the receiver, and it should not be disturbed unless necessary for repair.

13. Restrain the hammer, pull the trigger, and ease the hammer over past its normal forward position. Insert a tool inside the receiver to lift the front loop of the hammer pin retaining spring, and push the hammer pin out toward the left. Move the safety upward to clear the pin.

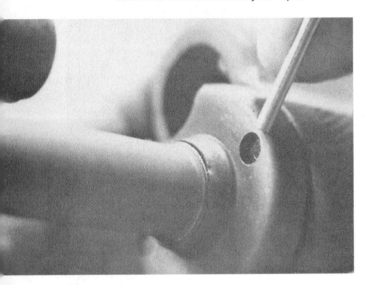

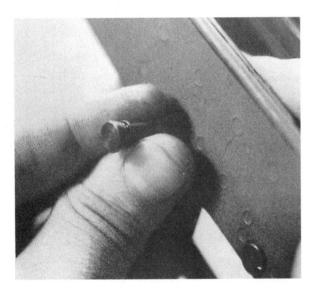

14. Restrain the hammer, and remove the hammer pin toward the left.

15. Insert a tool to unhook the rear tips of the hammer spring from the trigger, and move the hammer and its attached spring forward. Turn the hammer assembly to clear it, and remove the hammer and spring from the bottom of the receiver.

16. Insert a tool to slide the pin retaining spring forward, and remove it from the bottom of the receiver.

17. Push out the trigger pin and remove it toward the left. Restrain the sear while this is done.

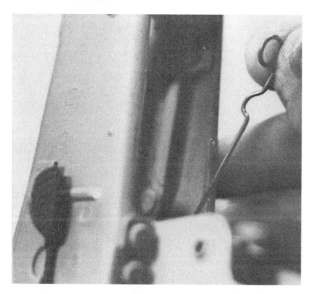

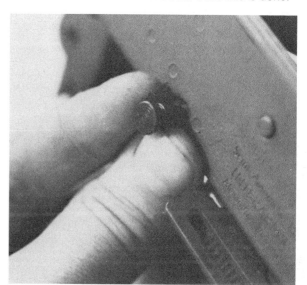

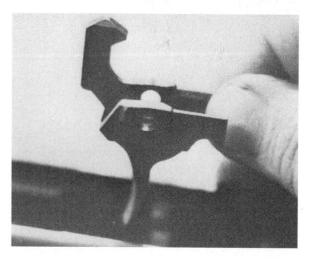

18. Remove the sear and its coil spring from the top of the receiver.

19. Remove the trigger from the top of the receiver.

20. Turn the safety lever up to the vertical position, move it toward the left, then slightly toward the rear. Remove the lever toward the right.

21. The magazine catch and its torsion spring are retained by a riveted cross pin, and these parts should be removed only for repair. The pistol grip piece is retained by a screw and lock-washer inside the receiver.

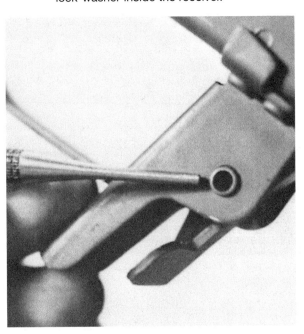

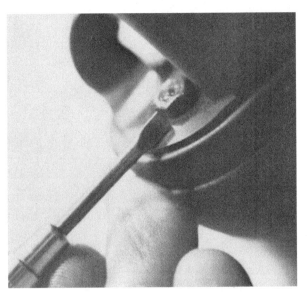

22. The folding buttstock is retained by a vertical hinge pin. After the pin is driven out downward, the stock latch spring can be slid toward the left, releasing the stock latch for removal downward.

23. The latch that holds the stock in folded position is retained on the back of the rear handguard plate by a hexagonal nut, and can be removed with a small wrench of the proper size.

Reassembly Tips:

1. When reassembling the internal components of the receiver, be sure to install the safety lever first, as this cannot be done with the sear and trigger assembly in place. Install the sear and trigger next, then the lock spring, being sure the rear tip of the spring is below the trigger pin. Install the hammer, lift the lock spring, and insert the hammer pin beneath the spring. Finally, hook the rear tips of the hammer spring back into the top rear of the trigger. The photo shows the interior of the receiver, with the parts properly installed, and the hammer in cocked position.

2. When replacing the bolt carrier assembly, position the rear of the carrier over the rear of the receiver as shown, then move it downward to engage its tracks with the flanges inside the receiver.

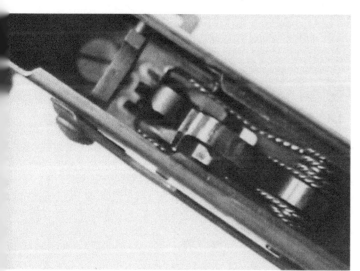

WILKINSON TERRY

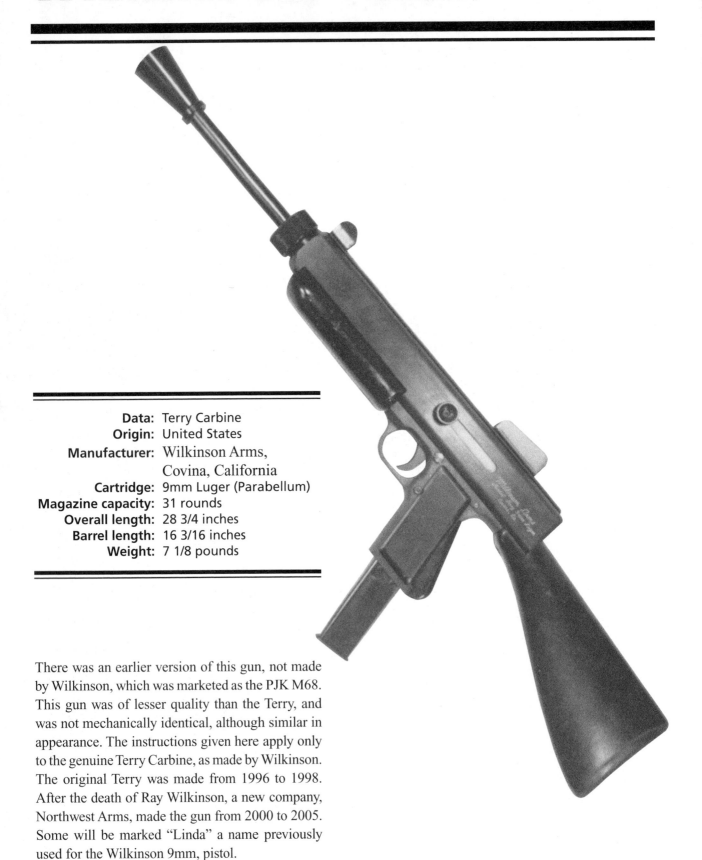

Data: Terry Carbine
Origin: United States
Manufacturer: Wilkinson Arms,
Covina, California
Cartridge: 9mm Luger (Parabellum)
Magazine capacity: 31 rounds
Overall length: 28 3/4 inches
Barrel length: 16 3/16 inches
Weight: 7 1/8 pounds

There was an earlier version of this gun, not made by Wilkinson, which was marketed as the PJK M68. This gun was of lesser quality than the Terry, and was not mechanically identical, although similar in appearance. The instructions given here apply only to the genuine Terry Carbine, as made by Wilkinson. The original Terry was made from 1996 to 1998. After the death of Ray Wilkinson, a new company, Northwest Arms, made the gun from 2000 to 2005. Some will be marked "Linda" a name previously used for the Wilkinson 9mm, pistol.

Disassembly:

1. Remove the magazine, and cycle the action to cock the hammer. Unscrew the knurled barrel retaining nut at the front of the receiver (counter-clockwise, front view), and remove the barrel assembly toward the front. If necessary, the flash hider can also be unscrewed from the muzzle, allowing removal of the barrel nut forward. If this is done, take care not to lose the twin half-rings at the rear of the flash hider.

2. With an Allen wrench, or an Allen bit in the Magna-Tip screwdriver, remove the vertical Allen screws at the front and rear of the grip frame. If the forend piece is also to be taken off, it is retained by two Allen screws of the same size. Remove the grip frame downward.

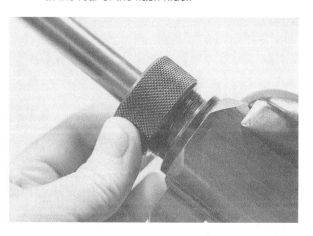

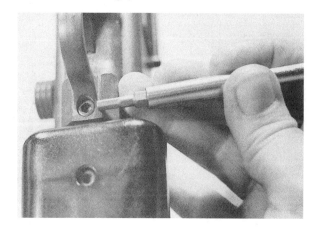

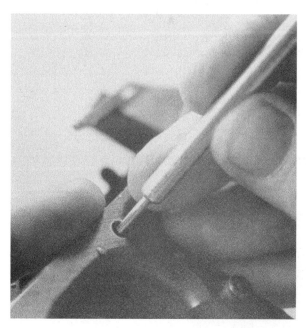

3. Remove the Allen screw in the backstrap of the grip frame, and remove the backstrap toward the rear. The grip side panels can now be lifted off the grip frame.

4. Hold a fingertip over the hole on top of the grip frame just above the safety, on the left side, and push the safety out toward the right. Use a drift punch near the size of the safety, to prevent loss of the safety detent ball.

5. Carefully withdraw the drift punch, and remove the safety detent ball and spring from their recess in the grip frame. If the spring sticks in the hole, a small screwdriver can be used to lift it out.

6. Removal of the safety will have partially released the cartridge guide, or feed ramp. Drifting out the small pin that crosses the lower end of the guide will allow its removal upward. All pins must be drifted out toward the right.

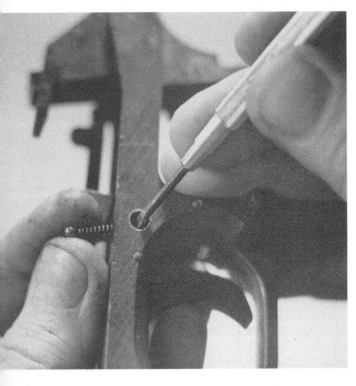

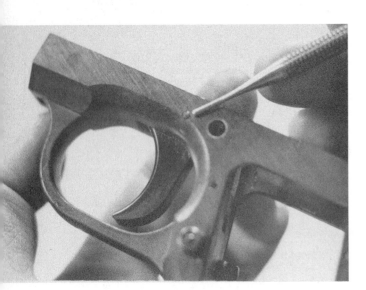

7. Restrain the trigger and trigger bar (disconnector) at the top of the grip frame, and drift out the trigger cross pin toward the right.

8. Remove the trigger assembly upward. Note that the trigger insert, or connector, is retained in the trigger by a cross pin. In normal takedown this is best left in place. The trigger spring is easily removed from its well in front of the trigger.

9. Depress the trigger bar (disconnector) at the rear to clear the sear wing, and move it forward until it can be lifted out of its guide at the front. As the bar is moved, control the rear disconnector spring beneath its rear tip to prevent loss. Remove the small spring inside the guide at the front. The guide is press-fitted into the grip frame, and should not be removed.

10. Remove the rear disconnector spring from its well at the rear.

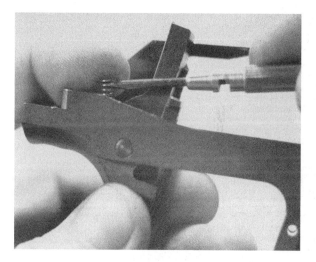

11. Restrain the hammer, trip the sear, and gently lower the hammer to fired position. Restrain the sear, inside the magazine well, and drift out the sear cross pin toward the right. Note the position of the sear spring before removal. **Caution:** *The sear spring will be released when the pin is removed, so control it.* Remove the sear and its spring forward, into the magazine well.

12. Drift the hammer cross pin toward the right, just enough to clear the ejector. Restrain the hammer, as the ejector is also the hammer stop.

13. While holding the hammer, remove the ejector upward.

14. Slowly allow the hammer to tip over forward into the magazine well, relieving the tension of its spring, and drift the hammer pin out toward the right.

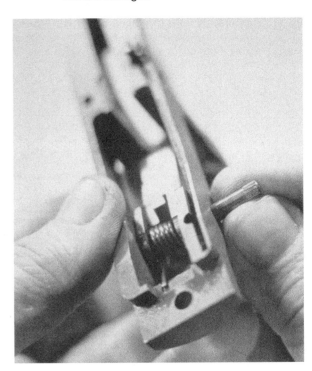

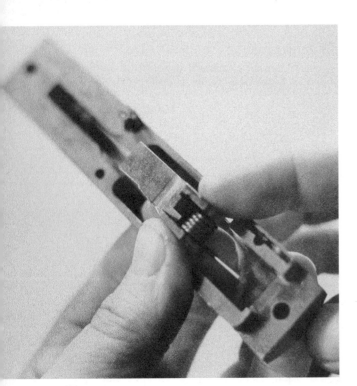

15. Remove the hammer and its spring from the top of the grip frame.

16. Grip the head of the magazine catch with non-marring smooth-jawed pliers, and unscrew the catch button from the cross-shaft of the catch (counter-clockwise, left side view). Remove the button and spring toward the left, and the magazine catch toward the right.

17. Remove the Allen screw on the underside at the forward end of the buttstock.

18. A hole is provided at the top of the rubber buttplate that will allow a slim, long-shanked screwdriver to reach the slotted screw in the front interior of the stock. The buttplate can also be easily pulled out to allow direct access to the screw. Remove the screw, and take off the butt-stock toward the rear. It should be noted that removal of the stock at this point is not necessary to further disassembly, and the remainder of takedown can be done with the stock in place.

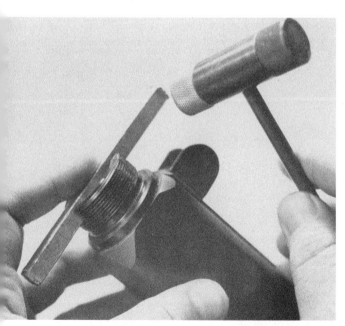

19. If you do not have an original Terry disassembly kit, use a piece of bar stock of suitable size, such as the aluminum piece shown, to engage the slots at the front of the barrel sleeve. The sleeve is then unscrewed from the receiver counter-clockwise (front view). If it is very tight, tap the end of the bar with a small hammer. An alternate method is to grip the bar in a vise, and turn the receiver. Note that the barrel timing pin is press-fitted in the sleeve, and is not removed. The rear receiver endpiece also should not be disturbed.

20. With an Allen wrench of the proper size, unscrew and remove the bolt handle, counter-clockwise (left side view). **Caution:** *Restrain the bolt as the handle is removed, as it will be released.* Note that the bolt handle may be tightly fitted, and may require that an Allen wrench be tapped with a hammer to free it.

21. Remove the bolt assembly from the front of the receiver. The twin recoil springs and their guides are easily removed from the rear of the bolt.

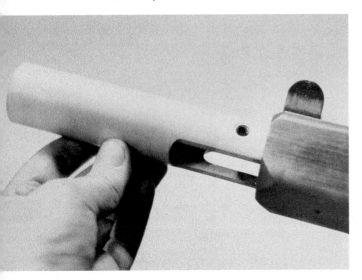

22. The extractor is retained by a vertical pin on the right side of the bolt, and the pin is drifted out downward.

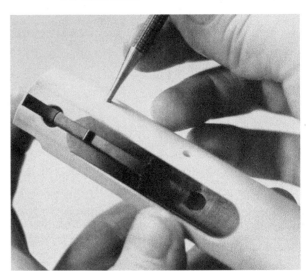

23. Gently lift the front of the extractor to free it, then remove it toward the right.

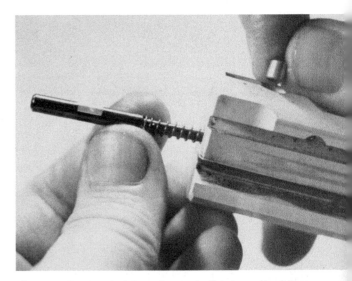

24. Removal of the extractor will expose the firing pin retaining button at the rear. Depress and restrain the firing pin at the rear, and tap the bolt with a nylon hammer to jar the button out of its recess. Remove the firing pin and its spring toward the rear.

25. The front sight is retained by twin Allen screws, and is taken off upward.

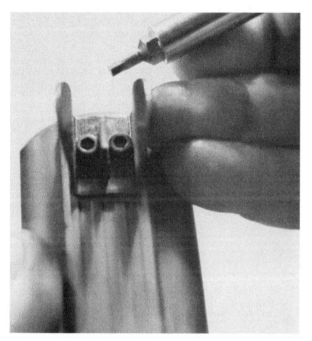

26. To remove the rear sight, first loosen the vertical adjustment screw on the left side, and slide the upper portion of the sight off forward and upward.

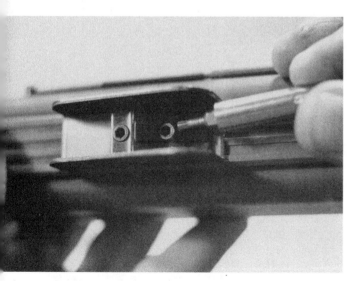

27. Removal of the sight slide will expose the rear retaining screw. Remove both Allen screws, and take off the sight and its protective bracket upward.

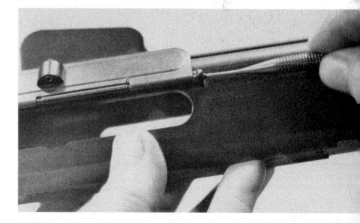

28. The ejection port cover can be removed by drifting out its hinge pin toward the rear. This pin is tightly fitted in the loops on the cover, so be sure the rear hinge post on the receiver is well supported during removal. Note that the cover spring will be released as the pin is removed, so control it. Unless removal is necessary for repair, the cover should be left in place. Also note that the cover latch plunger and spring are retained by riveting of the plunger tail, and the same advice applies to these parts.

Reassembly Tips:

1. When replacing the bolt in the receiver, be sure the bolt is in proper alignment, and insert a tool at the rear to ensure that the twin recoil spring guides enter their recesses in the receiver end-piece. As the bolt is moved to the rear, be sure that the springs do not twist and deform.

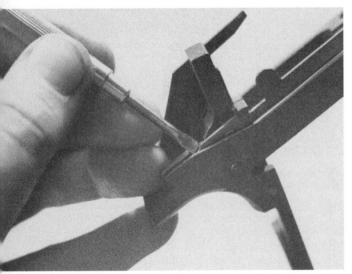

3. When replacing the trigger bar (disconnector), place it in its slot in the front guide, and use a tool to depress the rear spring while sliding the bar into place at the rear.

2. When replacing the sear and sear spring, start the sear pin into the sear, then insert a drift from the opposite side and push the spring into place, holding it with the tip of the drift until the pin is driven into place. If this proves difficult, a slave pin can be used.

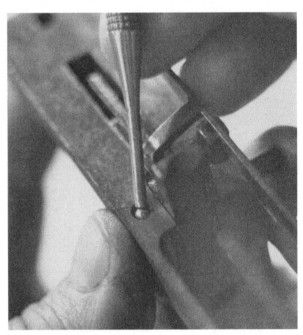

4. When replacing the safety system, remember that the twin grooves on the safety go on the left side. Being sure the cartridge guide is in upright position, insert the safety from the right. Move the safety until its left tip is even with the detent spring hole, then place the spring and ball in position, and while holding a fingertip over the safety opening on the left side, use a drift to compress the ball and spring, and push the safety toward the left into place.

When replacing the barrel, be sure the slot in the collar, midway on the barrel, mates with the locator or timing pin in the barrel sleeve before tightening the barrel retaining nut.

INGRAM MODEL 10

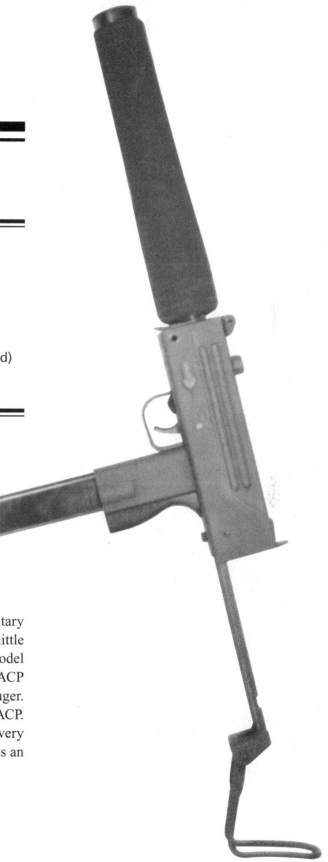

Data:	Ingram Model 10
Origin:	United States
Manufacturer:	RPB Industries, Inc., Atlanta, Georgia
Cartridge:	45 ACP
Magazine capacity:	30 rounds
Overall length:	31-3/4 inches (with silencer, stock extended)
Barrel length:	5-3/4 inches
Weight:	6-1/4 pounds

Originally made as the MAC-10 by Military Armament Corporation, this neat, flat little submachine gun is now called the Ingram Model 10 by RPB Industries. In addition to the 45 ACP chambering, it is also offered in 9mm Luger. A smaller gun, the Model 11, is in 380 ACP. The guns are mechanically the same. A very effective "suppressor" (silencer) is available as an accessory.

Disassembly:

1. Remove the magazine, and leave the bolt in the forward position. Unscrew the suppressor, and remove it from the barrel.

2. Push out the takedown pin, located at the lower front of the receiver, toward the right.

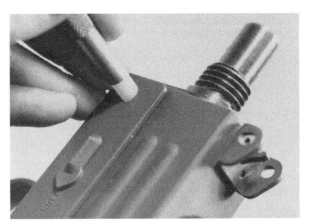

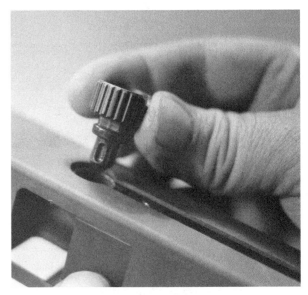

3. Lift the front of the receiver assembly, move the assembly forward, and detach it from the grip frame.

4. Move the bolt assembly to the rear of the receiver, and align the bolt handle with the larger opening at the rear of its track. Pull the bolt handle out upward. If it is very tight, insert a drift punch from below and nudge it out.

5. Remove the bolt assembly toward the rear.

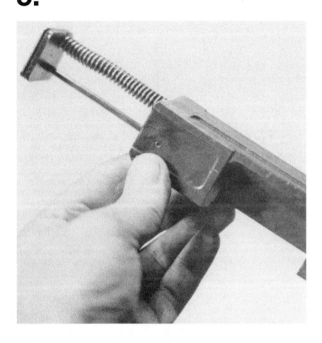

6. The barrel is threaded into the receiver and also retained by a large roll cross pin. Routine removal is not recommended.

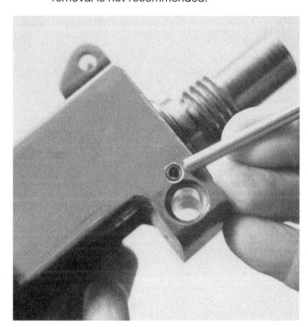

7. The recoil spring assembly is retained in the bolt by a roll cross pin at the front of the recoil spring guide. Compress the recoil spring slightly to push the guide out the front of the bolt, drift out the cross pin, and the spring and guide assembly can be removed toward the rear. **Caution:** *When the pin is out, control the compressed spring.*

8. The extractor is retained by a roll cross pin which is drifted out toward the right.

9. After the pin is removed, insert a drift punch from the rear, and nudge the extractor out toward the front.

10. The bolt handle retaining plunger and its spring are retained at the front of the bolt by a vertical roll pin, which is drifted out upward. Restrain the spring as the pin is removed, and take out the spring and plunger toward the front.

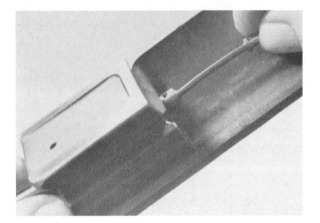

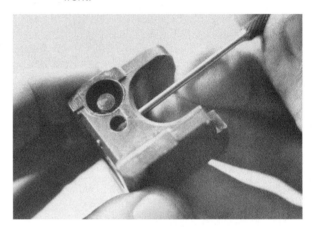

11. Lift the front L-shaped tip of the selector positioning spring slightly, and push the selector crosspiece toward the left.

12. Restrain the sear, and remove the selector toward the left.

13. Remove the sear and its spring from the top of the receiver.

14. Remove the disconnector from the top of the receiver.

15. Restrain the trigger, and push out the trigger pin toward the left.

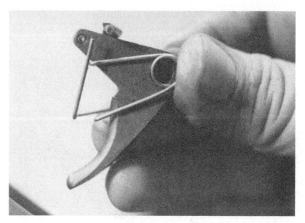

16. Remove the trigger assembly upward.

17. The spring is easily detached from the trigger. The sear trip is retained on the front of the trigger by a roll cross pin, and can be removed if necessary.

18. Remove the pivot pin locking spring.

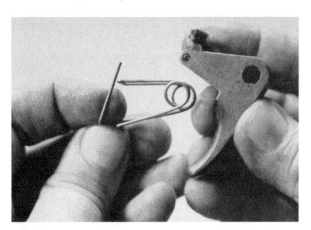

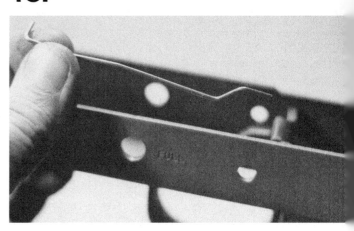

19. The safety assembly is retained by a roll cross pin in the safety button. After the pin is drifted out, the button is taken off downward, and the safety block, spring, and plunger upward.

20. Remove the screw at the center of the backstrap piece on the pistol grip.

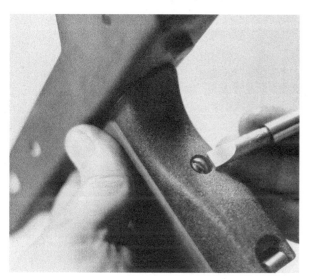

21. Move the backstrap piece toward the rear for removal. Note that the magazine catch spring bears on the backstrap, so remove it slowly.

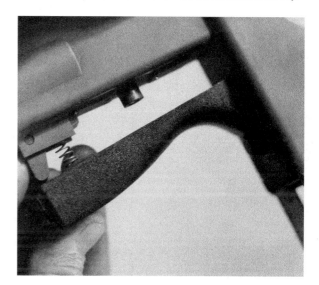

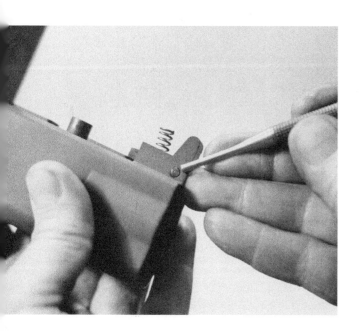

22. Push out the cross pin at the lower rear of the grip frame, and remove the magazine catch and its spring.

23. Depress and hold the stock latch button, and remove the stock toward the rear. The stock shoulder piece is retained by a C-clip on its hinge pin.

24. Inside the frame at the rear, depress the stock latch cross pin slightly, and move the pin out toward either side.

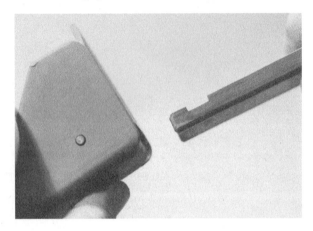

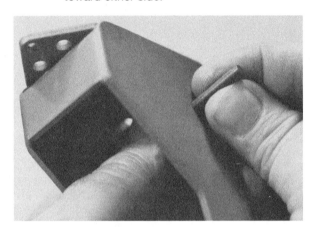

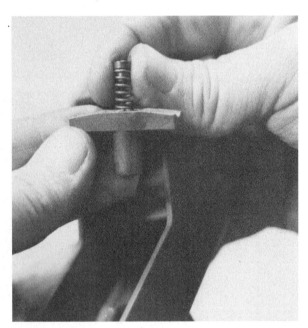

25. After the cross pin is removed, the stock latch and its plunger and spring can be taken out upward.

Reassembly Tips:

1. When replacing the trigger assembly, turn the sear trip in at the front to bear against the lower arm of the trigger spring, and use it to keep the spring to the rear while the cross pin is inserted.

2. This top view of the grip frame shows the parts installed in proper order.

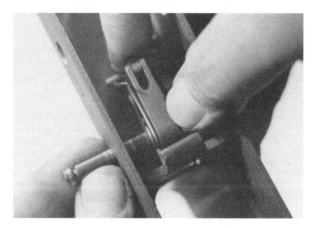

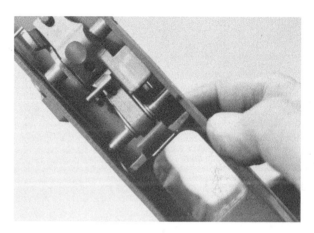

3. When replacing the extractor, note that it must be oriented so the hole in the extractor base will align with the cross-hole in the bolt. When the extractor is in position, insert a tapered drift punch to check this alignment before installing the cross pin.

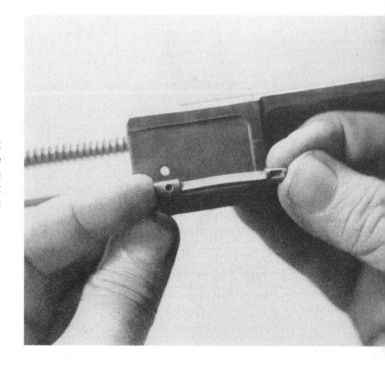

Reising Model 50

Data:	Reising Model 50
Origin:	United States
Manufacturer:	Harrington & Richardson, Worcester, Massachusetts
Cartridge:	45 ACP
Magazine capacity:	12 and 20 rounds
Overall length:	35-3/4 inches
Barrel length:	11 inches
Weight:	6-3/4 pounds

Designed by Eugene G. Reising, the Model 50 was made by Harrington & Richardson from 1940 through World War II, with a total production of about 100,000 guns. The Model 50 and a folding-stock version, the Model 55, were produced mainly for the U.S. Marines and the British Purchasing Commission. After the war, many of these guns were released to local law enforcement agencies in the United States.

Disassembly:

1. Remove the magazine, and set the fire selector in the full-auto position. Pull the trigger to drop the hammer to the fired position. Unscrew the takedown knob, located on the underside just behind the magazine housing. If the knob is tight, there is a slot for a coin or a large screwdriver. Lift the action out of the stock.

2. Unscrew the large endcap at the rear of the receiver, controlling it against the pressure of the hammer spring.

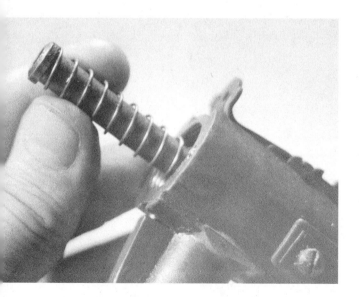

3. Remove the hammer spring toward the rear.

4. Tilt the action, pull the trigger, and remove the hammer from the rear of the receiver.

5. Drift out the front and rear magazine housing retainers toward the left.

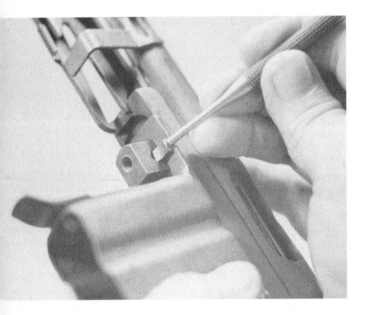

6. Remove the magazine housing downward.

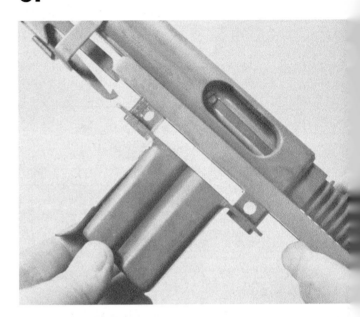

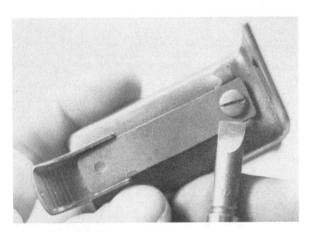

7. The magazine catch, which is its own spring, is retained on the back of the magazine housing by a single screw.

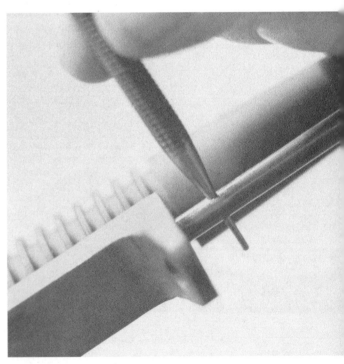

8. Move the action slide toward the rear until a hole is visible in the bolt spring guide. Insert a pin or tool in the hole and ease the slide forward, capturing the spring.

9. Move the slide assembly forward until it is stopped by the rear magazine housing mount, and move the front of the disconnector and connector away from the receiver for clearance. Tilt the front of the action slide away from the barrel.

10. Move the rear of the action slide outward, and twist it toward either side to clear the bolt contact lug from the receiver. Remove the slide assembly from the receiver. Restrain the bolt spring guide at the rear, remove the pin or tool, and remove the spring and guide toward the rear.

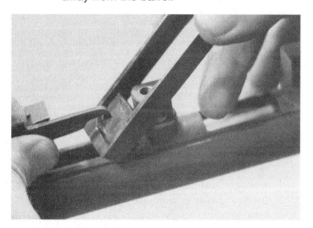

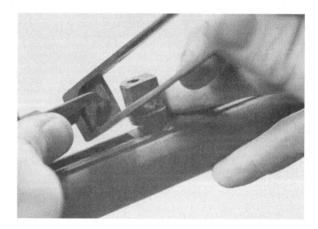

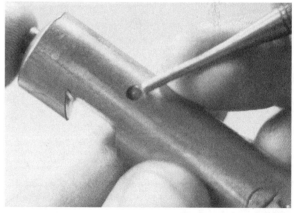

11. Tilt the action upward, pull the trigger, and remove the bolt from the rear of the receiver.

12. The firing pin and its return spring are retained in the bolt by a cross pin which is drifted out toward the left. Restrain the firing pin as this is removed.

13. The extractor is retained on the right side of the bolt by a screw. After the screw is removed, insert a tool to gently pry the extractor from its recess.

14. Remove the two screws that retain the selector and its positioning spring, and remove these parts toward the right.

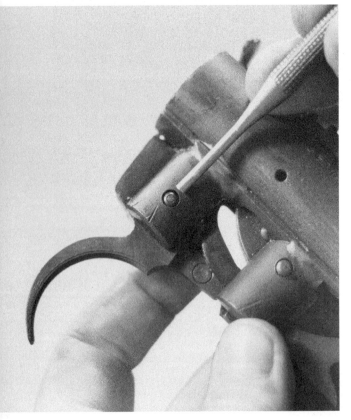

15. Push out the cross pin that retains the trigger and disconnector.

16. Remove the trigger and disconnector assembly downward. The trigger and disconnector can be separated by drifting out the link pin. The trigger spring and plunger, and the disconnector spring, can now be removed.

17. Push out the sear cross pin.

18. Remove the sear and connector assembly downward. The spring is easily removed from the top of the sear, and the connector and its spring and plunger can now be removed.

19. The rear sight is retained by a single screw.

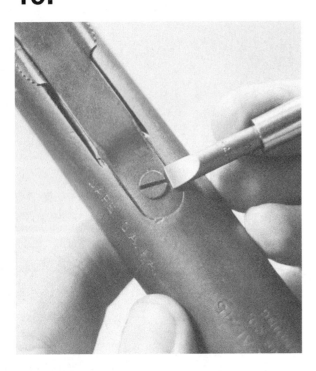

20. The front sight is retained in its dove-tail by a vertical Allen screw.

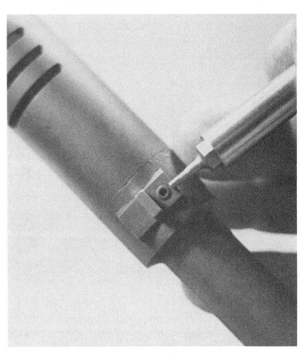

Reassembly Tips:

1. Here are right and left side views of the trigger, sear, disconnector, and connector assembly in proper order.

When replacing the action slide, be sure its upper rear lug engages the recess on the underside of the bolt.

SMITH & WESSON M76

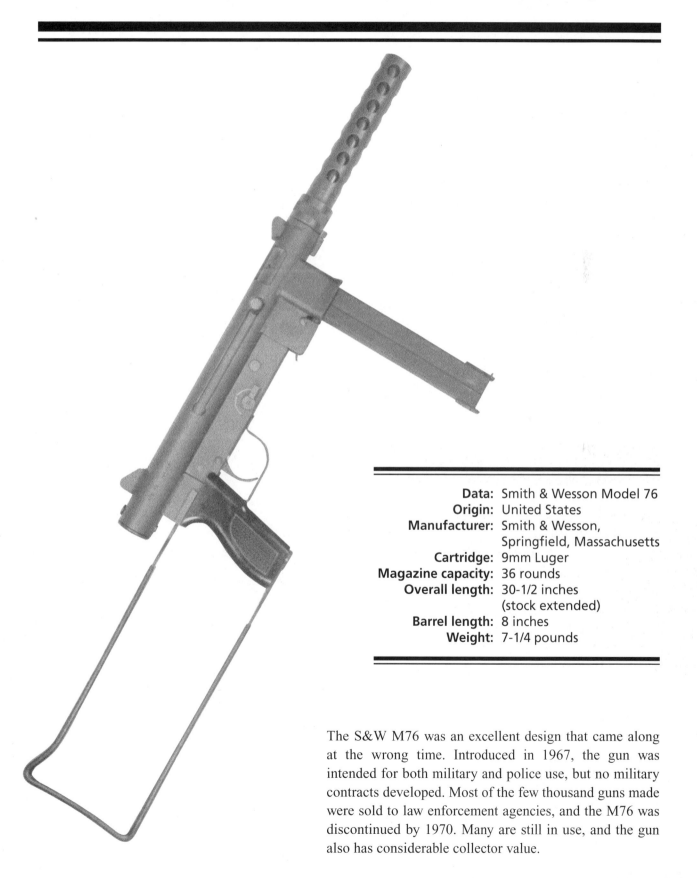

Data: Smith & Wesson Model 76
Origin: United States
Manufacturer: Smith & Wesson, Springfield, Massachusetts
Cartridge: 9mm Luger
Magazine capacity: 36 rounds
Overall length: 30-1/2 inches (stock extended)
Barrel length: 8 inches
Weight: 7-1/4 pounds

The S&W M76 was an excellent design that came along at the wrong time. Introduced in 1967, the gun was intended for both military and police use, but no military contracts developed. Most of the few thousand guns made were sold to law enforcement agencies, and the M76 was discontinued by 1970. Many are still in use, and the gun also has considerable collector value.

1. With the bolt in the forward position and the magazine removed, depress the barrel collar detent toward the rear, and unscrew the collar and cooling jacket for removal toward the front.

2. Remove the barrel toward the front.

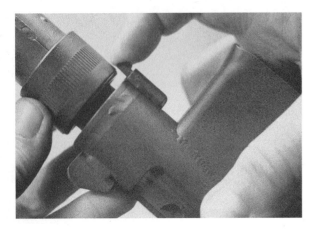

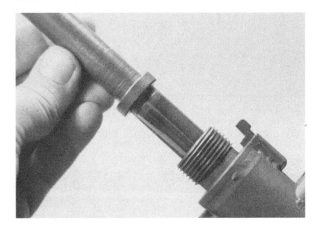

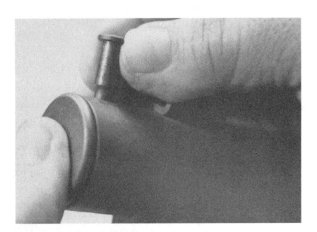

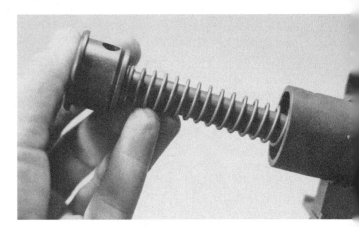

3. Fold the buttstock, restrain the receiver endcap, and push out the retaining pin upward. **Caution:** *Even with the bolt forward, the recoil spring has considerable tension, so keep the endpiece under control.*

4. When the pin is out, slowly release the spring tension, and remove the endcap, guide, and spring toward the rear.

5. Move the bolt back until the bolt handle aligns with the larger opening at the end of its track, and remove the bolt handle toward the right.

6. Remove the bolt toward the rear.

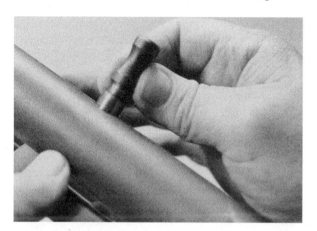

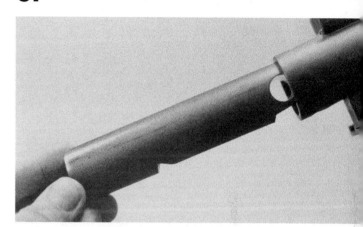

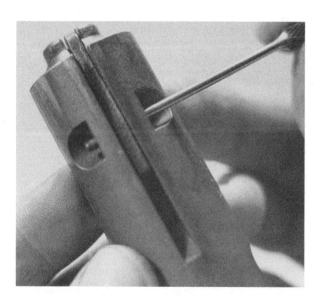

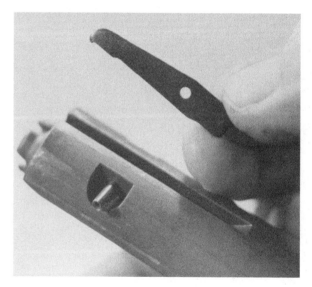

7. The extractor is retained by a roll cross pin at the front of the bolt. The pin can be drifted out toward either side.

8. Remove the extractor upward, and take out the extractor spring from its recess.

9. With a coin or a large screwdriver, unscrew the large bolt at the bottom of the pistol grip.

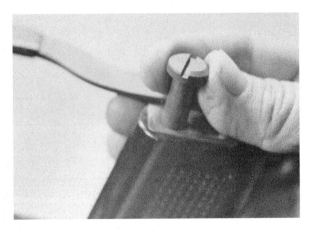

10. Flex the lower arm of the stock and its plate away from the bottom of the grip piece, and remove the pistol grip toward the rear and downward.

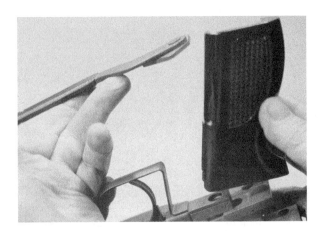

11. Unfold the stock to the rear, and tip the trigger sub-frame down at the rear. Remove the trigger sub-frame downward and toward the rear.

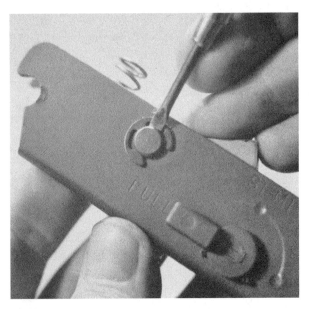

12. Remove the C-clip from the left tip of the sear pivot, and push out the sear pivot toward the right.

13. Remove the sear and its attached spring upward. The spring is easily removed from its post.

14. The selector (and its twin levers, balls, and springs) is heavily staked at the end of its cross-shaft on each side. Removal is not feasible in normal takedown.

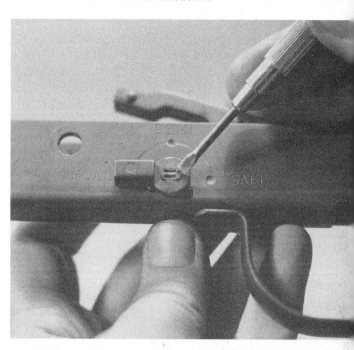

15. The trigger cross pin is roll-riveted on the left side, and this system is not removed in normal takedown. The forward trigger guard rivet also retains two leaf springs inside the frame, the springs powering the trigger and trigger bar. All of these parts should be removed only for repair purposes, and a new rivet and trigger pin will probably be needed for reassembly. The trigger bar can be separated from the trigger by drifting out the connecting cross pin.

16. Removal of the pistol grip bolt will have freed the buttstock base plates, and the buttstock can be removed toward the rear. The lower stock plate is retained by a riveted hinge-post. The upper mount hinge is also riveted over a washer at the top, retaining the mount and lock spring. Removal should be only for repair.

17. The ejector is spot-welded in place, and is not routinely removed. To replace a broken ejector, the spot-welds must be ground away, and the ejector is then driven out toward the left. The sights and sling loops are also welded in place.

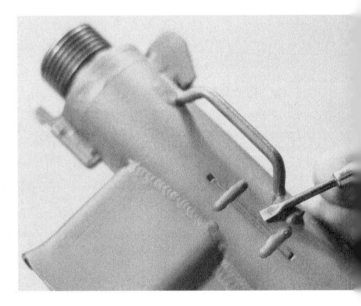

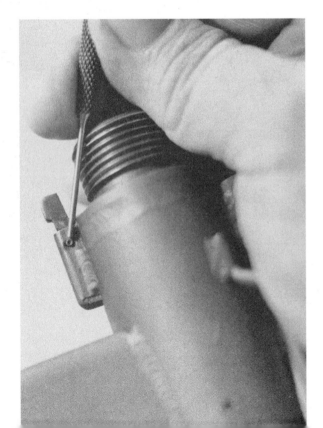

18. The barrel collar detent and its spring are retained by a small roll pin. The detent and its spring are removed toward the front.

19. The magazine catch and its spring are retained by a cross pin that is roll-riveted on the left side, and this system should be removed only for repair. If removal is necessary, use a drift punch small enough to enter the hollow end on the left, and drift the pin out toward the right. For replacement, a new pin may be necessary.

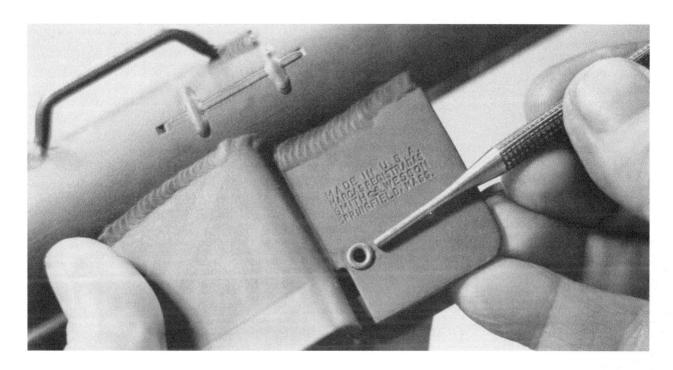

Reassembly Tips:

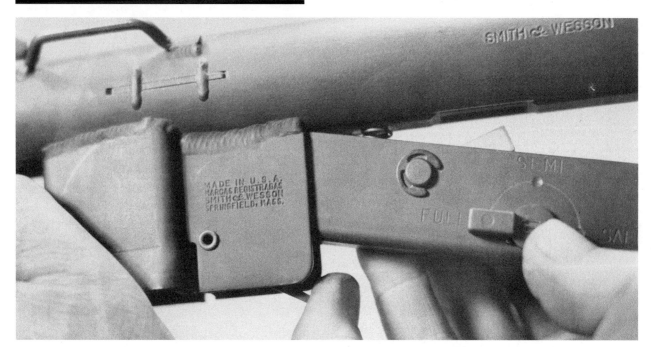

1. When replacing the trigger sub-frame, it is necessary to pull the magazine catch downward and hold it out of the way as the sub-frame is moved into place.

THOMPSON MODEL 1921

Data: Thompson Model 1921
Origin: United States
Manufacturer: Colt Firearms,
Hartford, Connecticut
Cartridge: 45 ACP
Magazine capacity: 20, 30, and 50 rounds
Overall length: 33-3/4 inches
Barrel length: 10-1/2 inches
Weight: 10-3/4 pounds

Apparently, quite a number of venerable Thompson guns are still in use with many departments around the country. In my own area, both the local police and the sheriff's department have a Thompson in the arms locker. Mechanically, there is very little difference between the Model 1921 and Model 1928, and most parts will interchange. The Model 1921 gun shown here has a Model 1928 recoil spring assembly.

Disassembly:

1. Remove the magazine, depress the stock release button, and slide the buttstock off toward the rear.

2. With the bolt in the forward position, set the safety to "fire" and the selector to "full auto." Pull the trigger and hold it to the rear. Depress the frame latch button on the underside at the rear.

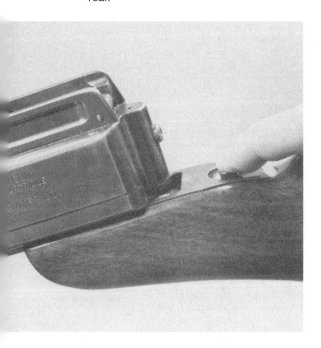

3. Keeping the trigger pulled to the rear, move the grip frame off toward the rear.

4. Fold a small piece of leather around the blade tip of a large screwdriver (to avoid marring the frame), and insert the tip on the right side between the upper part of the pivot plate and its short middle spring-arm. Turn the screwdriver to lever the arm downward, and push the rocker pivot pin toward the left.

5. Repeat this operation with the longer lower arm of the pivot plate, levering the spring arm clear of the notch in the safety shaft, and moving the safety toward the left.

6. Remove the safety toward the left.

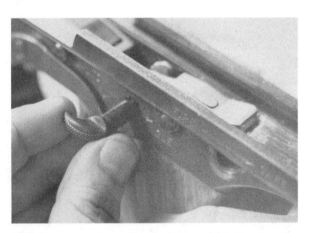

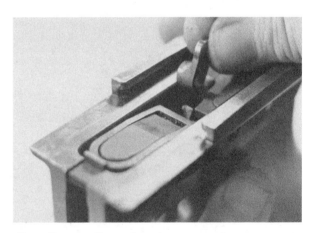

7. Remove the selector lever, which is also the rocker pivot, toward the left.

8. Remove the rocker piece upward.

9. The pivot plate is now removed toward the right. If the plate is tight, use a non-marring punch to nudge its two cross-shafts, the sear and trigger pivots, but do this alternately and equally to avoid deforming the plate. Take care to exert no pressure on the spring arms during removal. When the plate is free enough to be grasped and pulled out toward the right, restrain the sear and trigger assemblies, as they will be released.

10. Remove the sear assembly upward. The sear, sear lever, and their attendant springs are easily separated after removal.

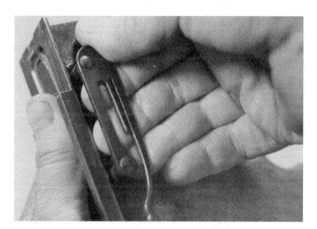

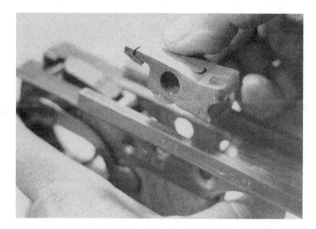

11. Remove the trigger assembly upward. The trip is easily lifted off the top of the trigger, and the spring can be taken out of its well at the front.

12. The disconnector is taken off the trigger toward the left, and its spring removed from its well in the trigger.

13. Move the magazine catch lever upward until its front projection is clear of its hole in the frame, and push the catch toward the left for removal. The catch spring is mounted on the cross-shaft of the magazine catch, and will come out with it.

14. The rear hand grip is retained by a large screw, and the grip is taken off downward.

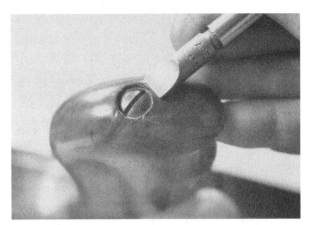

15. Depress the rear tip of the buffer rod (recoil spring guide) until the inside collar can be grasped. Move the assembly forward until its rear tip is clear, then lift it outward and remove the spring and guide toward the rear. Keep the spring under control.

16. Move the bolt to the rear of the receiver, and lift it out. Move the actuator forward until the H-block is pushed outward, and remove the H-block.

17. Move the actuator back until its knob aligns with the larger opening in its track, and remove the actuator downward. Inside the receiver, there is a thin steel bracket holding twin oiler pads. In normal takedown, this is best left in place.

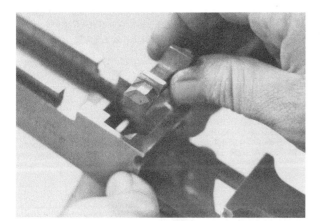

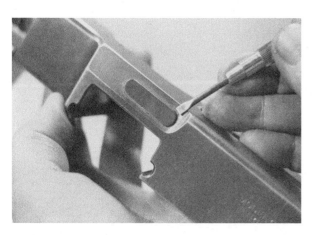

18. The ejector is removed by inserting a sharp tool to lift its rear tail until the lug is clear of its hole in the receiver, then unscrewing it, counter-clockwise (left side view). During this operation, a piece of cardboard should be used to protect the finish of the receiver from drag marks. Except for repair or refinishing, the ejector should not be removed.

19. If the gun has a compensator at the muzzle, as on the one shown, drift out the cross-pin, then unscrew the compensator counter-clockwise (front view). On guns without the compensator, driving out the cross-pin will allow the front sight ring to be nudged off toward the front. The rear sight is retained by its hinge-pin, and removal will also release a plunger and spring that bear on the sight.

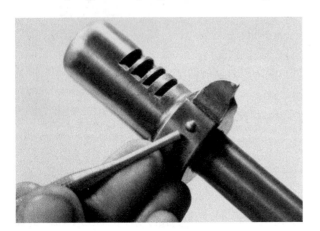

20. The forward hand grip is retained by a large screw, and is taken off downward.

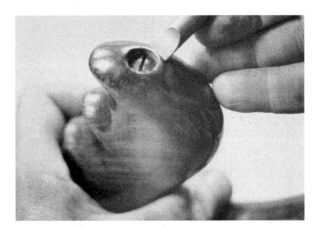

21. The frame latch button is retained in its well by an enlarged loop at the end of its spring. Pull it out while turning the button and spring counter-clockwise (bottom view). If the button and its spring are ever jammed in the well, an access hole is provided on top of the receiver for insertion of a drift punch to nudge it out.

22. Hook a screwdriver blade under the extractor beak, as shown, and lift it just enough to clear the underlug from its well in the bolt. Then, lever the extractor toward the front for removal. In normal takedown, the extractor is best left in place.

23. Push out the hammer pin toward either side.

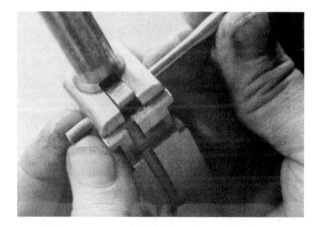

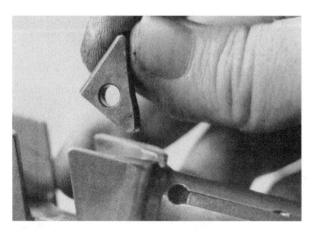

24. Remove the hammer from the bolt.

25. Remove the firing pin and its spring from the bolt.

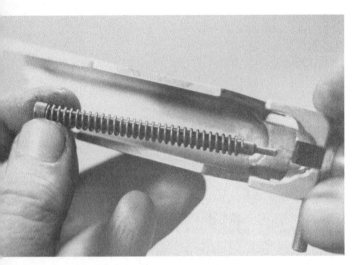

Reassembly Tips:

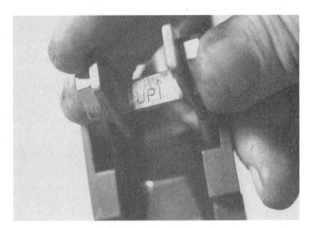

1. The H-block is marked with an arrow and the word "UP" to aid reassembly. The receiver is usually inverted during disassembly and reassembly, so the "UP" marking should be visible with the receiver in that position, and the arrow should point toward the muzzle.

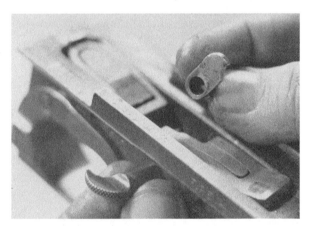

2. When replacing the rocker, be sure its "beak" is oriented toward the rear. If it is installed in reverse, the selector will not function, and the firing will be non-selective full-auto.

When replacing the selector ("rocker pivot") and the safety, use the leather-padded screwdriver, as in steps 4 and 5, to flex the spring arms as the parts are moved into place.

Note that the flat side of the collar on the recoil spring guide goes toward the inside top of the receiver.

U.S. M3A1

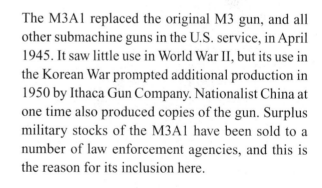

Data:	U.S. M3A1
Origin:	United States
Manufacturer:	Guide Lamp Division, General Motors Corporation, Detroit, Michigan
Cartridge:	45 ACP
Magazine capacity:	30 rounds
Overall length:	29.8 inches (stock extended)
Barrel length:	8 inches
Weight:	8-3/4 pounds

The M3A1 replaced the original M3 gun, and all other submachine guns in the U.S. service, in April 1945. It saw little use in World War II, but its use in the Korean War prompted additional production in 1950 by Ithaca Gun Company. Nationalist China at one time also produced copies of the gun. Surplus military stocks of the M3A1 have been sold to a number of law enforcement agencies, and this is the reason for its inclusion here.

Disassembly:

1. With the bolt in the forward position and the magazine removed, depress the barrel collar detent and unscrew the barrel and collar assembly for removal toward the front. The collar is retained on the barrel by a cross pin, and this is not removed in normal disassembly. If the gun is equipped with a flash hider, this can be removed by loosening the wing nut and slipping the flash hider off toward the front.

2. Depress and hold the stock latch, and pull the wire buttstock off toward the rear.

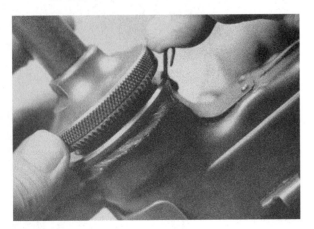

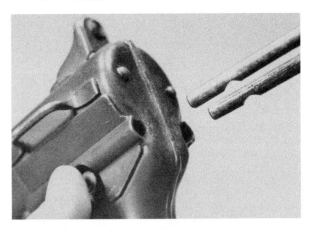

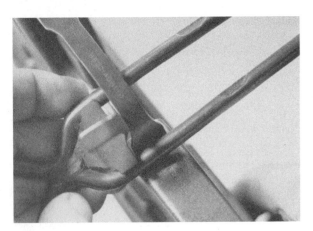

3. Insert the buttstock through the trigger guard as shown, and turn it to spring the guard out of its slot in the front of the pistol grip.

4. Tip the trigger guard over toward the front, and remove it.

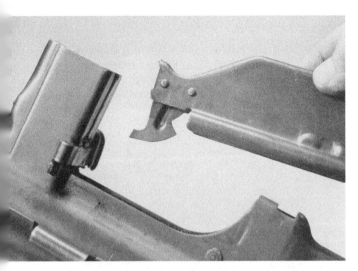

5. Tip the housing assembly downward at the rear, and remove it. The ejector is riveted to the housing, and is not removed in normal takedown.

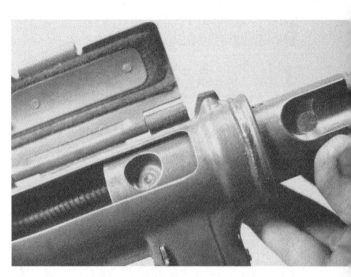

6. Open the ejection port cover, and remove the bolt and recoil spring assembly toward the front.

7. Restrain the springs and guide rod assembly at the rear, and remove the guide rod retaining clip at the front of the guide rod locating plate. Caution: Keep the springs under control.

8. Remove the guide rod locating plate, keeping the spring system under control.

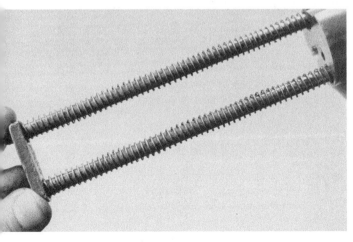

9. Release the spring tension slowly, and remove the springs and guide rod assembly toward the rear.

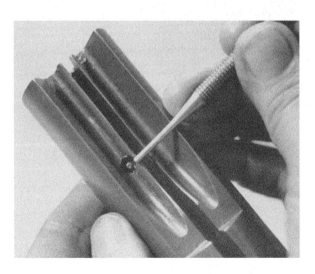

10. Drift out the extractor retaining pin upward.

11. If the extractor is not tightly fitted, hook a screwdriver blade under the extractor beak, and pull the extractor out toward the front. The extractor is its own spring.

12. If the extractor is tightly fitted, insert a rod into the small hole at the rear of the bolt, and push the extractor out toward the front. This method is also used if the extractor beak is broken off.

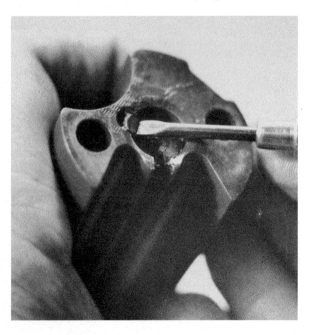

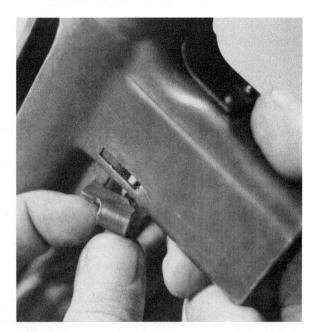

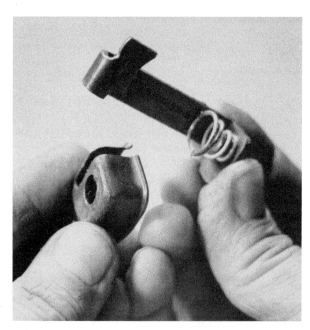

13. Push the magazine catch cup toward the rear, off the magazine housing, and when it clears unhook the right tip of the cross-piece from its slot in the housing.

14. After the catch is removed, the cup and spring are easily separated from the catch cross-piece.

15. The ejection port cover hinge can be drifted out toward the rear to free the cover for removal. The hinge pin will usually be tightly fitted, and removal should be done only for repair.

16. Push out the sear pin toward either side. When the pin is removed, the combination trigger and sear spring will pull the sear downward, but the sear will remain attached to the trigger bar.

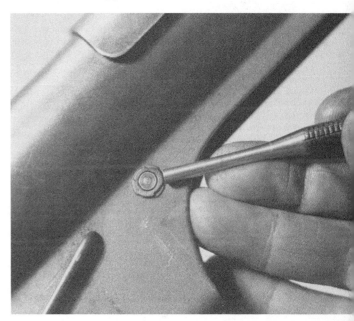

17. Remove the trigger pivot toward the right.

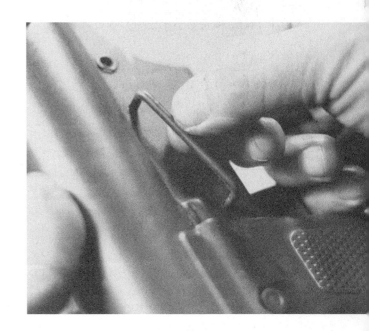

18. Move the trigger and sear assembly upward into the receiver, move the assembly forward, and take it out downward.

19. Push out the sear connector pin toward either side, and remove the sear from the front of the trigger bar ("connector").

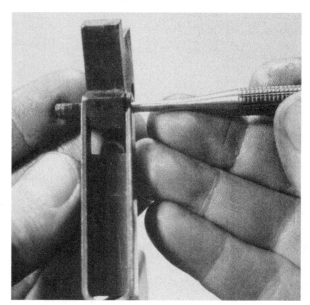

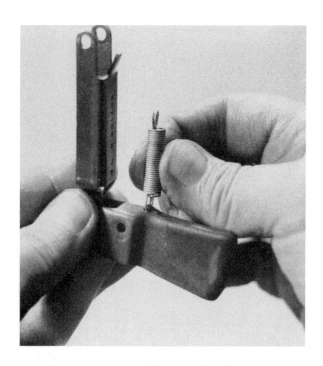

20. The combination sear and trigger spring is easily unhooked from the front of the trigger bar. The trigger bar cross pin at the top of the trigger is semi-riveted in place, and is not routinely removed. The rear spring hook, on the front of the trigger, may be clinched, and will have to be bent outward to free the spring.

21. The stock retaining latch is retained by a collar on the right side that is cross pinned to the latch shaft. The collar is taken off toward the right, and the latch and spring toward the left.

22. Unscrew and remove the cap and oiler rod from the oil bottle at the bottom of the pistol grip, and use a wrench of the proper size to unscrew and remove the oil bottle.

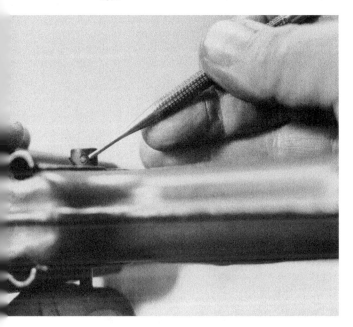

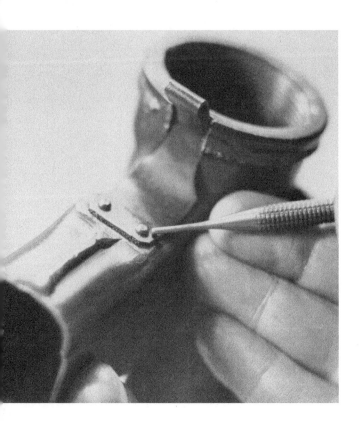

23. The barrel collar detent is retained by two rivets, and is not routinely removed.

Reassembly Tips:

1. When replacing the trigger and sear assembly, position the trigger and install the trigger pivot first. Then, elevate the sear and bar, and pull the trigger to move the sear into alignment for replacement of the sear cross pin.

2. When replacing the bolt and spring assembly, be sure the rear tips of the guide rods snap into their holes in the rear of the receiver and protrude slightly, as shown.

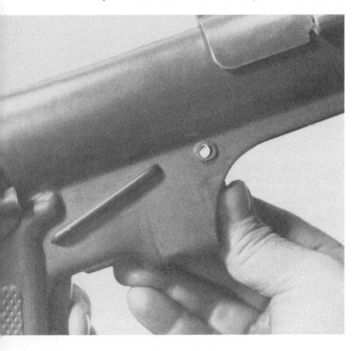

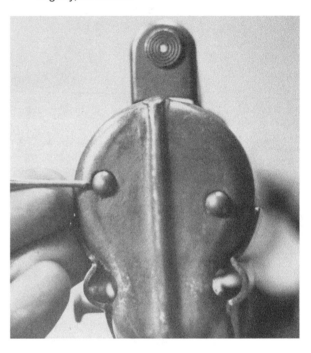

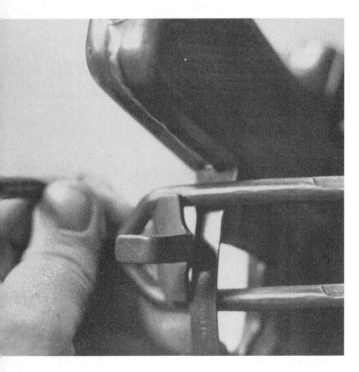

3. When replacing the trigger guard, use the stock again, this time at the rear, to snap the rear tip of the guard into its slot.

Index/Cross-Reference

A

American Arms AKC-47 315
American Arms AKF-39 315
American Arms AKY-39 315
AMT Back-Up 12
AMT Combat Government Model 25
AMT Hardballer 25
AMT Long Slide 25
AMT Skipper 25
Argentine Model 1927 25
Armalite AR-10 197
Armalite AR-15 197
Armalite AR-180 151
Armalite AR-30 144
Armalite AR-50 144
Armalite AR-50A1 144
Austrian StG 58 215
Austrian StG 58 250
Auto-Ordnance M1911A1 Pit Bull 25
Auto-Ordnance M1911A1 Thompson 25

B

Barrett Model 98B 161
Barrett MRAD 161
Benelli M2 Tactical 97
Benelli M4 105
Benelli MR1 176
Beretta Cx4 Storm 181
Beretta Px4 Storm 18
British L1A1 215
British L1A1 250
Bushmaster ACR 186
Bushmaster XM-15 197

C

Chinese Type 56 323
Colt 1911 Series 25
Colt AR-15 197
Colt AR-15 Collapsible Stock Model 197
Colt AR-15 Delta HBAR Match 197
Colt AR-15A2 Carbine 197
Colt AR-15A2 Delta HBAR 197
Colt AR-15A2 Government Model Carbine 197
Colt AR-15A2 Government Model Target 197
Colt AR-15A2 HBAR 197
Colt AR-15A2 Sporter II 197
Colt Combat Commander 25
Colt Combat Elite 25
Colt Combat Grade Government 25
Colt Commander 25
Colt Delta Elite 25
Colt Gold Cup 25
Colt Gold Cup 38 Special 25
Colt Lightweight Commander 25
Colt Mark IV Series 70 25
Colt Mark IV Series 80 25
Colt Model 1911 25
Colt Super 39 25

Colt National Match 45 25
Colt Officers ACP 25
Colt Sporter Lightweight Rifle 197
Colt Sporter Match Delta HBAR 197
Colt Sporter Match HBAR 197
Colt Sporter Target Model 197

D

Daewoo DT 200 207
Detonics Scoremaster 25
DPMS A-15 197
DPMS LR-308 197
DS Arms SA58 215
DS Arms SA58 250

E

Eagle Arms EA-15 197
Egyptian Maadi AK-47 315
Essex Model 1911A1 25

F

Falcon Portsider 25
Federal Ordnance Ranger M1911A1 25
FN FAL 215
FNH F2000 227
FNH Five-Seven 34
FNH FNS 42
FNH FS2000 227
FNH FS2000 CQB 227
FNH P90 240
FNH PS90 240
FNH SLP 115
FNH SLP Mk 1 115
FNH SLP Mk 1 Tactical 115
FNH SLP Tactical 115

G

German G1 215
German G1 250
German G3 250

H

Heckler & Koch HK 91 250
HK 33 250
HK 41 250
HK 53 250
HK 93 250
HK USP Tactical 51

I

Ingram Model 10 391
Iver Johnson M-1 Carbine 366
IWI Tavor 262

J

JP Enterprises CTR-02 197
JP Enterprises JP-15 197

K

Kel-Tec KSG 125

Kel-Tec PLR-16 60
Kel-Tec RFB 275
Kel-Tec SU-16 290
Kel-Tec SUB 2000 285

L

Llama Model IIIA 25
Llama Model VIII 25
Llama Model IXA 25
Llama Model XA 25
Llama Model XI 25
Llama Model XV 25

M

M-S Safari Arms Enforcer 25
M-S Safari Arms Model 81 25
M-S Safari Arms Model 81 BD 25
M-S Safari Arms Model 81 BP Super............25
M-S Safari Arms Model 81NM.....................25
Marlin M9 297
Marlin Model 45 297
Mitchell Arms AK-47
Mitchell Arms AK-47 Heavy Barrel..............315
MSAR STG-556..356
MSAR STG-E4..356

N

Norinco Type 84S AK................................315

O

Olympic Arms AR-15 Heavy Match..............197
Olympic Arms AR-15 Service Match............197
Olympic Arms CAR-15 197
Olympic/Safari Arms Enforcer 25
Olympic/Safari Arms Matchmaster...............25

P

Plainfield M-1 Carbine 366
Poly Tech AKS-47S...................................315
Poly Tech AKS-762...................................315
Polytech M14S...344
PSG-1...250

R

Randall Compact Service Model....................25
Randall Curtis LeMay Four Star 25
Randall Raider 25
Randall Service Model 25
Reising Model 50 400
Remington Model 870R 136
Remington R-15 197
Rock River Arms LAR-15............................197
Ruger Mini Thirty 307
Ruger Mini-14 307
Ruger Mini-14 Ranch Rifle 307
Rusian AK-47 315
Russian SKS 323

S

SIG 550 333

SIG 551 333
SIG 552 333
SIG 553 333
SIG SAUER 551 A1 333
SIG SAUER 556 333
Smith & Wesson M76 407
Smith & Wesson Model 439 65
Smith & Wesson Model 459 65
Smith & Wesson Model 469 65
Smith & Wesson Model 639 65
Smith & Wesson Model 645 65
Smith & Wesson Model 659 65
Smith & Wesson Model 669 65
Spanish CETME 250
Springfield Armory 25
Springfield Armory M1911A1 25
Springfield Armory M1911A1 Compact 25
Springfield Armory M1911A1 Commander
  Vega 45 25
Springfield Armory M1911A1 Defender 25
Springfield Armory SAR 48 215
Springfield Armory SAR 48 250
Springfield Armory SAR 48 Bush Rifle 215
Springfield Armory SAR 48 Bush Rifle 250
Springfield Armory SAR 4800 215
Springfield Armory SAR 4800 250
Springfield Armory SAR Para Model 215
Springfield Armory SAR Para Model 250
Springfield M1A 344
Springfield M1A Scout 344
Springfield M21 Tactical............................344
Springfield SOCOM 16 344
Springfield SOCOM II................................344
Steyr AUG 356

T

Taurus 24/7 82
Taurus 45/410 74
Thompson Model 1921 414

U

U.S. 30 M1A1 366
U.S. M-1 Carbine 366
U.S. M-14 344
U.S. M3A1 423
Universal M-1 Carbine 366

V

Valmet 76/FS 374
Valmet Model 62......................................315
Valmet Model 71......................................315
Valmet Model 78......................................315

W

Wilkinson Terry 382
Wilson ADP 89

Y

Yugoslavian Model 59/66...........................323